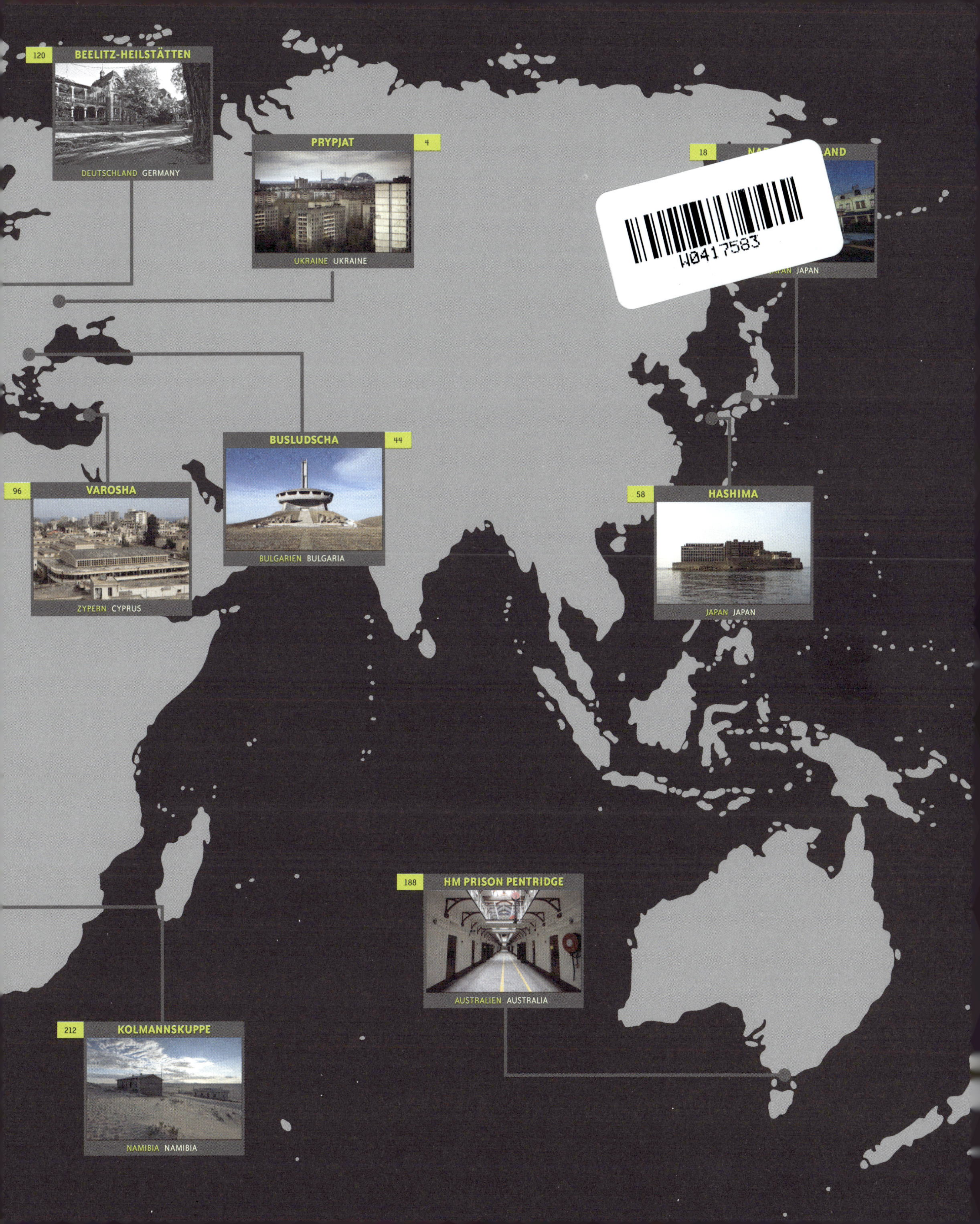
120 BEELITZ-HEILSTÄTTEN
DEUTSCHLAND GERMANY
PRYPJAT 4
UKRAINE UKRAINE
18
JAPAN
BUSLUDSCHA 44
BULGARIEN BULGARIA
96 VAROSHA
ZYPERN CYPRUS
58 HASHIMA
JAPAN JAPAN
188 HM PRISON PENTRIDGE
AUSTRALIEN AUSTRALIA
212 KOLMANNSKUPPE
NAMIBIA NAMIBIA

DIE WELT DER VERLASSENEN ORTE
WORLD'S LOST PLACES

DIE WELT DER VERLASSENEN ORTE

URBEX-FOTOGRAFIE

WORLD'S LOST PLACES

URBAN EXPLORATION PHOTOGRAPHY

MIT TEXTEN VON WITH TEXTS BY PETER TRAUB

mitteldeutscher verlag

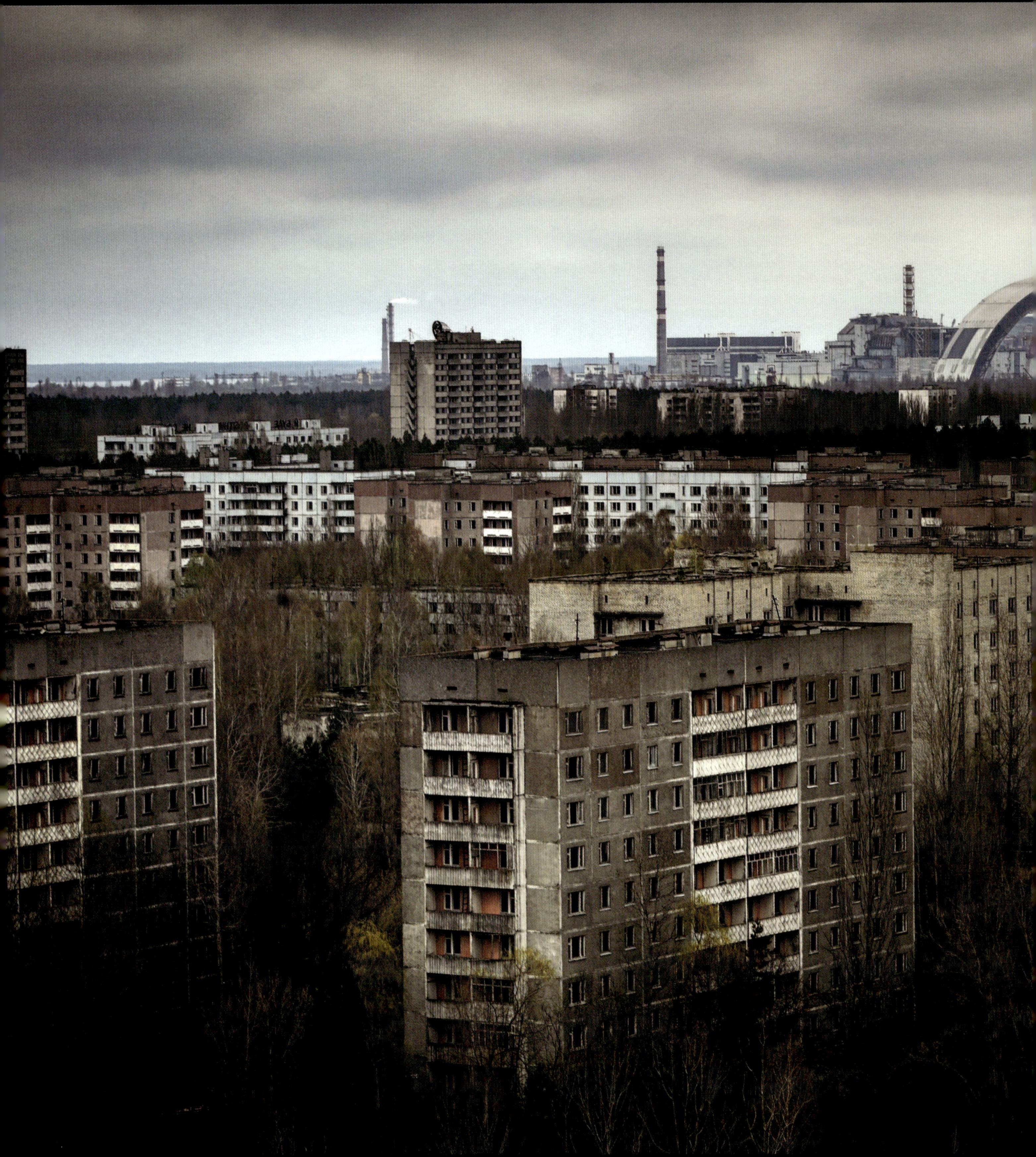

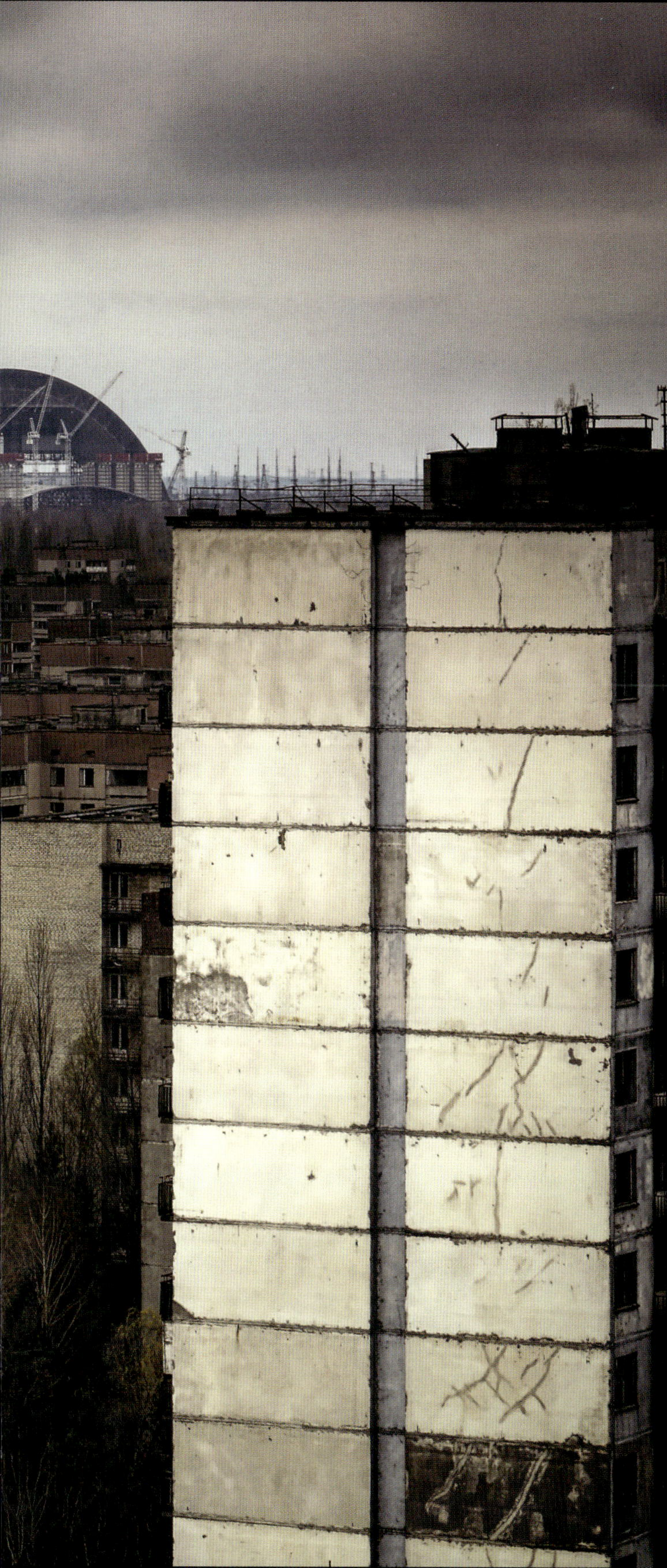

PRYPJAT

UKRAINE UKRAINE

FOTOS VON PHOTOS BY ANDY KAY

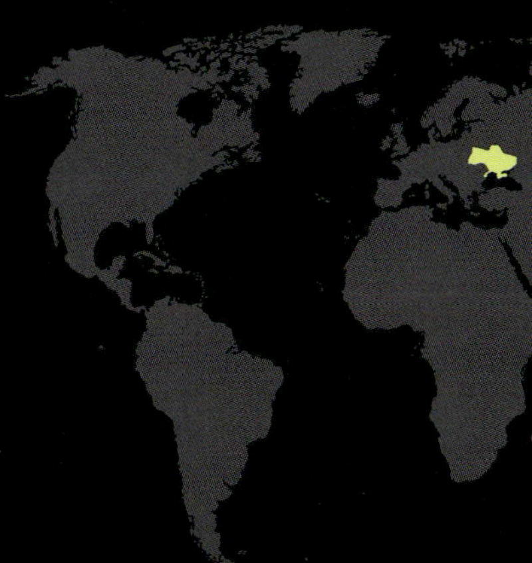

Unsicherheit herrschte am Vormittag des 28. April 1986 im schwedischen Kernkraftwerk Forsmark, als das Alarmsignal erklang: Auf dem Betriebsgelände wurde zu hohe Radioaktivität gemessen. Die Techniker rieben sich die Augen vor den Parametern in den Leitwarten, alle Anzeigen verwiesen auf einen intakten Betrieb. Das Gras aber wies extreme Strahlungswerte auf. Es hatte geregnet. Der Wind blies aus Südost, aus der Sowjetunion. Im Norden der Ukrainischen SSR, an der Grenze zur Belorussischen SSR, etwa 1.200 Kilometer von Forsmark entfernt, hatten zu diesem Zeitpunkt viele Menschen für immer ihr Zuhause verloren, ohne es zu wissen. Am 27. April mittags war die Bevölkerung der Stadt Prypjat aufgefordert worden, sich auf drei Tage Abwesenheit einzustellen. Ab 14 Uhr begann die Evakuierung mit 1.225 Bussen, 160 Lkws und etlichen Sonderzügen, die nach zweieinhalb Stunden abgeschlossen war.
Durch den goldenen Korridor des Kernkraftwerks Tschernobyl, an den die Kontrollräume anschließen, liefen zur selben Zeit die Ingenieure mit desillusionierten Blicken. Für die Kraftwerker war eine neue Zeitrechnung angebrochen: die Zeit nach dem GAU, dem größten anzunehmenden Unfall. In der Nachtschicht des 26. April 1986, um 1.23 Uhr, war der Reaktor 4 außer Kontrolle geraten und explodiert. Radioaktive Materie wurde in die Atmosphäre geschleudert; was nicht in der unmittelbaren Umgebung niederfiel, trieb in einer Wolke über die Grenzen, um vom Regen aus der Atmosphäre herausgewaschen zu werden.
Eine nach Moskau übermittelte Nachricht durch die Kraftwerksleitung, dass der Reaktor 4 noch intakt sei, allein nur der Kühlung bedürfe, wurde als Begründung für die um viele Stunden verspätete Evakuierung Prypjats angegeben.
Erst 1970 war die Stadt im Zuge des Kraftwerkbaus, wenige Kilometer davon entfernt, gegründet worden. Sie zählte knapp 50.000 Einwohner, deren Durchschnittsalter bei 26 Jahren lag. Auf dem Rummelplatz, der am 1. Mai 1986 für die 15.500 Kinder Prypjats und die Kinder der umliegenden Ortschaften eröffnet werden sollte, rostet heute das Riesenrad. In der 30 Kilometer-Sperrzone um den havarierten Reaktor, der seit November 1986 unter einem Sarkophag aus Stahlbeton liegt, begegnen sich mittlerweile Wolf, Luchs und Bär; Adler durchqueren den Luftraum. Die Seen gelten wieder als fischreich. Für die Bevölkerung von Prypjat wurde die Stadt Slawutytsch errichtet, über eine Bahnverbindung gelangen die Beschäftigten nun zu ihren Arbeitsplätzen im Kernkraftwerk Tschernobyl.
Neben Miliz und Bauleuten – 2015 soll ein neuer Sarkophag über dem havarierten Reaktor fertiggestellt sein – betreten zunehmend Touristen die verlassene Stadt. Die Hauptstraßen von Prypjat wurden dekontaminiert. Zwei Stunden Zeit bleibt den Besuchern im Sperrgebiet, um den Zerfall und die Melancholie mit ihren Kameras einzufangen: Karussell und Autoscooter, das Hallenbad, den Kulturpalast, die Plattenneubauten. Sie sind ausgerüstet mit Handschuhen und Staubmasken für das Betreten von Innenräumen. Sie werden aufgefordert, nichts zu berühren. Die Stille in der Stadt setzt sich fort in den Besuchern. Das knackende Geräusch des Geigerzählers erzeugt Anspannung. Staub am Schuh bekommt plötzlich eine schwerwiegende Bedeutung. Die Strahlungswerte variieren. Sie steigen an, nähert man sich dem Sarkophag. Vor ihm steht das Denkmal für Hunderttausende Liquidatoren, für jene, die an den Räumungsarbeiten im nuklear verstrahlten Gebiet beteiligt waren.

There was a heavy feeling of apprehension when the alarm sounded on the morning of April 28, 1986 in the Forsmark power plant in Sweden. A high level of radioactivity had been measured on the plant grounds. The technicians couldn't believe their eyes as they studied the parameters in the control room; all indicators pointed to an intact operation. However, the grass showed extremely high levels of radiation. It had rained. The wind was blowing from the south east, from the Soviet Union. In the north of the Ukrainian SSR on the border to the White Russian SSR, about 1,200 kilometers from Forsmark, many people had at that moment lost their homes forever, without knowing it. On April 27, residents of the city of Pripyat were instructed to be prepared to leave for three days. At 2:00 p.m. the evacuation began with 1,225 buses, 160 trucks and various special trains. It was completed two and a half hours later.

At the same time, engineers with disillusioned expressions walked through the golden corridor of the Chernobyl power plant past the control rooms. For the power plant operators, a new era had started: the time after the worst case scenario. During the night shift of April 26, 1986, at 1:23 a.m., reactor 4 was out of control and exploded. Radioactive material was cast up into the atmosphere. Whatever didn't fall in the immediate vicinity was carried in a cloud across the borders to be washed out of the atmosphere by rain. A message sent to Moscow by the power plant management that reactor 4 was still intact and only needed cooling was the reason given for the delayed evacuation of Pripyat many hours later.

The city was only founded in 1970 as part of the construction of the power plant a few kilometers away. It had almost 50,000 residents with an average age of 26 years old. On the fairgrounds that was to open on May 1, 1986 for the 15,500 children of Pripyat and the surrounding municipalities, the large Ferris wheel is still rusting today. In the 30 kilometer restricted zone around the stricken reactor, which has been covered under a sarcophagus of reinforced concrete since November 1986, wolves, lynxes and bears now meet and eagles cross the sky. The lakes are considered to be rich with fish once again. The city of Slavutych was built for the population of Pripyat, and now the employees reach their places of work at the Chernobyl power plant by a train connection.

Besides military and construction personnel, increasing numbers of tourists visit the lost city. In 2015, a new sarcophagus is to be completed over the stricken reactor. The main streets of Pripyat have been decontaminated. Visitors are given two hours in the restricted zone to capture the decay and melancholy with their cameras: the carousel and bumper cars, the swimming pool, the palace of culture, the flattened new buildings. They are equipped with gloves and dust masks to enter the inner rooms. They are asked not to touch anything. The stillness in the city settles on the visitors. The crackling sound of a Geiger counter creates tension. Dust on shoes suddenly takes on very serious significance. The radioactivity levels vary. They increase when you get closer to the sarcophagus. In front of it is a monument to the hundred thousand liquidators, for those who took part in the clean-up work in the nuclear radiated area.

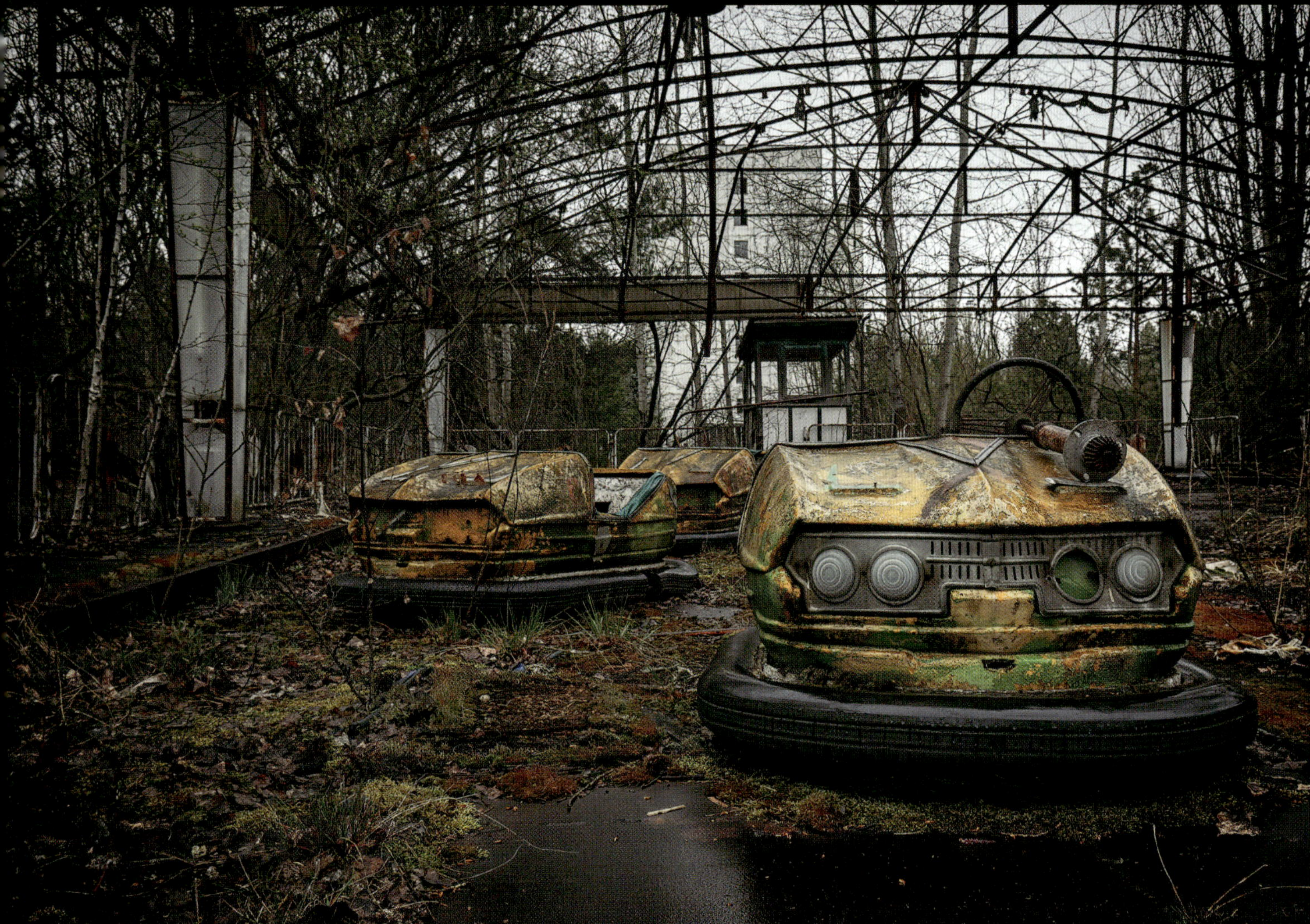

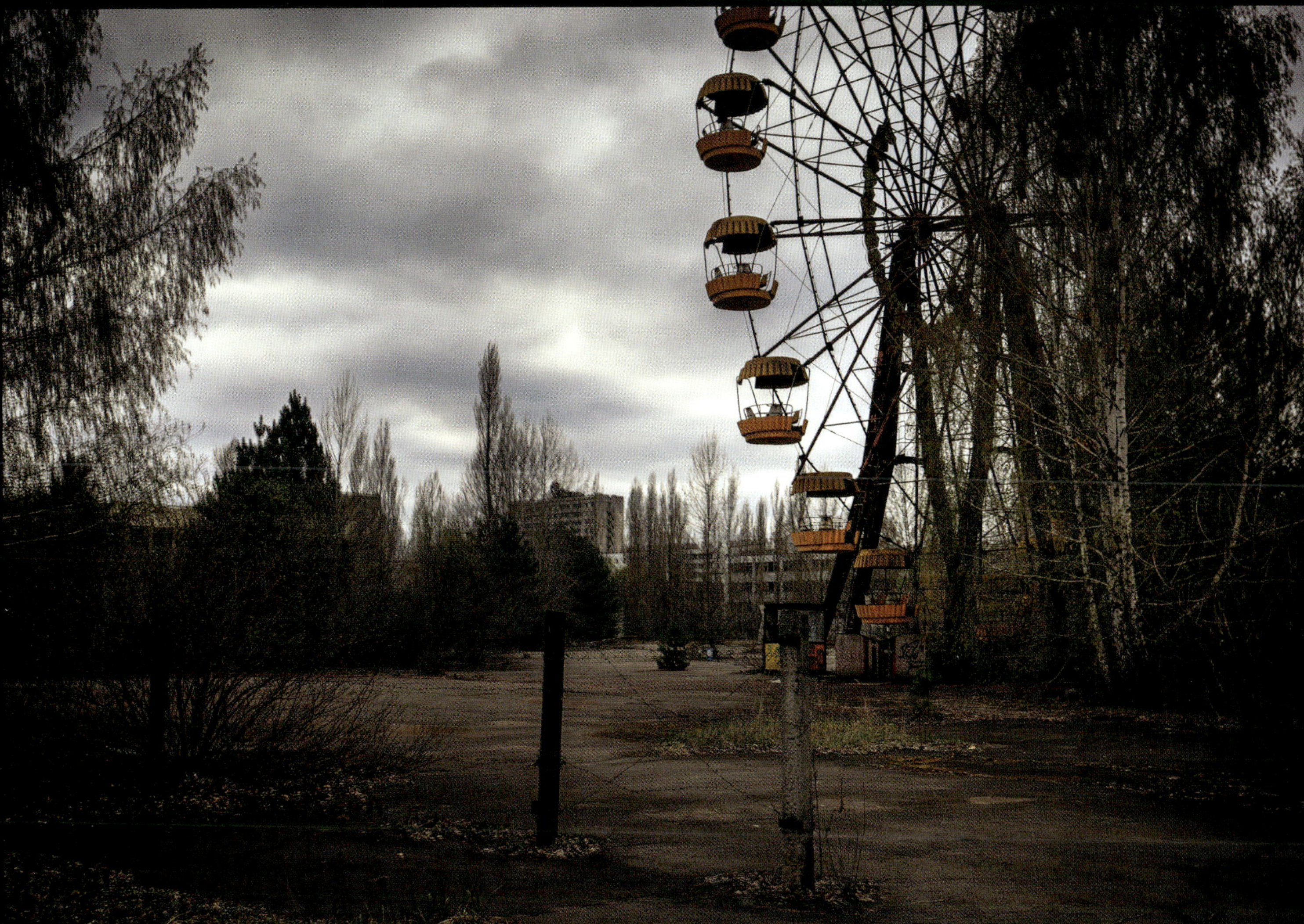

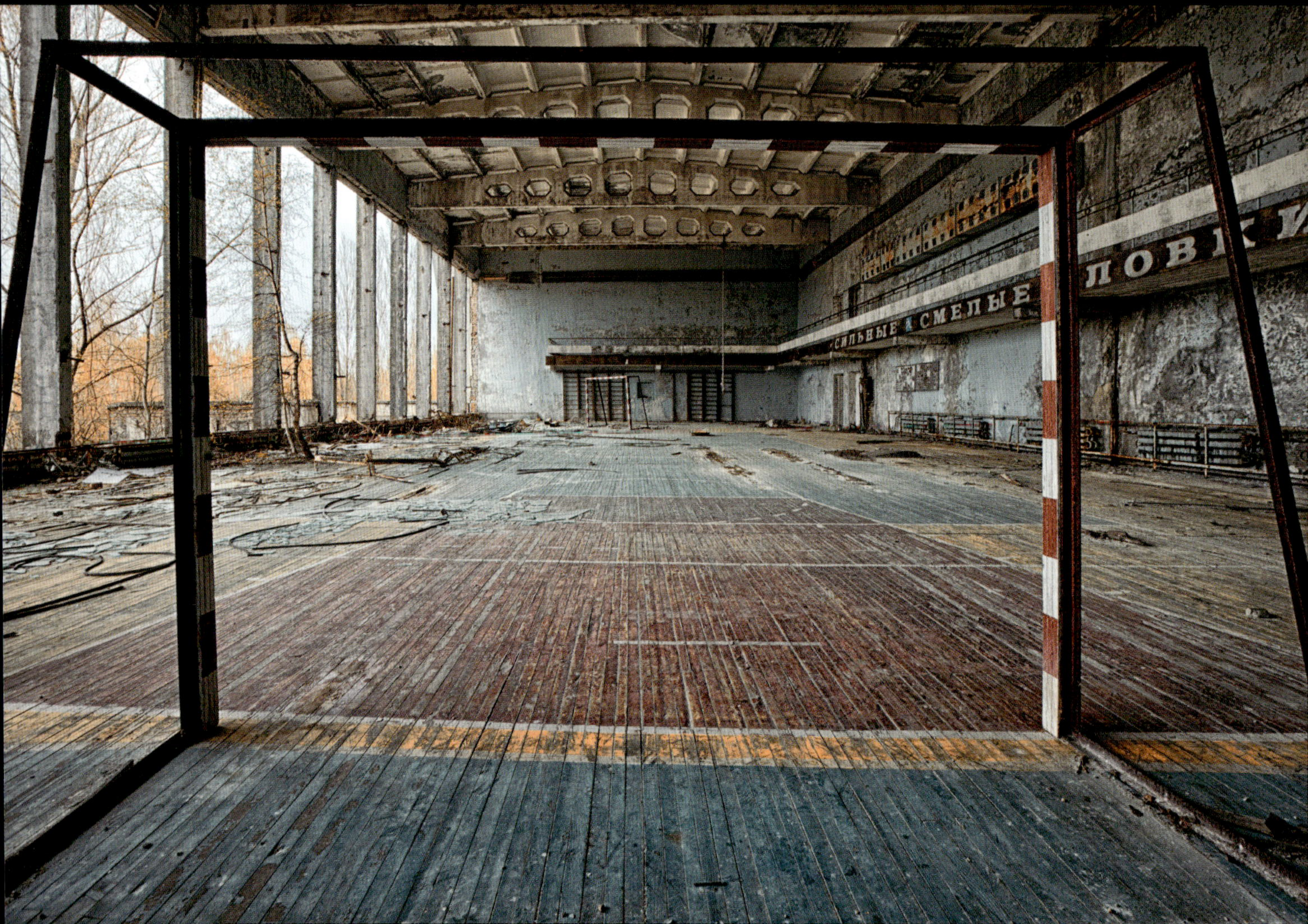
СИЛЬНЫЕ СМЕЛЫЕ

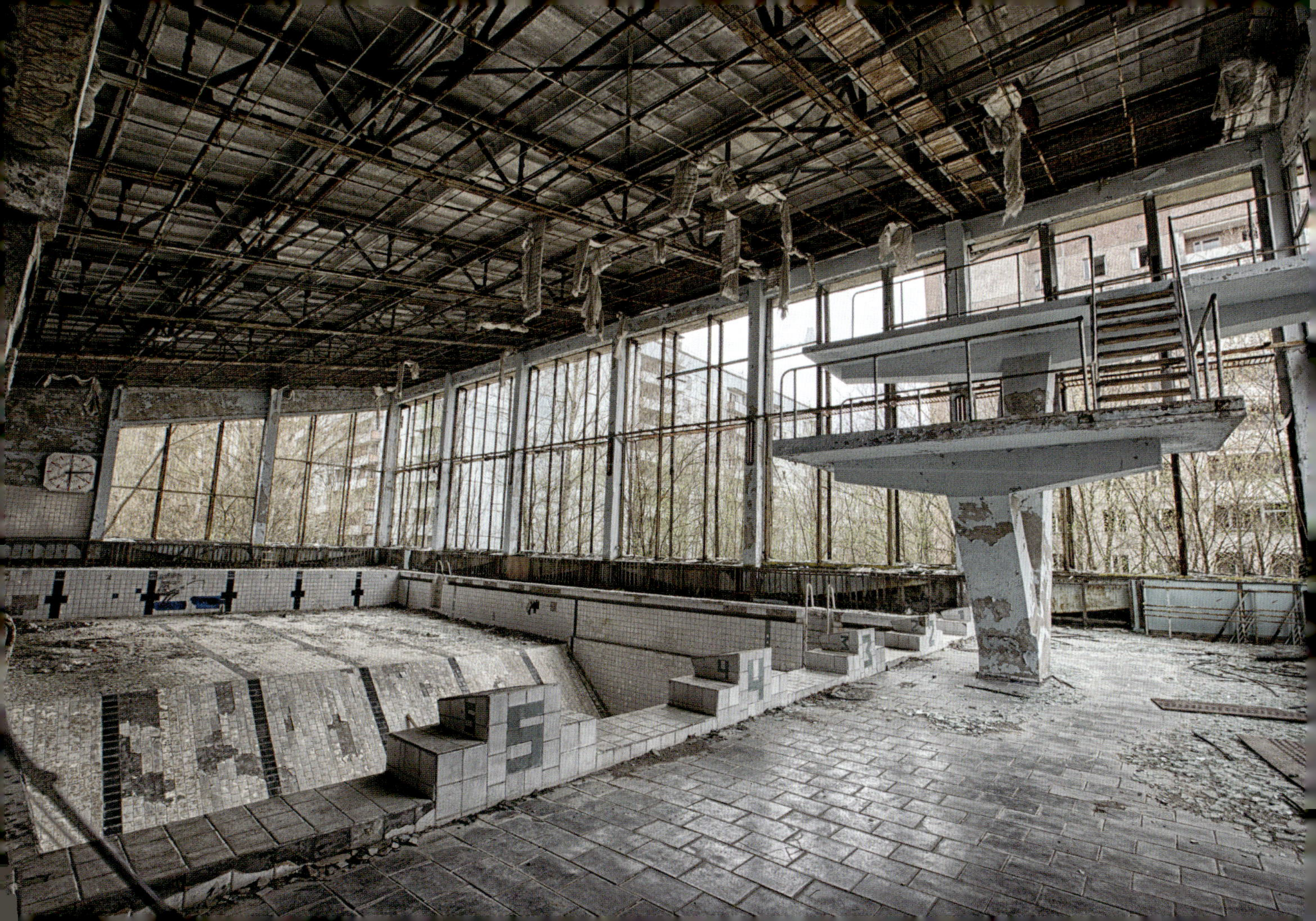

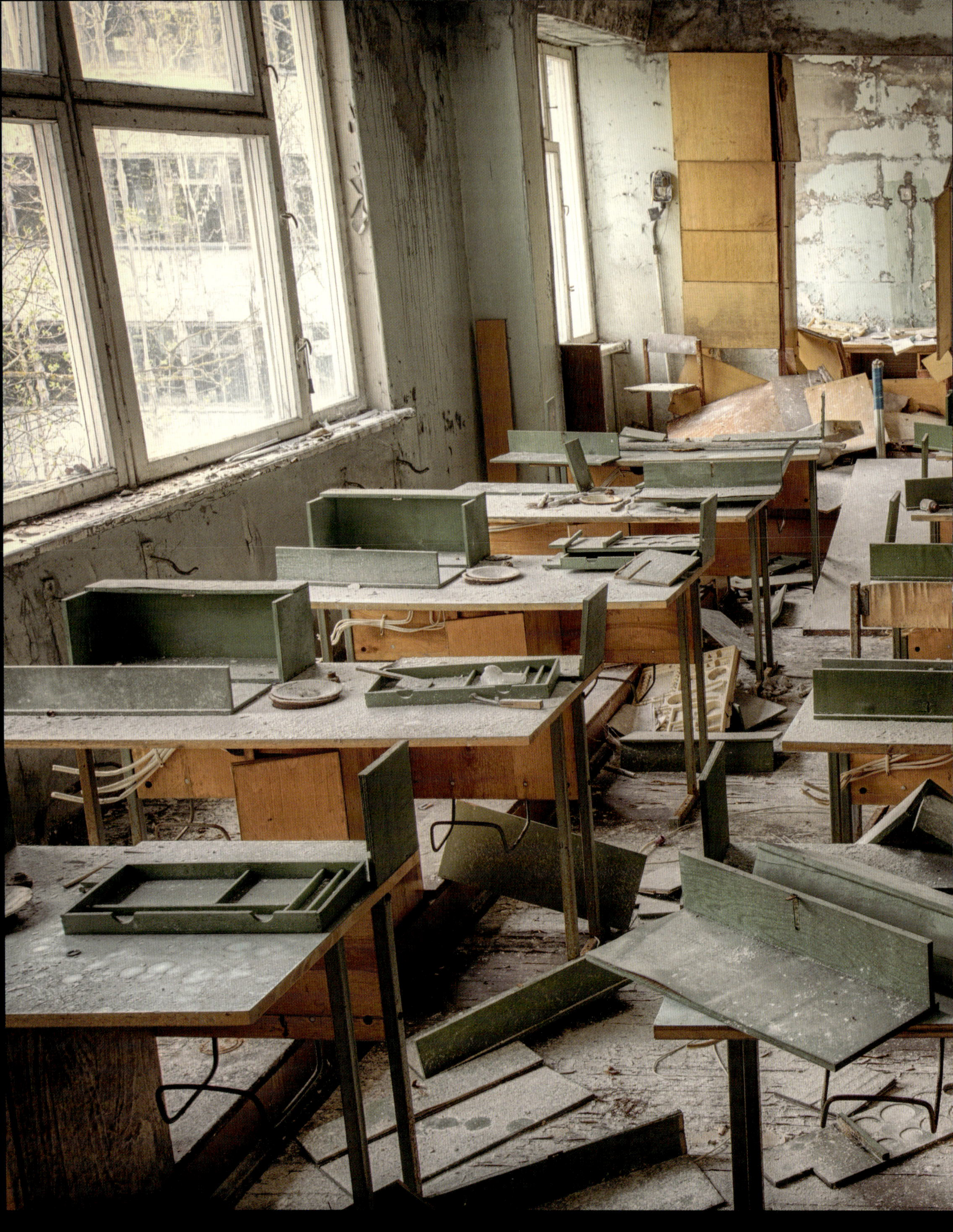

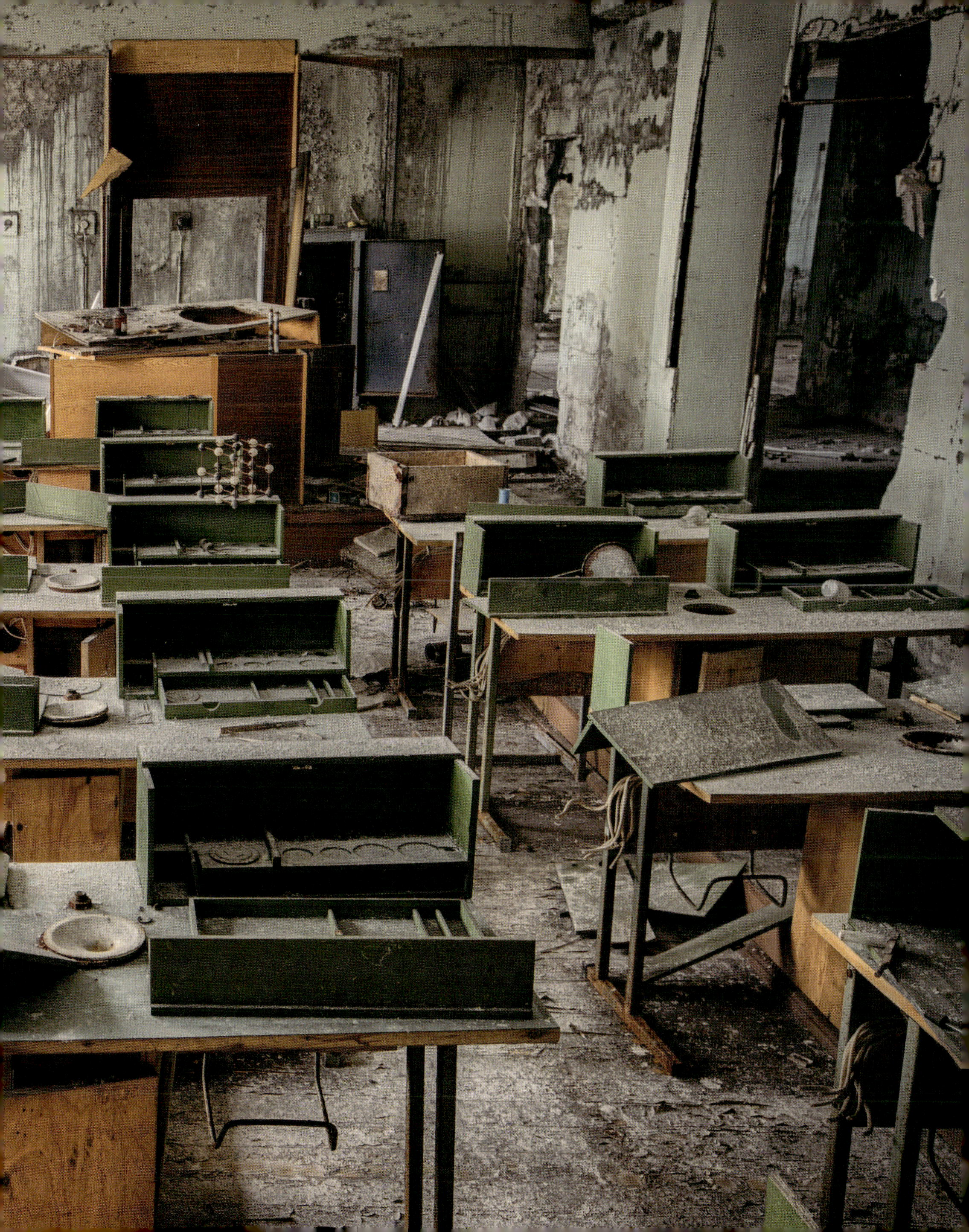

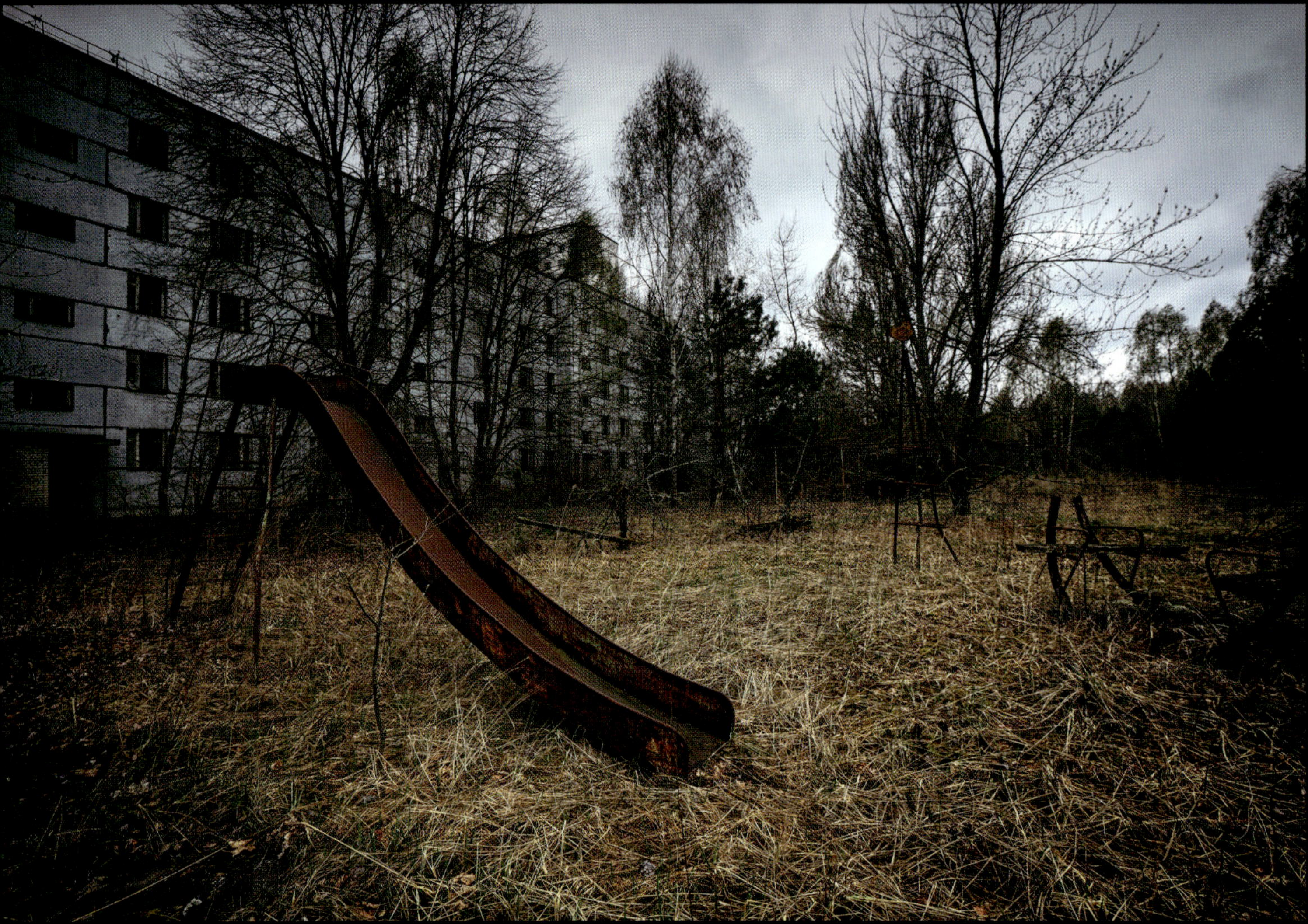

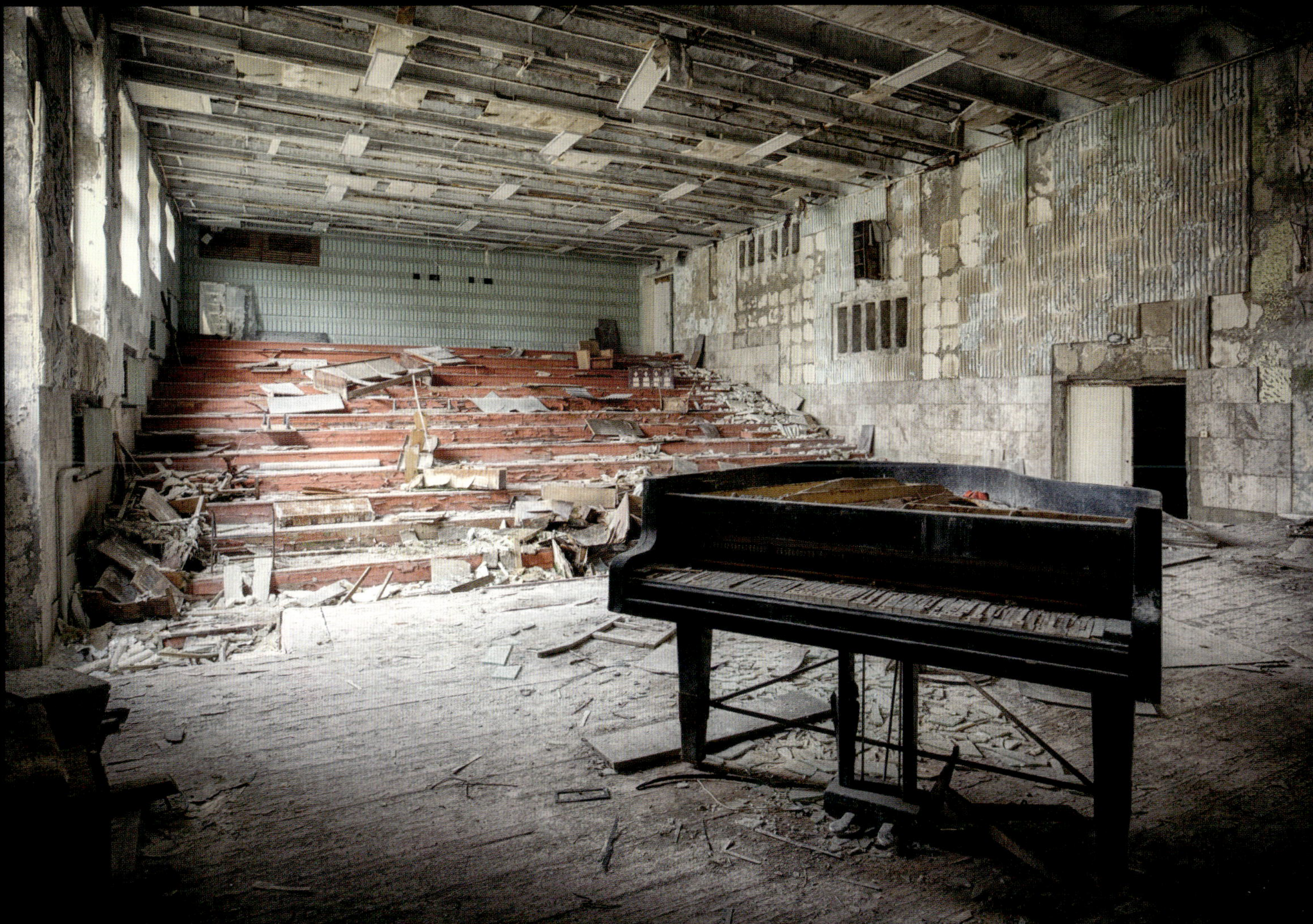

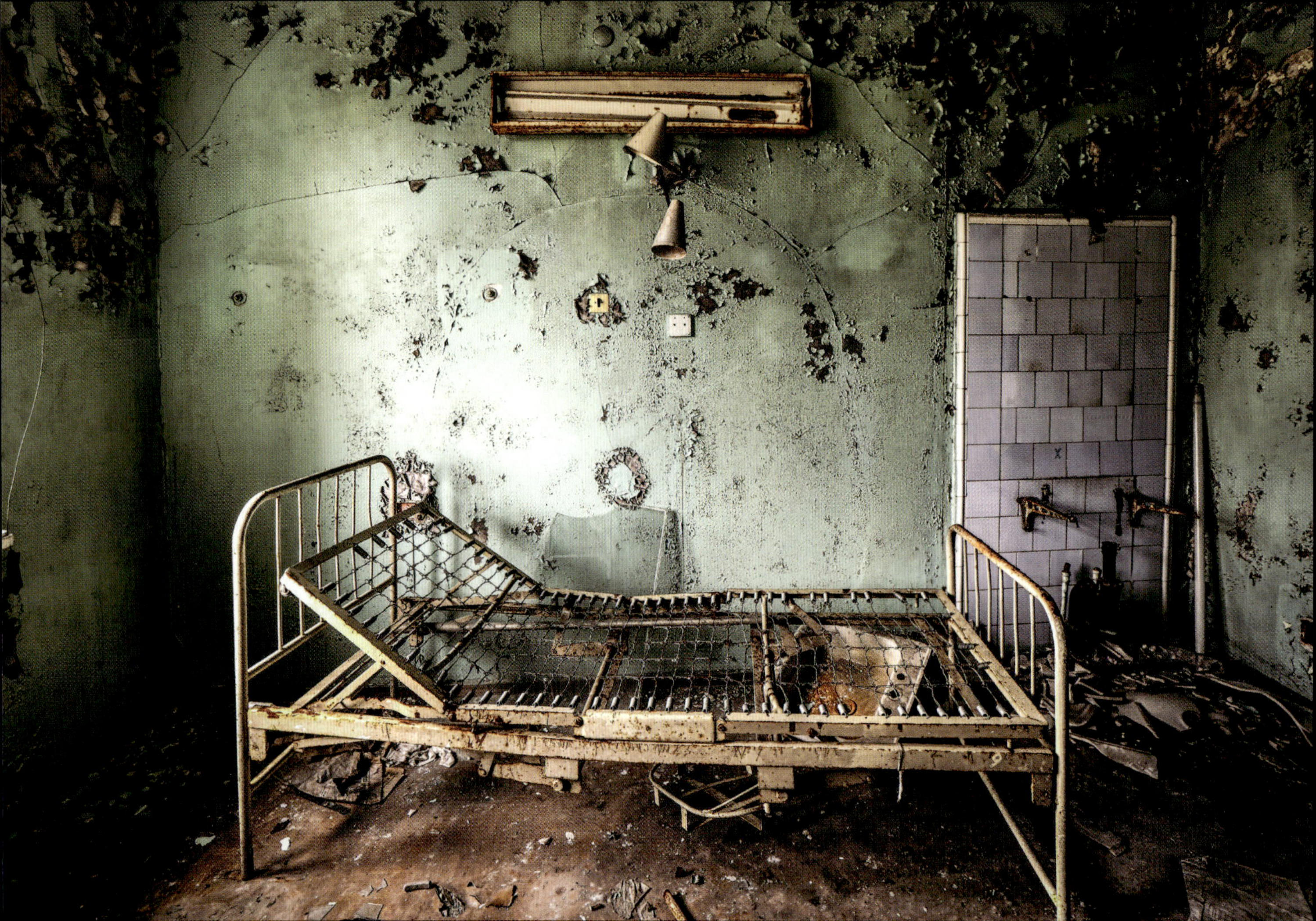

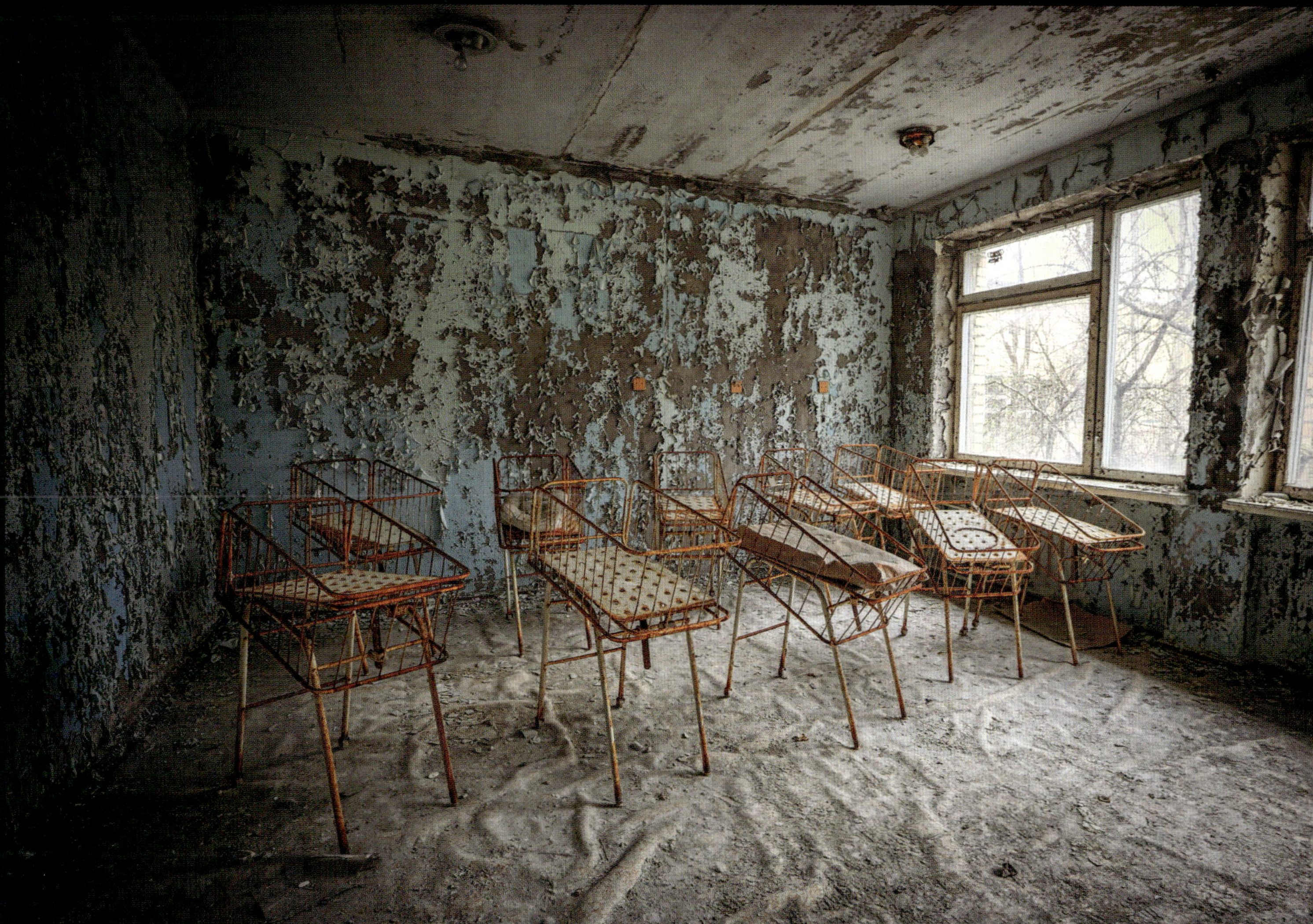

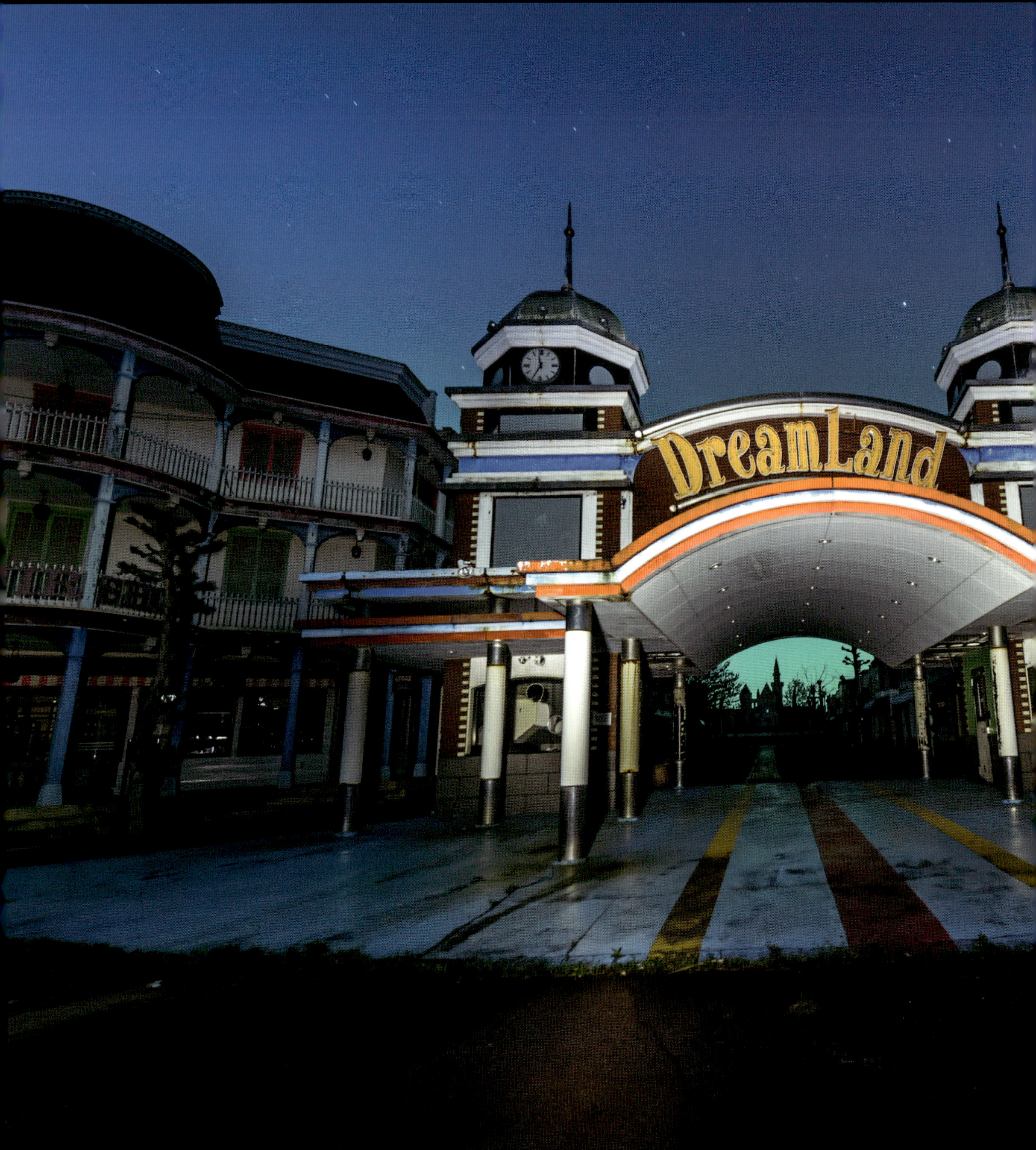
DreamLand

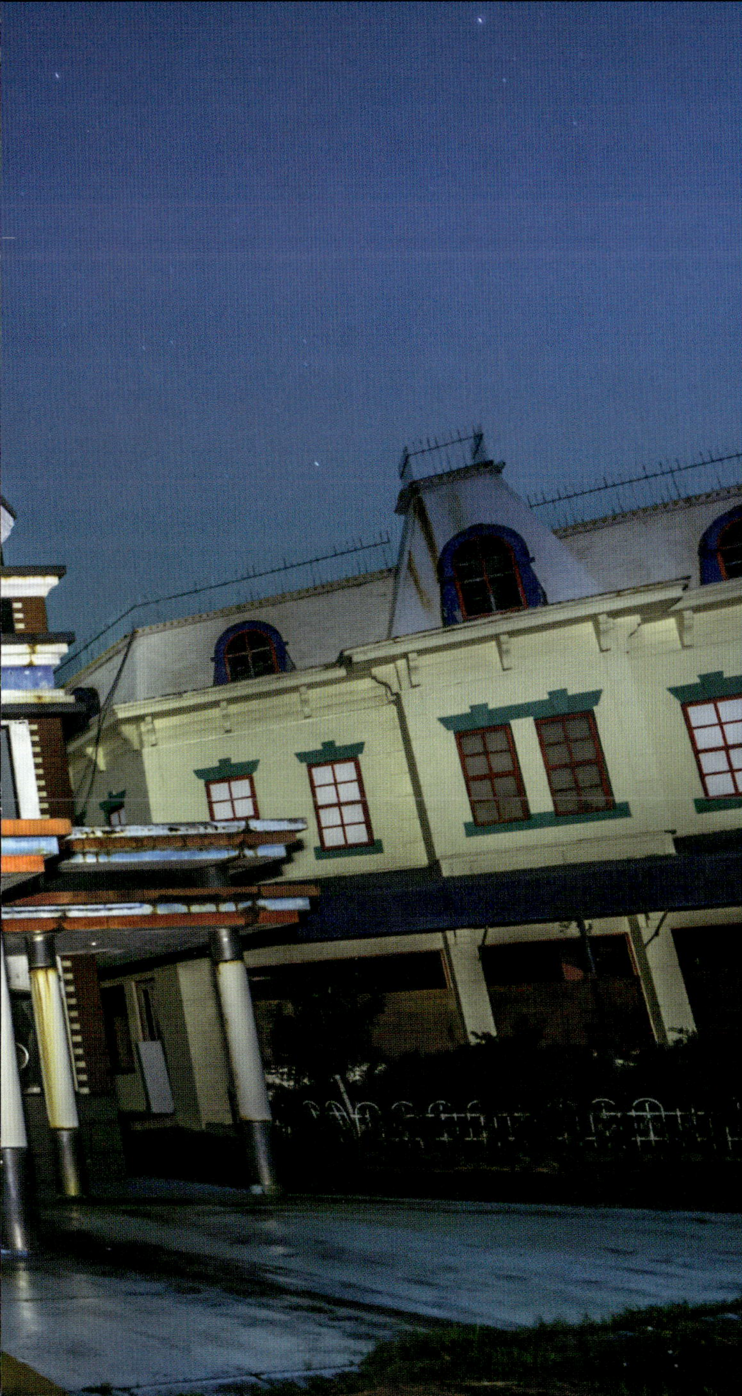

NARA DREAMLAN

JAPAN JAPAN

FOTOS VON PHOTOS BY JORDY MEOW

Alles begann mit Kunizo Matsuo und seiner Begeisterung für die Welt Walt Disneys. Auf einer Amerikareise besuchte er das im Juli 1955 eröffnete Disneyland in Anaheim, Kalifornien, und war fasziniert von dem farbenfrohen Bahnhof, der Paradestraße unter der Burg der schlafenden Schönen und der Matterhornnachbildung mit Achterbahn. Er wollte dieses Land der Träume mit der Autorennbahn für Kinder und der Hochseilbahn, die quer durch den Park verlief, so detailgetreu wie möglich nach Japan bringen. Die nach seiner Rückkehr gegründete Japanese Dream Sightseeing Company verhandelte deshalb mit Disney über den Bau des neuen Erlebnisreiches. Genügend Platz dafür hatte man am Rand von Nara, der einstigen Hauptstadt Japans, gefunden.

Gemeinsam mit den Ingenieuren von Disneyland wurde bald darauf der Aufbau des Nara Dreamland vorangetrieben. Dann kam es jedoch zum Zerwürfnis wegen der Lizenzgebühren. Die japanische Company gab die Kooperation auf, beglich Disneyland die bisherigen Leistungen und entwickelte eine eigene Figurenwelt, die ihr Land der Träume nun anstelle von Micky Maus, Goofy, Donald Duck und deren Freunden beleben sollte. Im Jahr 1961 wurde es eröffnet und von den Besuchern schier überrannt. Der Vergnügungspark florierte 22 Jahre lang mit immer neuen, noch spektakuläreren Fahrbetrieben wie dem Screw und dem Fantasy Coaster oder der Aska genannten riesigen Holzachterbahn. Unerschöpflich schien der Wunsch seiner Gäste nach einem Kurzurlaub mit der ganzen Familie im parkeigenen Hotelkomplex.

Erst die Eröffnung des Tokyo Disneyland im Jahr 1983 erschütterte diesen Geschäftserfolg. Die Besucherzahlen begannen zu sinken. Das Unternehmen Daiei, eine der großen Supermarktketten Japans, kaufte 1993 die Japanese Dream Sightseeing Company mitsamt dem Park auf. Acht Jahre später nahm im 40 Kilometer entfernten Osaka der Freizeitpark Universal Studios Japan seinen Betrieb auf. Für das zu alt gewordene Land der Träume in Nara bedeutete es das Ende. Im August 2006 wurden hier die Tore geschlossen. Bei widerrechtlichem Betreten des umzäunten Geländes drohen nun Geldstrafen bis 900 Euro.

Wer einen Eindringling beobachtet, ist verpflichtet, ihn der Polizei anzuzeigen. So fordert es der Eigentümer, die Firma Daiei. Sie hat ihr ehemaliges Freizeitparadies nie aufgegeben. Keine der Attraktionen wurde verkauft oder abgebaut. Keines der Ausstattungsdetails bereitet andernorts Kindern und Erwachsenen erneut Vergnügen. Die Gebäude entlang der Paradestraße, die Kassenhäuschen, die Parkplätze und die Hotelanlagen scheinen einfach eingeschlafen zu sein. Wäre nicht der jahrelange Stillstand und die damit einhergehende Verwahrlosung des Parks und seiner Einrichtungen, könnte man meinen, es würde ein kurzes Klingelzeichen genügen, damit alles wieder erwacht.

Nara Dreamland ist heute ein Ziel für Fotografen und Anhänger der Urban Exploration. Die neuzeitlichen Entdecker suchen, was an die enormen Besucherströme früherer Tage erinnert, was ihre Fantasie beflügelt und ihnen einen gewissen Nervenkitzel verspricht. Sie lassen sich weder von hohen Geldbußen abschrecken noch von dem beauftragten Wachdienst. Vielleicht ist für sie beides sogar ein Teil der besonderen Anziehungskraft. So gesehen hält der einstige Vergnügungspark bis heute, was sein Name verspricht.

It all began with Kunizo Matsuo and his enthusiasm for the world of Walt Disney. On a trip to the US, he visited Disneyland in Anaheim, California, which opened in July 1955, and was fascinated with the colorful train station, the main street under the castle of Sleeping Beauty and the copy of the Matterhorn with the rollercoaster. He wanted to bring this land of dreams with the car racetrack for children and the cable car that runs right through the park, back to Japan as close to the original as possible. After his return, he founded the Japanese Dream Sightseeing Company that negotiated with Disney for construction of a new realm of adventure. There was enough room for it at the edge of Nara, the one-time capital of Japan. Together with the engineers from Disneyland, the construction of the Nara Dreamland continued soon afterwards. Then, however, it there was a disagreement over the license fees. The Japanese company gave up on the cooperation, paid Disneyland for its services thus far and developed its own world of characters that was to bring their land of dreams to life, instead of Micky Mouse, Goofy, Donald Duck and their friends. In 1961 it opened and was almost overrun with visitors. The amusement park flourished for 22 years with consistently new, even more spectacular rides like the Screw and the Fantasy Coaster or the Aska, the giant wooden roller coaster. It seemed that the desire of its guests was insatiable for a short holiday with the whole family in the hotel complex set in its own park. The business success was only shaken after the opening of Disneyland Tokyo in 1983. The numbers of visitors began to drop. One of Japan's biggest supermarket chains, the Daiei corporation, bought the Japanese Dream Sightseeing Company with its park in 1993. Eight years later and 40 kilometers away in Osaka, the Universal Studios Japan amusement park began operations. That signified the end of the too old Land of Dreams in Nara. In August 2006, the doors closed. There is now a fine of €900 for anyone caught trespassing on the fenced area.

Anyone who sees a trespasser is required to report it to the police. That is the requirement of the owner, the Daiei company. It has never abandoned its one-time recreational paradise. None of the attractions have been sold or dismantled. None of the details are enjoyed by children and adults anywhere else. The buildings along the main street, the sales kiosks, the parking lots and the hotel facilities seem to have simply fallen asleep. If it were not for the years of stagnation and resulting neglect of the parks and its facilities, you could imagine it would take only a little tinkle of a bell to wake everything back up.

Today, Nara Dreamland is a destination for photographers and followers of urban exploration. Modern day explorers look for something to remind them of the enormous streams of visitors of former days and that which captivated their imaginations and promised them a certain thrill. They are not deterred by the expensive fine or by the contract security service. Perhaps both of these are even part of the special attraction for them. Looking at it that way, the former amusement park still keeps that which its name promises to this day.

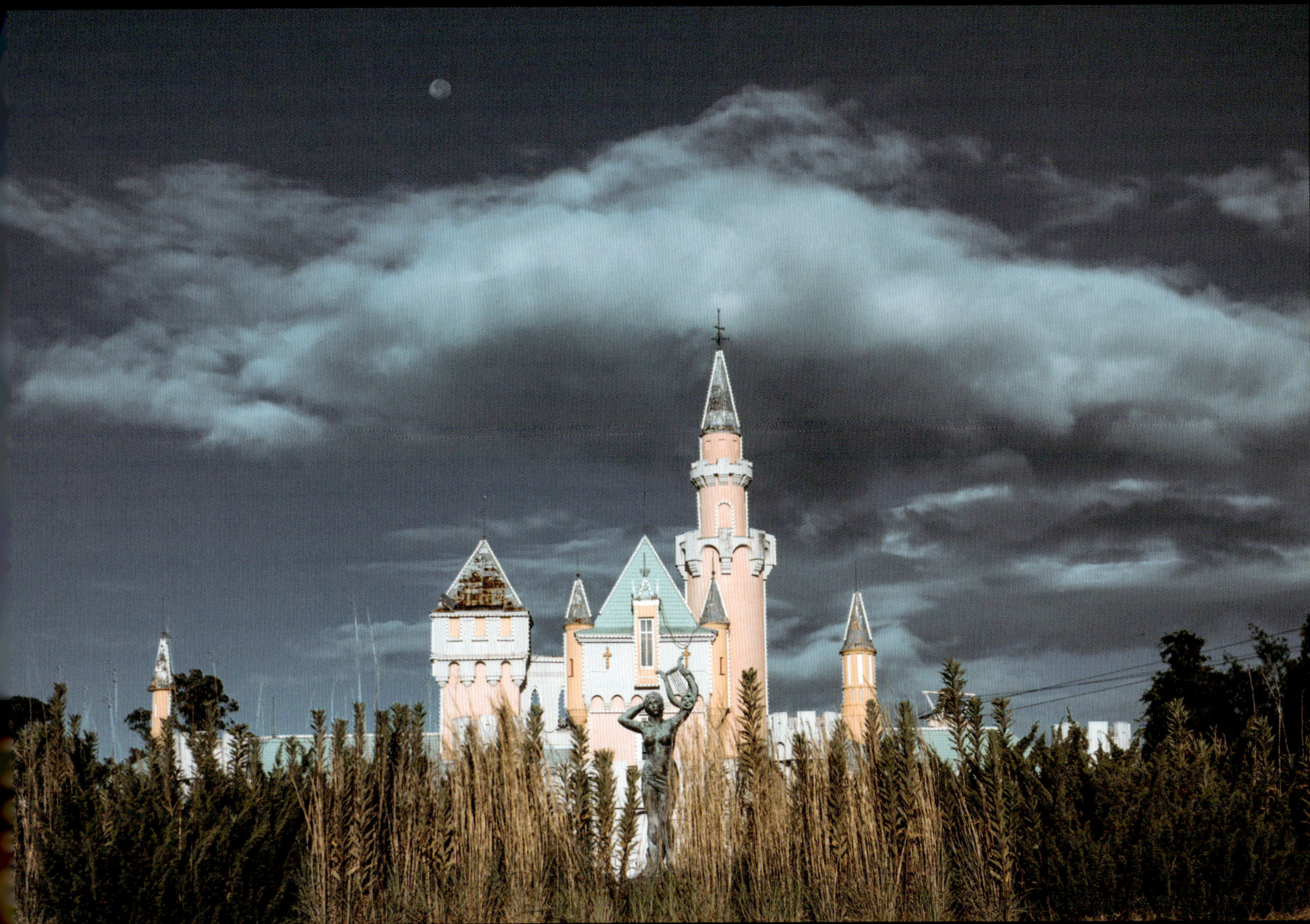

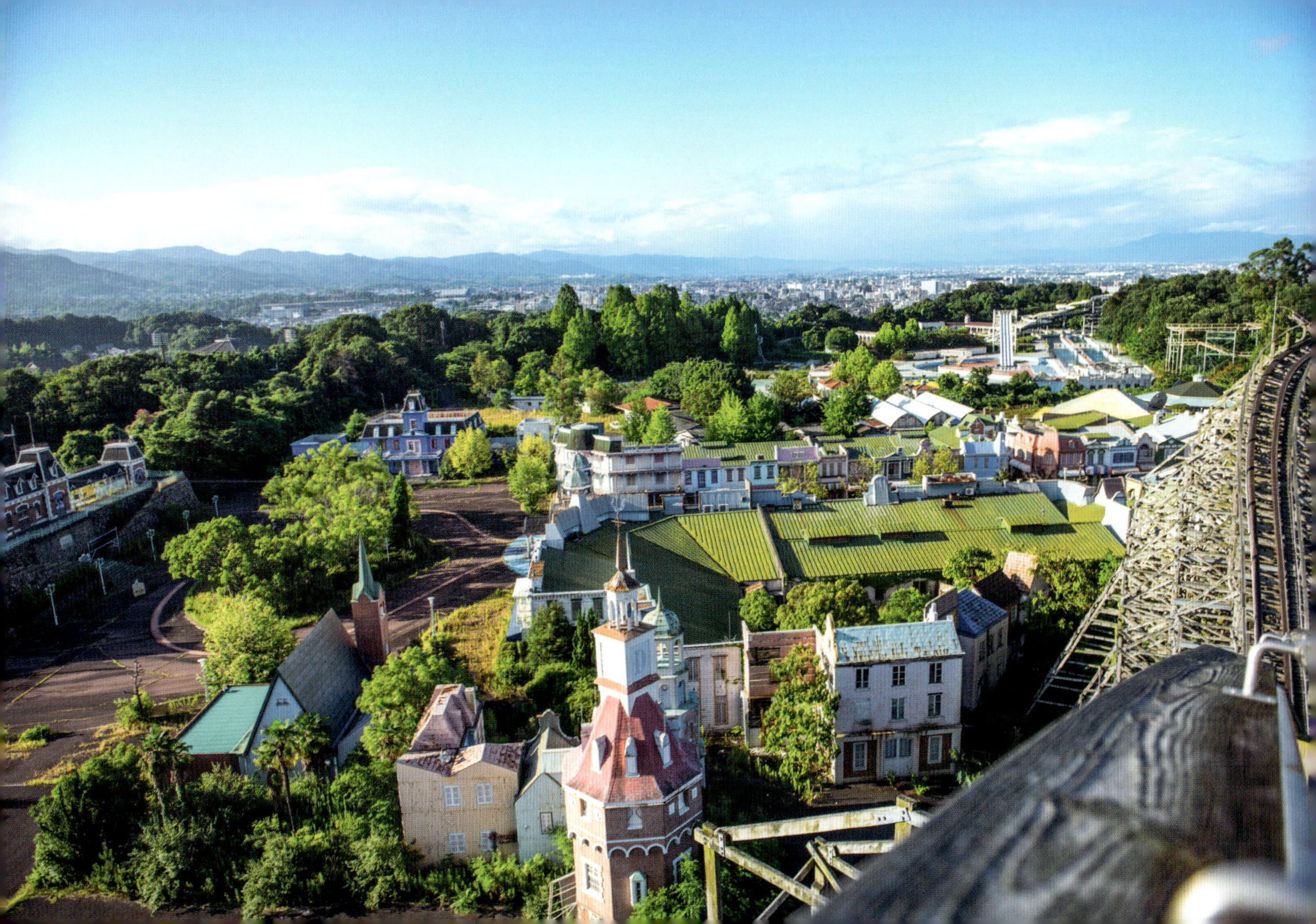

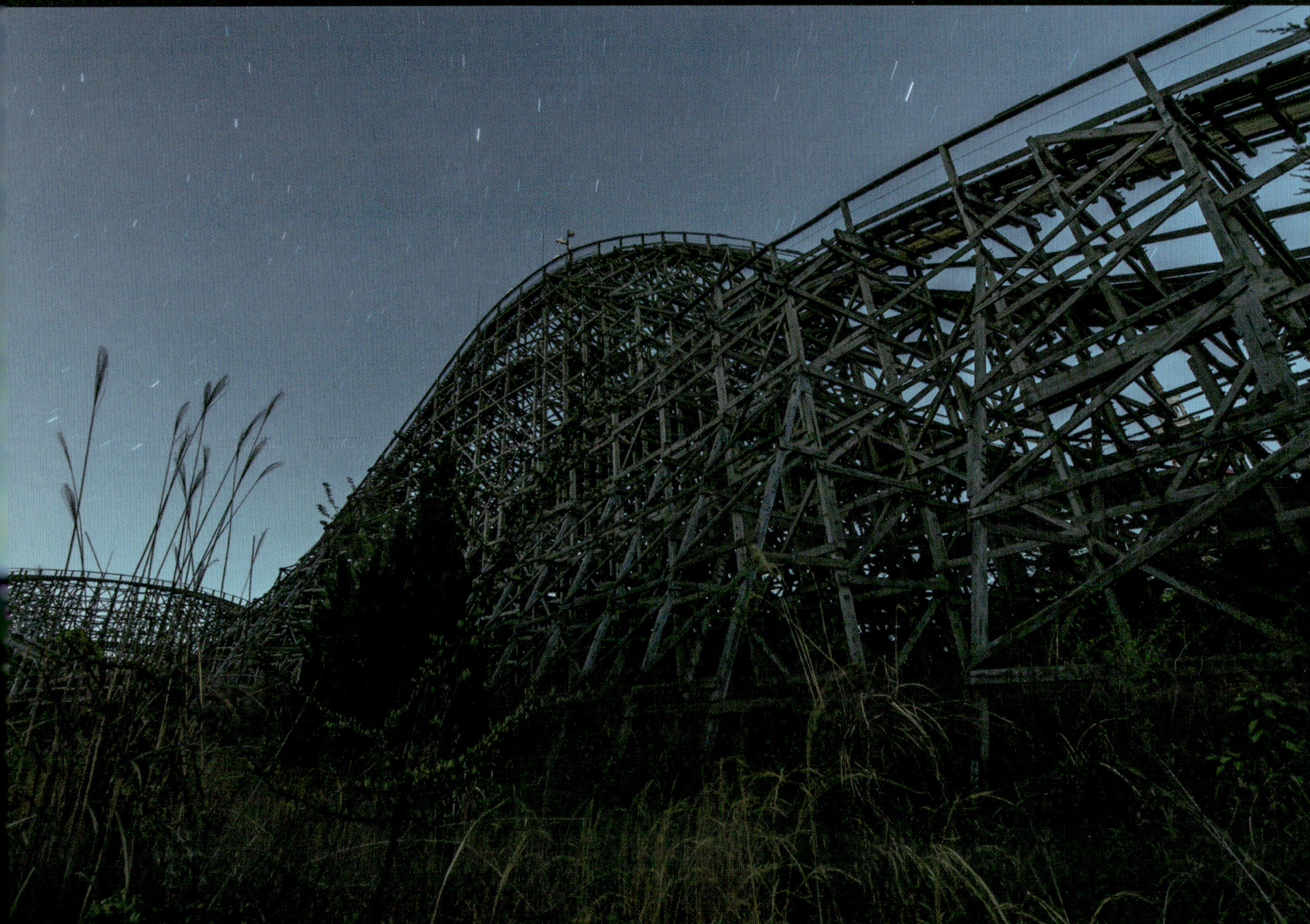

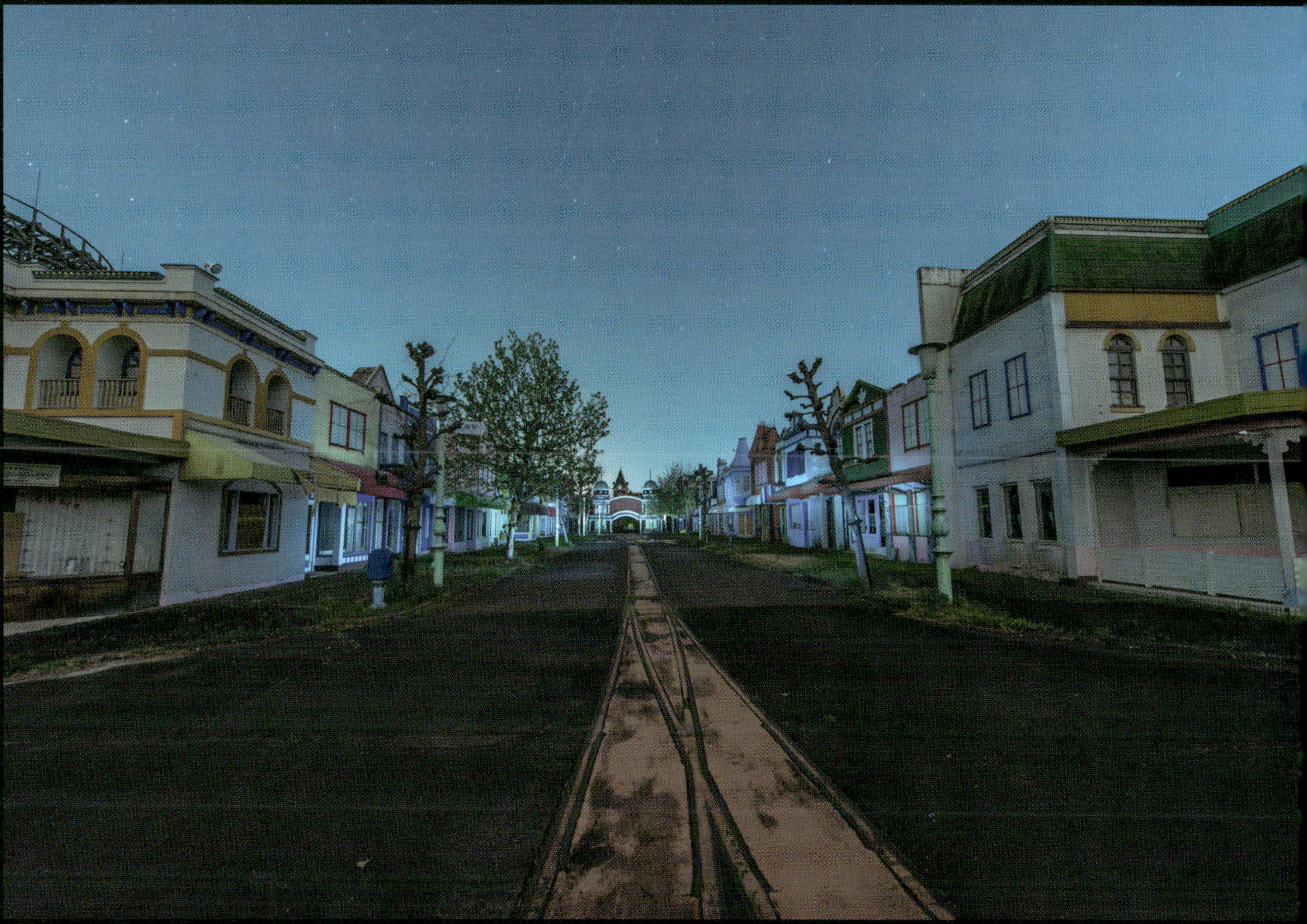

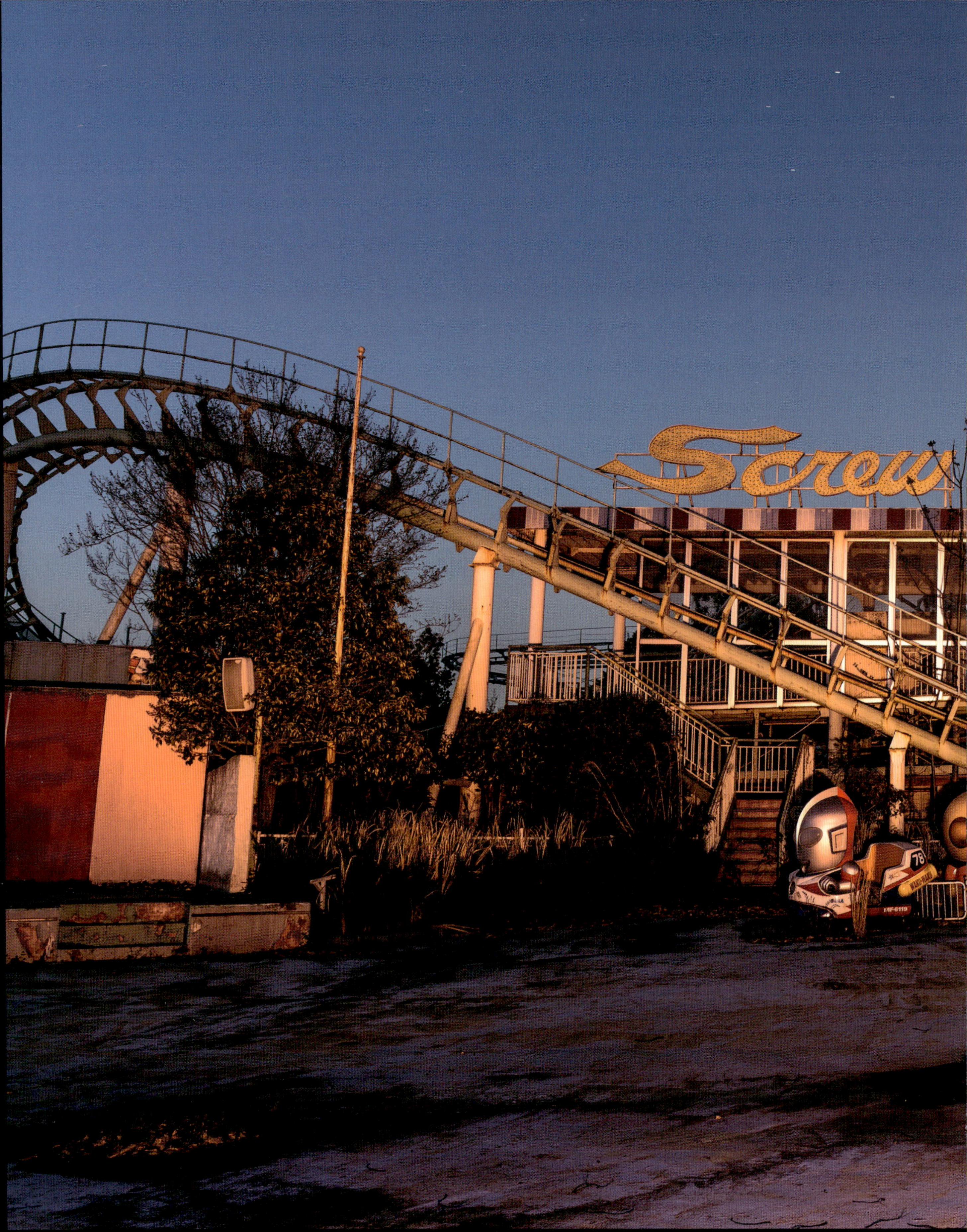
Screw

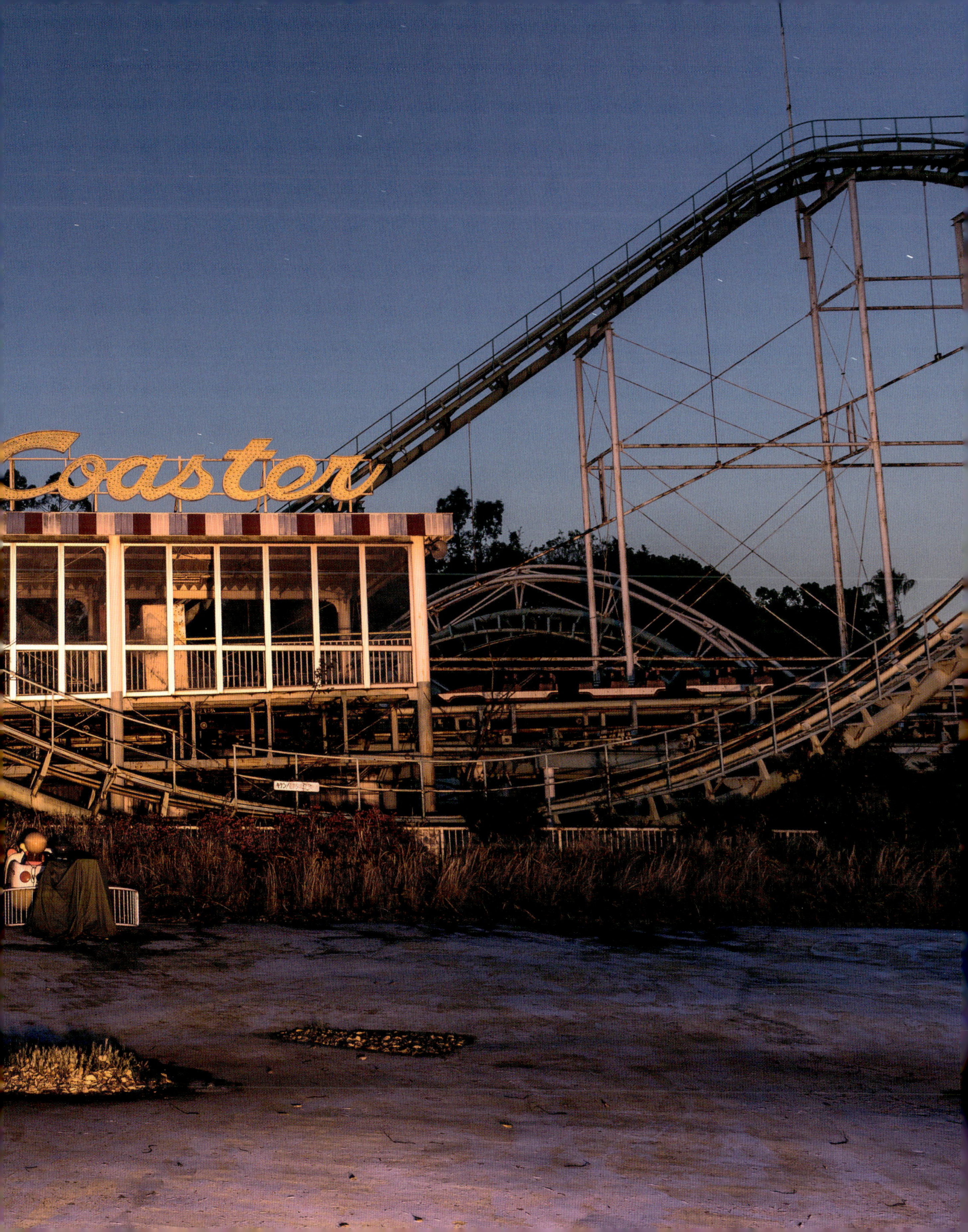
Coaster

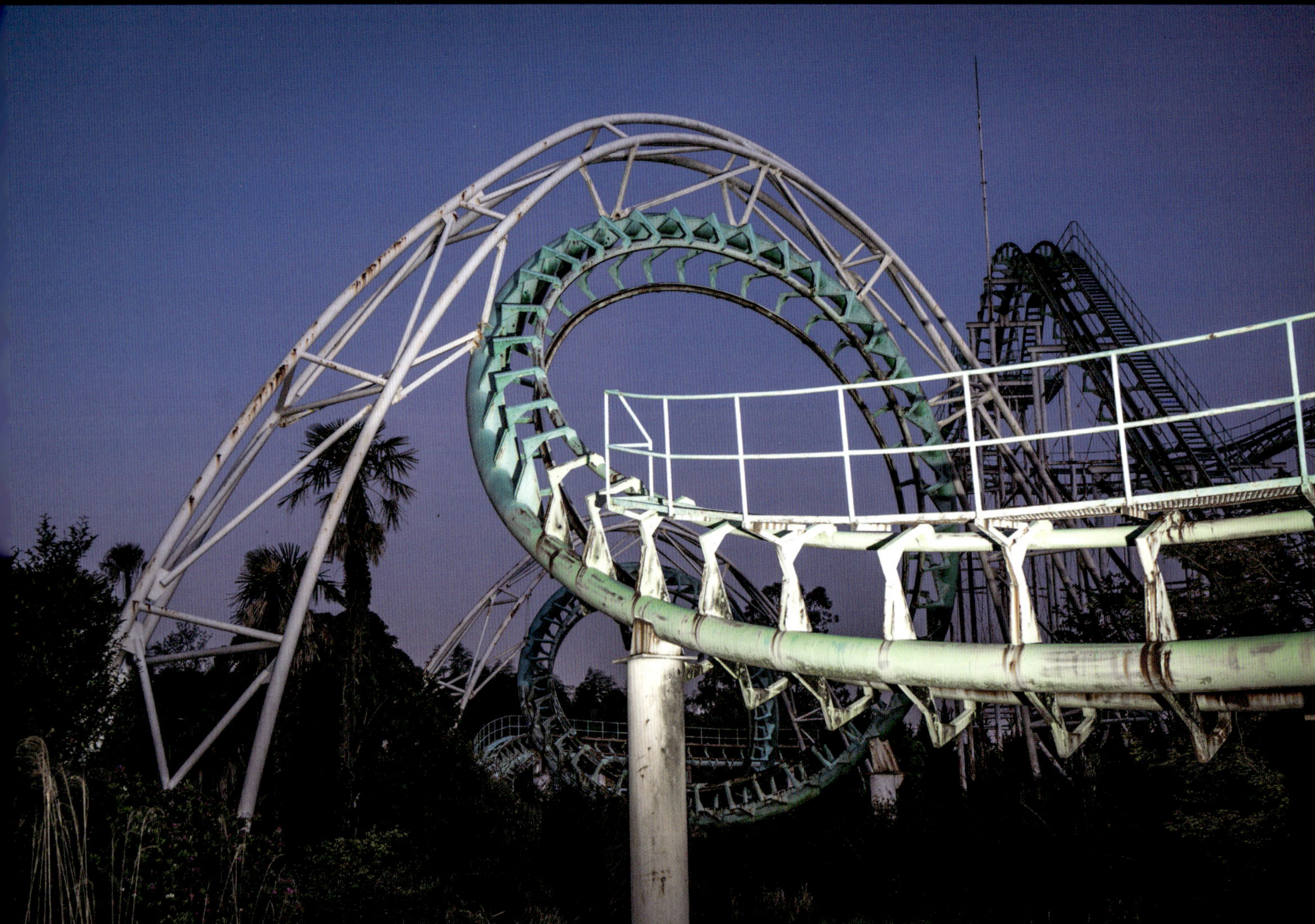

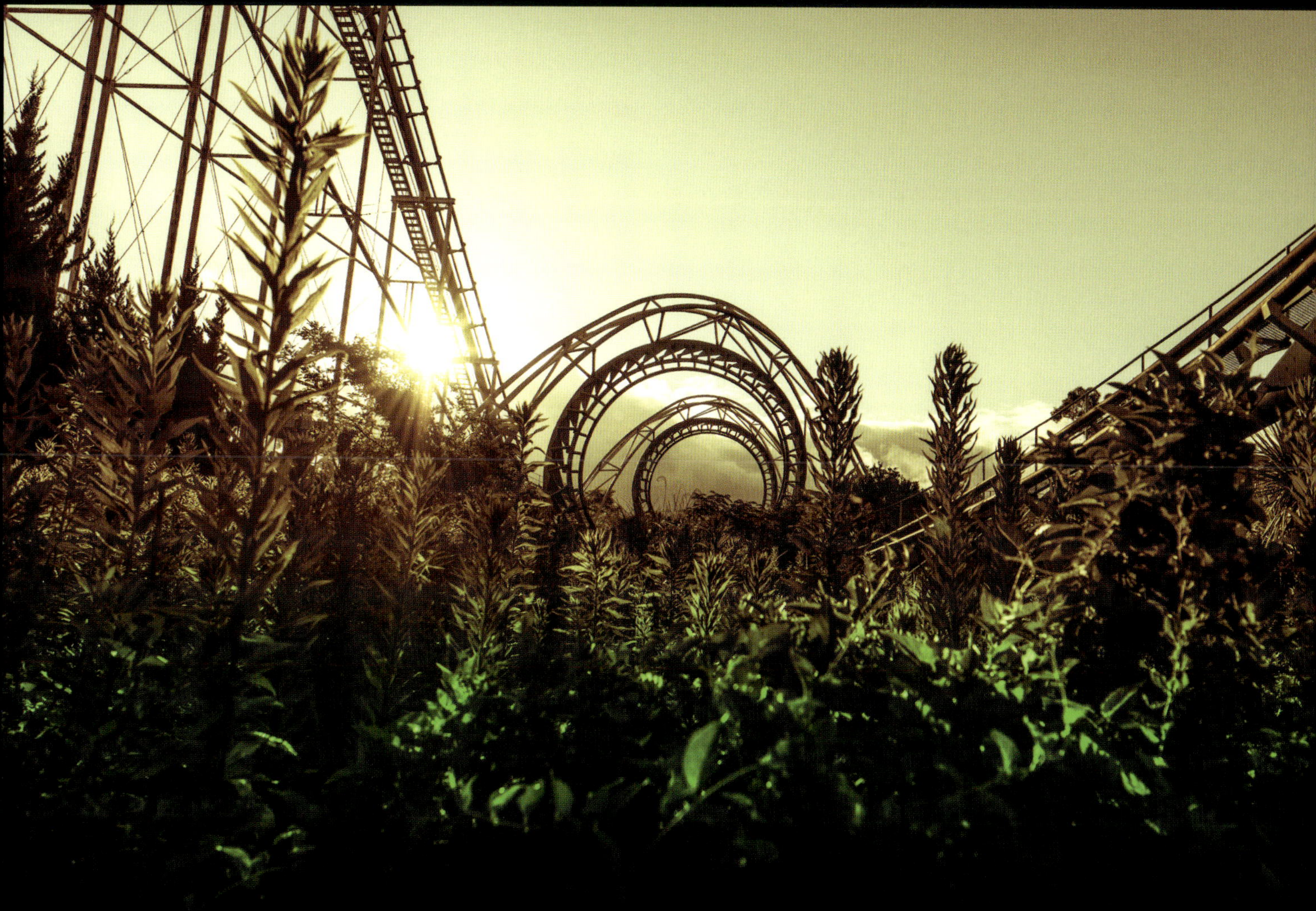

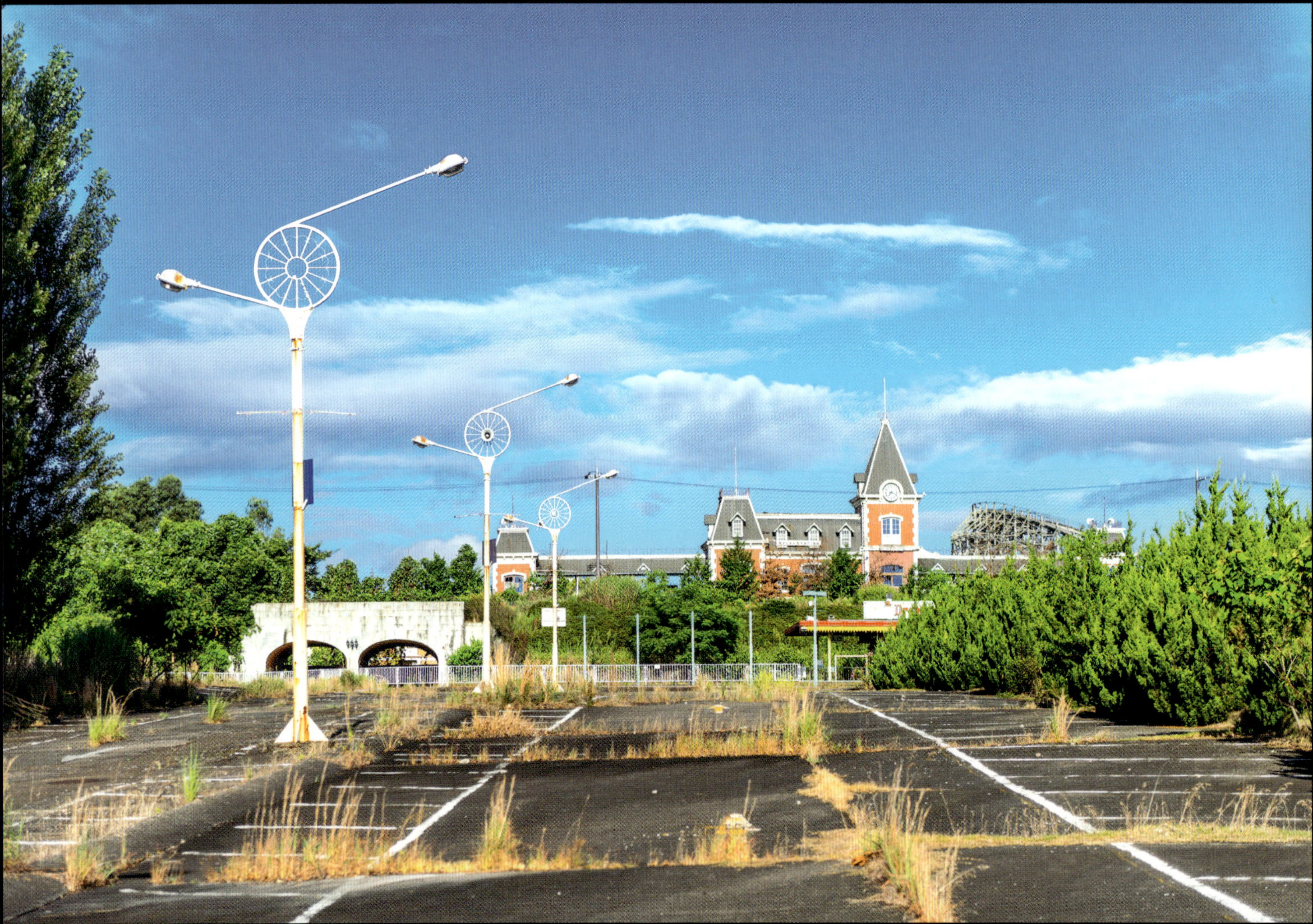

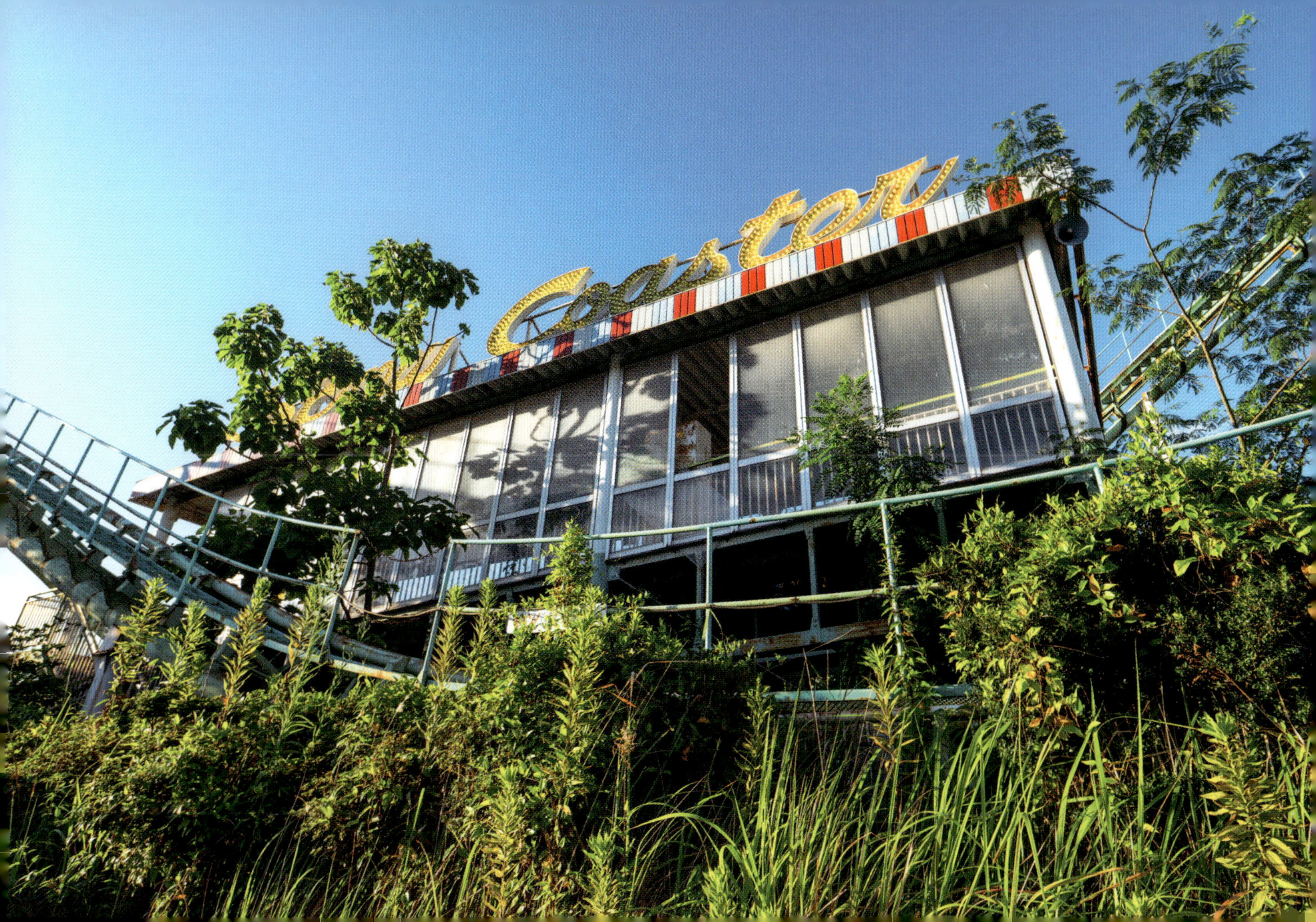
Coaster

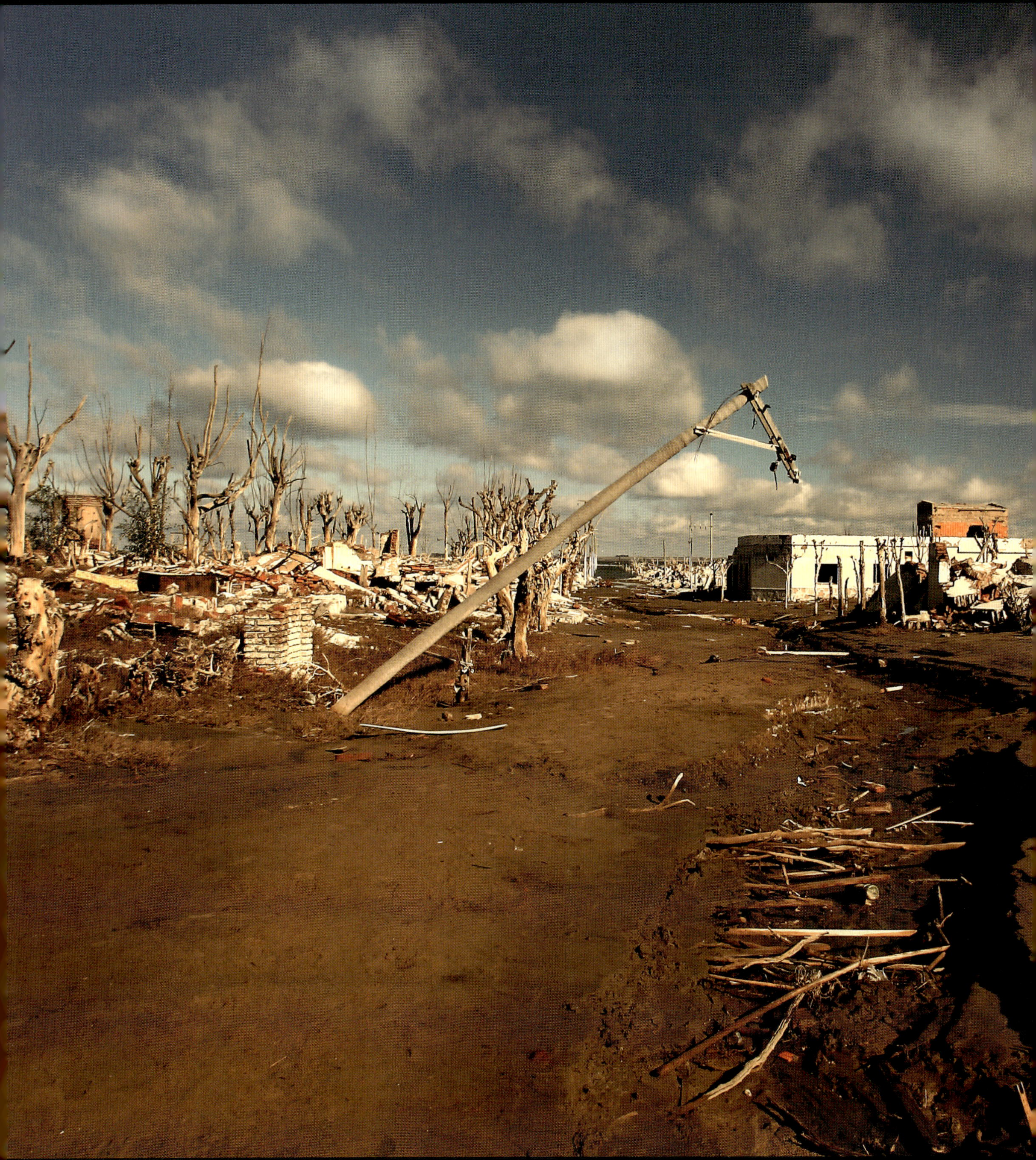

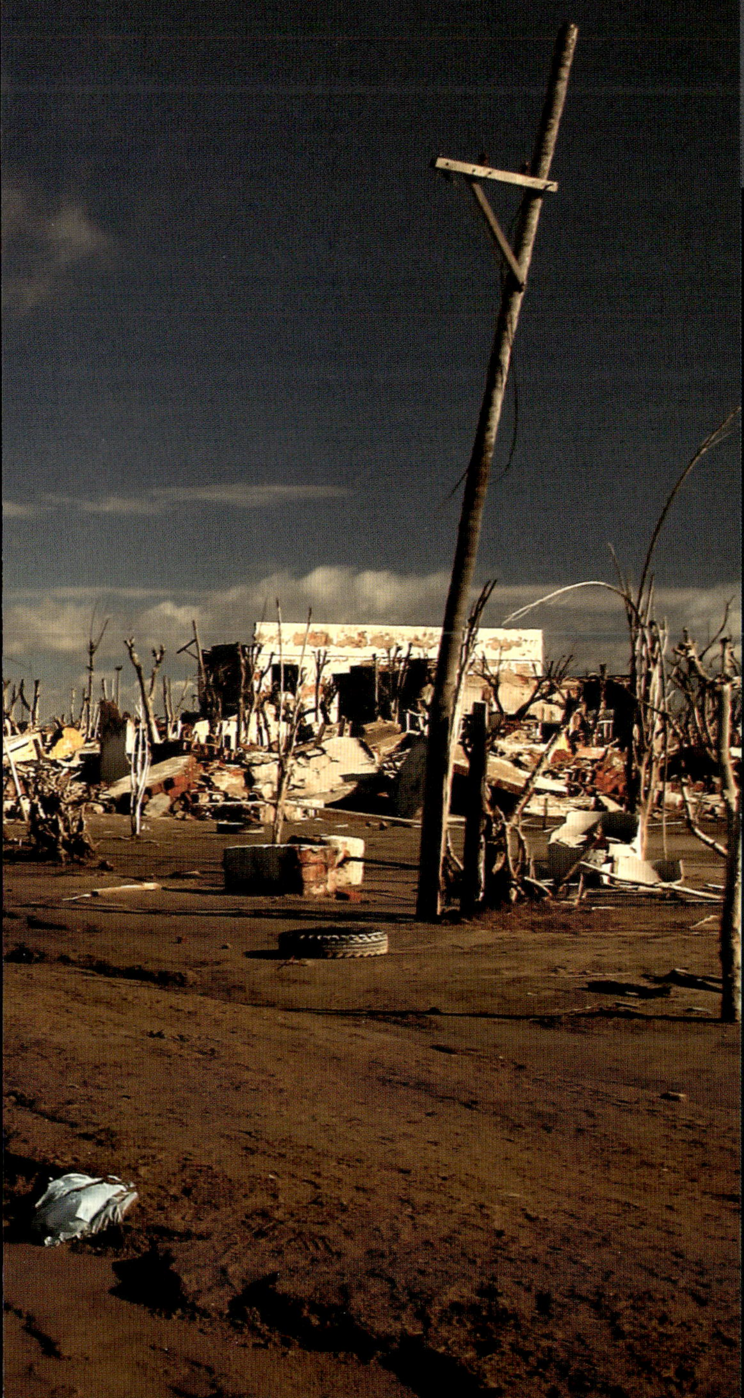

VILLA EPECUÉ

ARGENTINIEN ARGENTINA

FOTOS VON PHOTOS BY ALBERTO CLAVERÍA

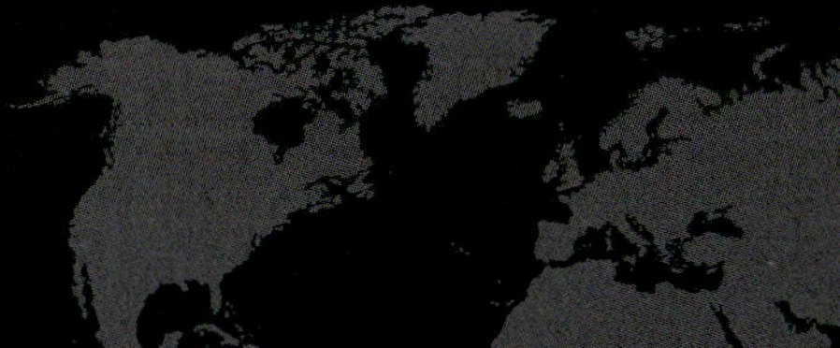

Einer der vielen Legenden zufolge wurde Carhue, ein Häuptling des Puelche-Stammes, von einer Lähmung geheilt, als er in dem See aus Tränen seiner Geliebten Epecuén ein Bad genommen hatte.
Der reale, etwa 10.000 Hektar große Lago Epecuén wies 1934 eine Salzkonzentration von 382 Gramm pro Liter auf, weswegen er mit dem Toten Meer auf der anderen Seite der Erdkugel gern im Zusammenhang genannt wurde. 1922 offiziell gegründet, entwickelte sich Villa Epecuén am Ufer des Salzsees zu einem Badeparadies mit einem eigenen Eisenbahnanschluss und Elektrizitätswerk. Elegante Thermalanlagen, Hotels verschiedener Kategorien und vielversprechende medizinische Behandlungen lockten Familien von Minenarbeitern wie auch vermögende Kurgäste in den 550 Kilometer südwestlich von der argentinischen Hauptstadt Buenos Aires gelegenen Ort.
Rheuma, Hautkrankheiten, Diabetes, Atemwegbeschwerden, Depression, Arthritis: Die Heilungschancen durch das Salzwasser sprachen sich herum und zogen auch internationale Urlauber an. 25.000 Badegäste begegneten jährlich in der Urlaubssaison von Dezember bis März den etwa 1.500 Einwohnern. Man lebte gut in Villa Epecuén. Obschon die niederschlagsarmen Dreißiger- und Vierzigerjahre den See schwinden ließen. Deswegen wurde in den Siebzigerjahren ein Kanal gebaut, der, im Verbund mit fünf weiteren großen Seen, den Lago Epecuén speiste, seinen Salzgehalt aber senkte. Ein Damm zum Schutz vor Hochwasser wurde 1980 errichtet.
Im Jahr 1985 jedoch, am 10. November, nach wochenlangen heftigen Regenfällen – die Bewohner hatten schon lange Zeit das Anschwellen des Sees mit Sorge beobachtet –, brach der Lehmdamm an mehreren Stellen und Villa Epecuén wurde überflutet. Einige Einwohner flohen auf die Dächer ihrer Häuser, weil sie es blieb. Im Jahr 1993 lag der Ort zehn Meter unter Wasser.
Der Salzgehalt des Sees maß 1987 nur noch 37 Gramm pro Liter. Die Aussichten, an die Tradition des Gesundheitstourismus anzuknüpfen, erschöpften sich.
Erst ab 2009, nach lang anhaltenden Trockenperioden, zog sich das Wasser zurück. Nach einem Vierteljahrhundert tauchten nun die Reste der Thermalanlagen und der 250 Hotels oder Pensionen – von einer weißen Salzschicht überzogen – wieder auf. Erhalten gebliebEN war das am Stadtrand liegende El Matadero, das ehemalige Schlachthaus im Stil des Art déco, in dem sich Tauben eingenistet haben. Verrottete Fahrzeuge, eine Badewanne, schiefe Strommasten, verwüstete Häuser und Straßen, die zusammengebrochene Kirche, Möbel und abgestorbene Bäume sind die Wegmarken für ehemalige Bewohner, die nach Villa Epecuén zurückkehren, wenn auch nur für kurze Zeit.
Einige gehen in milden Tagesstunden auf Schrottsuche oder räumen einige Trümmer ihres ehemaligen Anwesens zur Seite, in der Hoffnung etwas aus der Vergangenheit zu finden. Andere beobachten mit Interesse Fotografen, Touristenführungen oder argentinische Kameraleute, die unter azurblauem Himmel einen Film drehen über den aufgetauchten Ort. Im Gedächtnis der Einwohner haften die Bilder einer goldenen Zeit und das frohsinnige Flair eines Kurbetriebs, welches Schwarz-Weiß-Postkarten, die im Nebenort Carhue verkauft werden, zu vermitteln suchen: Badegäste mit Sonnenschirmen spazieren auf mehrere Meter breiten Holzstegen über den Lago Epecuén.

According to one of many legends, Carhue, a chief of the Puelche tribe, was healed of paralysis after taking a bath in the lake of tears from his beloved Epecuén.

The real, approximately 10,000 hectare Lake Epecuén, had a salt concentration of 382 grams per liter in 1934, which is the reason it is often mentioned in connection with the Dead Sea on the other side of the world. Officially founded in 1922, Villa Epecuén on the bank of the salt lake developed into a bathing paradise with its own train connection and power plant. Elegant thermal baths, hotels of various categories and promising medical treatments attracted the families of miners and well off spa guests to the location 550 kilometers southwest from the Argentinian capital of Buenos Aires.

Rheumatism, skin diseases, diabetes, respiratory diseases, depression, arthritis: Word about the healing power of the salt water spread and also attracted international vacationers. Every year in tourist season from December to March, 25,000 spa guests met the approximately 1,500 residents. Life was good in Villa Epecuén. Inevitably, the low precipitation in the thirties and forties caused the lake to disappear. For that reason, a canal was built in the seventies connecting five other large lakes that fed into Lago Epecuén, but lowered its salt content. In 1980, a dam was built as protection against flooding.

In the year 1985, however, on November 10, after weeks of heavy rainfall during which the residents watched with concern as the level of the lake rose, the clay dam broke in several places and Villa Epecuén was flooded. Some residents fled to the roofs of their houses hoping that the water would subside quickly, but it stayed. In 1993 the town was under ten meters of water.

In 1987, the salt content of the lake was only 37 grams per liter. The hopes of continuing in the tradition of health tourism came to an end.

The water only receded in 2009, after a long period of drought. After a quarter of a century, the remaining thermal baths and the 250 hotels and guest houses surfaced again, covered in a white layer of salt. The El Matadero survived on the edge of town, the former slaughterhouse in the art deco style in which pigeons nested. Rusted vehicles, a bathtub, crooked power poles, devastated houses and streets, the collapsed church, furniture and dead trees are the signposts for former residents who return to Villa Epecuén, even if just for a short time.

Some go searching for scrap in the mild daytime hours or push some debris from their former property to the side in the hope of finding something from the past. Others observe photographers with interest, guided tours or Argentinian camera crews filming the resurfaced town under the azure blue sky. Still in the memories of the residents are the images of a golden era and the cheerful flair of a spa business that black and white postcards sold in neighboring Carhue try to portray: bathing guests carrying sun umbrellas walking along a several meter wide wooden piers above Lake Epecuén.

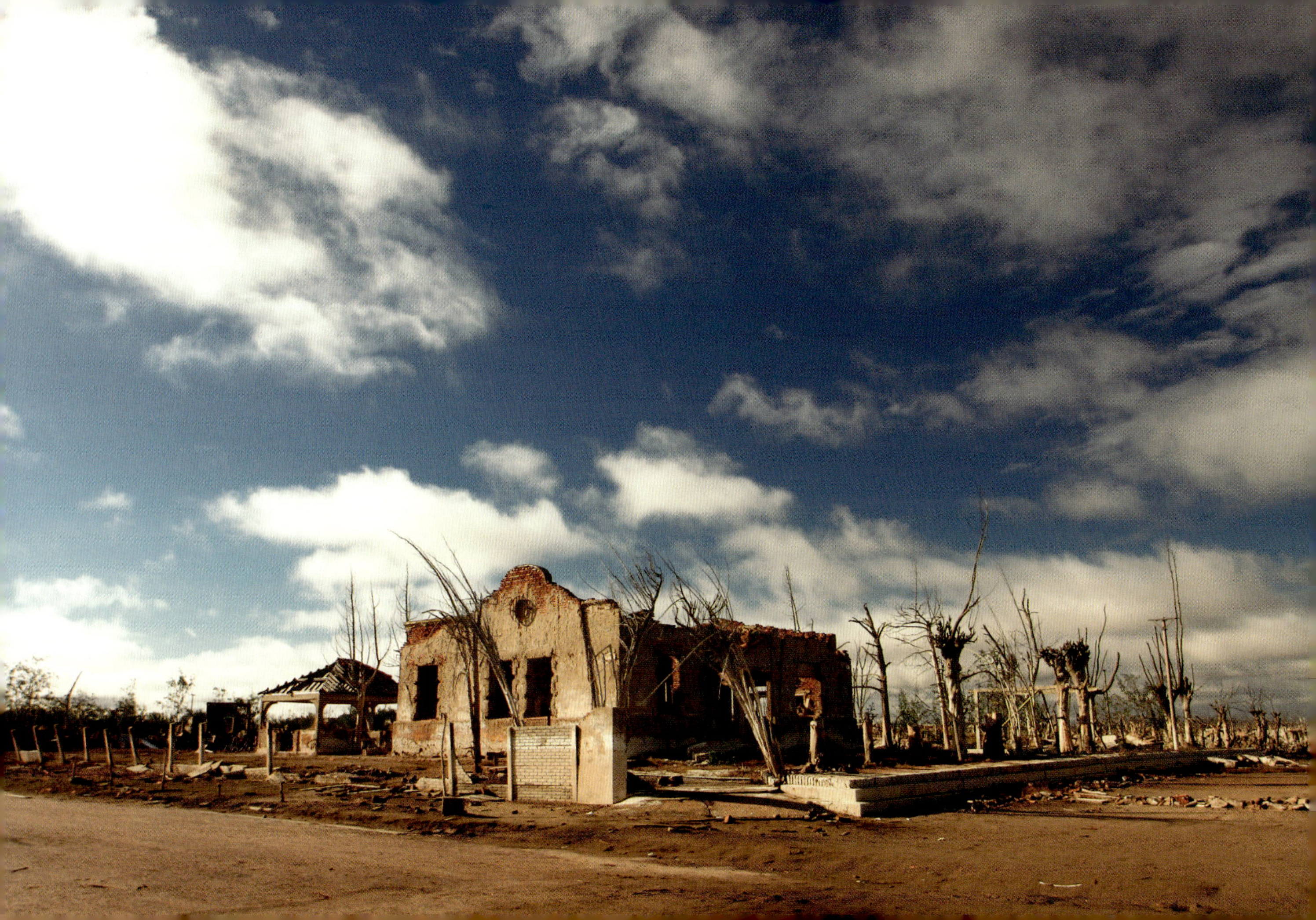

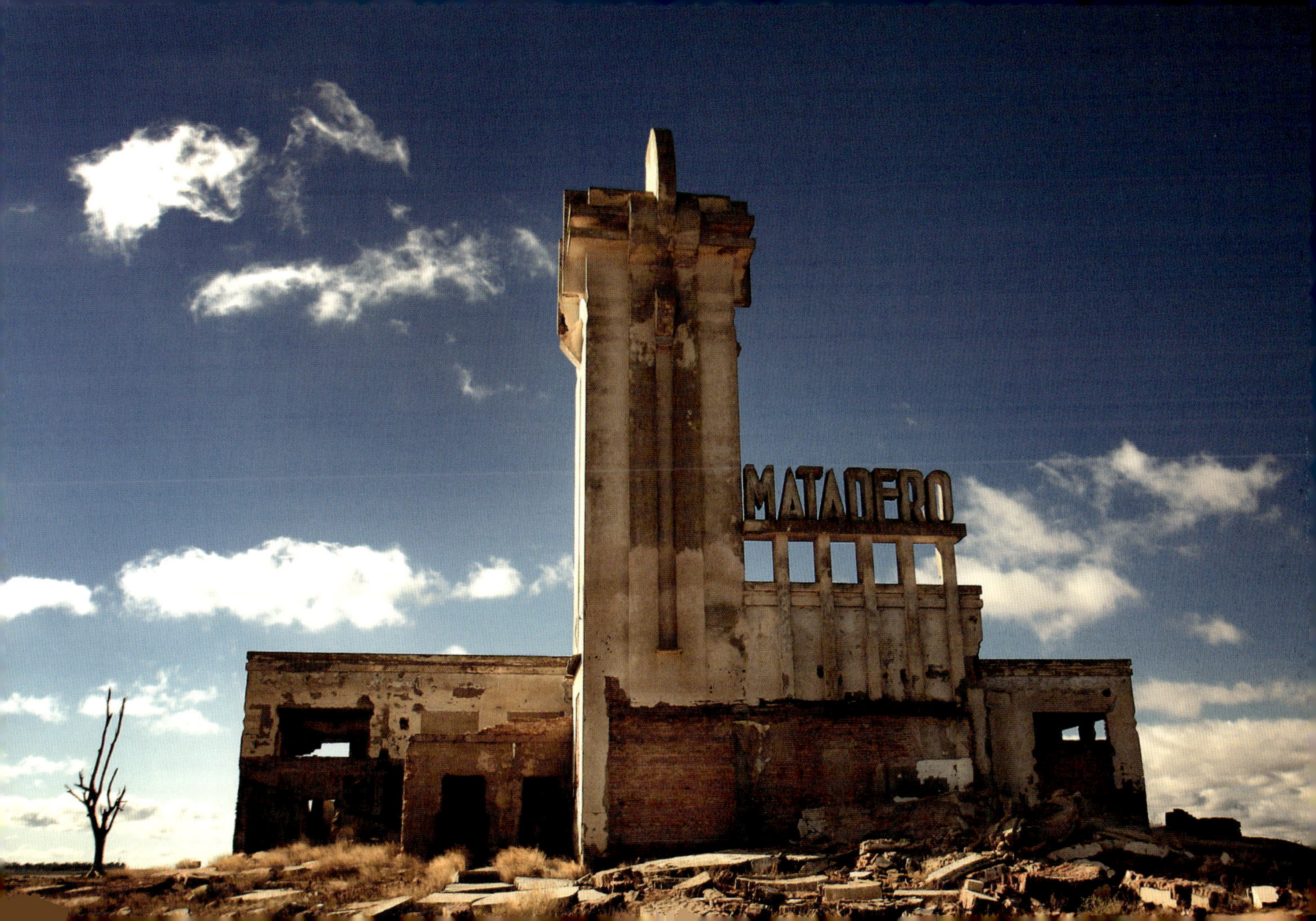
MATADERO

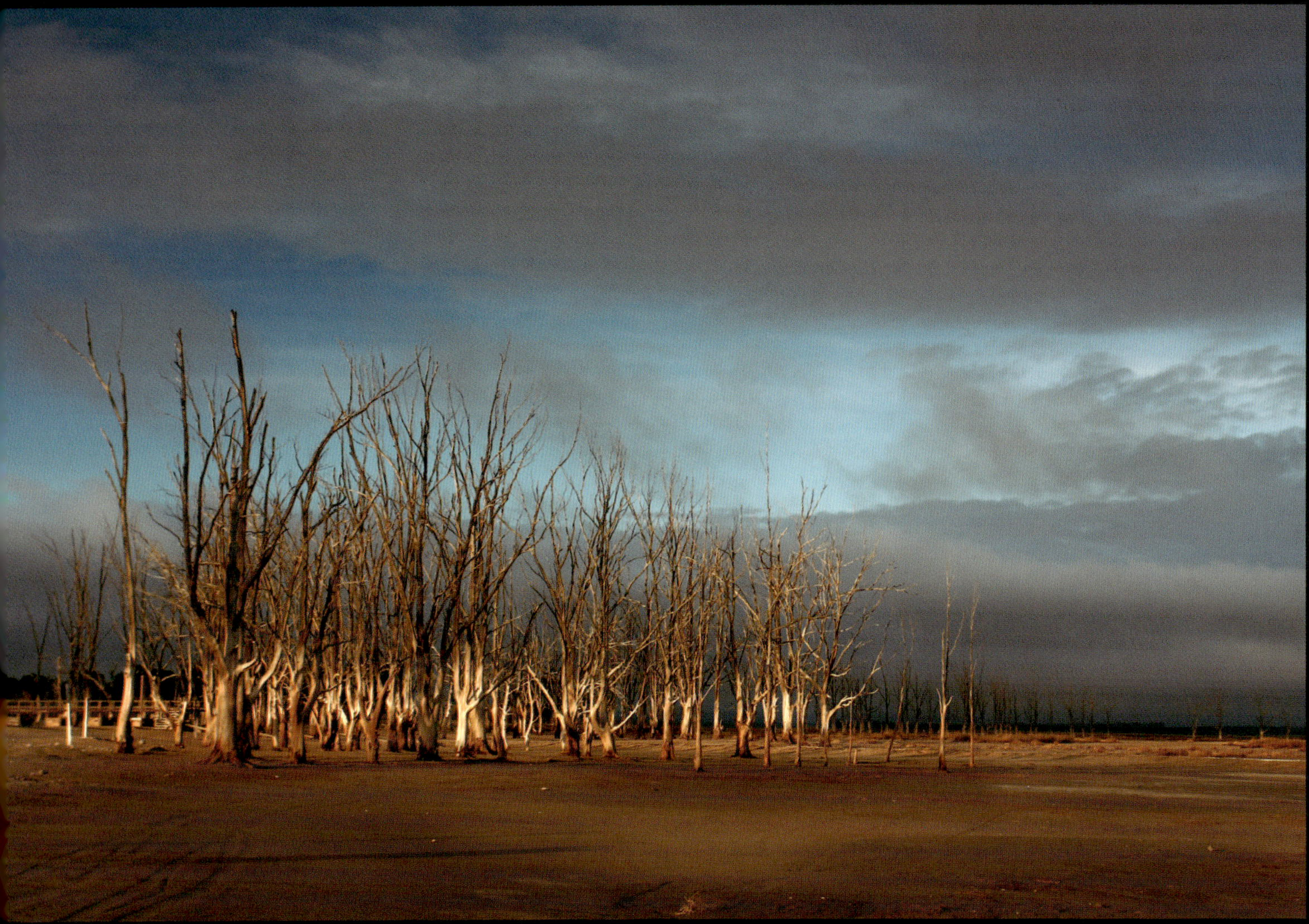

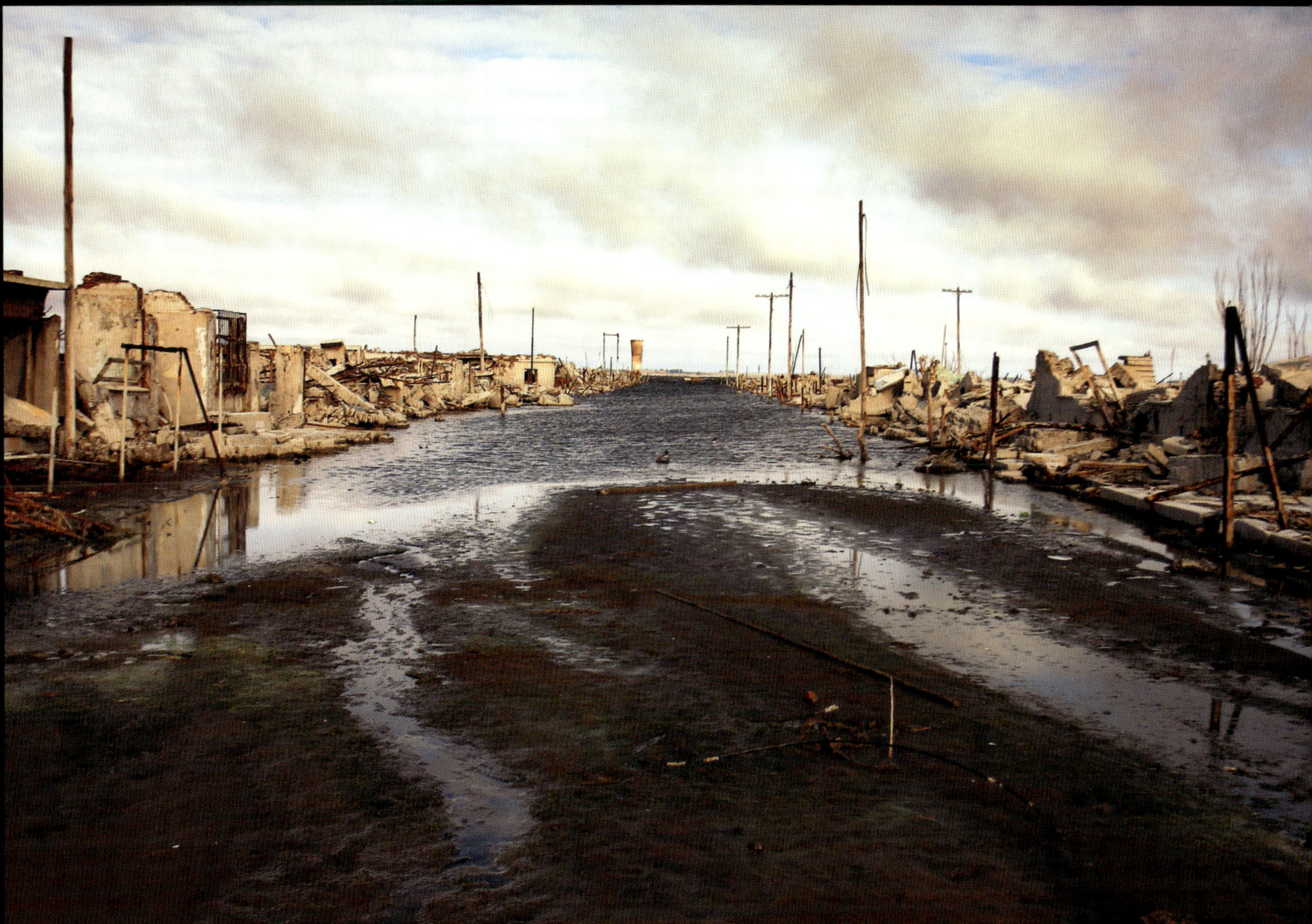

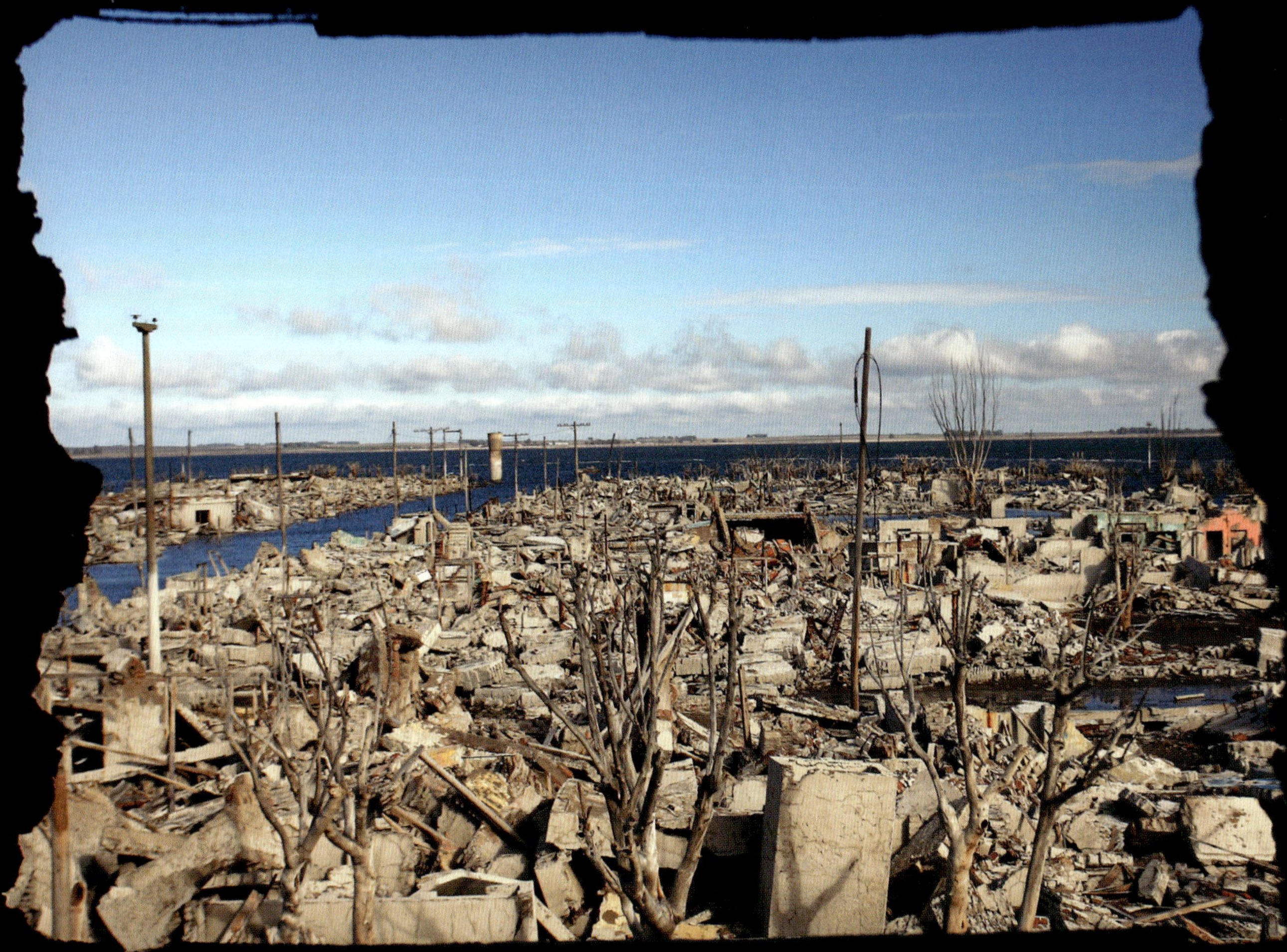

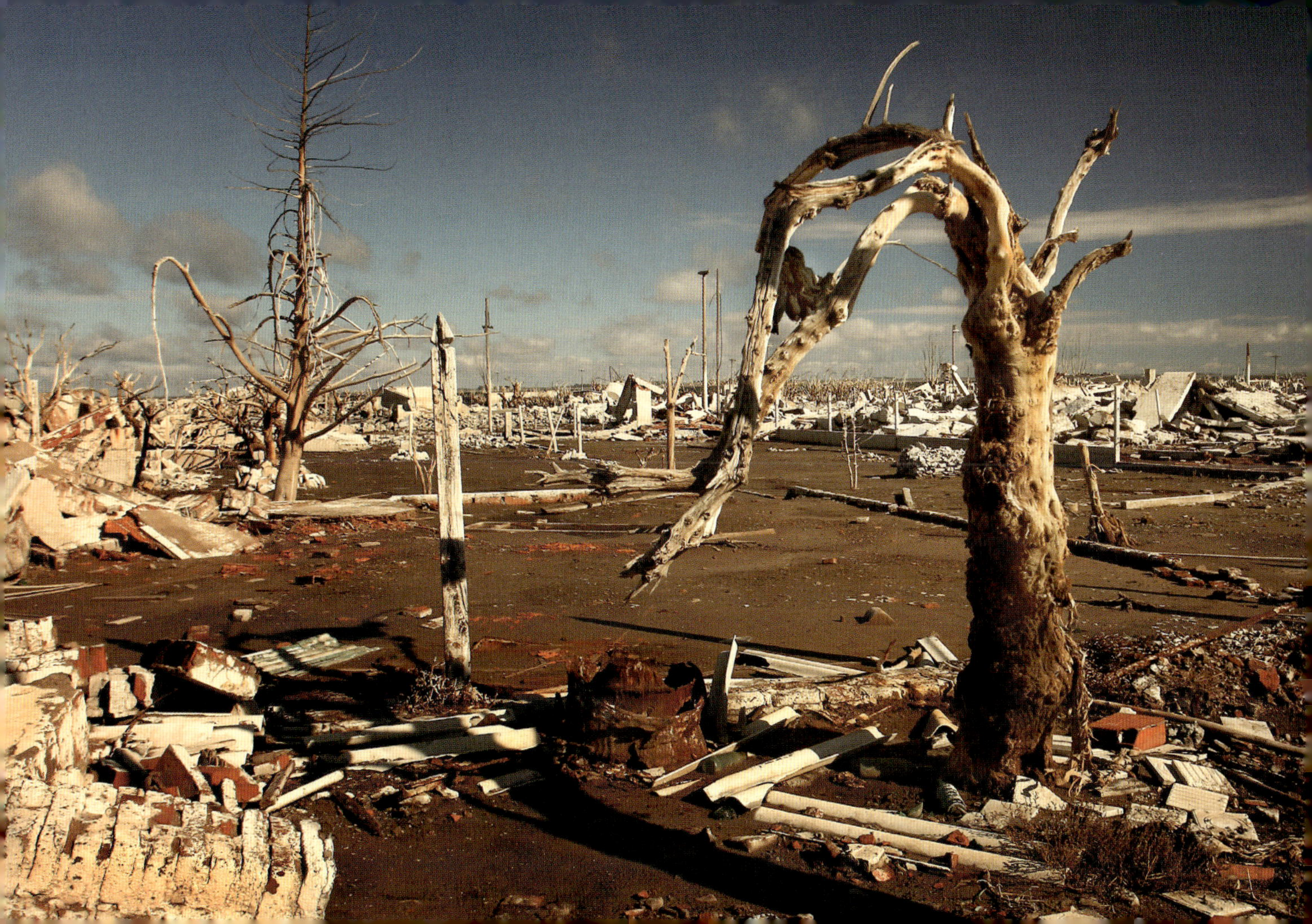

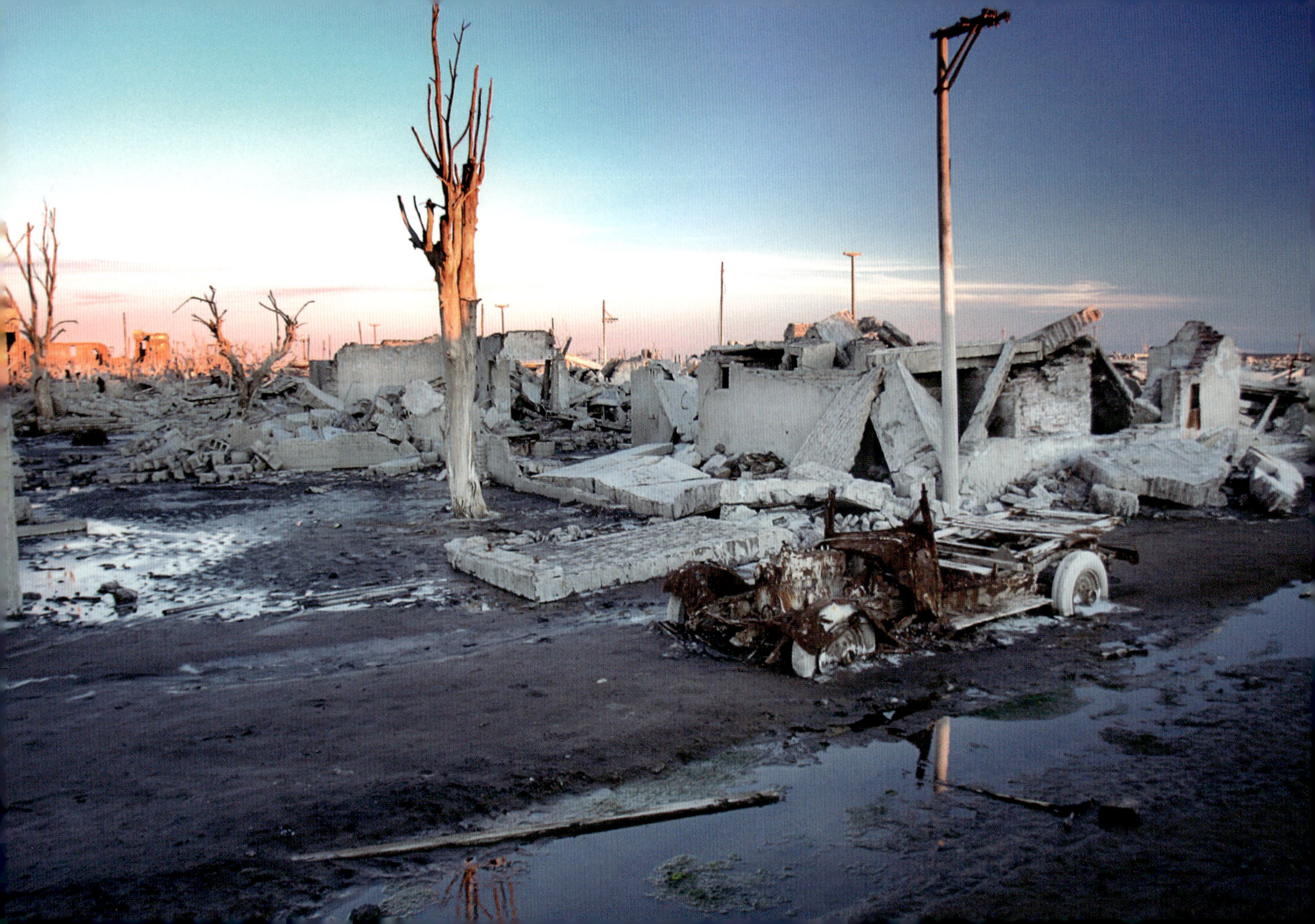

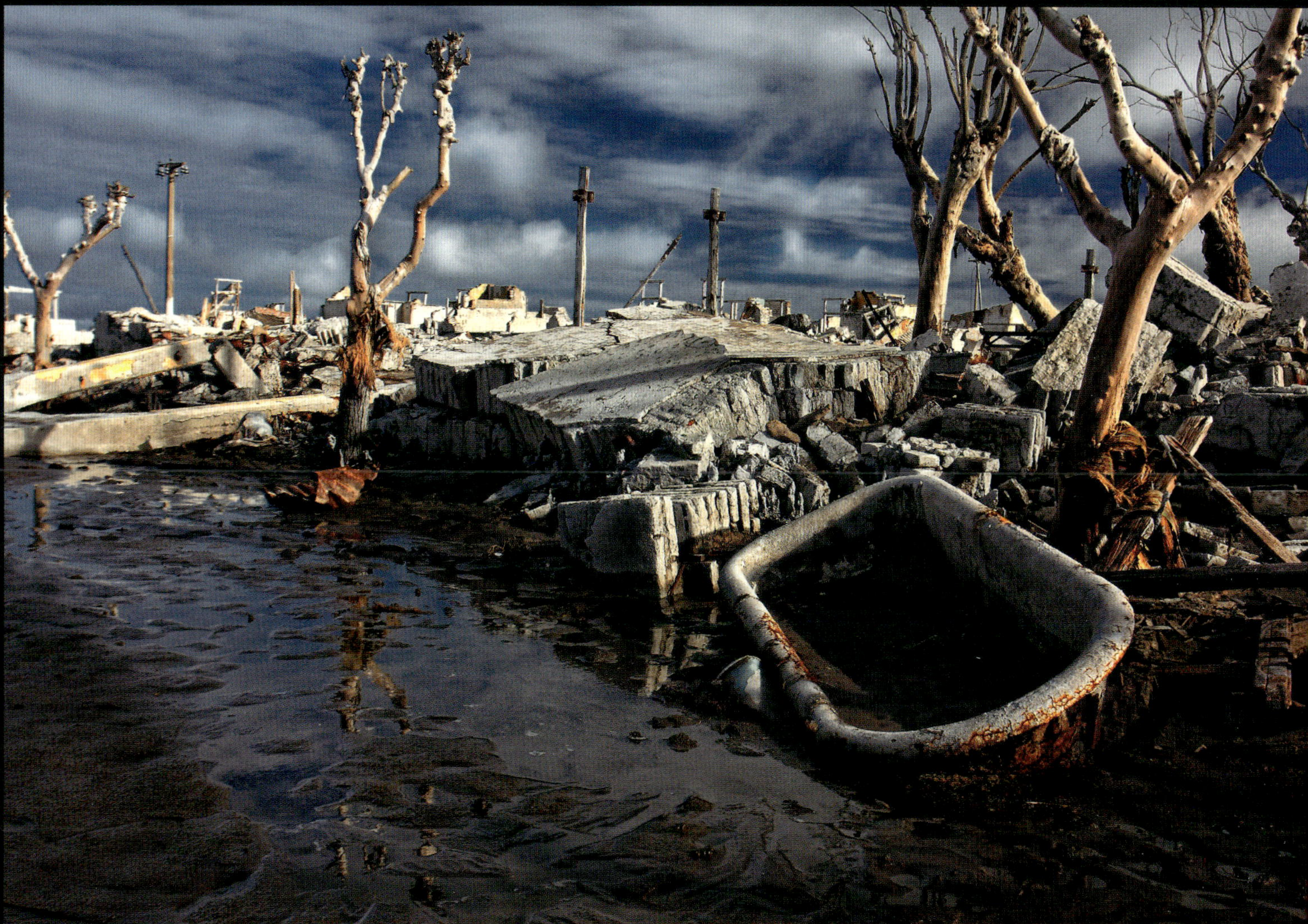

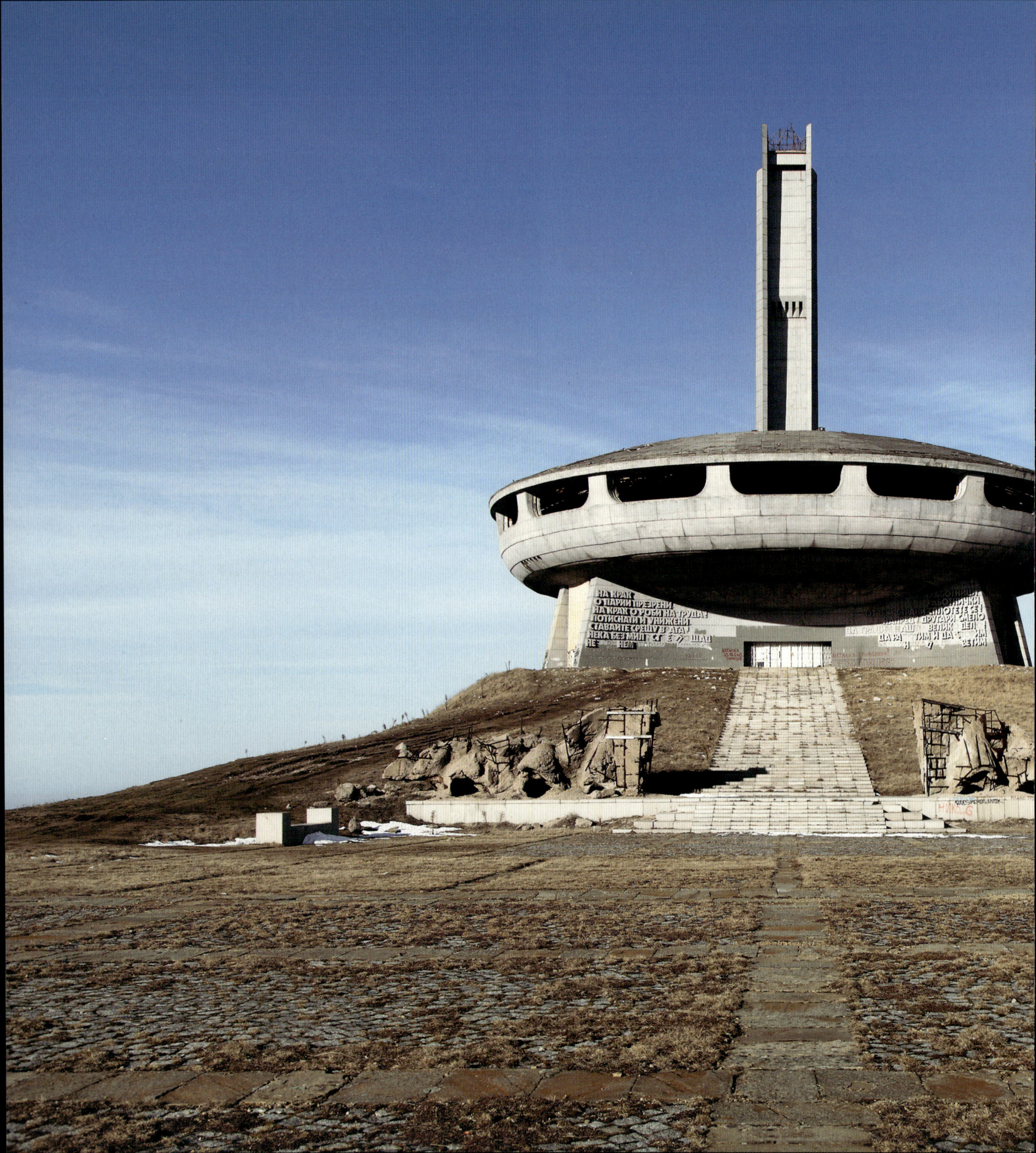
НА КРАК
О ПАРИИ ПРЕЗРЕНИ
НА КРАК О РОБИ НА ТРУДА!
ПОТИСНАТИ И УНИЖЕНИ
СТАВАЙТЕ СРЕЩУ В АГА!
ДРУГАРИ СМЕЛО

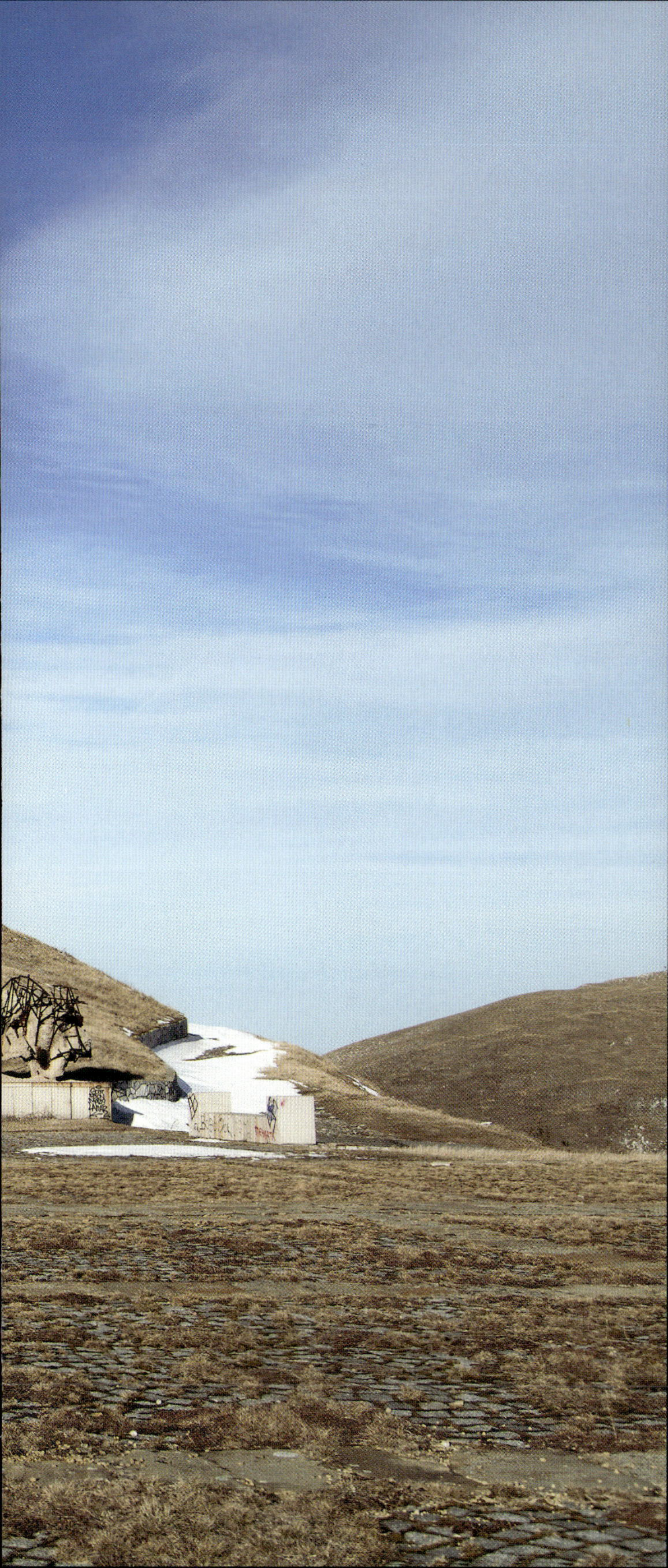

BUSLUDSCHA

BULGARIEN BULGARIA

FOTOS VON PHOTOS BY DANIEL BARTER

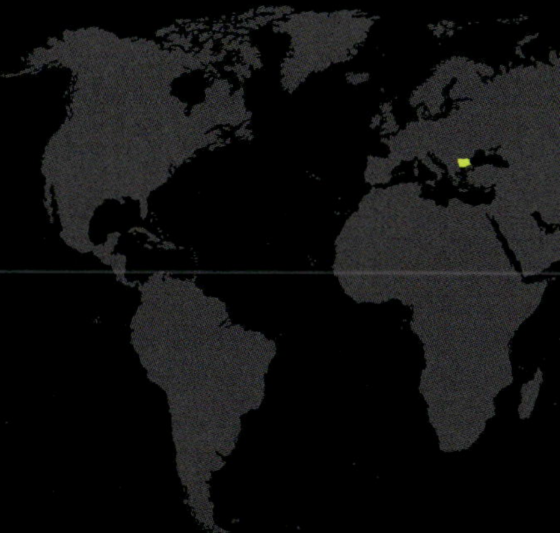

Über die Hänge und Wiesen des Balkangebirges, das in Bulgarien auch Stara Planina: „Altes Gebirge" heißt, zieht der Nebel, in dem die Silhouetten weidender Pferde eher einem Traum entlehnt als der Wirklichkeit anzugehören scheinen. Am Horizont, auf dem 1.440 Meter hohen Chadschi Dimitar, einem im Volksmund auch Busludscha genannten Berg, liegt das Busludscha-Denkmal. Es wirkt wie ein vom Himmel gefallenes Raumschiff, über dem immer noch – als wäre es ein abgefeuertes Notsignal – der rote Stern auf einem 70 Meter hohen Turm am Himmel steht. Entworfen von dem Architekten Georgi Stoilow, wurde das utopisch anmutende Gebäude 1981 zur 1.300-Jahr-Feier der Gründung Bulgariens als Versammlungsort der sozialistischen Regierung eröffnet. In dieser Gegend, am Schipkapass, ereignete sich im August 1877 eine entscheidende Schlacht im Russisch-Osmanischen Krieg (1877/1878). Der für die Bulgaren günstige Ausgang und die dem Krieg vorausgegangenen Aufstände gegen die türkische Herrschaft unter dem Rebellenführer Chadschi Dimitar machten den Berg zu einem Symbol der Freiheit.

Im Innern des Gebäudes beeindruckt der einem antiken Auditorium nachempfundene 500 Quadratmeter große Sitzungssaal, in dem sich Vogelrufe mit den Stimmen der Besucher hallend vermischen. Ein Panoramamosaik hält die Ikonografie einer vergangenen Zeit fest: Abbilder von Engels, Marx und Lenin – und ihnen gegenüber, hinter den wichtigsten Ratssitzen, eine weitere Dreiergruppe, wovon eine Figur sorgsam entfernt wurde. Hinter dieser Abwesenheit soll sich der Politiker Todor Schiwkow (Staatschef bis November 1989) verbergen, der neben Dimitar Blagoew und Georgi Dimitroff einst Aufnahme gefunden hatte. Auch die Außenwand des Saales wurde mit Mosaiken ausgestattet, die jedoch durch Wind, Schnee, Regen und Plünderung stark fragmentiert sind; der äußere, fensterlose Rundgang gibt auch heute noch das Gefühl eines umfassenden Überblicks. Hebt sich der Nebel, erblickt der Besucher die waldreichen und sanft abgerundeten Berge des Balkangebirges, dessen Name türkischen Ursprungs ist.

In dem seit der politischen Wende 1989 verlassenen Denkmal haben inzwischen Vögel Unterschlupf gefunden. Über das skelettartige Dach des Gebäudes fliegen sie herein. Rötel- und Mehlschwalbe, Mauersegler, Hausrotschwanz und Gebirgsstelze fanden auf der Bergkuppe beste Brutbedingungen und unternehmen ihre waghalsigen Flugmanöver im Zuge der Brautwerbung auch in der unverbrauchten Luft des Sitzungssaals. Abenteurer durchstreifen im Winter nach heftigen Schneefällen auf Skiern den Versammlungssaal und schauen nachdenklich auf die mit Schnee bedeckten Sitzreihen. Andere erkunden wie Höhlenforscher mit Stirnlampe das Netz aus Gängen und Tunneln, zerreißen die Spinnweben und finden unter anderem Läden, den Kesselraum, elektrische Betriebsräume und mit Schutt angefüllte Sackgassen. Einige Parkour-Sportler erobern springend, sich drehend, ja fliegend das Labyrinth Busludschas.

Nur wenige Kilometer im Süden, um die Stadt Kasanlak, breitet sich betörender Duft aus. Geschützt von den Bergen liegt ein herrlicher Garten im Tal: ein Anbaugebiet rosa blühender Damaszener-Rosen, die – von französischen und amerikanischen Parfümeuren gleichsam geschätzt – zur Gewinnung des weltweit kostbarsten Rosenöls hier seit mehreren Jahrhunderten kultiviert werden.

Along the cliffs and meadows of the Balkan Mountains, also called Stara Planina in Bulgarian, "Old Mountains", the fog makes the silhouette of grazing horses appear more like a dream than reality. On the horizon, the Buzludzha monument stands on the 1,440 meter high Hadzhi Dimitar, the mountain also called Buzludzha in the local dialect. It looks like a space ship fallen from the sky over which the red star still stands on a 70 meter high tower like an emergency signal that has been fired off. Designed by the architect Georgi Stoilov, the seemingly utopian building was opened in 1981 for the 1,300 year celebration of the founding of Bulgaria as the meeting place of the socialist government. In August 1877, this area in the Shipka pass was the site of a decisive battle in the Russian-Ottoman War (1877/1878). The mountain became a symbol of freedom for the Bulgarians following the favorable outcome of the war and the previous revolts against Turkish rule before the war under rebel leader Hadzhi Dimitar.

The interior of the building is impressive with its large 500 square meter courtroom resembling an antique auditorium where bird calls blend in with the voices of visitors. A panoramic mosaic records the iconography of a past time: images of angels, Marx and Lenin – and across from them, behind the most important council seats, another group of three where one figure has been carefully removed. Politician Todor Zhivkov is

Since the political turning point in 1989, the monument has been abandoned and birds have taken shelter there. They fly in through the skeleton-like roof of the building. Red and house martins, swallows, black restarts and grey wagtails have found the best conditions for nesting on the hilltop where they perform their daring flight maneuvers as part of their courtship in the open air of the courtroom as well. Adventurers also crisscross the meeting room on skis in the winter after heavy snowfalls and ponder the snow covered rows of seats. Others explore the network of hallways and tunnels like spelunkers with headlamps, pulling away spider webs and finding among other things, shops, the boiler room, electrical utility rooms and dead ends filled with debris. Some parkour athletes take the Buzludzha maze by storm by jumping, spinning, even flying.

Only a few kilometers to the south, around the city of Kazanlak, an enchanting scent fills the air. A magnificent garden lies in a valley protected by the mountains: an agricultural region of pink blooming Damascus roses that have been cultivated here for many centuries as they are equally prized by French and American perfumeries to be harvested for the most valuable rose oil in the world.

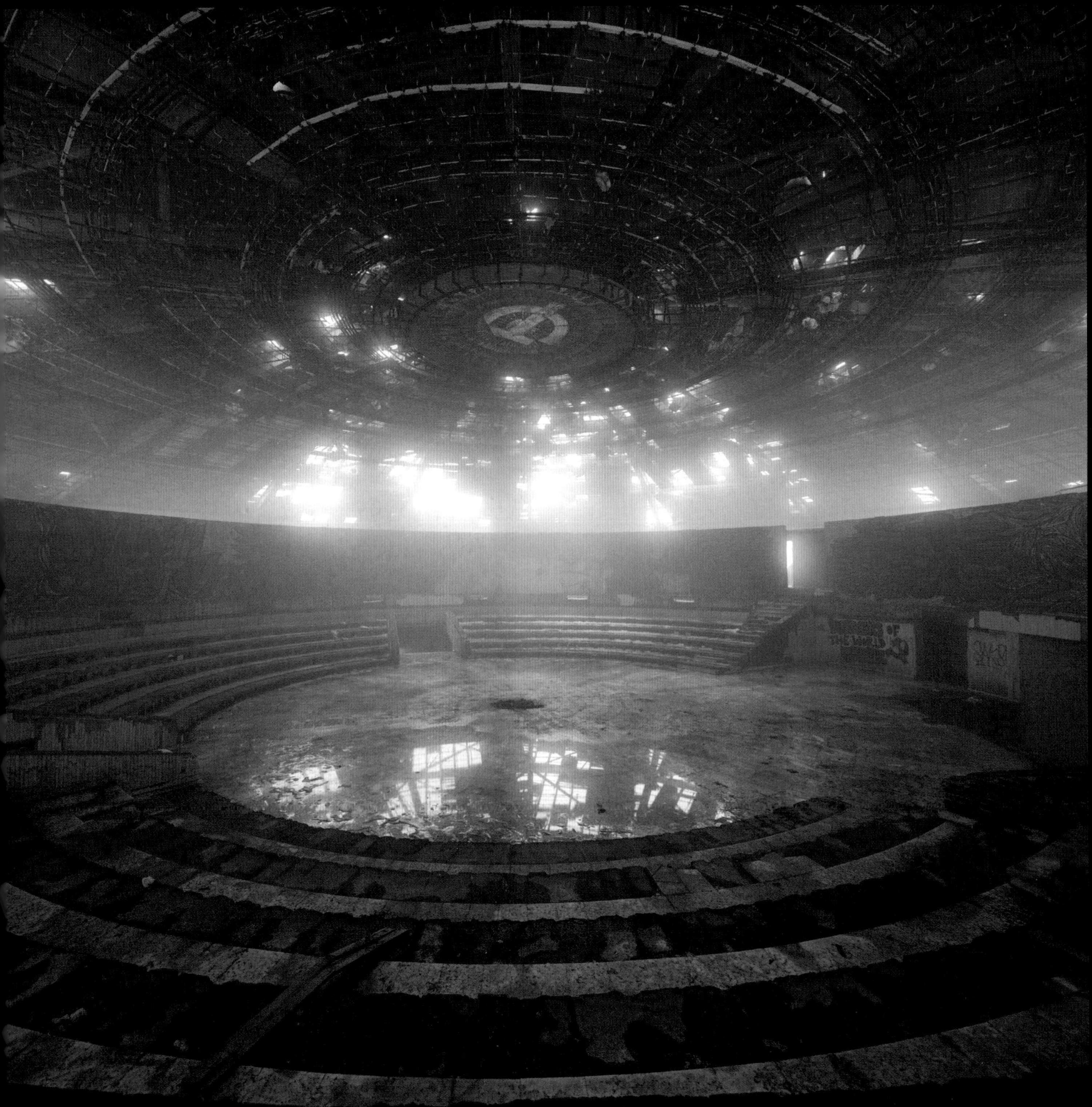

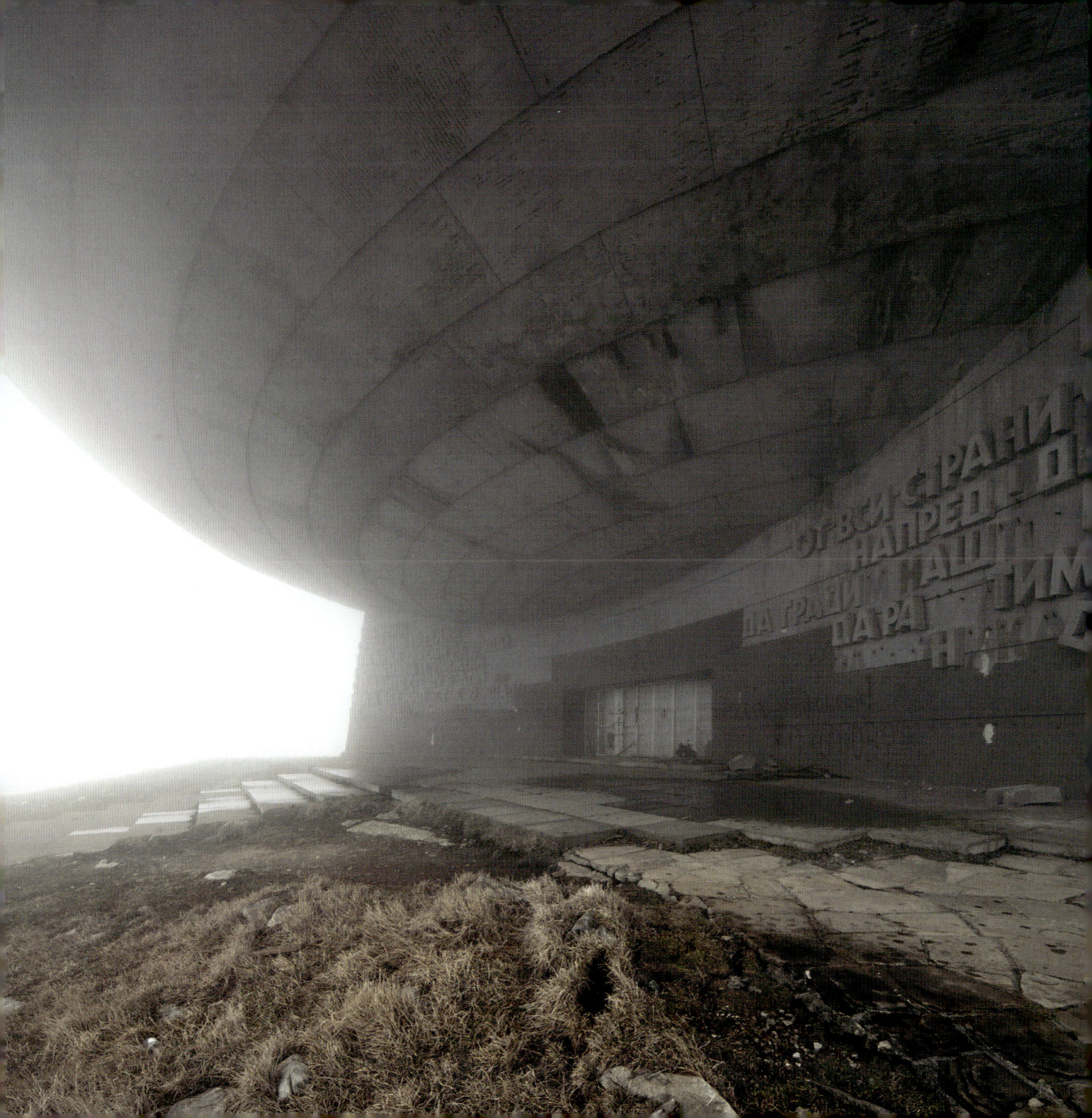
ОТ ВСИ СТРАНИ
НАПРЕД

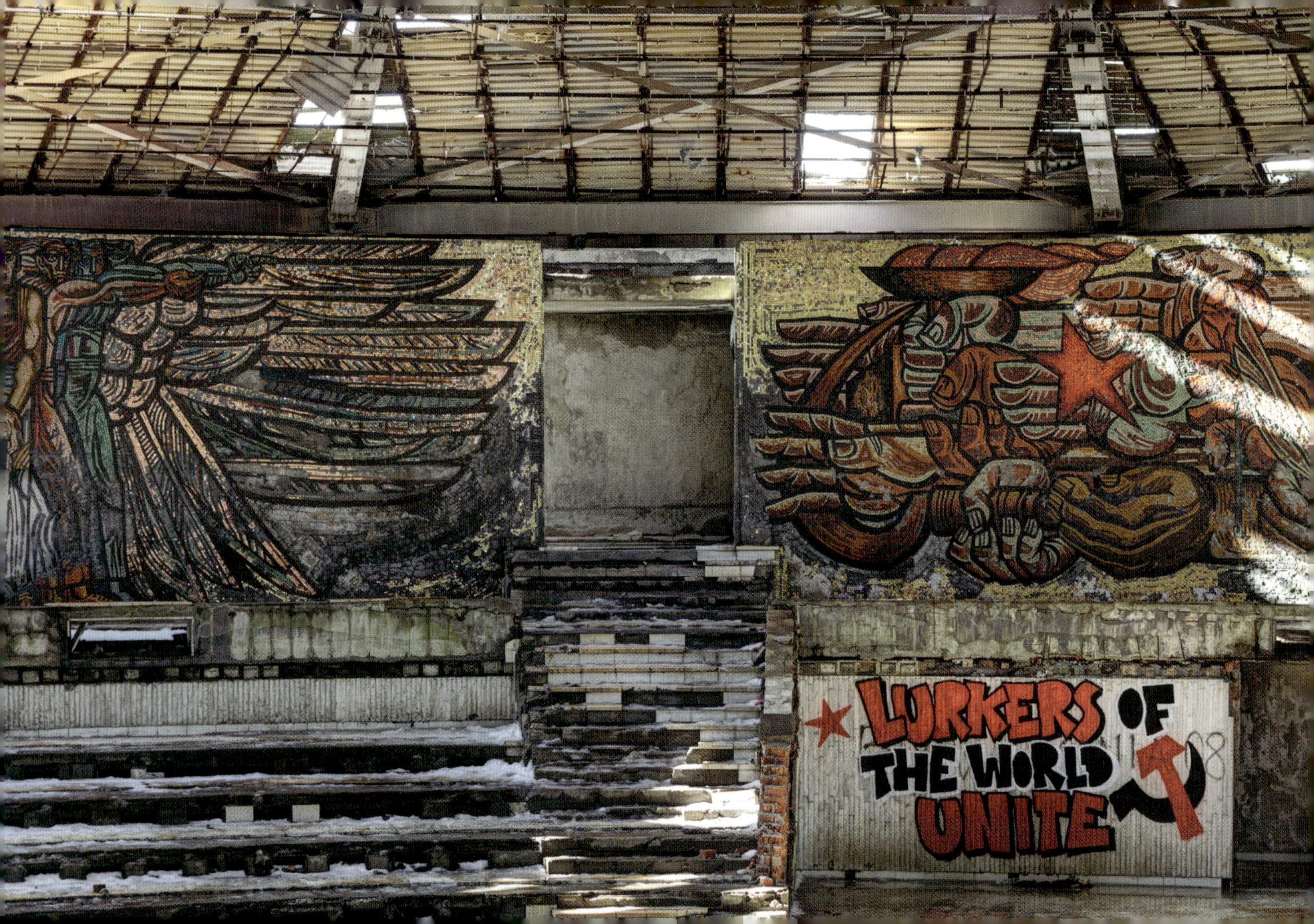
LURKERS OF
THE WORLD
UNITE

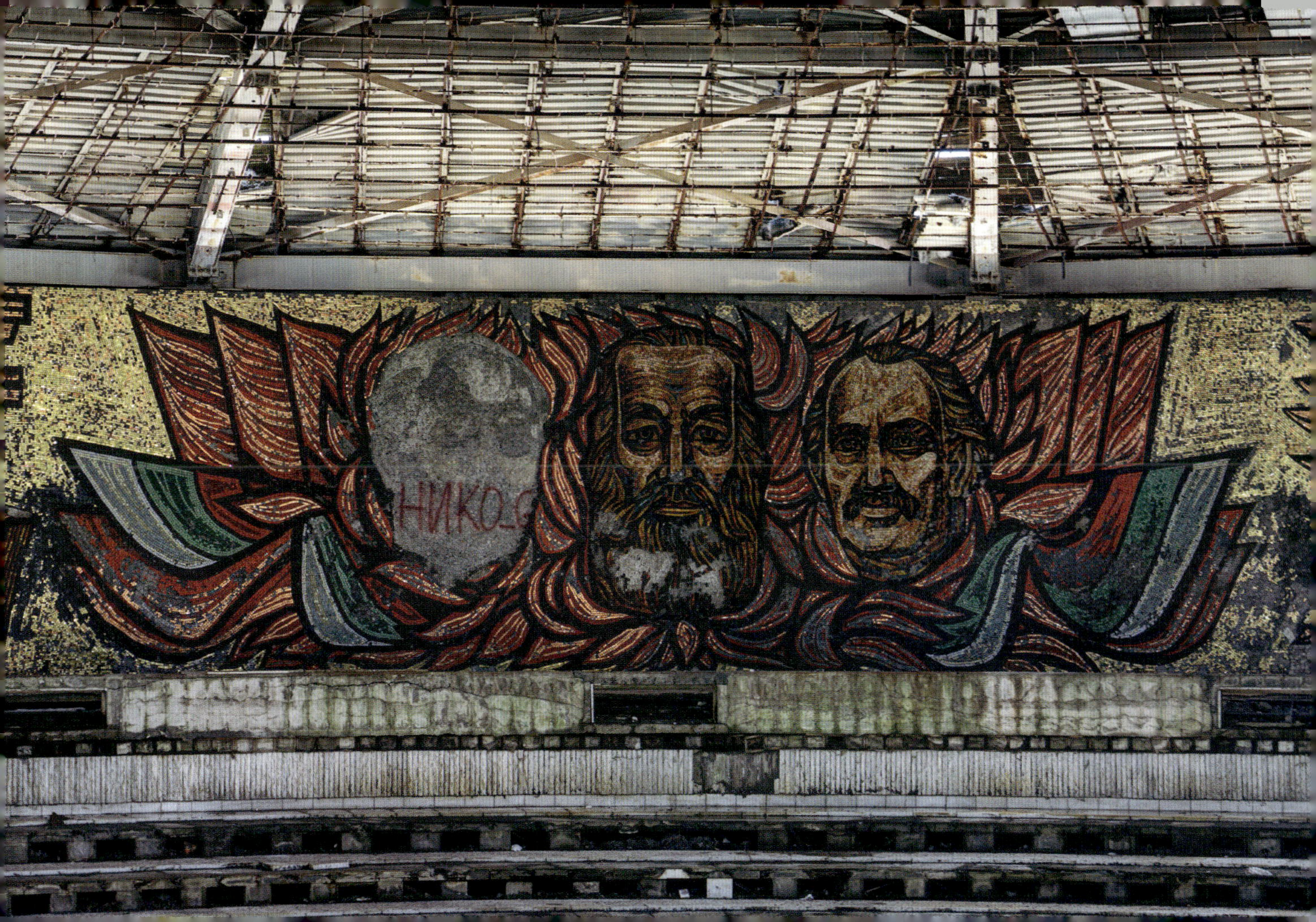

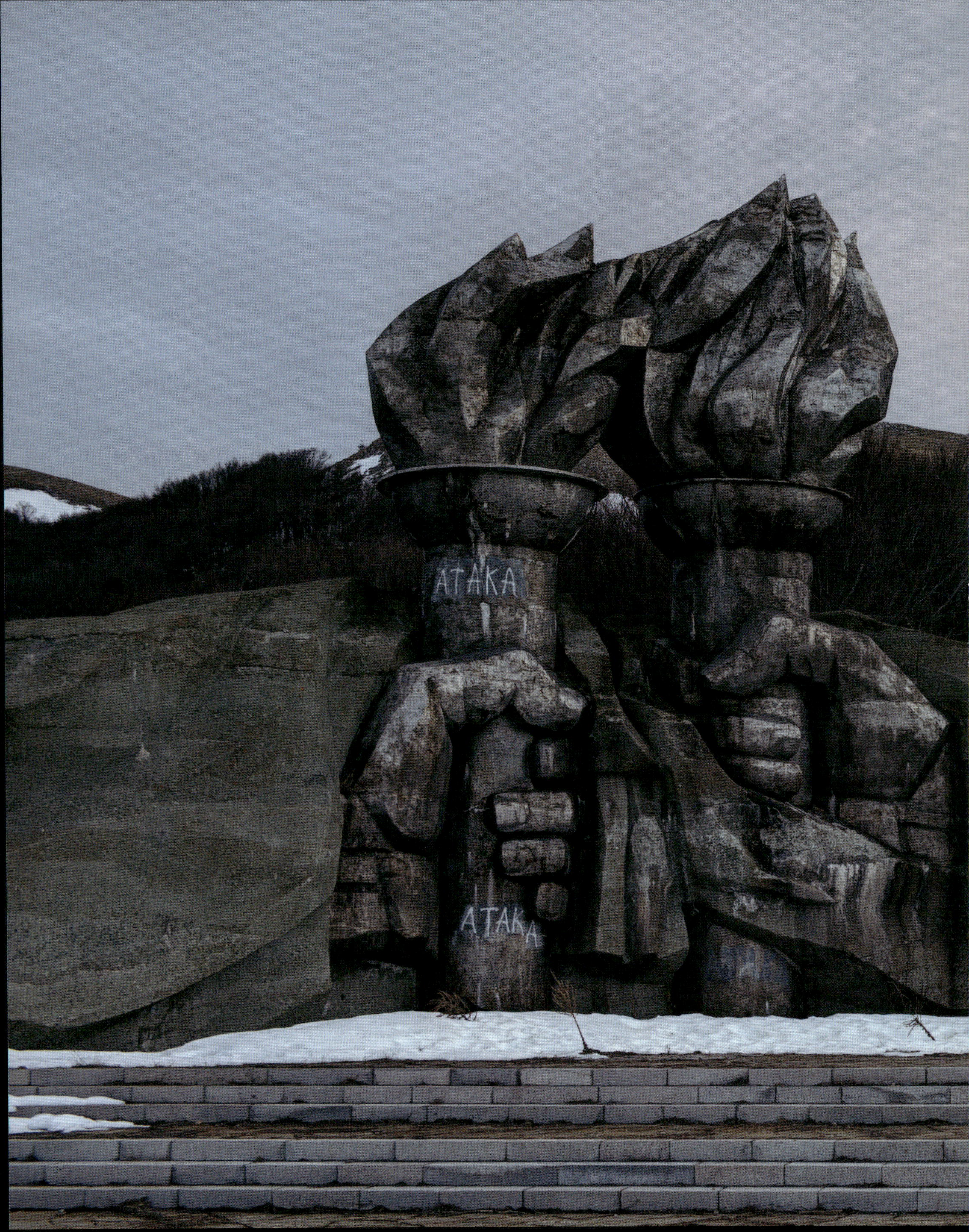
ATAKA
ATAKA

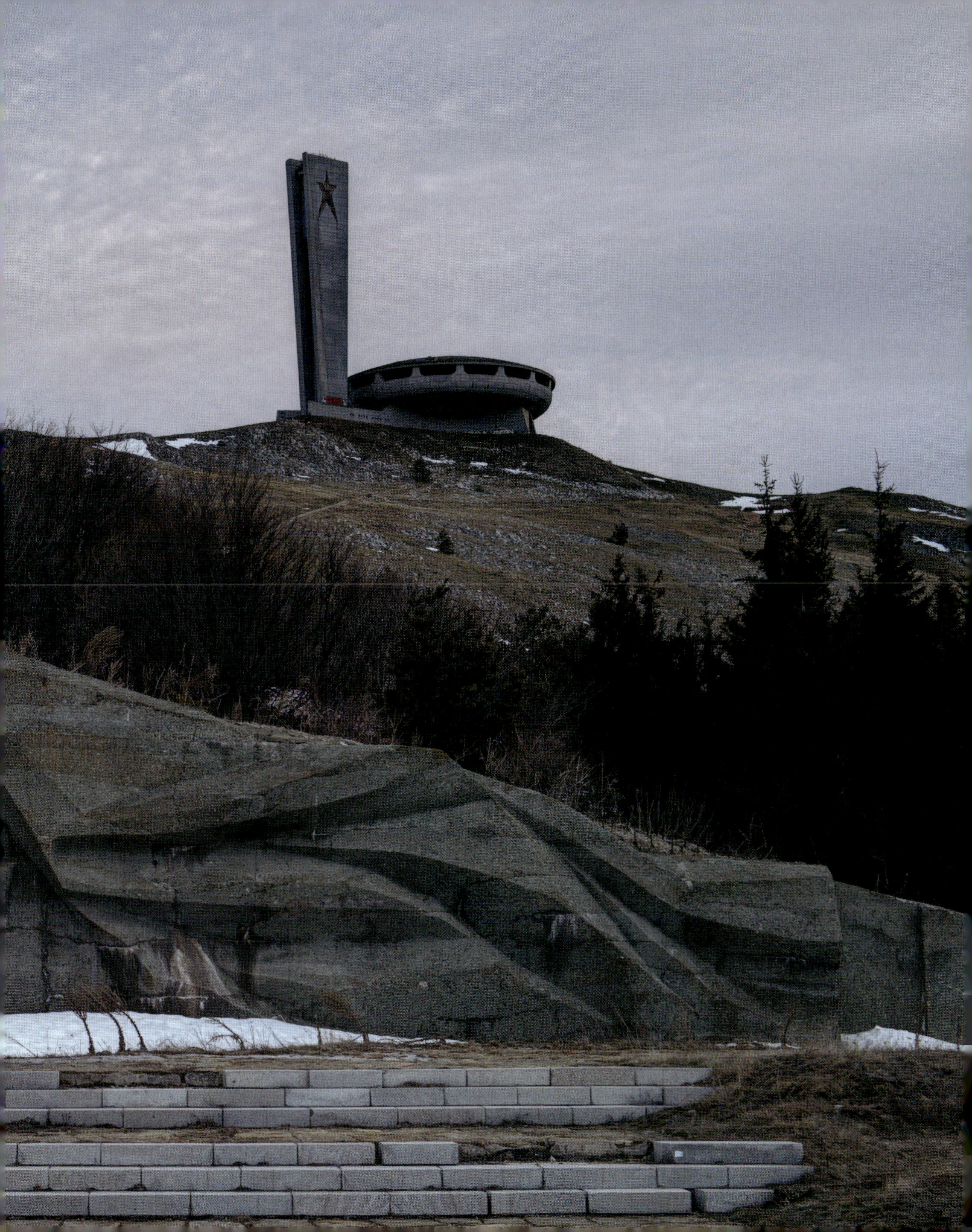

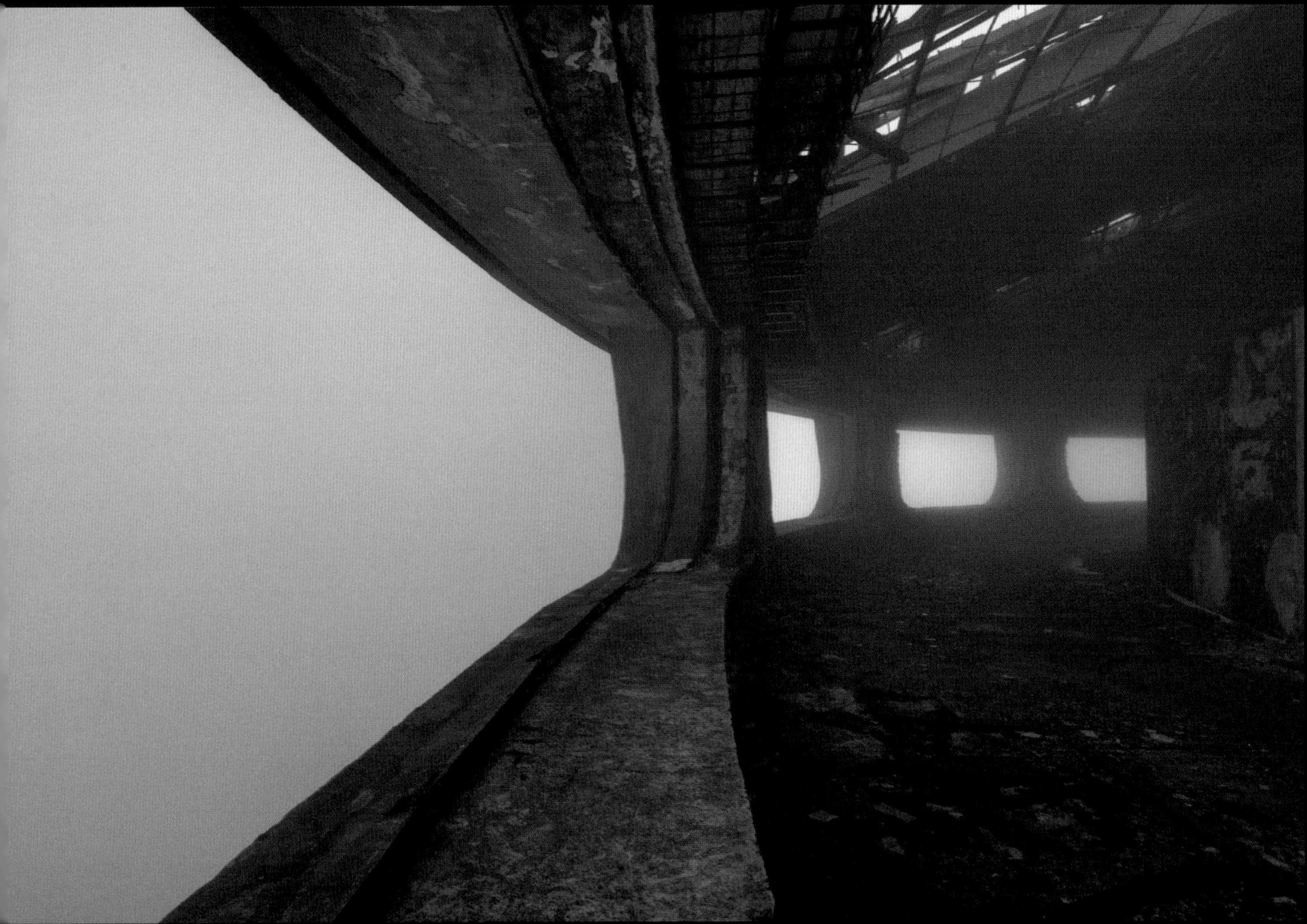

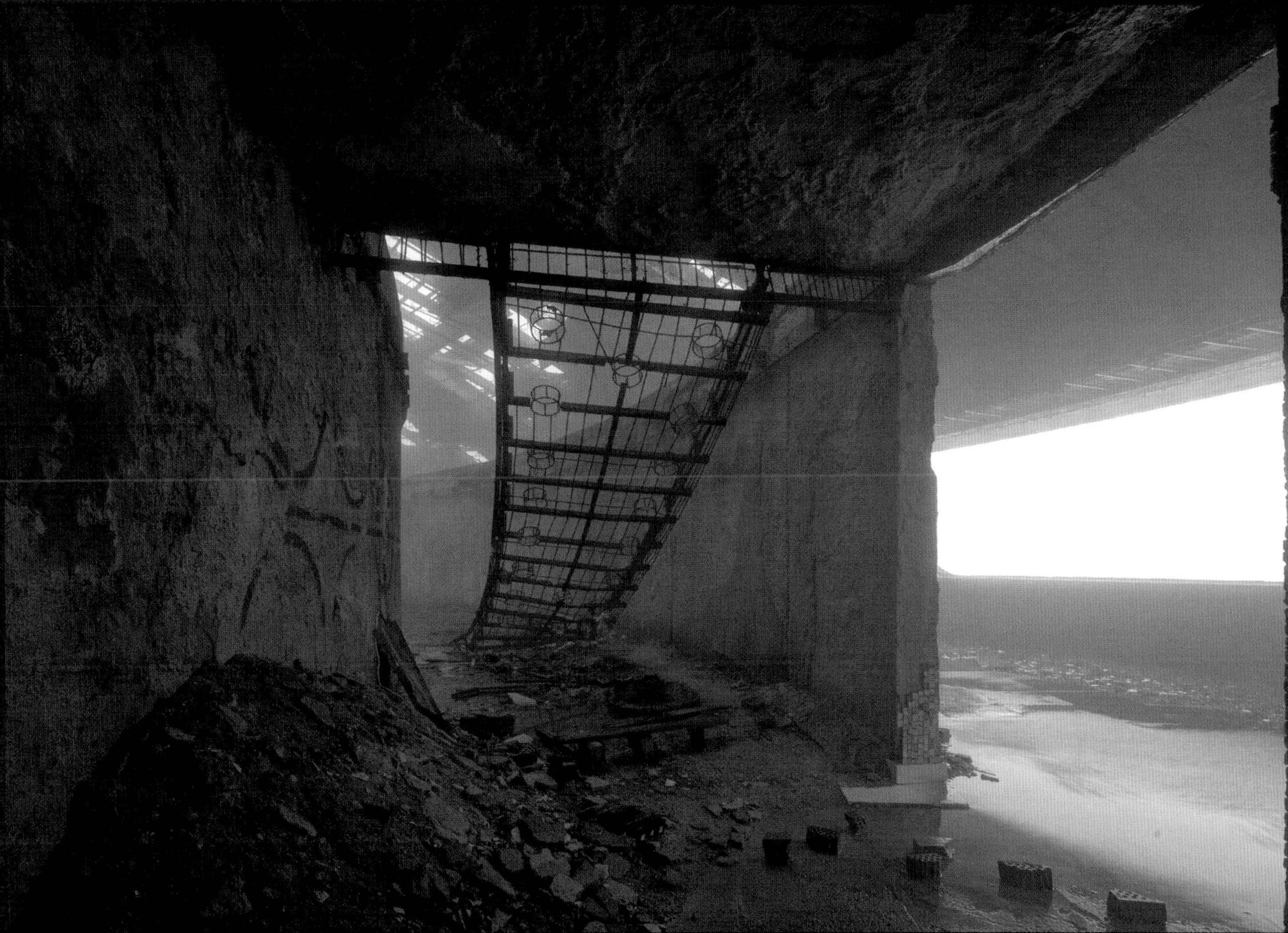

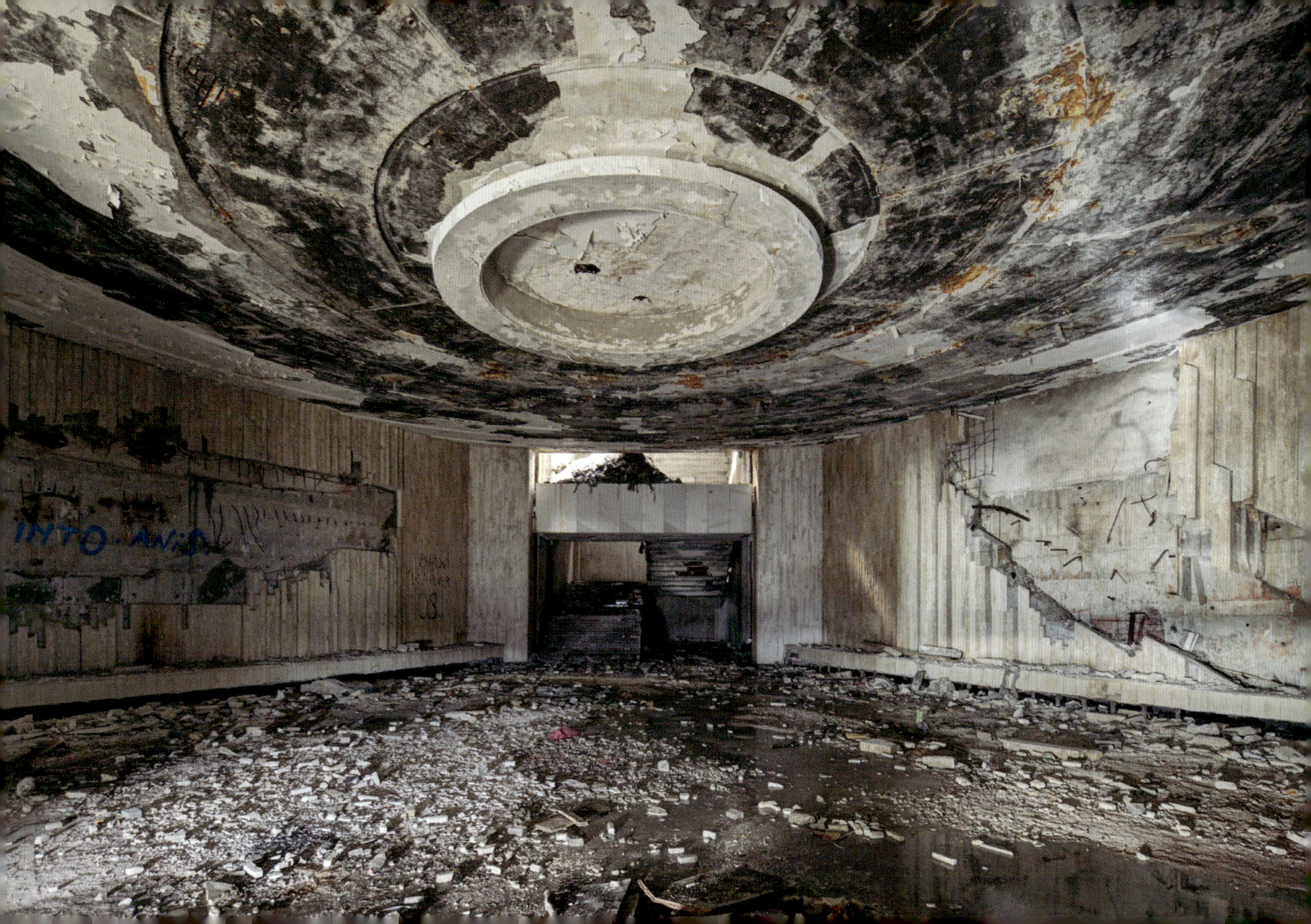

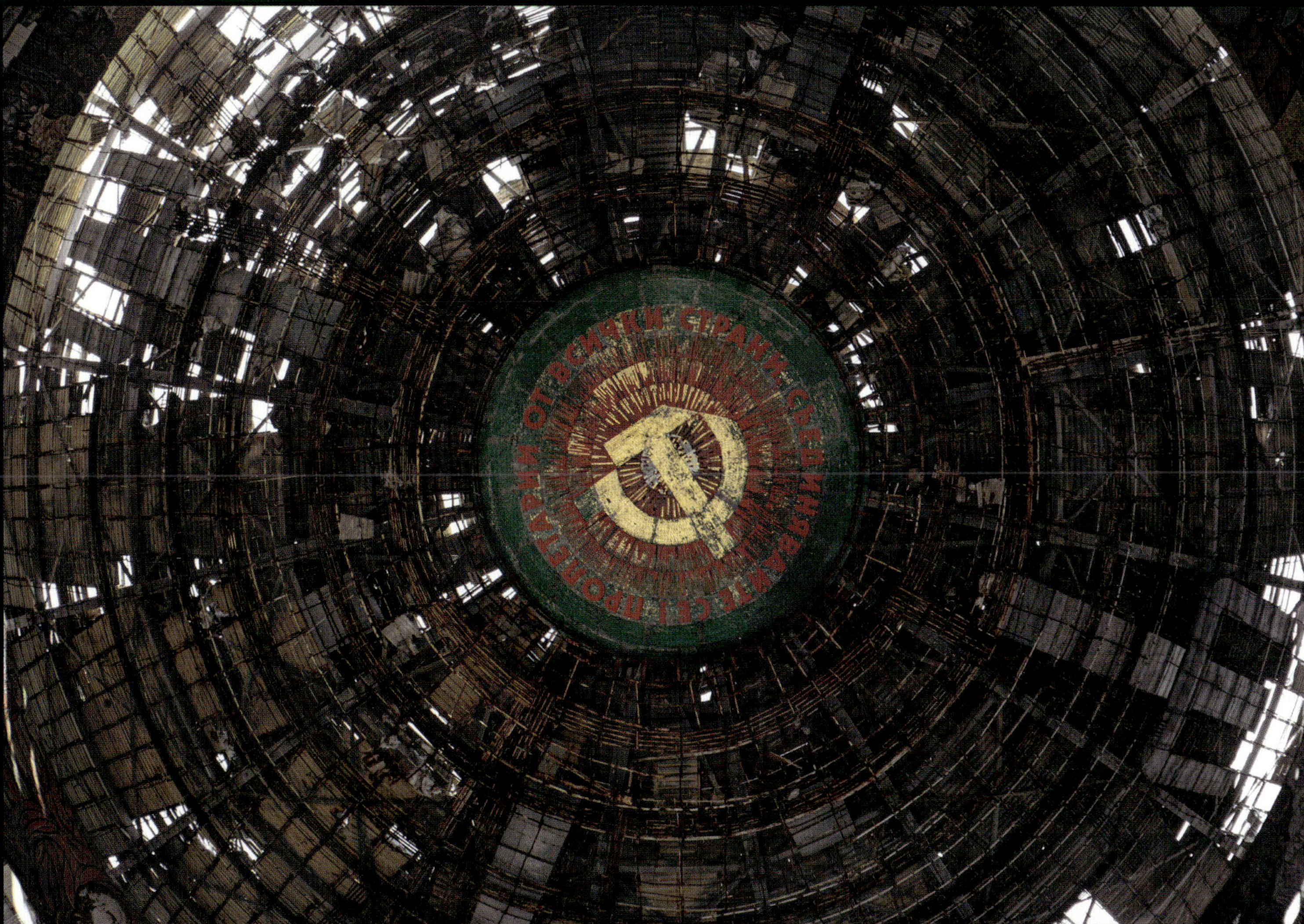
ПРОЛЕТАРИИ ОТ ВСИЧКИ СТРАНИ СЪЕДИНЯВАЙТЕ СЕ!

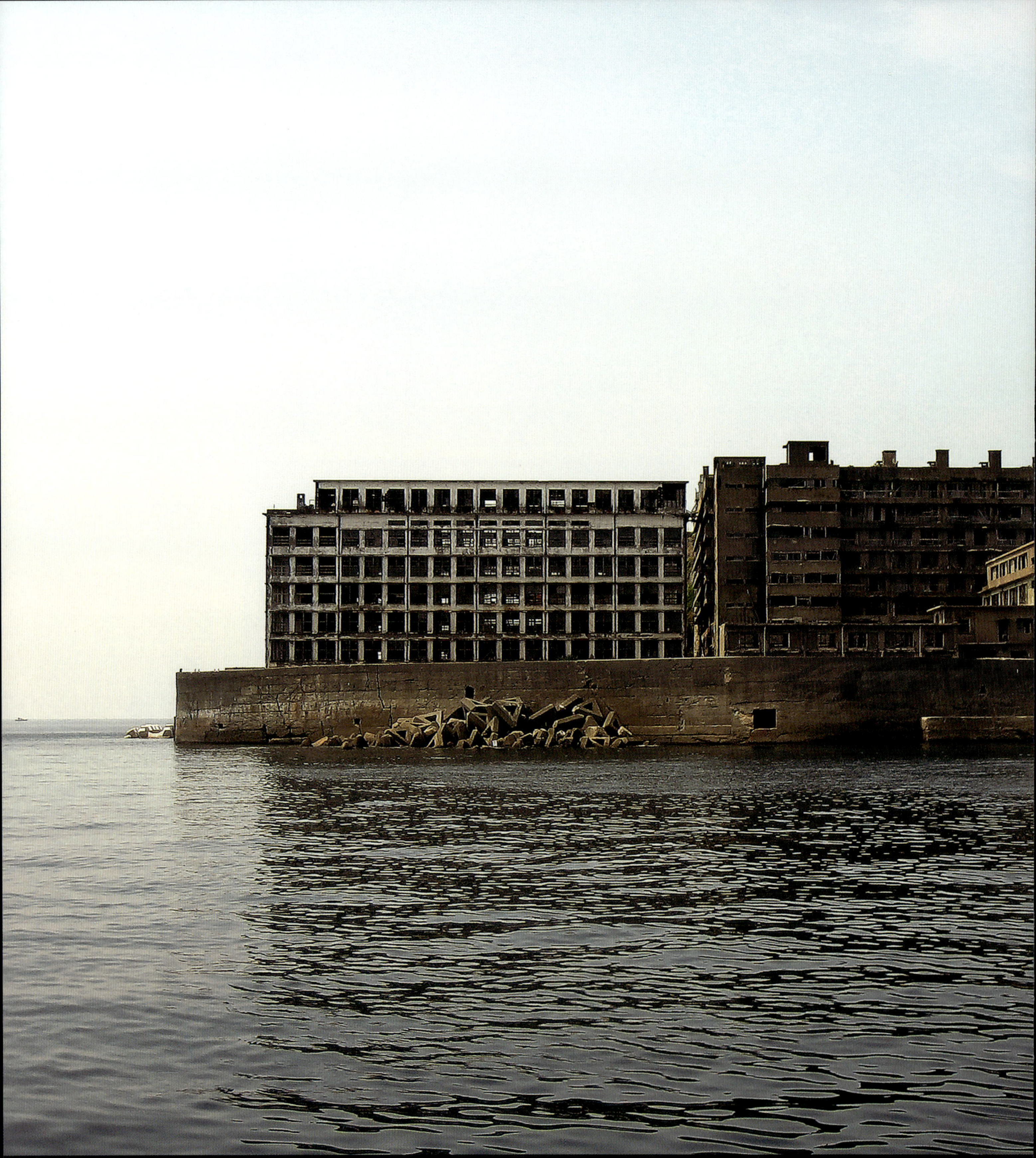

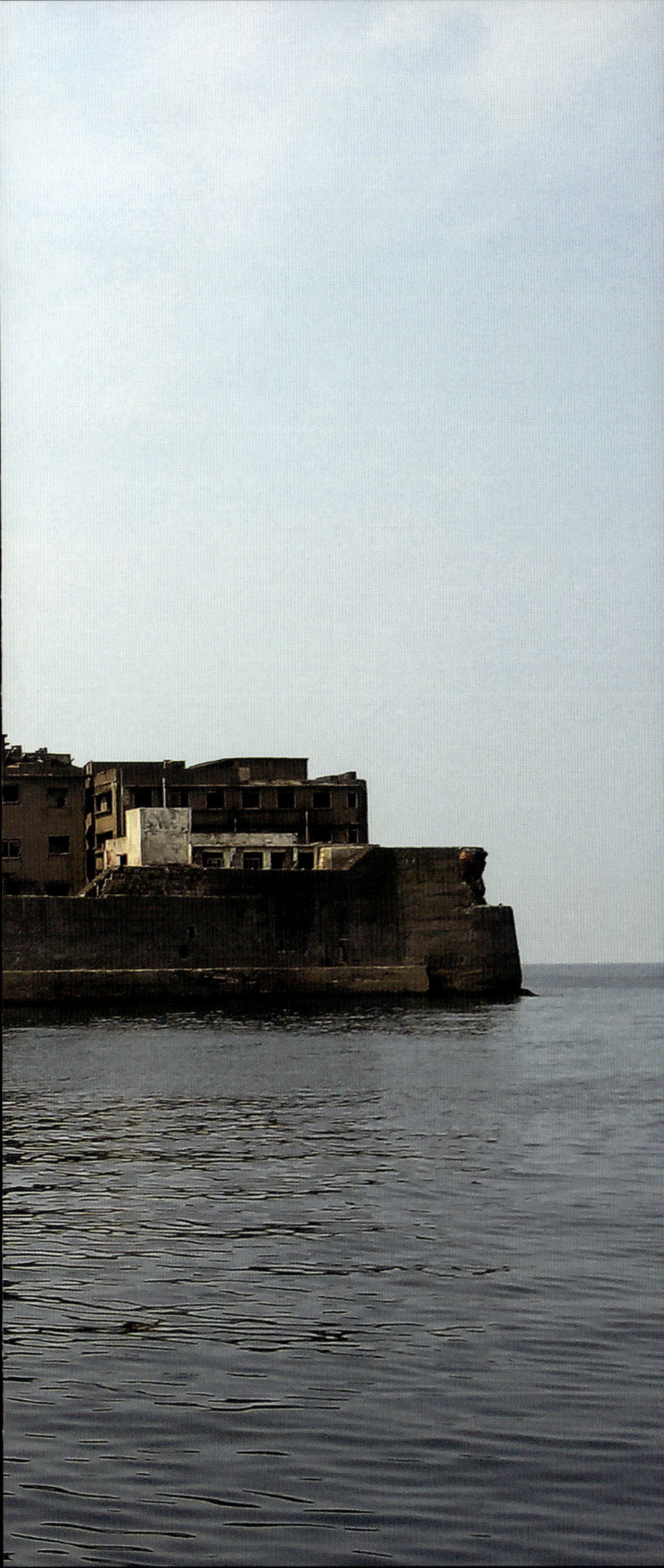

HASHIMA

JAPAN JAPAN

FOTOS VON PHOTOS BY CHAD CHATTERTON

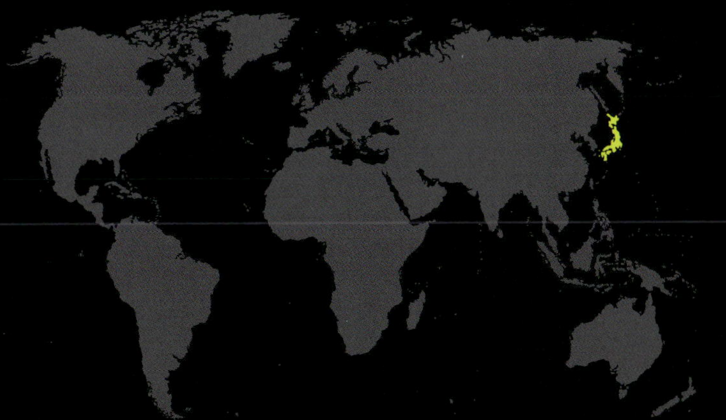

Es ist ein Eiland im Ostchinesischen Meer. Drei Kilometer von der größeren Nachbarinsel Takashima entfernt, liegt es vor der Küste der Großstadt Nagasaki. Die Insel ist 160 Meter breit und 480 Meter lang. Der Name Hashima bedeutet „Grenzinsel". Taifune gehen über das Areal hinweg. Wellenberge drängen immer wieder gegen seine acht bis zehn Meter hohen Uferbefestigungen. Doch der unnachgiebigste Gegner ist die Zeit. Unter ihrem Ansturm zerfallen die ehemaligen Kohleminen- und Wohnanlagen und verstreuen sich in kleiner werdenden Brocken über den Boden.

Die Insel wuchs, nachdem die Firma Mitsubishi sie wegen ihrer hochwertigen Kohlevorkommen 1890 erworben hatte, durch den Abraum des unterseeischen Bergbaus und durch moderne Stahlbetonkonstruktionen bis auf ihre heutige Größe an. Als zu Beginn des 20. Jahrhunderts die mächtigen Schutzmauern gegen die raue See fertiggestellt waren, erhielt sie von der japanischen Presse ihren zweiten Namen: Gunkanjima, was übersetzt „Schlachtschiff-Insel" heißt. Denn aus der Ferne betrachtet, ähnelte das Eiland nun mit seinen Türmen sowie den Industrie- und Wohnkomplexen hinter der hohen Uferwand den größten Kriegsschiffen seiner Zeit.

Im Jahr 1959 galt die 6,3 Hektar große Inselfläche als das am dichtesten bevölkerte Gebiet der Erde. Hier lebten über 5.000 Männer, Frauen und Kinder in einer extrem effizient strukturierten Umgebung. Wohn-, Arbeits- und Verwaltungsbauten, die wegen des Platzmangels teils unterirdisch angelegt waren, gingen ineinander über. Ein einzelner Kohlearbeiter erhielt eine 9,9 Quadratmeter große Wohnung. Familien verfügten über einen Wohnraum, der doppelt so viel maß. Bäder und Toiletten mussten jeweils von mehreren Wohnparteien genutzt werden.

Dafür kam der moderne Komfort schneller auf die Insel als in andere Regionen Japans. Anfang der Sechzigerjahre besaßen die Bewohner Hashimas bereits Waschmaschinen, Kühlschränke und Fernsehgeräte. Ihr Arbeits- und Wohnort bot die Annehmlichkeiten einer Stadt: mit eigenem Krankenhaus, Postamt, Kindergarten, einer Schule, Turnhalle, Kegelbahn und dem Kino, einem Bordell, einigen Bars, Tempeln, Schreinen, Badeanstalten, etlichen Geschäften, Restaurants, dem Hotel und einer eigenen Polizeistation – nur einen Friedhof gab es nicht. Unterseeisch verlegte Leitungen führten Energie und Trinkwasser heran, und auf den Häuserdächern kultivierten die Inselbewohner in ihren kleinen Gärten Küchenkräuter und Gemüsearten.

Durch die Umstellung von Japans Industrie auf Erdöl wurde die Kohleförderung unrentabel. Mitsubishi entschied im Januar 1974, die Förderstätten auf Hashima aufzugeben. Den Arbeitern, die als Erste gehen würden, versprach das Unternehmen auf dem Festland einen neuen Arbeitsplatz. Was folgte, glich eher einem Wettrennen als einem besonnenen Abschied. Schon im April desselben Jahres fuhr zum letzten Mal ein Boot von hier ab. Was keinen besonderen Wert besaß, wurde liegen gelassen. Noch sollen zum Essen gedeckte Tische von einst zu finden sein. Dann war es jahrzehntelang verboten, die Insel zu betreten.

Im April 2009 gab Nagasaki das eingemeindete Eiland für die touristische Nutzung frei. Man bietet Bootstouren dorthin an und hat einen Besichtigungspfad auf der Insel angelegt. Viele Japaner sehen in Hashima aber auch ein Mahnmal. Es erinnert sie an die rücksichtslos betriebene Ausbeutung der Natur und an die hier im Zweiten Weltkrieg verstorbenen Kriegsgefangenen.

It is an island in the East China Sea. It lies off the coast of the big city of Nagasaki, three kilometers away from the larger neighboring island of Takashima. The island is 160 meters wide and 480 meters long. The name, Hashima means "Border Island". Typhoons blow right over this area. Mountainous waves constantly surge against its eight to ten meter high shoreline reinforcements. However, the unrelenting enemy is time. Under its advance, the former coal mine and residences are falling apart, being scattered in smaller and smaller pieces across the ground.
After Mitsubishi bought the island in 1890 due to its high quality coal deposits, the island grew to its current size from the material excavated from the undersea mine and through modern reinforced steel structures. At the beginning of the 20th century, when the mighty protective walls against the rough sea were completed, the island got its second name from the Japanese press: Gunkanjima, which translated means "Battleship Island". That's because, from the distance the island resembled the biggest war ship of its time with its towers as well as the industrial and residential complexes behind the high waterfront wall.
In 1959, the 6.3 hectare island area was the most densely populated area in the world. More than 5,000 men, women and children lived there in an extremely efficiently structured environment. Residential, work, and administration buildings, some of which were underground because of a lack of space, flowed together. A single coal worker had a 9.9 square meter apartment. Families had twice as much living space. Bathrooms and toilets each had to be shared by multiple residents.
In return, modern comforts arrived sooner on the island than in other regions of Japan. At the beginning of the 1960s, the residents of Hashima already owned washing machines, refrigerators and televisions. Their work and living areas offered the conveniences of a city with its own hospital, post office, kindergarten, a school, gymnasium, bowling and a cinema, a brothel, several bars, temples, shrines, swimming pools, a number of businesses, restaurants, a hotel and its own police station - the only thing missing was a cemetery. Underwater pipelines carried electricity and drinking water, and island residents grew small gardens on their roofs with herbs and different varieties of vegetables.
When Japan's industry changed over to oil, coal production became unprofitable. Mitsubishi decided to abandon mining operations on Hashima in January 1974. The company promised new jobs on the mainland to the first workers to leave. What followed was more of a race than a relaxed farewell. The last boat left the island in April of the same year. Everything that was of no special value was left behind. It is reported that tables laid for dinner can still be found. That's because it was forbidden to land on the island for decades.
In April 2009, Nagasaki allowed the incorporated island to be opened up for tourism. Boat tours to it were offered and a sightseeing trail was built on the island. However, many Japanese consider Hashima to be a memorial. It reminds them of the ruthless exploitation of nature and of the prisoners of war who died there in the Second World War.

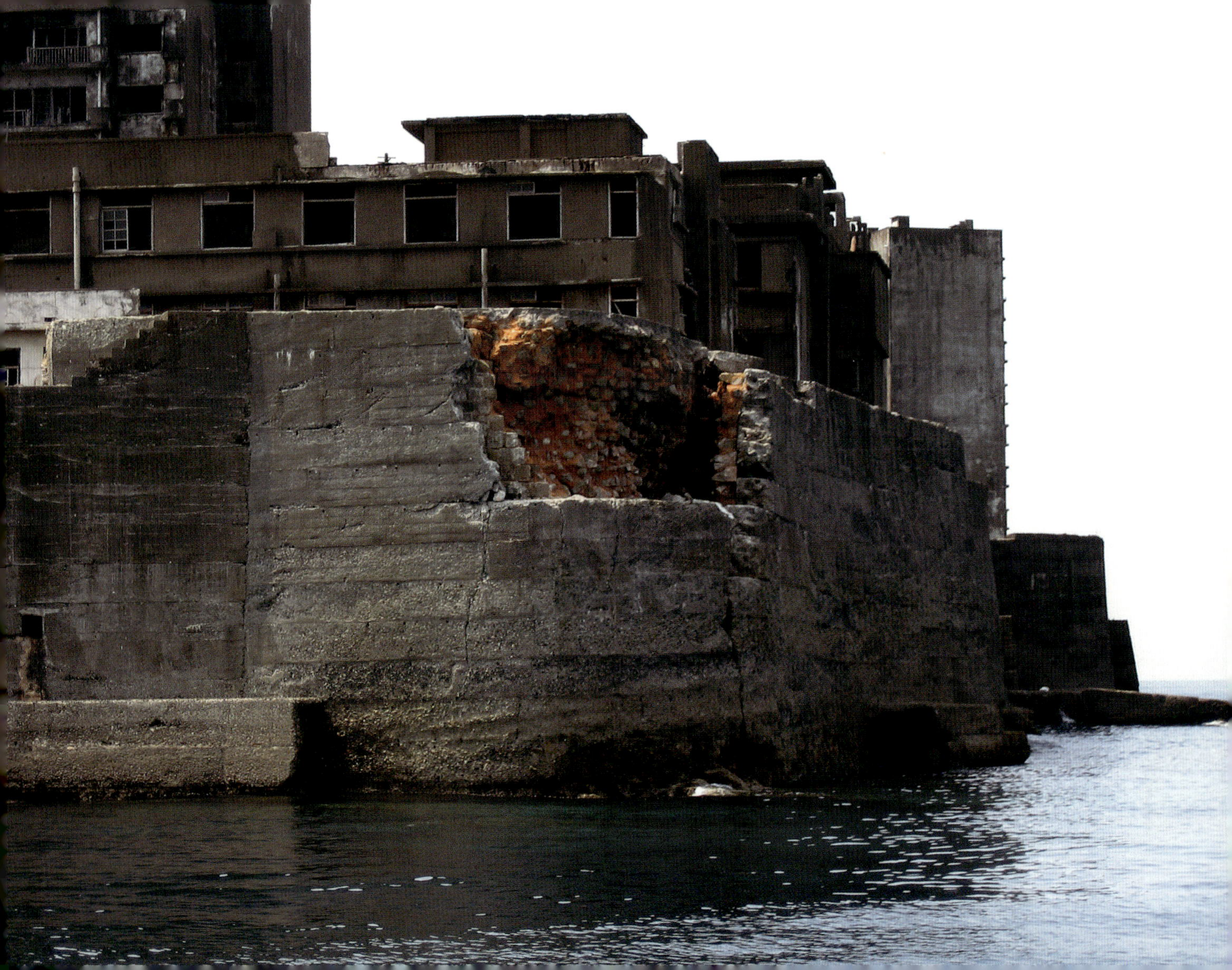

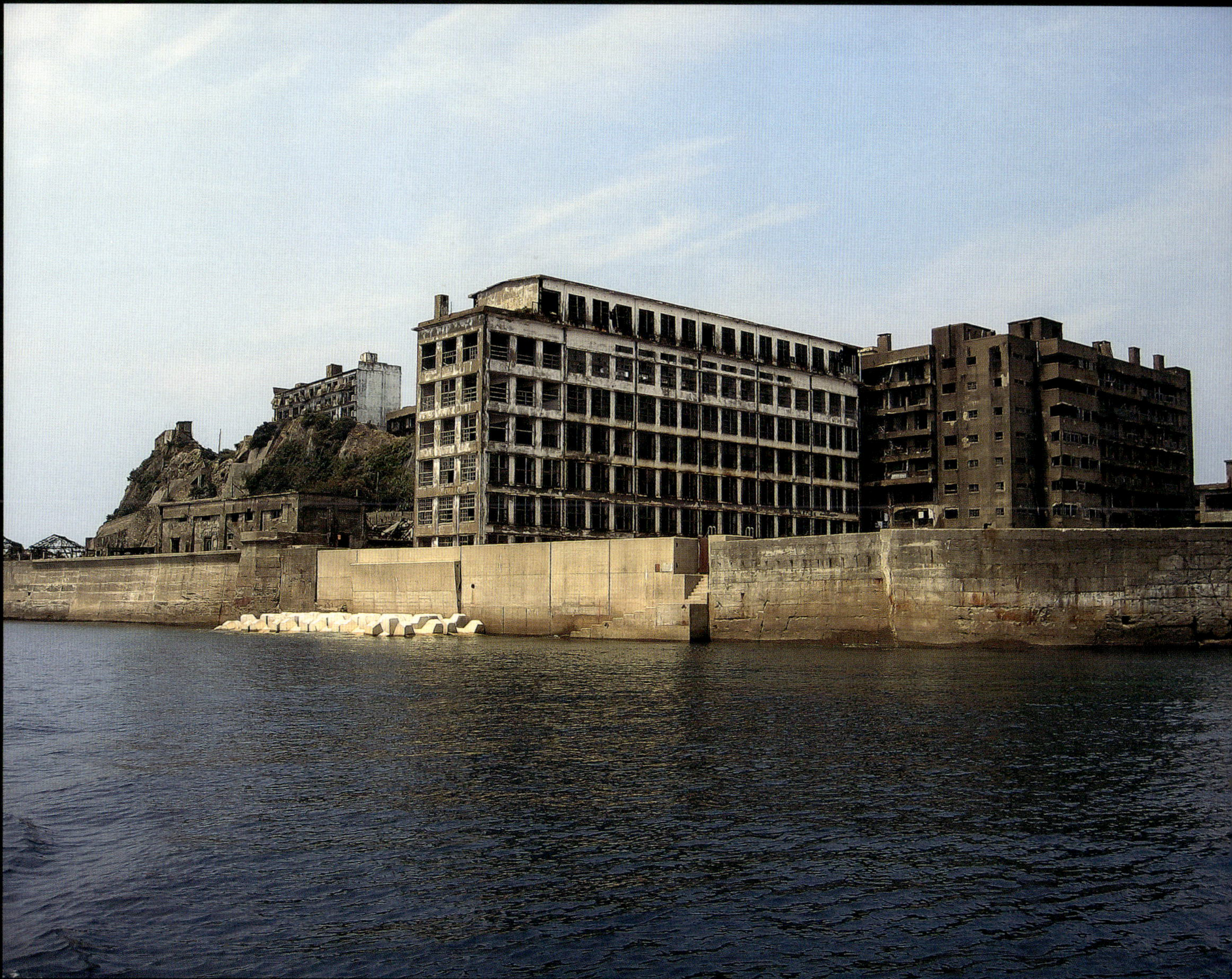

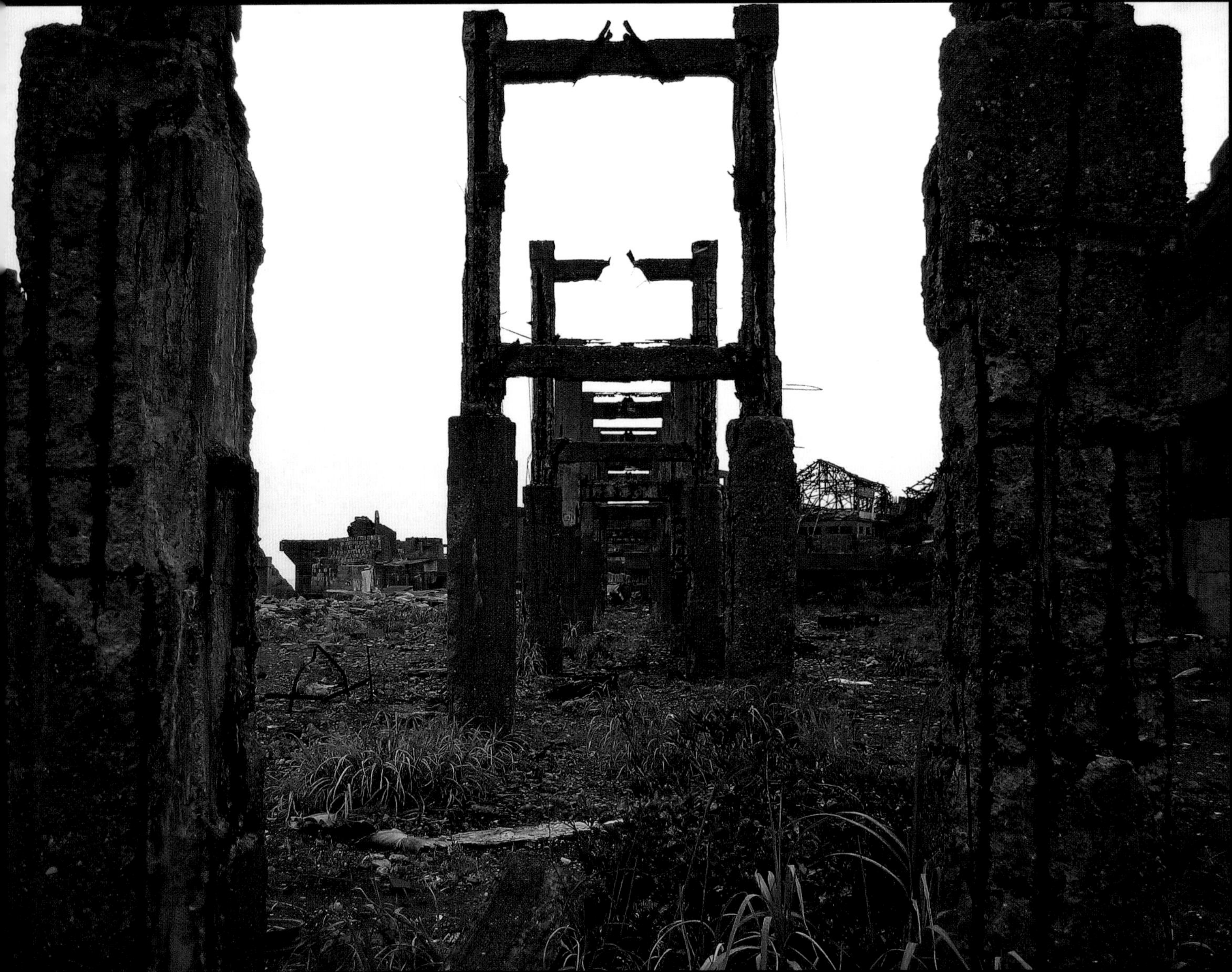

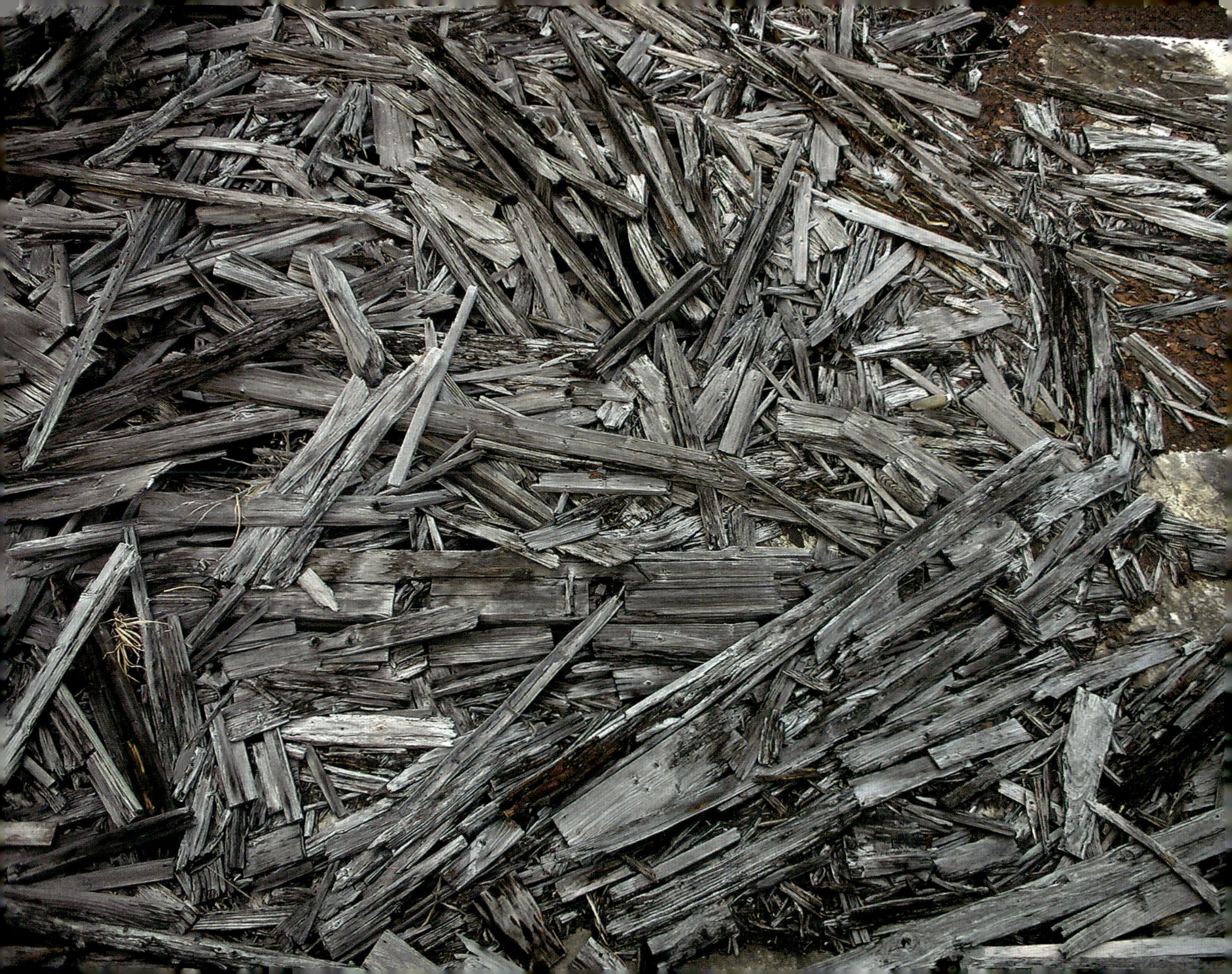

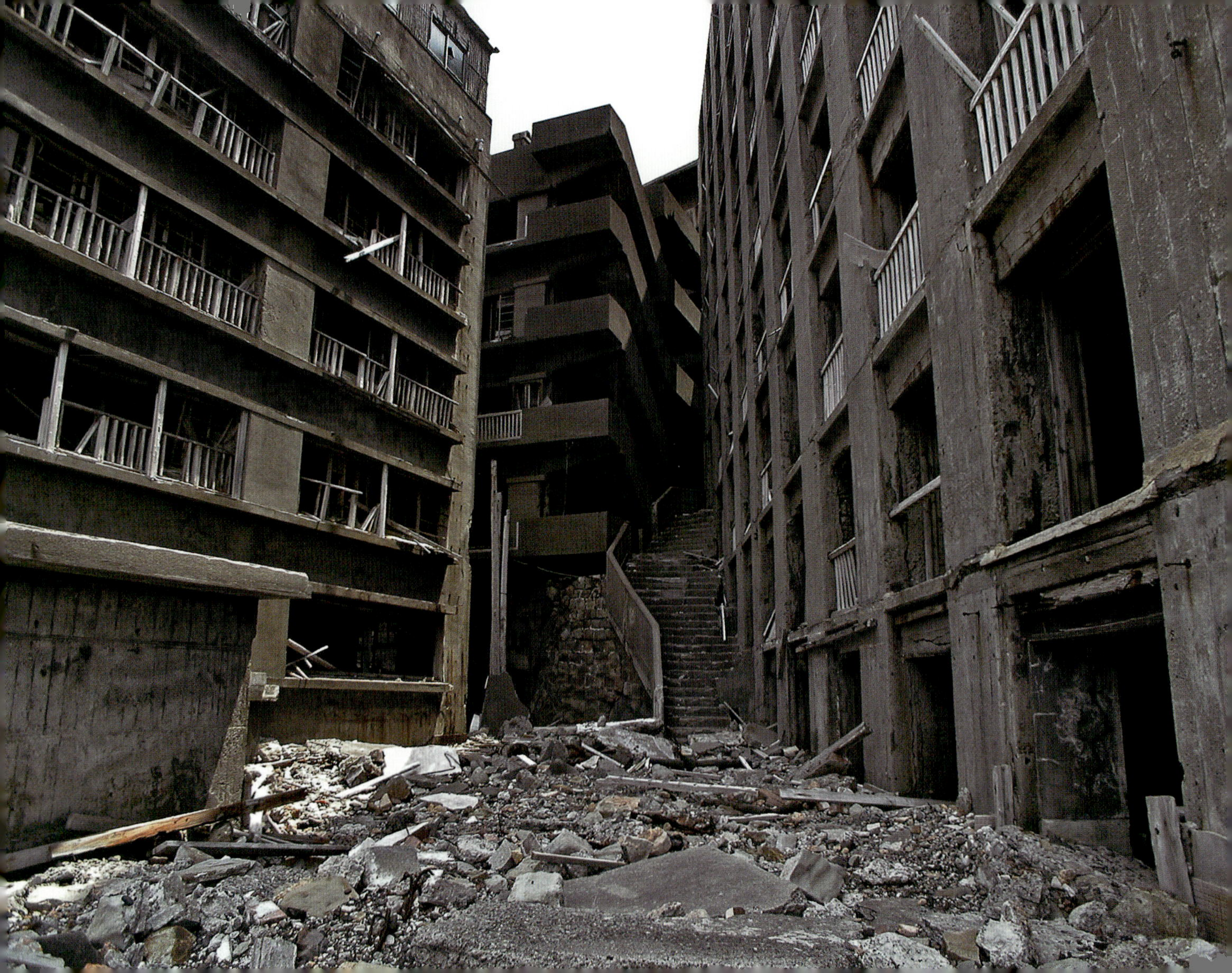

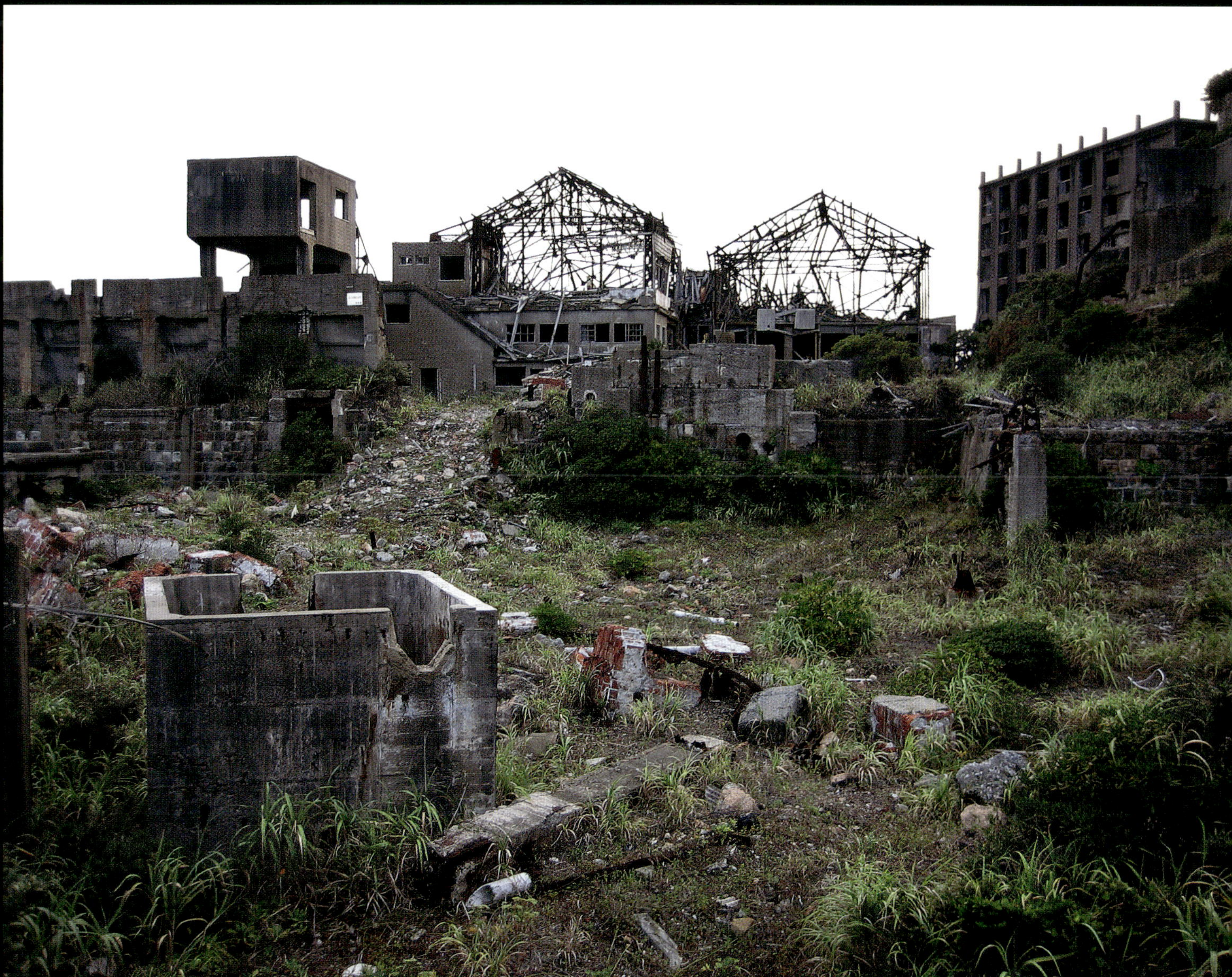

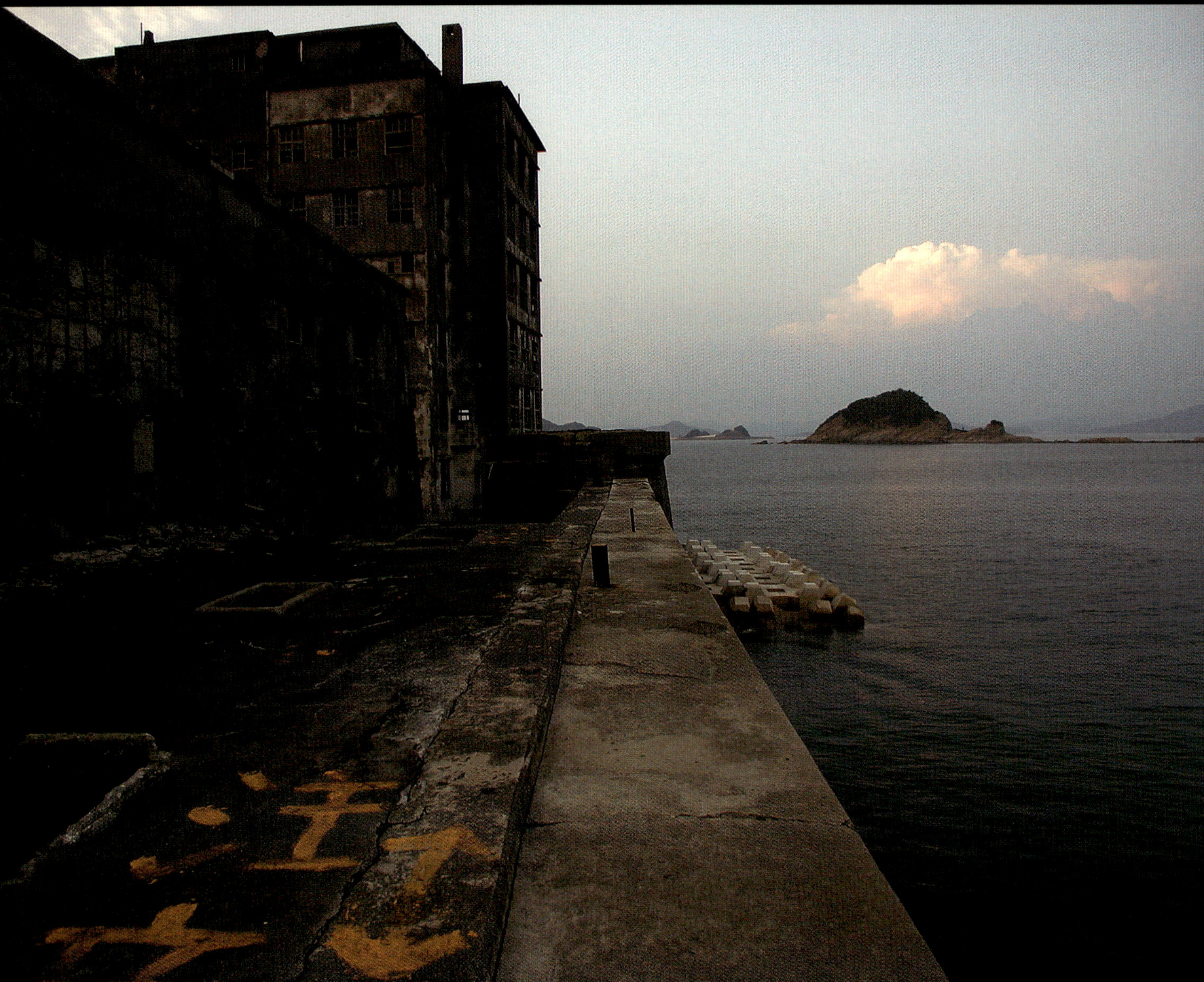

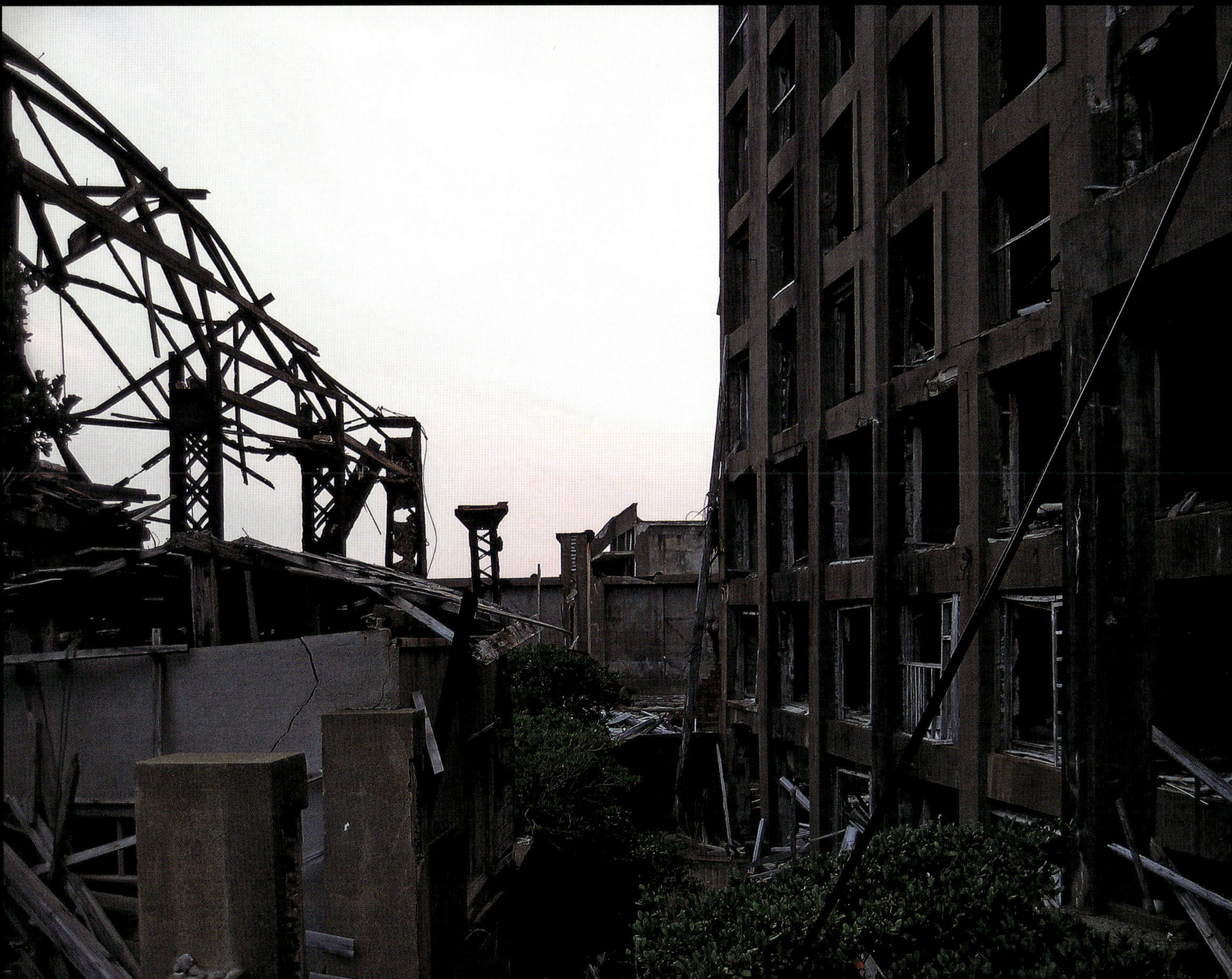

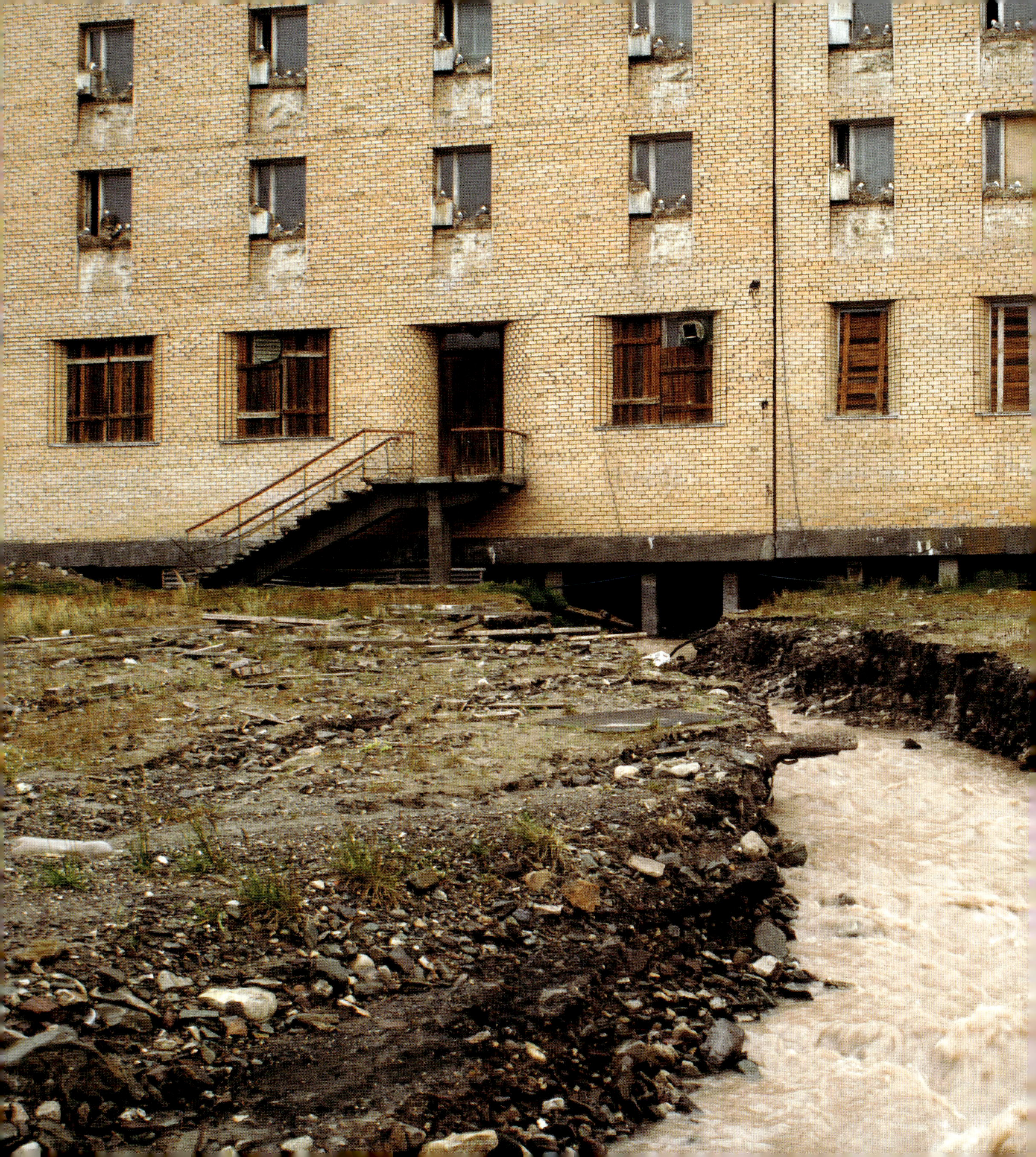

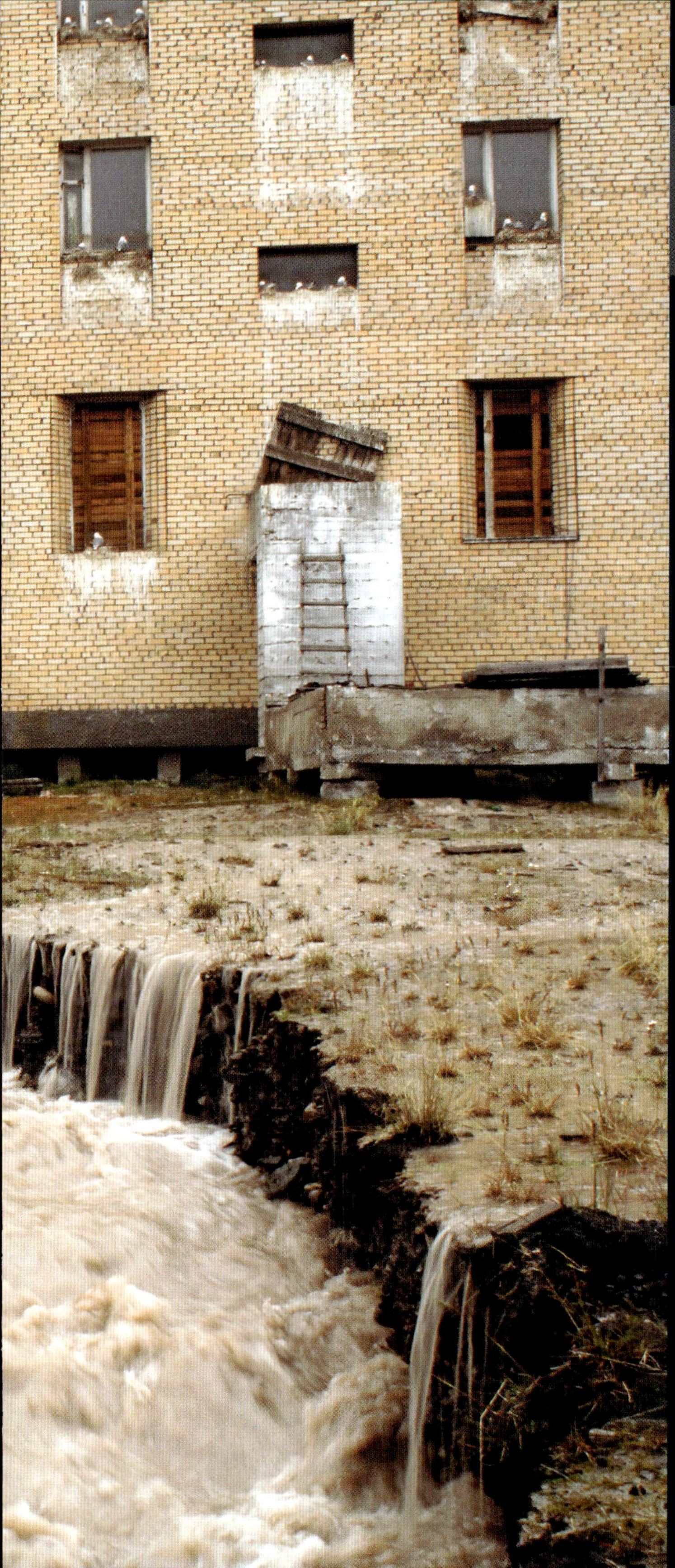

PYRAMIDEN

NORWEGEN NORWAY

FOTOS VON PHOTOS BY ELIN ANDREASSEN

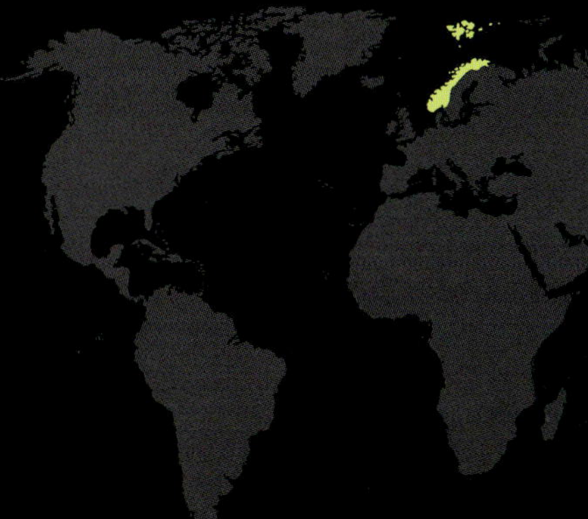

In der Arktischen See, dem kleinsten Ozean der Erde, liegt Hunderte Kilometer von Grönland, Norwegen und Russland entfernt der Archipel Spitzbergen. Etwa 1.300 Kilometer beträgt die Entfernung zum geografischen Nordpol. Laut einem Vertrag aus dem Jahr 1920 gehört die Inselgruppe zum Staat Norwegen und wird als Verwaltungsbezirk Svalbard – „Kühle Küste" – genannt. Von ihrer größten Insel, die norwegisch Spitsbergen heißt, hat sie den bis heute bekannteren Namen. Der Archipel bleibt entsprechend dem „Svalbardtraktaten", das auch als „Spitzbergenvertrag" bezeichnet wird, ein entmilitarisiertes Gebiet und jedem Vertragsunterzeichner wird das Recht eingeräumt, es wirtschaftlich zu nutzen. Allein die Fischereirechte in der 200-Meilen-Zone beansprucht Norwegen für sich.

Die im kurzen Sommer nicht mehr untergehende Sonne, die sogenannte Mitternachtssonne, und das während der langen Polarnacht faszinierende Spiel bewegter Vorhänge, Bänder, pulsierender Bogen, Flammen und Strahlenkränze des Nordlichts, der Aurora borealis, beeinflussen den Rhythmus des Lebens in dieser Region. Seit Jahrtausenden inspirieren diese Phänomene Sagen und Legenden. Den Menschen offenbarte sich darin einst die Welt der Götter und sie glaubten, an deren Begegnungen und Auseinandersetzungen teilzuhaben. Nun widmen sie sich mehr der Wechselwirkung von Sonnenwind und Erdmagnetfeld, finden Risiken für die weltweite Telekommunikation und den Flugverkehr oder sie untersuchen die Zusammenhänge des Klimawandels.

Am Kongsfjord bei Ny-Ålesund auf der Insel Spitzbergen haben Norwegen, Italien, Großbritannien, Frankreich, Deutschland, China, Japan, Südkorea und Indien ihre Forschungsstationen eingerichtet. Die internationalen Teams bilden einen nicht unerheblichen Teil der hiesigen Bevölkerung. Auf dem 39.044 Quadratkilometer großen Eiland leben und arbeiten sie zusammen mit den 1.800 Einwohnern von Longyearbyen am Isfjord, den 500 Bergleuten der russischen Siedlung Barentsburg sowie den Wissenschaftlern der dort errichteten russischen Polarstation. Noch bis zum Jahr 2000 war am Ausläufer des Isfjords, dem Billefjord, auch der Bergbauort Pyramiden bewohnt. Zwei Jahre zuvor hatte man dessen Kohleförderanlage stillgelegt. Von den russischen Bergarbeitern blieb daraufhin keiner länger als nötig.

Bis zu tausend Menschen lebten in Pyramiden. Angeregt von der Form eines nah gelegenen Bergs, gaben die Erbauer dem Ort seinen Namen. Sie fühlten sich durch den Bergrücken an die Grabmale ägyptischer Pharaonen erinnert. Eine schwedische Minengesellschaft begann ab 1921 mit dem Abbau der Kohle. Einige Jahre später übernahm der sowjetische Bergwerkbetrieb Arktikugol mit den Förderrechten auch die Siedlung. Die Sowjetunion war Unterzeichnerin des Spitzbergenvertrags und der Trust Arktikugol kann bis heute Rohstoffe und Kohle auf dem Archipel gewinnen. Pyramiden wurde nach dem Zweiten Weltkrieg zum bedeutendsten arktischen Bergbaustandort für die Sowjetunion.

Jetzt vergeht die Siedlung unter dem Anprall von Wind und Wetter. Touristen blicken ihren Reiseleiter verblüfft an, wenn er berichtet, dass hier zur Zeit des intensiven Kohlebergbaus Paprika, Tomaten und Salat geerntet wurden – 1975 etwa 5,7 Tonnen Gemüse. Es fällt inzwischen nicht leicht, sich vorzustellen, wie man im selben Jahr 35 Tonnen Fleisch, 110.000 Eier und 48.000 Liter Milch erzeugte oder für die harte Arbeit Ausgleich im Schwimmbad oder dem Kulturhaus fand.

The Svalbard Archipelago is hundreds of kilometers from Greenland, Norway and Russia in the Arctic Ocean, the smallest ocean in the world. It is about 1,300 kilometers from the geographic North Pole. According to an agreement from 1920, the group of islands belongs to the state of Norway and is known as the Administrative District of Svalbard or "cool coast". It still has its better-known name today from the largest island, called Spitsbergen in Norwegian. According to the "Svalbardtraktaten", or the Svalbard Agreement, the archipelago remains a demilitarized zone and everyone who signed the agreement was given the right to use it commercially. Norway only claims the fishing rights in the 200 mile zone for itself. The short summers with no sunset, the so called midnight sun, and the fascinatingly playful moving curtains, bands, pulsing crescents, flames and coronas of the northern lights, the aurora borealis during the long winter night both influence the rhythm of life in this region. For thousands of years, these phenomena have inspired myths and legends. In them, the world of the gods was revealed to the people at one time, and they believed in their encounters and that they took part in their disputes. Today, they dedicate their time more to the interactions of the solar wind and earth's magnetic field, they find risks to worldwide telecommunications and air traffic, or they study the correlations of climate change.

Norway, Italy, Great Britain, France, Germany, China, Japan, South Korea and India have set-up research stations at Kongsfjord near Ny-Ålesund on the island of Spitsbergen. The international teams make up a considerable amount of the current population. They live and work together on the 39,044 square kilometer island with the 1,800 residents of Longyearbyen on Isfjord, the 500 miners of the Russian settlement of Barentsburg as well as the scientists of the Russian polar station built there. On an offshoot of the Isfjord, the Billefjord, the mining town of Pyramiden was still occupied up until the year 2000. Two years prior, its coal production facility was shut down. Afterwards, none of the Russian miners stayed longer than necessary. Up to one thousand people lived in Pyramiden. The builders gave the town its name from the shape of the mountain nearby. The mountain ridges reminded them of the tombs of the Egyptian pharaohs. A Swedish mining company started mining the coal in 1921. Some years later, the Soviet mining operation, Trust Arktikugol, took over the claim as well as the settlement. The Soviet Union was a signee of the Svalbard Agreement and Trust Arktikugol can still mine raw materials and coal from the archipelago today. Pyramiden became the most important Arctic mining location for the Soviet Union after the Second World War.

Now the settlement is disappearing under the onslaught of wind and weather. Tourists look at their travel guide amazed when they hear that during the time of the most intensive coal mining, paprika, tomatoes, and lettuce were harvested – in 1975 about 5.7 tons of vegetables. In the meantime, it is not easy to imagine how, in the same year, people produced 35 tons of meat, 110,000 eggs and 48,000 liters of milk, or that they found relaxation from the hard work in the swimming pool or leisure center.

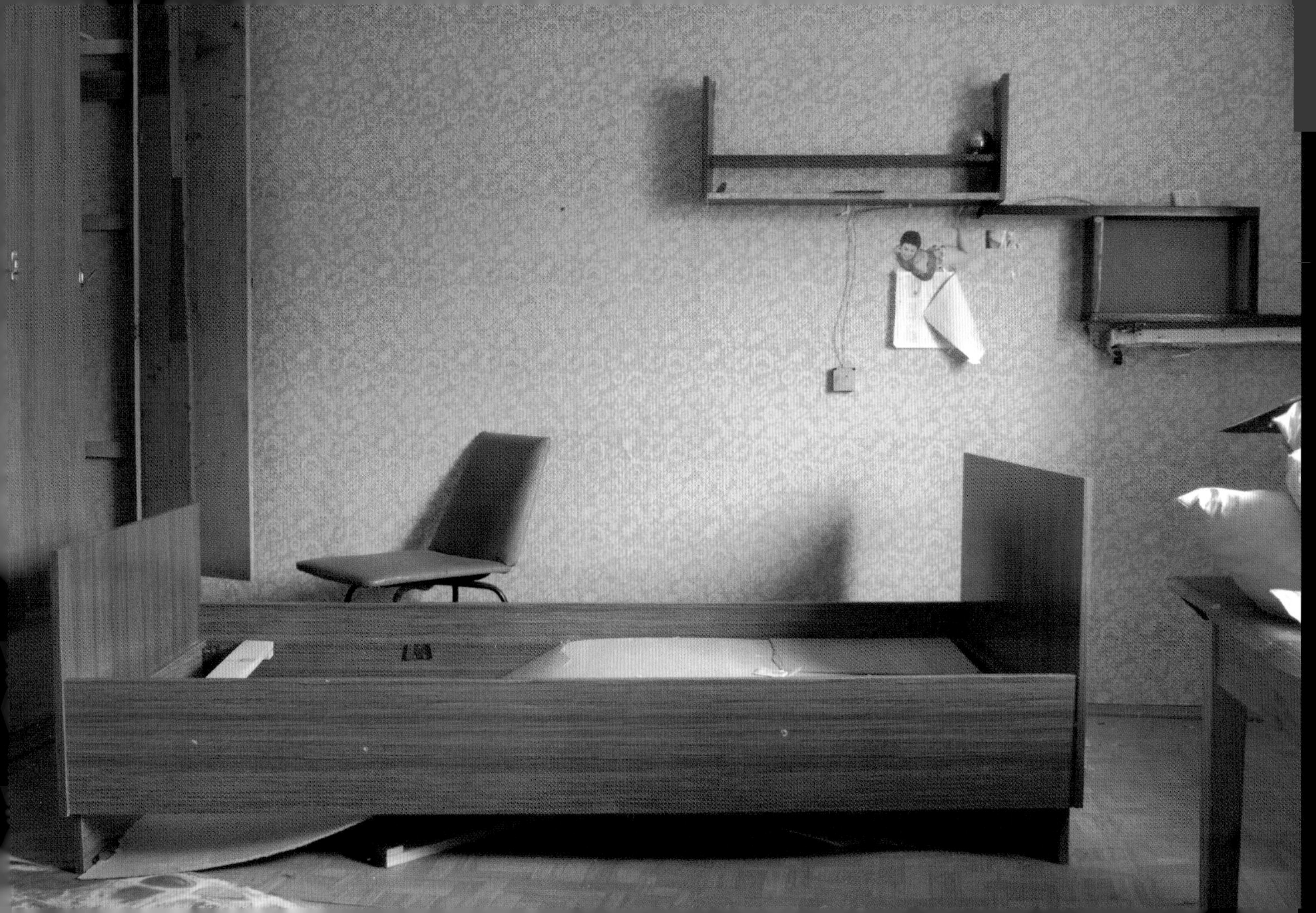

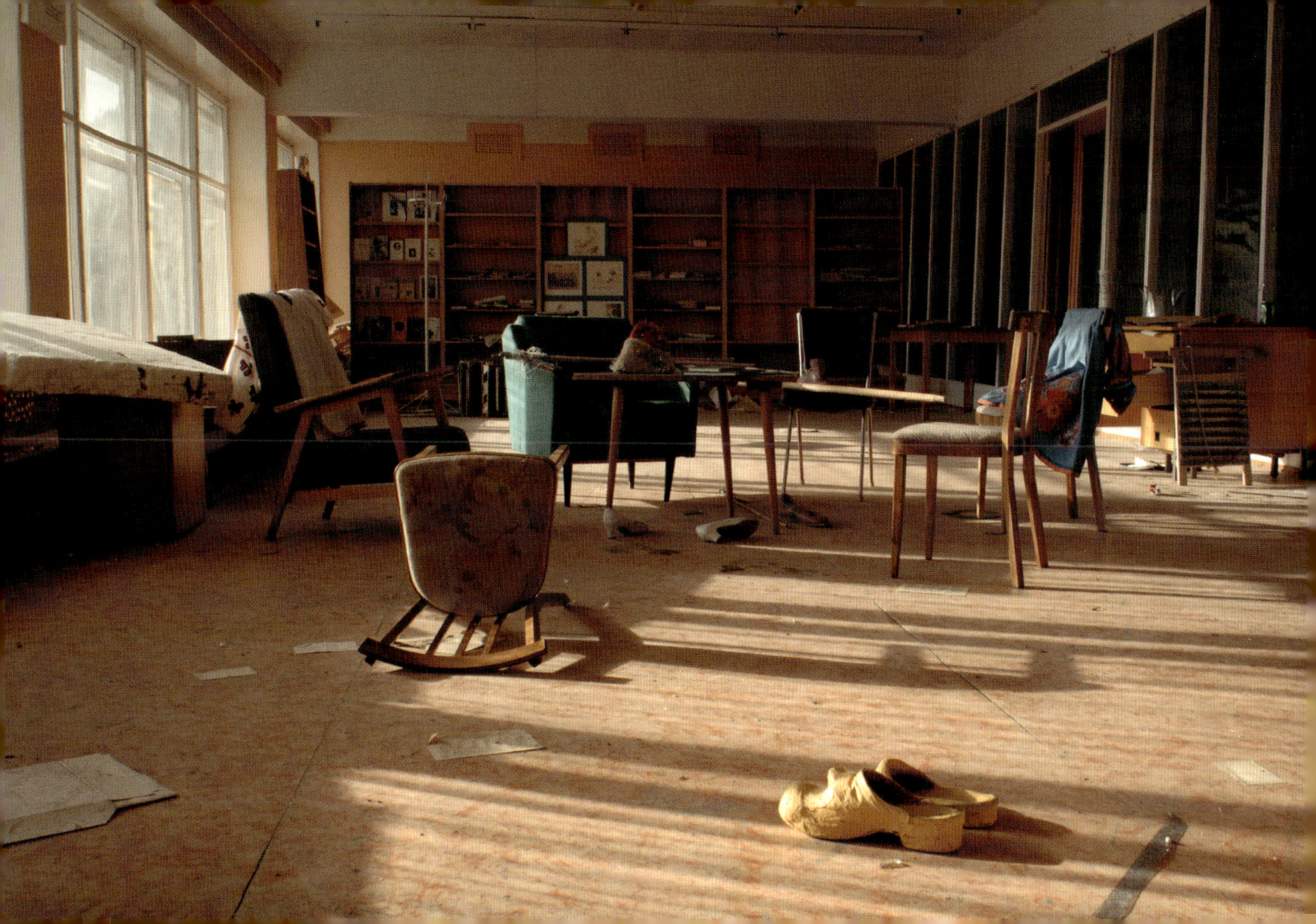

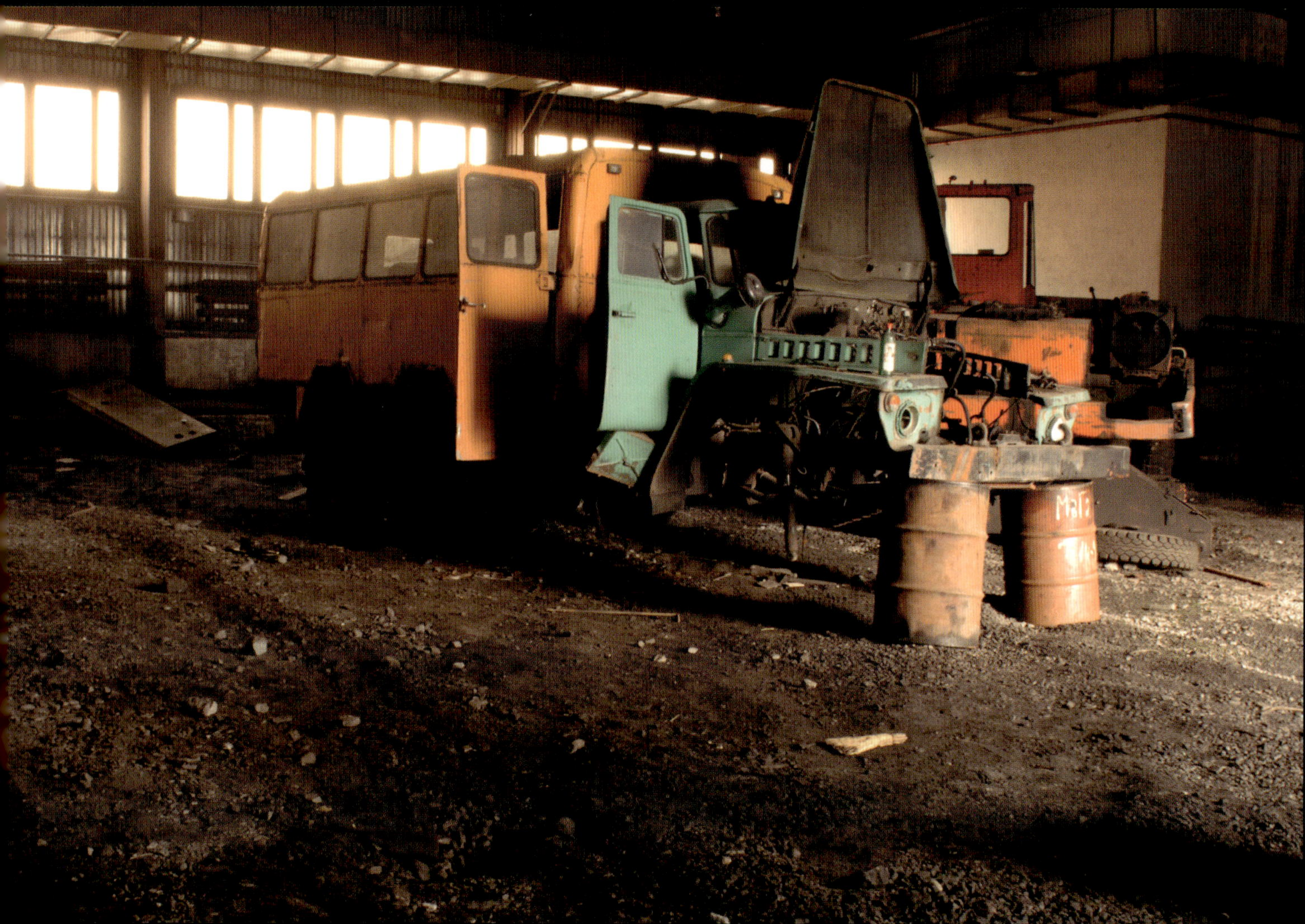

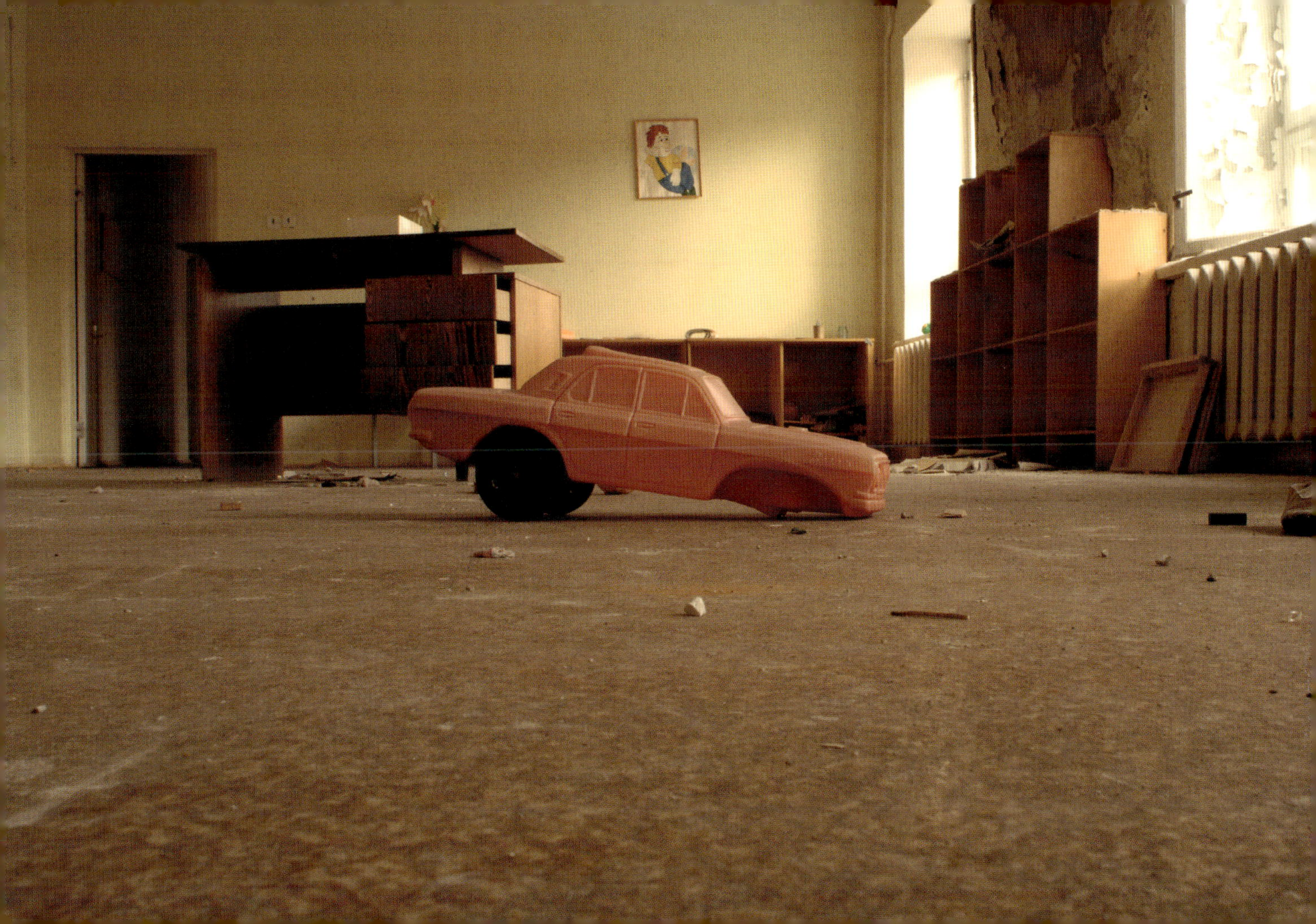

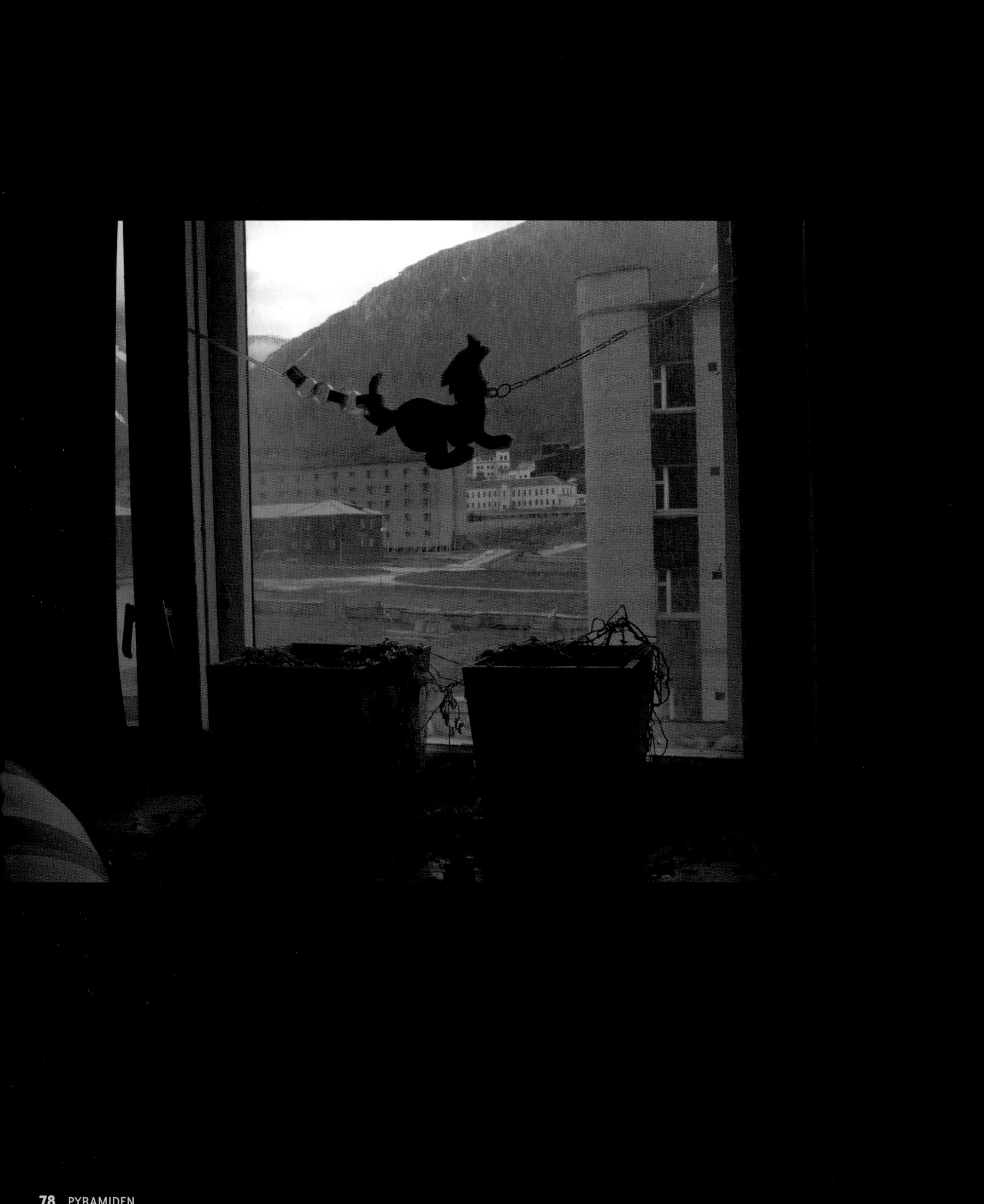

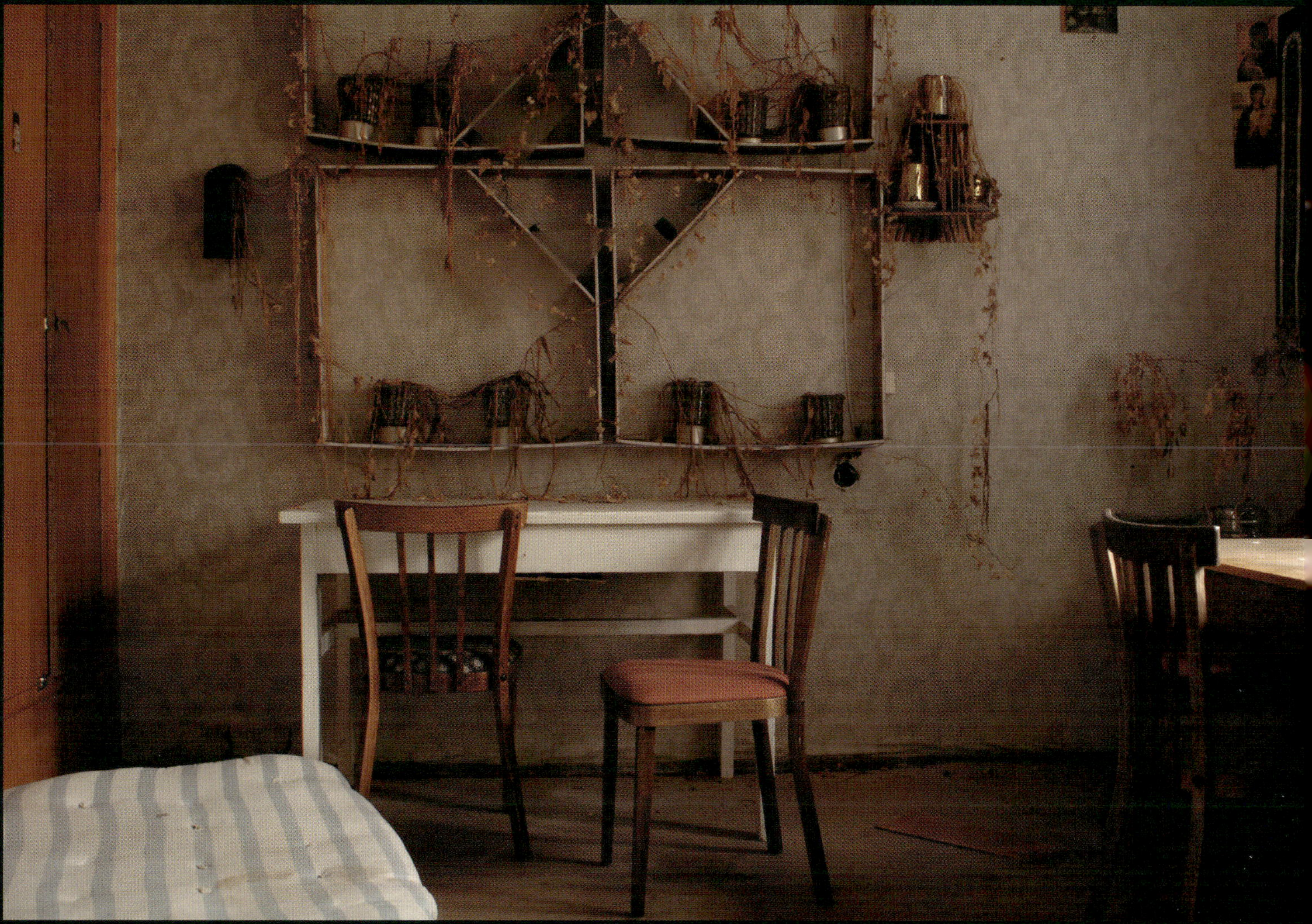

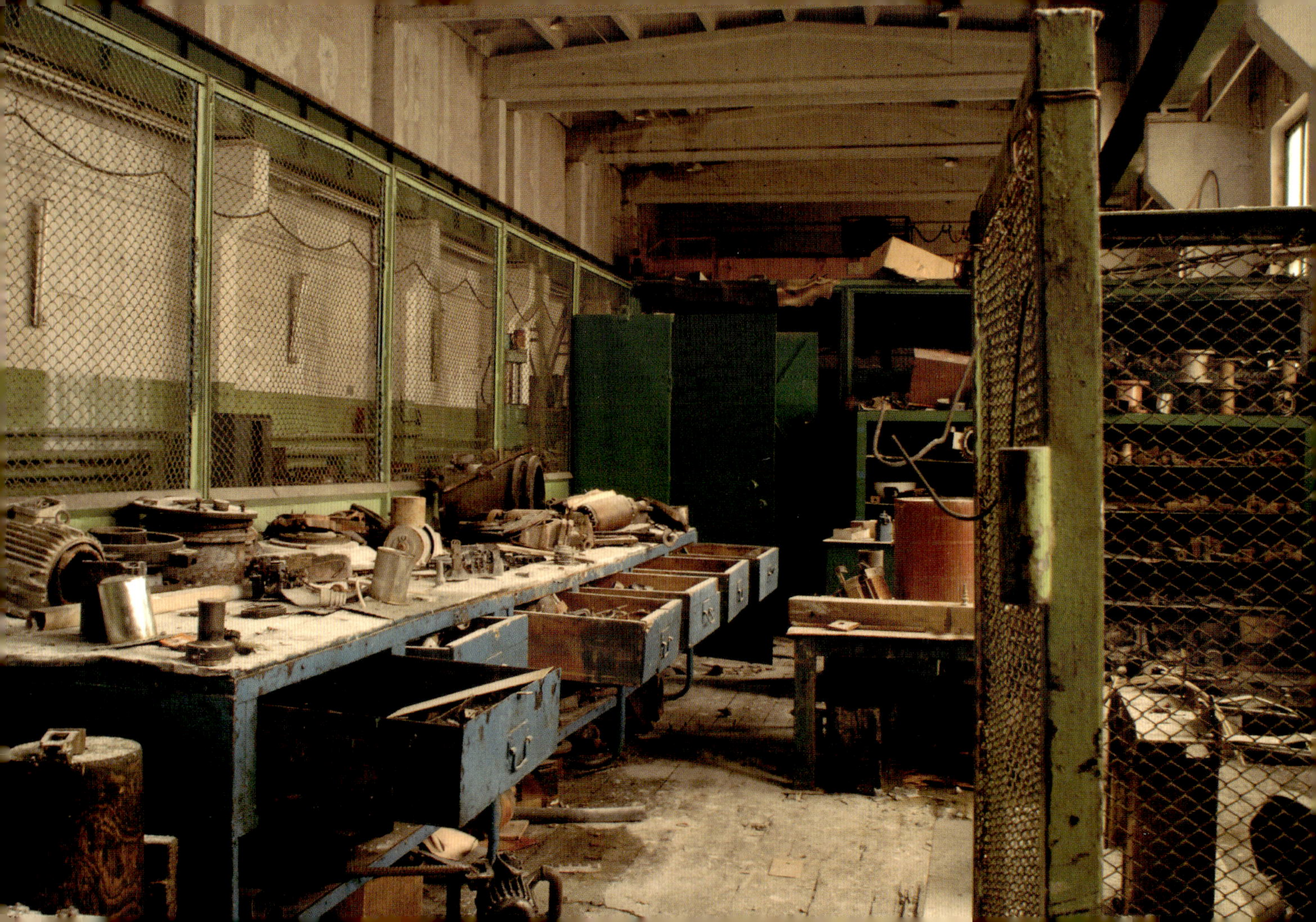

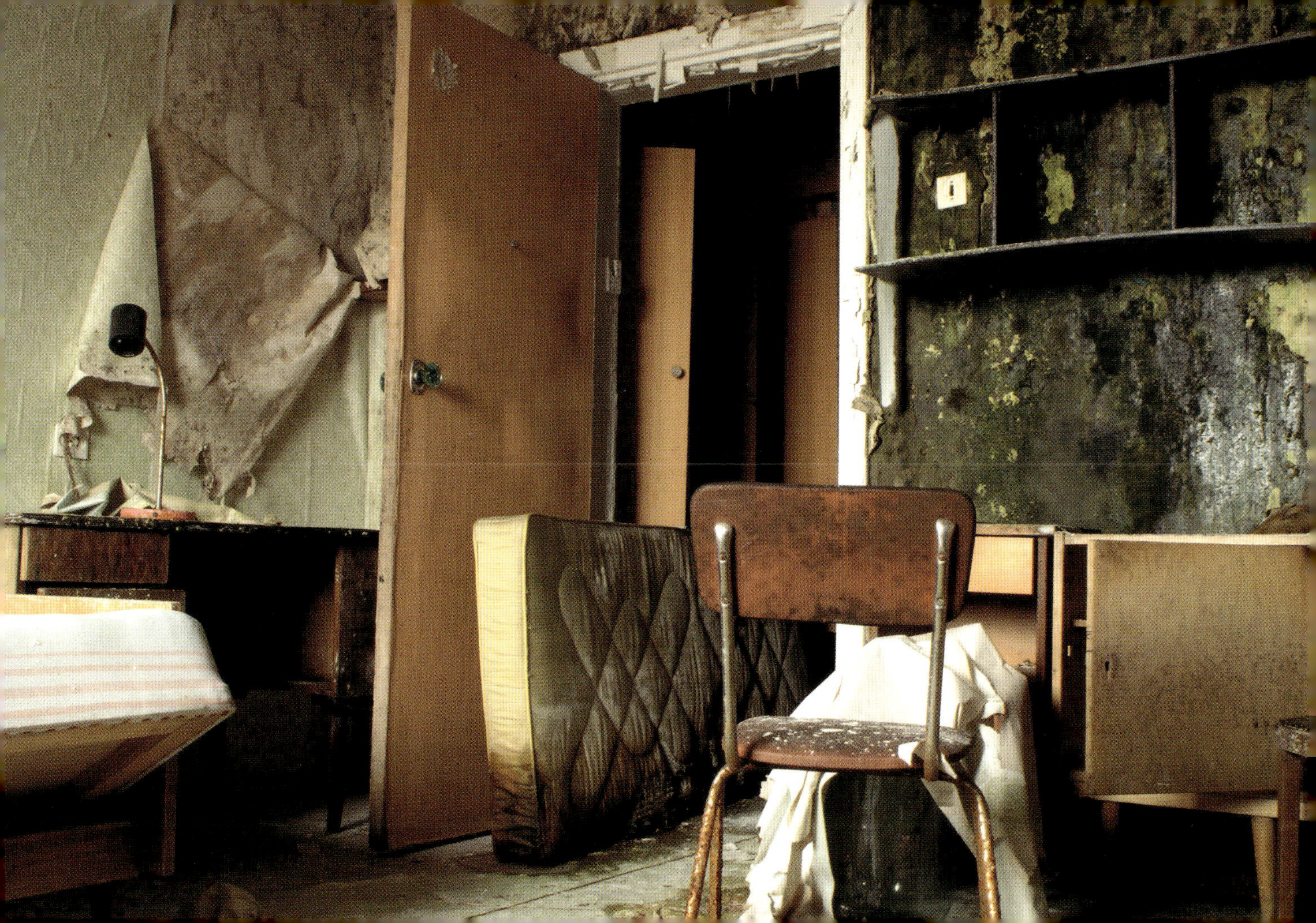

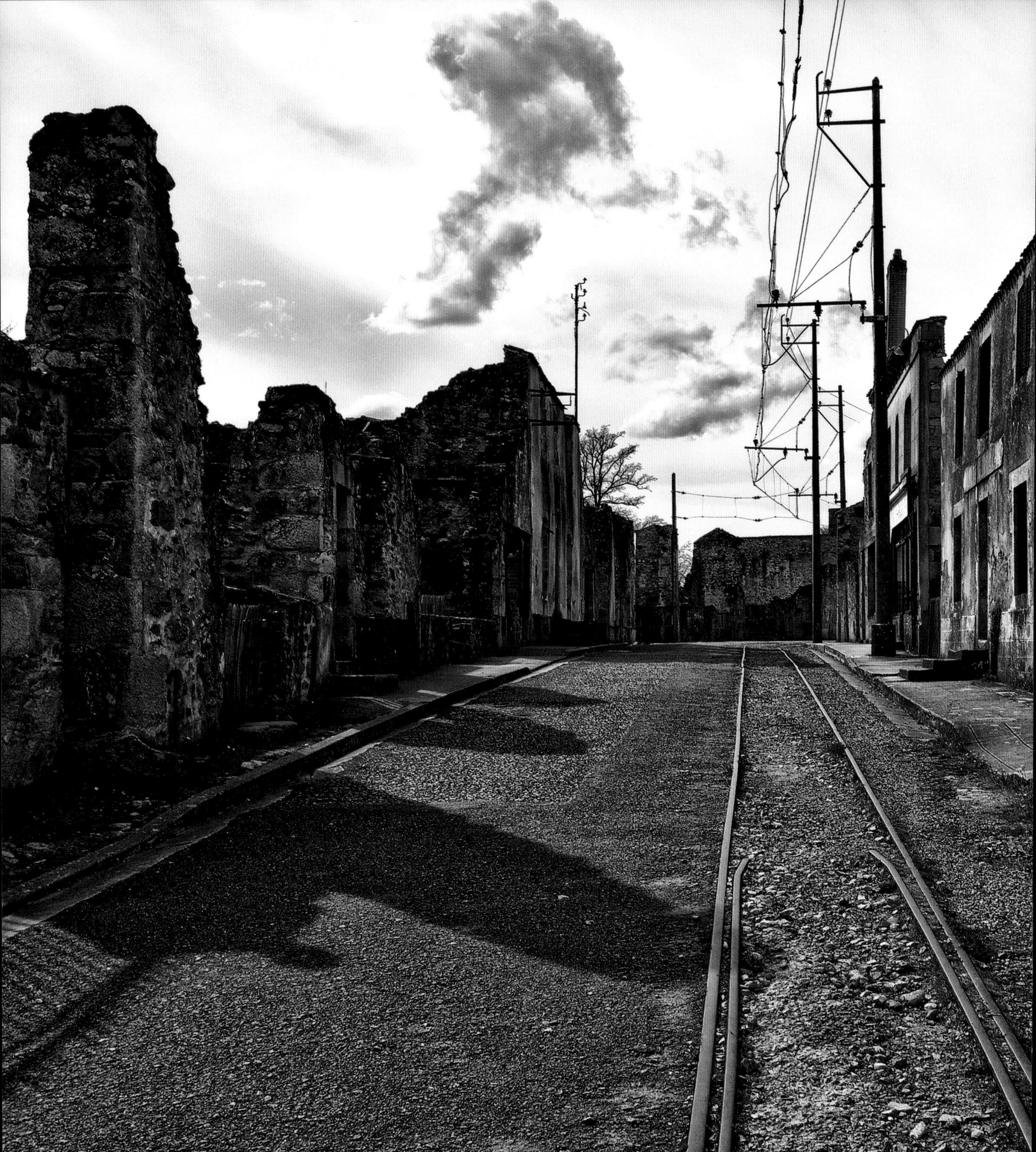

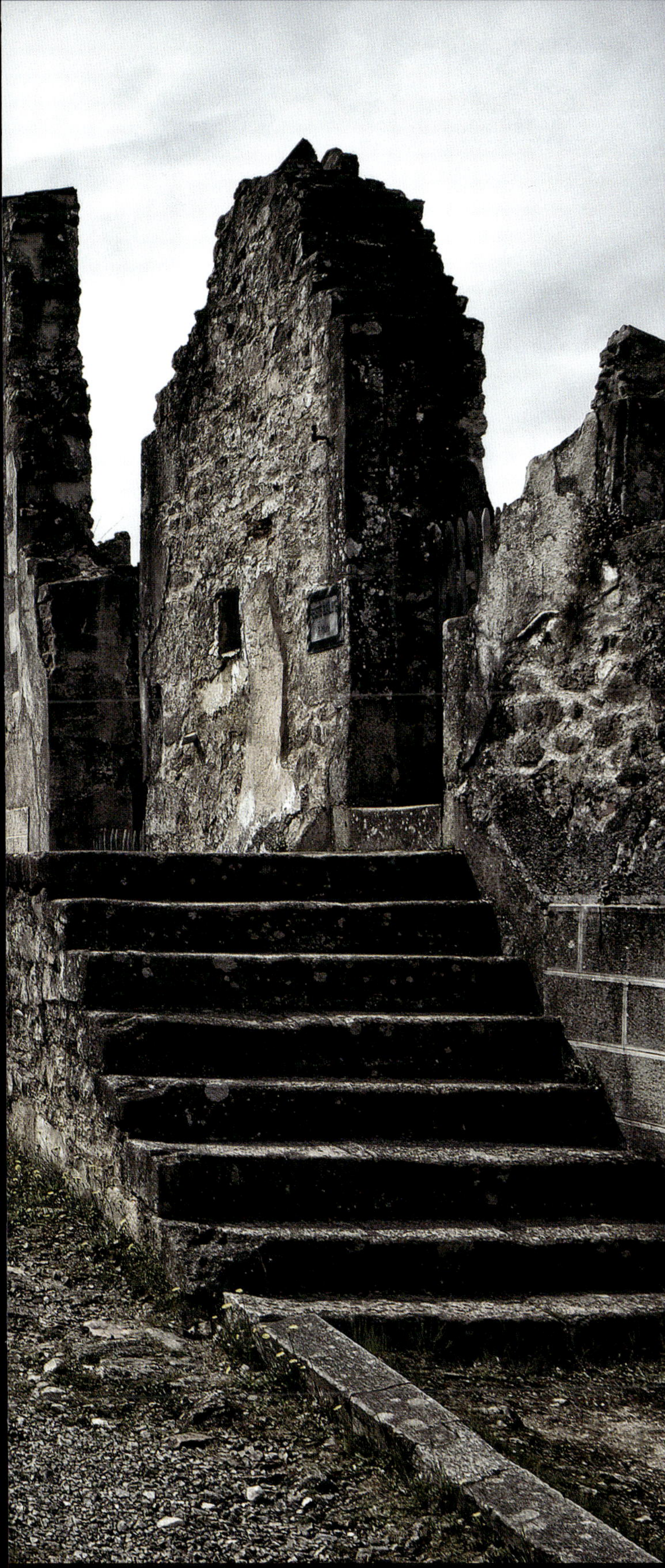

ORADOUR-SUR-GLANE

FRANKREICH FRANCE

FOTOS VON PHOTOS BY MARTIN GRAF

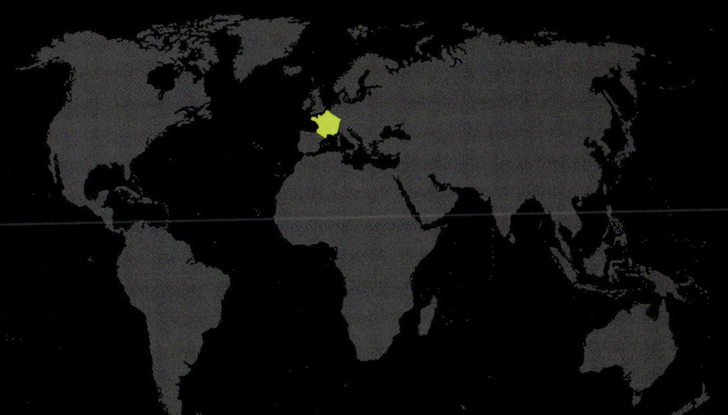

Es war für die Jahreszeit zu kühl an diesem Samstag, dem 10. Juni 1944. Die Kinder des Ortes Oradour-sur-Glane und die der umliegenden, Dutzenden Weiler waren noch nicht von der Schule heimgekehrt. Auch wenn es nun Zeit schien, dass sie nach Hause zu ihren Familien kamen und etwas zu Mittag aßen. Da drang ein 120 Mann starkes Kommando der Zweiten SS-Panzerdivision „Das Reich“ um 14 Uhr in den Ort ein und trieb Kinder, Frauen und Männer, insgesamt 642 Menschen, auf dem Markt zusammen. Die deutschen Soldaten sperrten die Männer aus Oradour-sur-Glane in Schuppen und Garagen, wo sie bald darauf getötet wurden. Sie schlossen Frauen und Kinder in die Kirche ein, steckten diese in Brand, sprengten den Kirchturm, sodass er auf das Kirchenschiff stürzte, warfen Handgranaten und schossen in das Kircheninnere. Als Einzige konnte Marguerite Rouffanche von dort flüchten.

Vor dem Militärgericht bestätigten ihren Augenzeugenbericht später mehrere der beteiligten SS-Soldaten. Es überlebten nur wenige Menschen in Oradour-sur-Glane. 207 Kinder, 254 Frauen und 181 Männer starben. Kaum wurde das Massaker bekannt, legte die Vichy-Regierung bei der deutschen Behörde für strittige Angelegenheiten während des deutsch-französischen Waffenstillstands Protest ein. Der verantwortliche Offizier wurde aber wenig später, bei Kampfhandlungen während der Landung der Alliierten in der Normandie, getötet und seine Kompanie aufgerieben. Acht Jahre nach dem Zweiten Weltkrieg konnte in Frankreich noch gegen 65 der in Oradour-sur-Glane beteiligten Soldaten Anklage erhoben werden. In Bordeaux verurteilte im Februar 1953 das Militärtribunal 21 von ihnen, 14 stammten aus dem Elsass.

Da in Frankreich ein Gesetz die gemeinsame Anklage von Deutschen und Franzosen untersagte, verkündete das Tribunal sein Urteil getrennt für die deutschen und französischen Angeklagten. Es verhängte zwei Todesstrafen, entschied 18-mal die Verurteilung zur Zwangsarbeit bis zu zwölf Jahren und sprach einen Soldaten frei. Vor allem im Elsass führte das Gerichtsurteil zu so erheblichen Unruhen in der Bevölkerung, dass die französische Regierung sich genötigt sah, eine Amnestie zu beschließen. Man wandelte die beiden Todesstrafen in Haft um und 1959 wurden auch diese am Massaker in Oradour-sur-Glane Beteiligten freigelassen. In der Bundesrepublik Deutschland musste sich keiner der übrigen Angeklagten verantworten, einer Überstellung nach Frankreich zum Prozess in Bordeaux wurde nicht zugestimmt. Erst im Jahr 2014 erhob die Staatsanwaltschaft von Dortmund Anklage gegen einen mutmaßlich Beteiligten.

Heute befindet sich eine neu errichte Ortschaft neben dem als Monument im Zustand von 1944 belassenen Oradour-sur-Glane. Einzig der Friedhof und das sogenannte „Maison d’Oradour“ blieben unzerstört erhalten. Auf dem Friedhof hat die Vereinigung der Märtyrerfamilien ein eigenes Denkmal für die getöteten Angehörigen errichten lassen. Es liegt entfernt von dem des Staates Frankreich, welchem man bis heute nicht die Generalamnestie für die Täter vergessen hat. Spät, aber intensiv bemüht sich die deutsche Regierung um Versöhnung. Der Besuch des Bundespräsidenten Joachim Gauck, im September 2013, war für Oradour-sur-Glane ein wichtiges Signal.

It was cool for this time of year on Saturday, the 10th of June 1944. The children of the town of Oradour-sur-Glane and the surrounding dozen hamlets were not yet home from school – even though it seemed to be time for them to come home to their families and eat something for lunch. That's because a 120 man detachment of the second SS tank division, "Das Reich" invaded the town and rounded up the children, women and men, a total of 642 people, into the market. The German soldiers locked the men from Oradour-sur-Glane in sheds and garages where they were soon killed. They locked women and children in the church, set it on fire, blew up the church tower, so that it crashed into the sanctuary, threw hand grenades and shot into the church interior. Marguerite Rouffanche was the only one who was able to escape. In front of a military court, her eye witness account was confirmed later by many of the SS soldiers who participated. Only a few people survived in Oradour-sur-Glane. 207 children, 254 women and 181 men died. As soon as the massacre was known, the Vichy government registered a protest with the German authorities for disputed matters during the German-French ceasefire. The officer responsible was killed soon afterwards and his company disbanded in fighting during the landing of the Allies in Normandy. Eight years after the Second World War, it was possible in France to bring charges against 65 of the soldiers who participated in Oradour-sur-Glane. In Bordeaux, in February 1953, a military tribunal sentenced 21 of them; 14 of them were from Alsace.

Due to a law in France forbidding common sentencing of German and French citizens, the tribunal handed down its decision separately for the German and French defendants. It handed down two death sentences, decided on 18 sentences of forced labor of up to twelve years and let one soldier go free. The court sentencing resulted in such massive unrest in the population, especially in Alsace, that the French government decided it was necessary to grant amnesty. The two death sentences were changed to imprisonment and in 1959 these two massacre participants were also set free. In the Federal Republic of Germany, none of the remaining defendants had to take responsibility. Extradition to France to the trial in Bordeaux was not approved. It was only in 2014 that the public prosecutor's office in Dortmund brought charges against one of the alleged participants.

Today a newly built town is near the original Oradour-sur-Glane, which has been left as it was in 1944 as a memorial. Only the cemetery and the so called, "Maison d'Oradour" were not destroyed. The Association of Martyred Families erected its own memorial at the cemetery to the murdered family members. It stands a distance away from the one from the French government, which stops people from forgetting the general amnesty granted to the perpetrators. It was late, but the German government made an intensive effort at reconciliation. The visit of the Federal President, Joachim Gauck in September 2013 was an important sign for Oradour-sur-Glane.

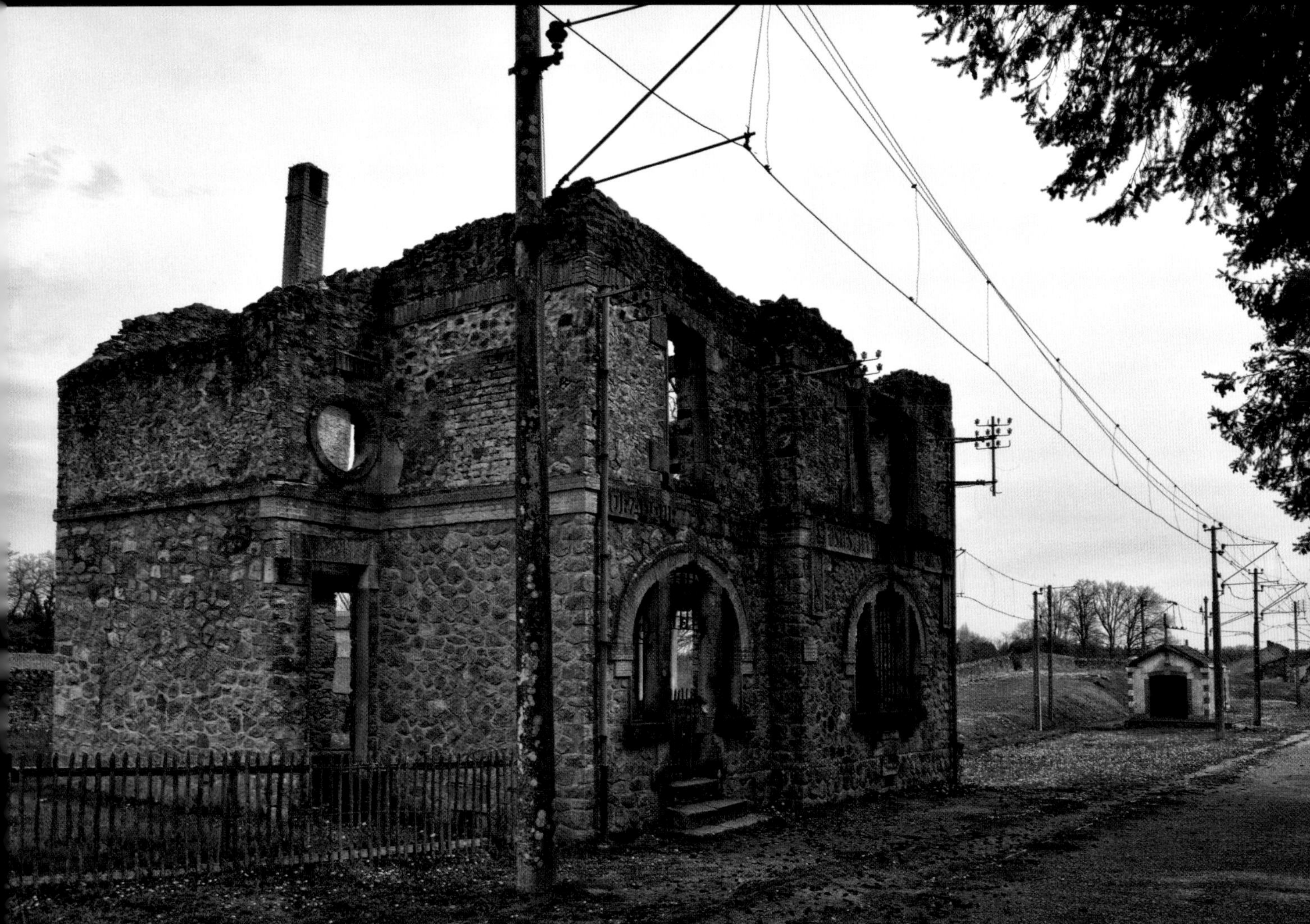

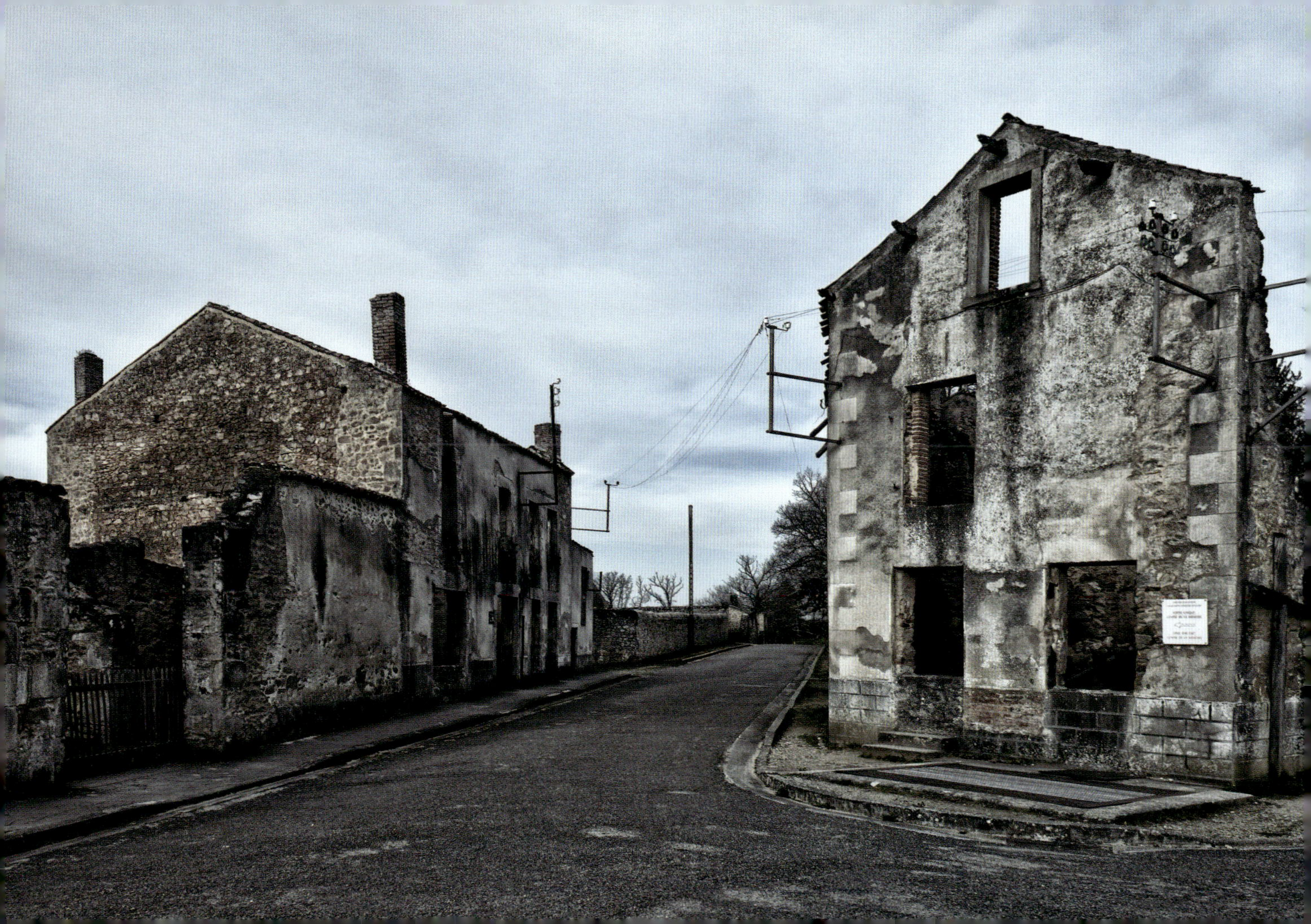

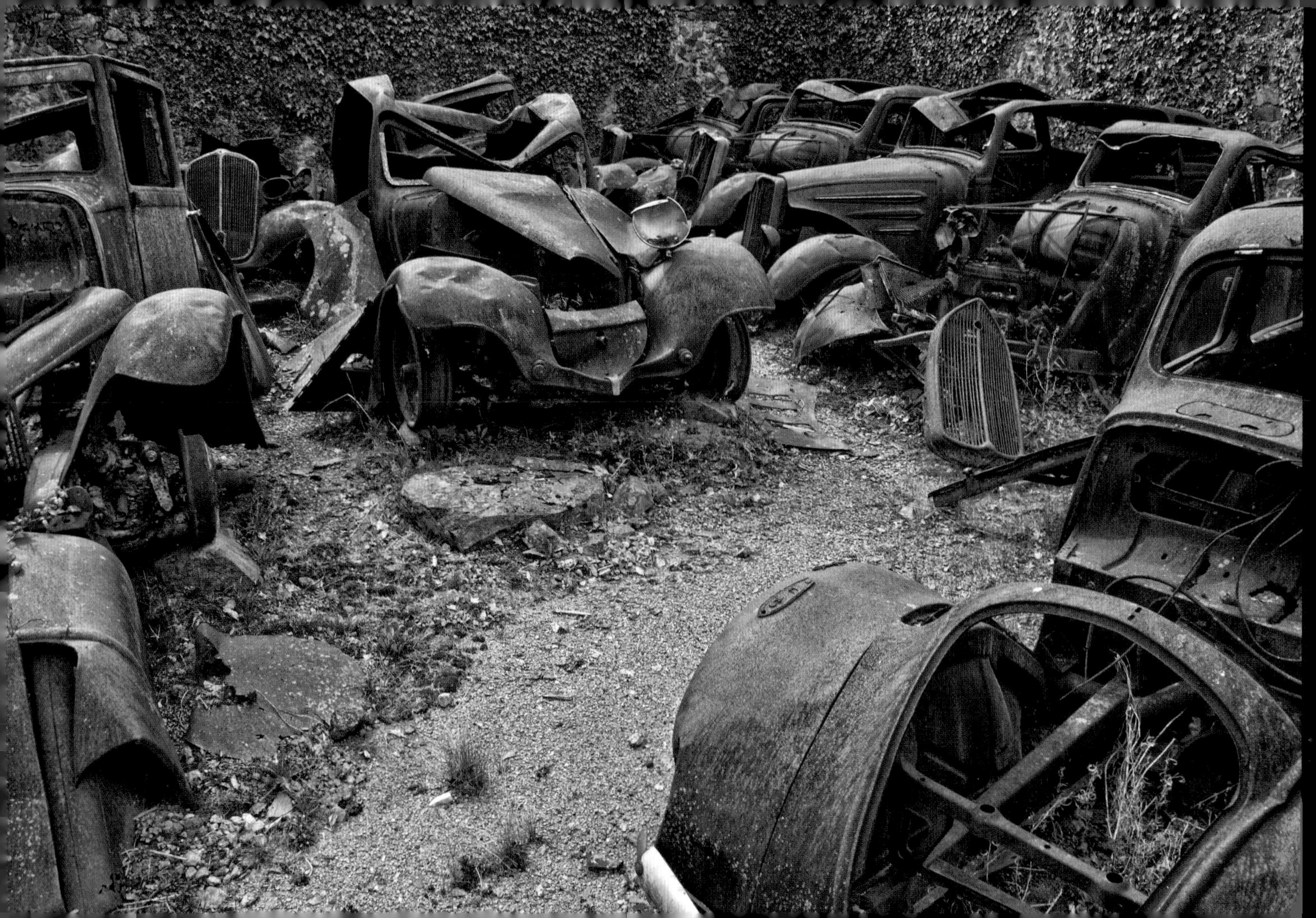

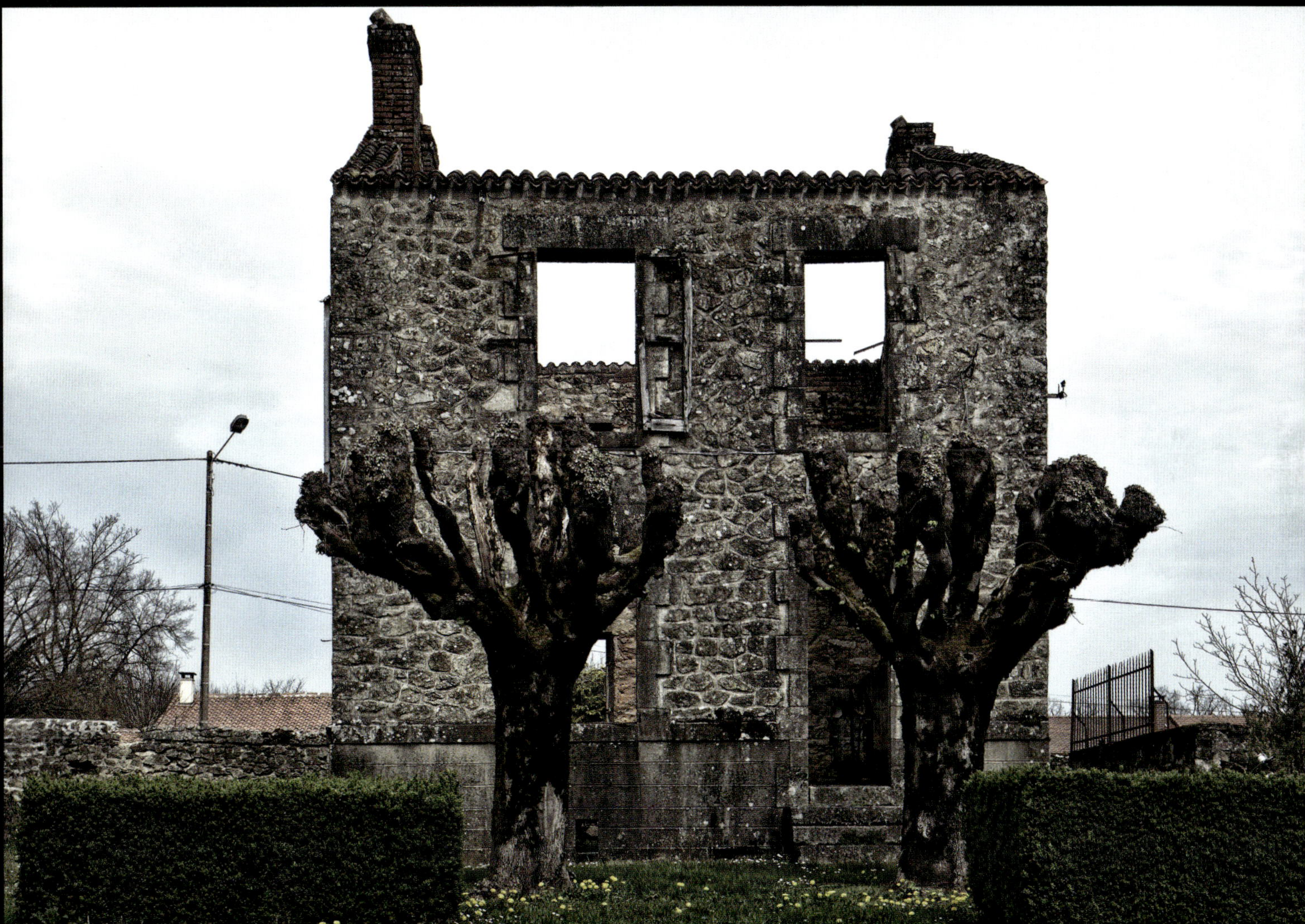

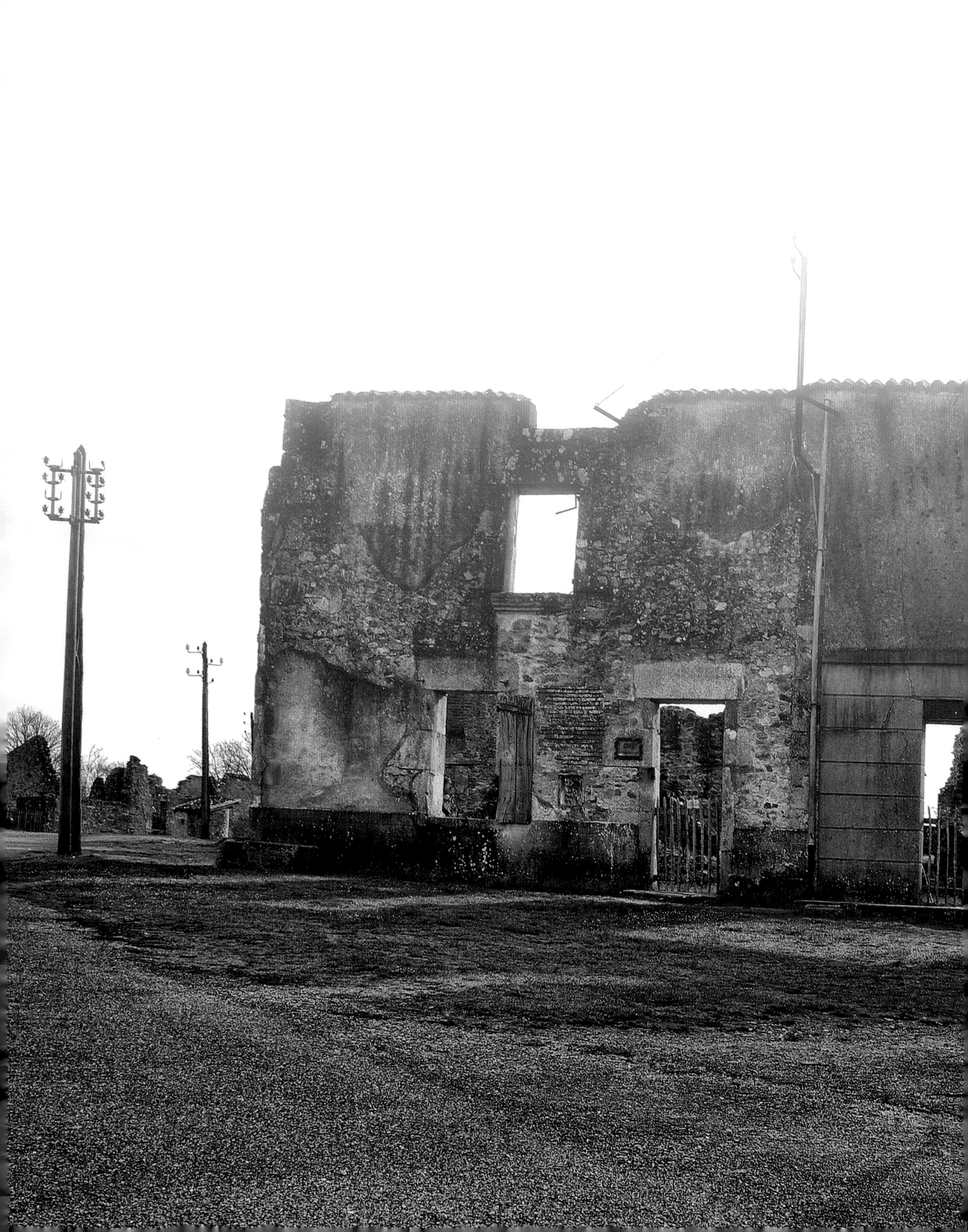

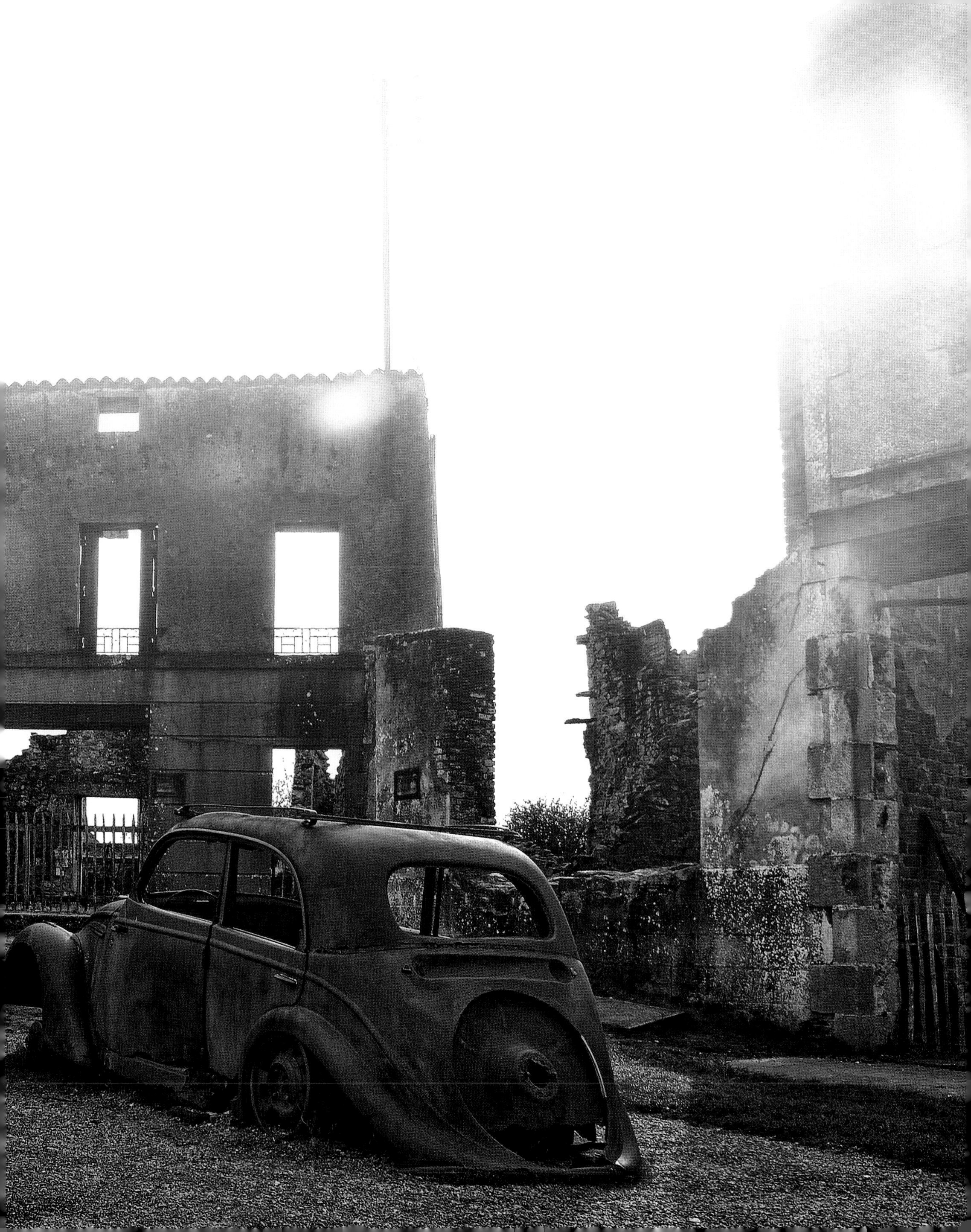

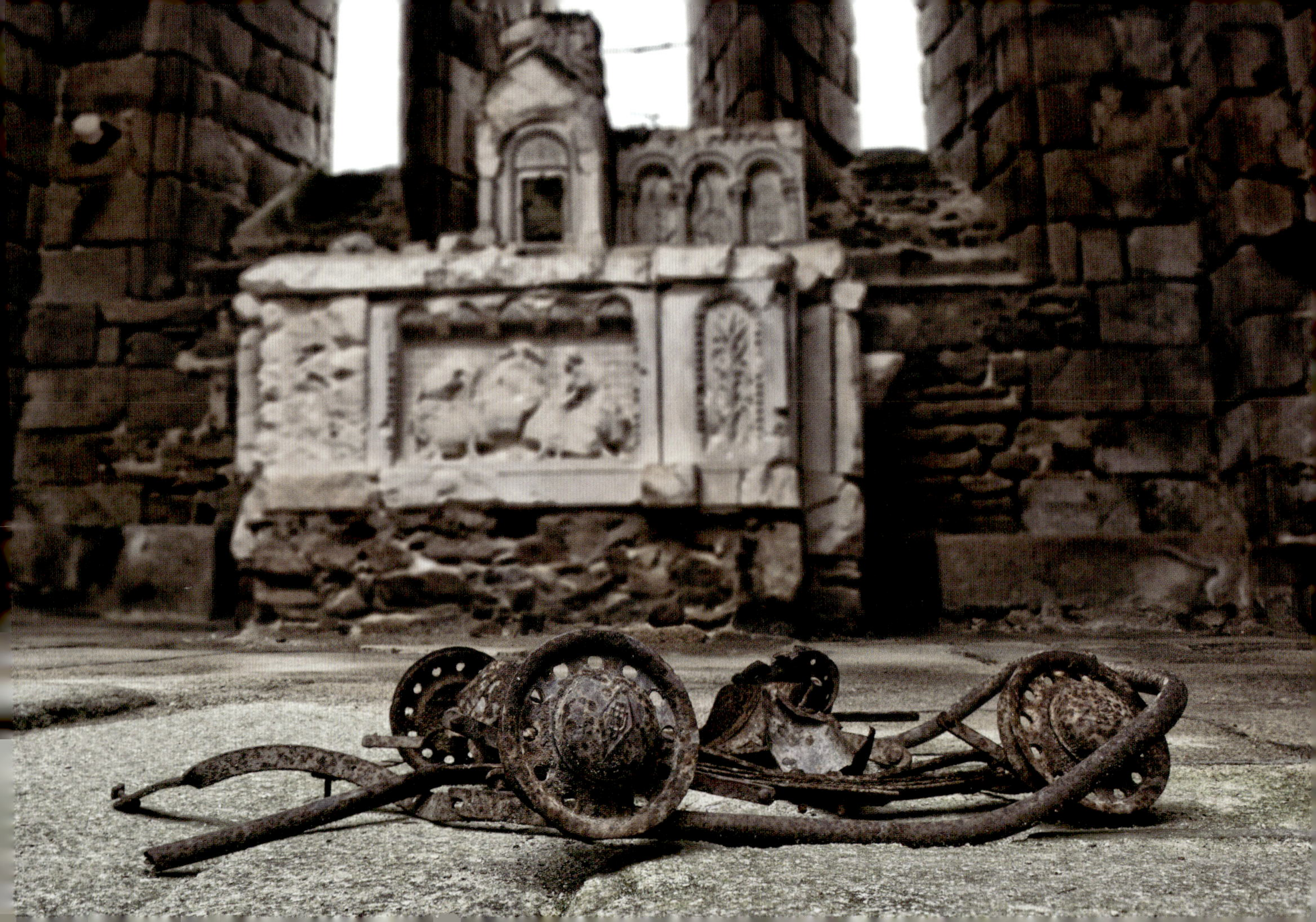

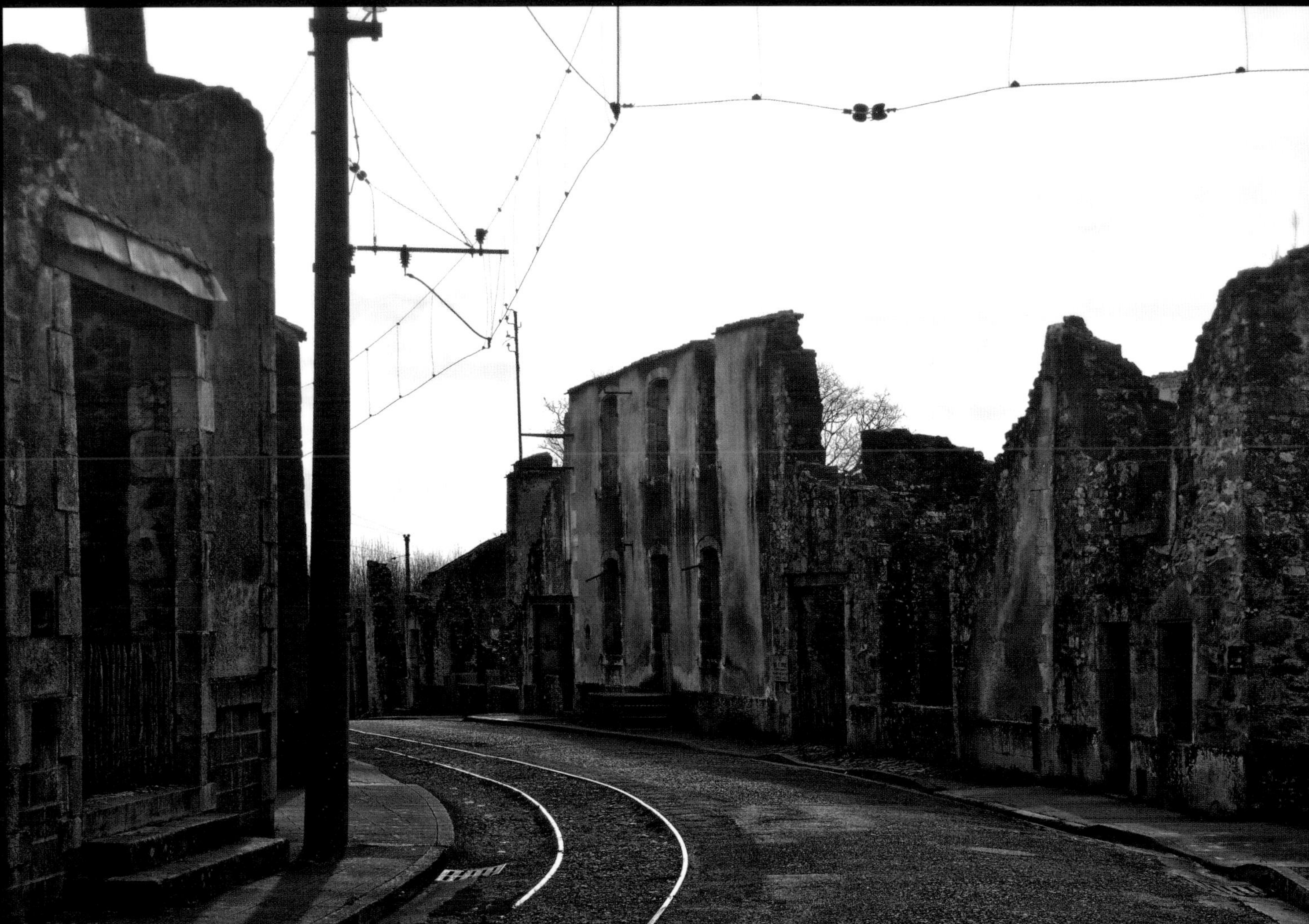

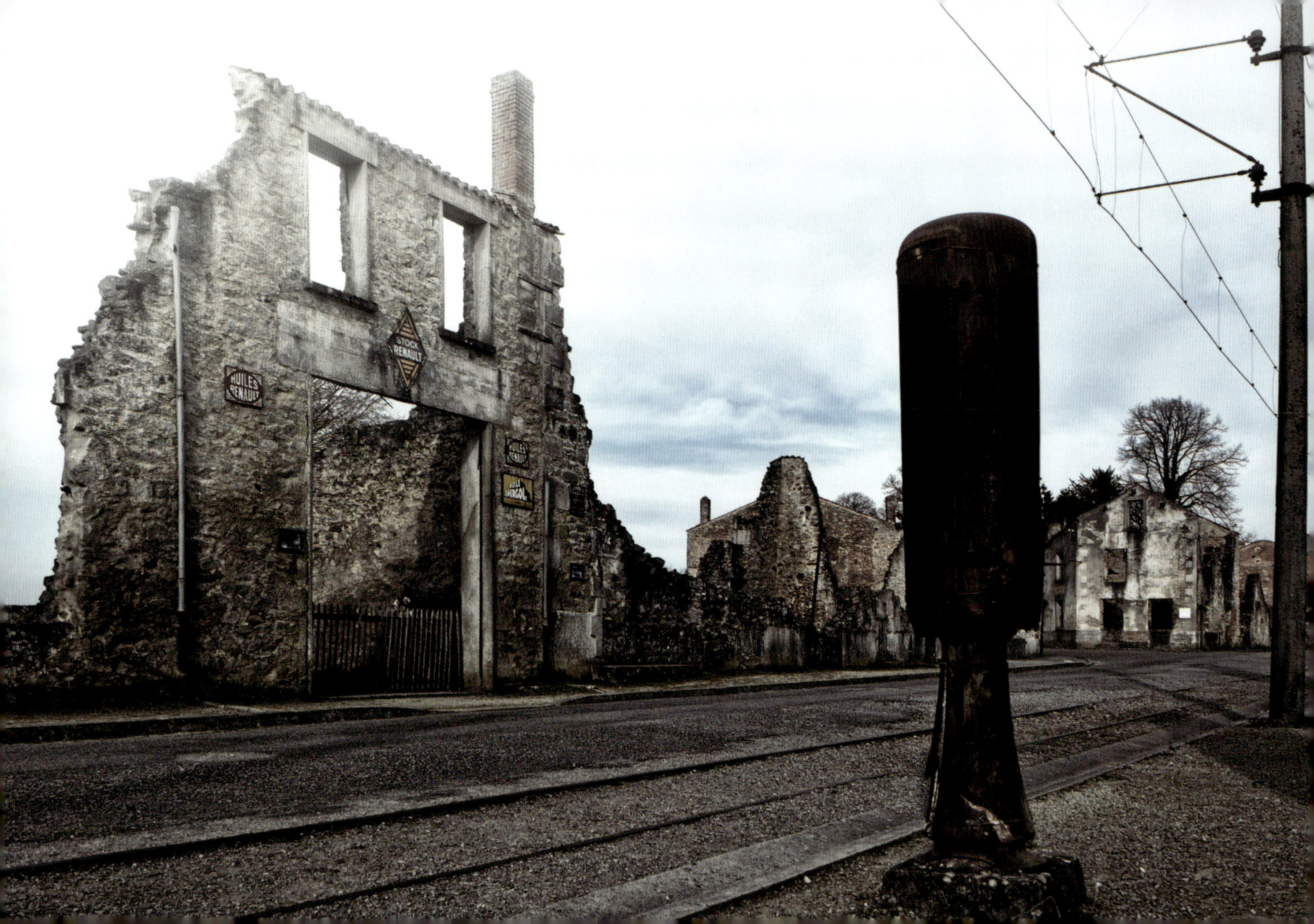
STOCK RENAULT
HUILES RENAULT

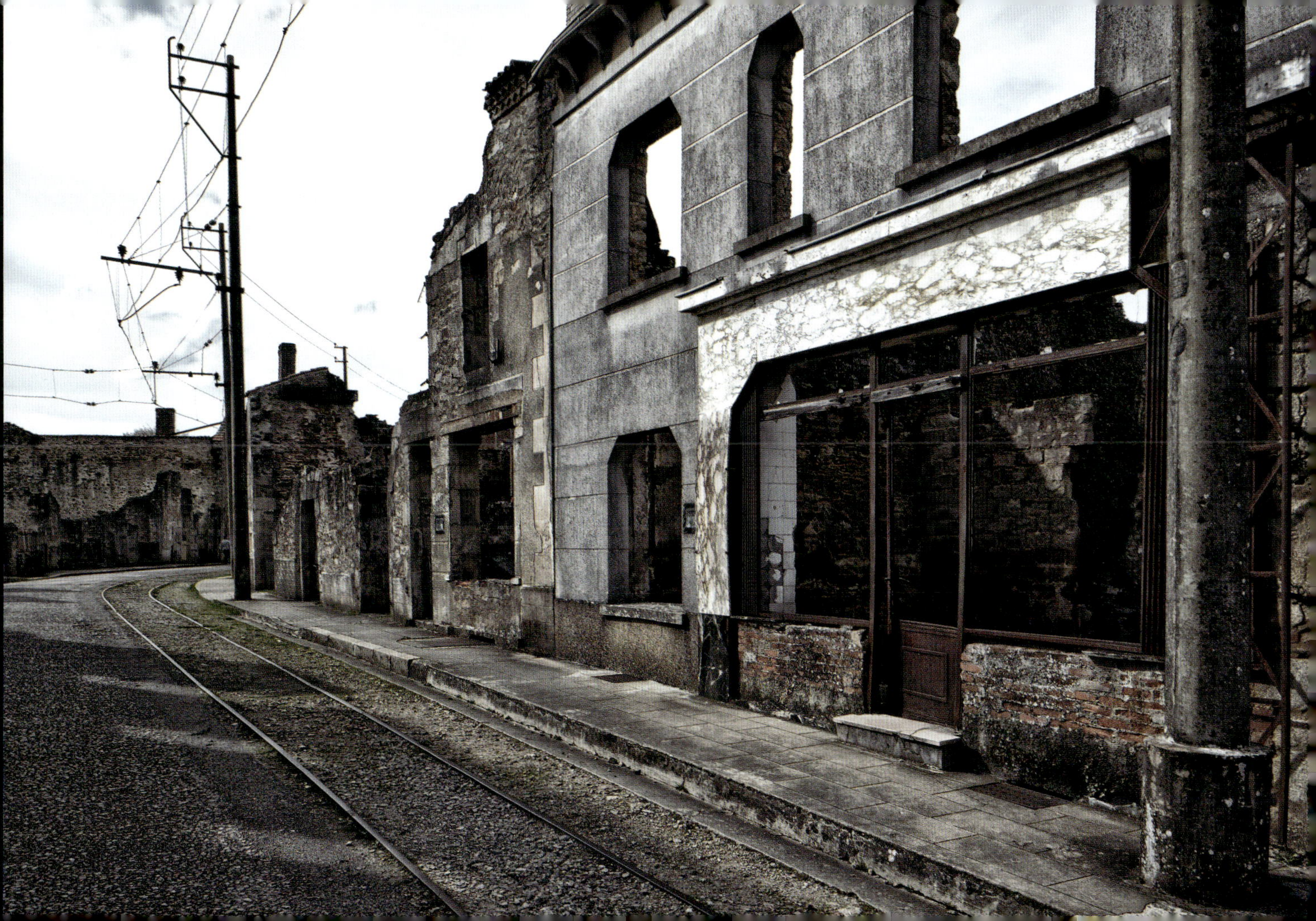

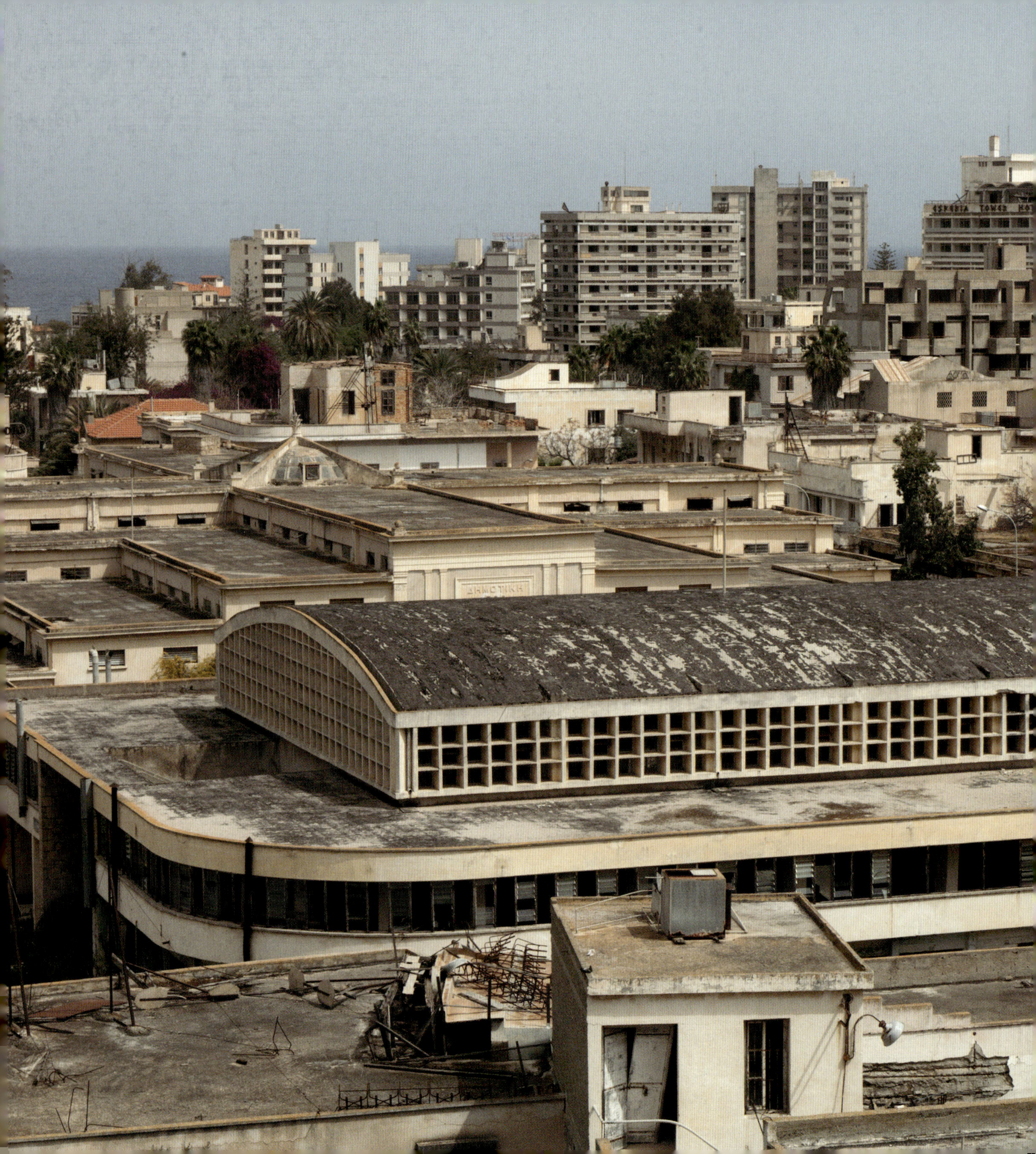
ΔΗΜΟΤΙΚΗ

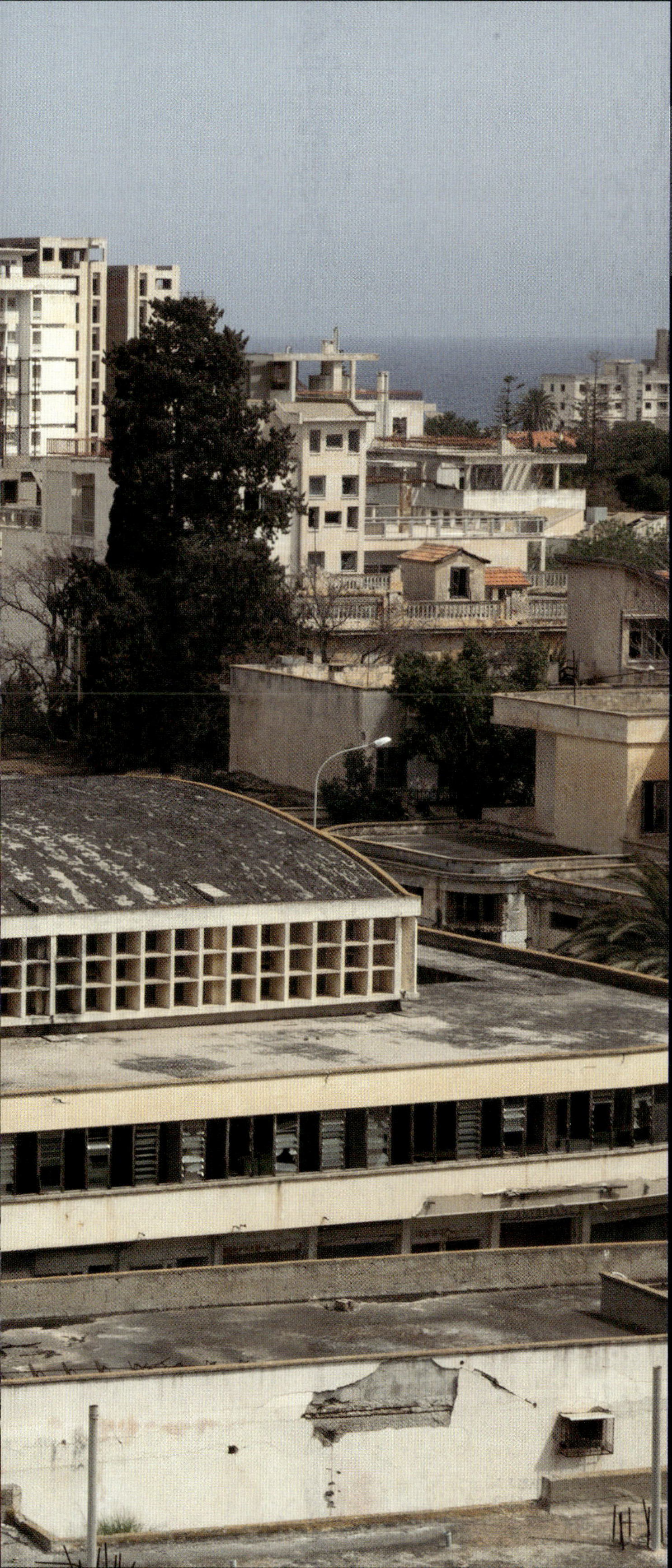

VAROSHA

ZYPERN CYPRUS

FOTOS VON PHOTOS BY PAUL DOBRASZCZYK

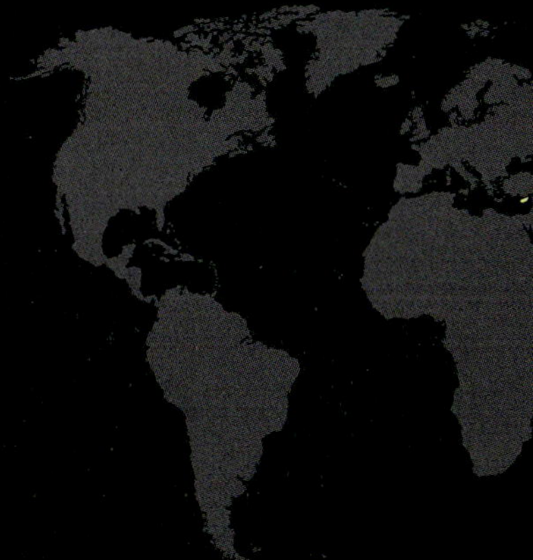

Heiß dringt der Wüstenwind über das levantinische Meer und erwärmt das Wasser an Zyperns Küste. Noch im Winter bei 17 Grad Celsius, erreicht es 28 Grad während des langen Sommers. Niederschlag fällt vor allem in den wenigen Wintermonaten. Dann bildet sich zuweilen Schnee in Höhen von 1.500 Metern, der die Gipfel des waldreichen Troodos-Gebirges bedeckt. Aber nur selten sinkt in den tiefer gelegenen Regionen zur Winterzeit die Tageswärme auf 15 Grad ab. Von Mai bis Oktober ist es meist trocken und die Temperaturen steigen auf 30 bis 35 Grad. Bereits die Dichter der Antike, wie Ovid in seinem berühmten Werk „Metamorphosen", widmeten sich dem fruchtbaren und umkämpften Eiland. Dem frühen Leben auf der Insel begegnet man in Ovids Versen über Pygmalion. König von Zypern und Künstler, war Pygmalion von einer besonderen Sehnsucht erfüllt. Er wünschte sich die vollkommenste Schöne als Gefährtin und fand sie auch. Sein Begehren zeigte nicht wenig Ähnlichkeit mit dem dichterischen Schaffen Hesiods und Homers über Aphrodite, die Göttin der Schönheit und der Liebe, die vor den zyprischen Gestaden geboren wurde.

Die geschichtsträchtige Insel mit ihren duftenden Zitrushainen und immer blühenden Gärten zog seit jeher Abenteurer und Weltenbummler an. Ab den Sechzigerjahren auch Urlauber – und das kaum minder intensiv als zuvor Eroberer und Kolonialherren aus den verschiedensten Nationen. Der breite Strand von Varosha bei Famagusta war von Touristen bis in die Siebzigerjahre dicht bevölkert. Hier erwirtschaftete man 1973 mehr als die Hälfte der Tourismuseinnahmen Zyperns. Es gab 99 Freizeitanlagen, 60 Appartementkomplexe, 45 Hotels mit etwa 10.000 Betten, eine Vielzahl an Theatern, Kinos und einige Tausend große und kleine Geschäfte. Am Montag, dem 15. Juli 1974, fand das vergnügliche Badeleben ein Ende, als die Zyprische Nationalgarde gegen ihren Staatspräsidenten Erzbischof Makarios III. revoltierte, um die Insel Griechenland anzuschließen. Fünf Tage später, am Samstag, dem 20. Juli, landeten Invasionseinheiten der türkischen Armee auf Zypern und besetzten den Norden, auch die Hafenstadt Famagusta und das ihr vorgelagerte Varosha. Der viel besuchte Badeort wurde militärisches Sperrgebiet und seine touristische Anziehungskraft ging verloren.

Seit August 1974 gilt ein Waffenstillstandsabkommen und UN-Truppenkontingente wachen über dessen Einhaltung. Der türkisch besetzte Norden rief 1983 die Türkische Republik Nordzypern aus, was die Vereinten Nationen jedoch als Verletzung des Völkerrechts ansahen. Hinter der sogenannten Green Line besteht die Republik Zypern im Süden weiter. Sie wurde im Mai 2004 Mitglied der Europäischen Union. Die Bemühungen um Ausgleich hatten zum Jahresbeginn 2007 ein überraschendes Ergebnis: Türkische Zyprer zerstörten in Nikosia eine Barrikade, die seit vielen Jahren Inbegriff für die Teilung war. Im März desselben Jahres folgte die griechische Seite und riss auf ihrem Gebiet eine Barrikade nieder. Seit April 2008 gibt es in Nikosias Altstadt einen Grenzübergang für Radfahrer und Spaziergänger. Varosha jedoch bleibt verlassen. Nur für einen kurzen Zeitraum, wenn die Meeresschildkröten ihre Eier im warmen Sand vergraben, belebt sich der Strand des Sperrgebiets. Die an Land eher schwerfällig wirkenden Tiere bleiben dort laut Regierungsbeschluss ungestört.

The desert wind blows hot over the Levantine Sea warming the waters of Cyprus' coast. Even in winter, it is 17 degrees Celsius, reaching 28 degrees during the long summer. Rain falls mainly in the few months of winter. Then, from time to time, it becomes snow at elevations of 1,500 meters that covers the peaks of the forested Troodos Mountains. It is only very seldom that the heat of the day drops to 15 degrees in the lower lying regions during the wintertime. From May to October, it is mainly dry and the temperature climbs to 30 or 35 degrees. The poets of antiquity have dedicated their work to the fertile and contested island, like Ovid in his famous work, "The Metamorphoses". The earlier life on the island is seen in Ovid's verses about Pygmalion. Pygmalion, King of Cyprus and artist, was filled with a special passion. He wished for the most perfect beauty as his wife, and he found her too. His longing was very similar to the poetic creations of Hesiod and Homer about Aphrodite who was the goddess of beauty and love and was born by the beaches of Cyprus.

The historic island with its scented lemon groves and continuously blossoming gardens has attracted adventurers and world travelers since time began. And since the 1960s, vacationers have also come, and no less intensively than previous conquerors and colonial rulers of a great variety of nations. The wide beach of Varosha near Famagusta was densely populated with tourists until the 1970s. In 1973 more than half of the tourism revenue of Cyprus was generated there. There were 99 recreational facilities, 60 apartment complexes, 45 hotels with about 10,000 beds, a multitude of theatres, cinemas and a few thousand large and small businesses. On Monday, the 15th of July 1974, the luxurious bathing life came to an end when the Cyprus National Guard revolted against their state president, Archbishop Makarios III, in order to annex the island to Greece. Five days later on Saturday, the 20th of July, invasion units of the Turkish army landed on Cyprus and occupied the north, as well as the port city of Famagusta and offshore Varosha. The much visited spa town became a military restricted area and it lost its touristic attraction.

A truce has been in effect since August 1974, and detachments of UN troops watch over its enforcement. The Turkish-occupied north declared the Turkish Republic of North Cyprus in 1983 which the United Nations, however saw as a violation of human rights. Behind the so-called Green Line, the Republic of Cyprus continues to exist in the south. It became a member state of the European Union in May 2004. Efforts for reconciliation at the beginning of 2007 had a surprising result: Turkish Cypriots destroyed a barricade in Nicosia that had represented the separation for many years. In March of the same year, the Greek side followed and tore down a barricade in their territory. Since April 2008, there has been a border crossing for bicyclists and pedestrians in the old part of Nicosia. Varosha, however remains abandoned. The beach of the restricted area only comes to life for a short period of time when the sea turtles bury their eggs in the warm sand. The animals that look cumbersome on land remain there undisturbed according to a government resolution.

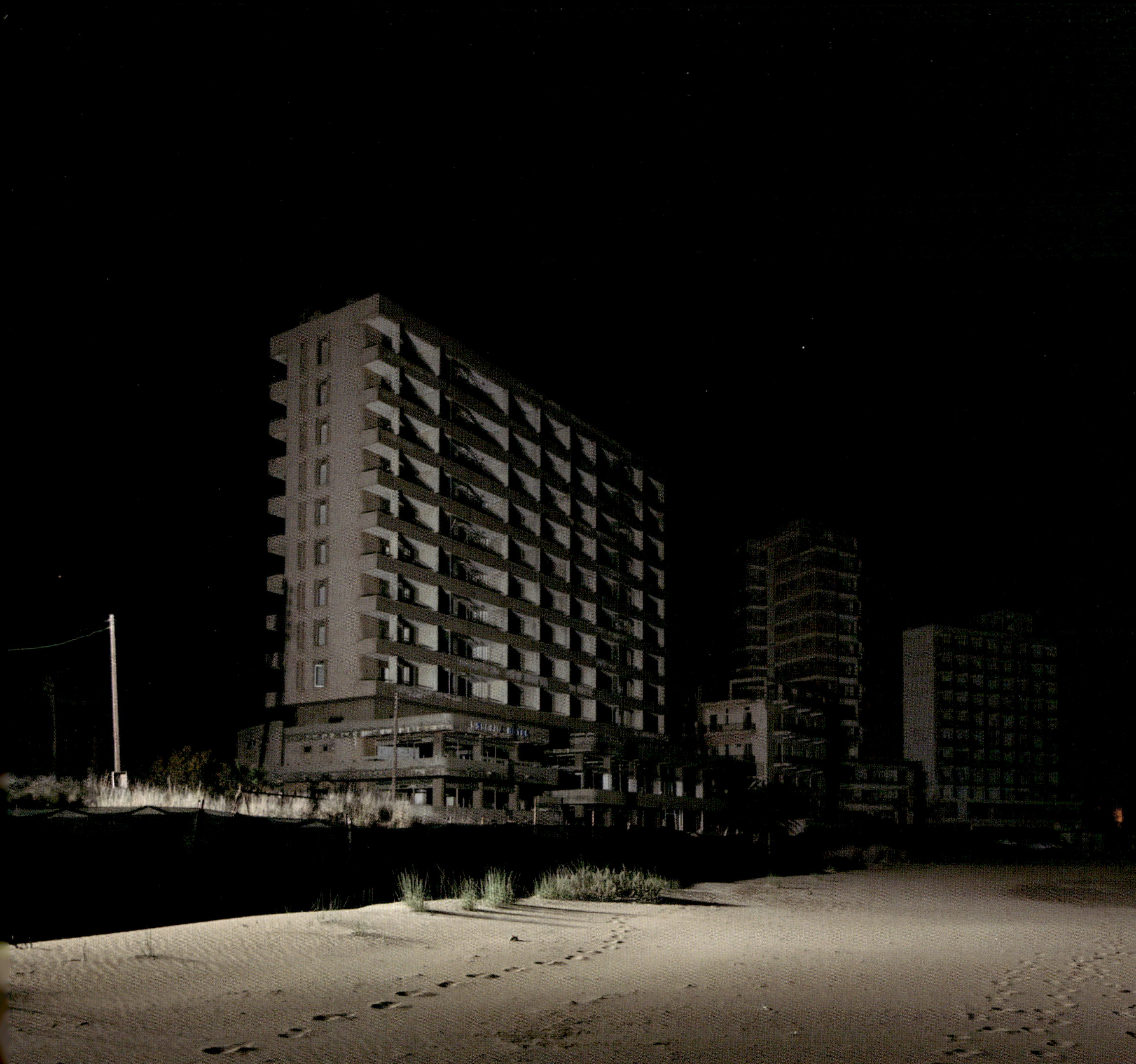

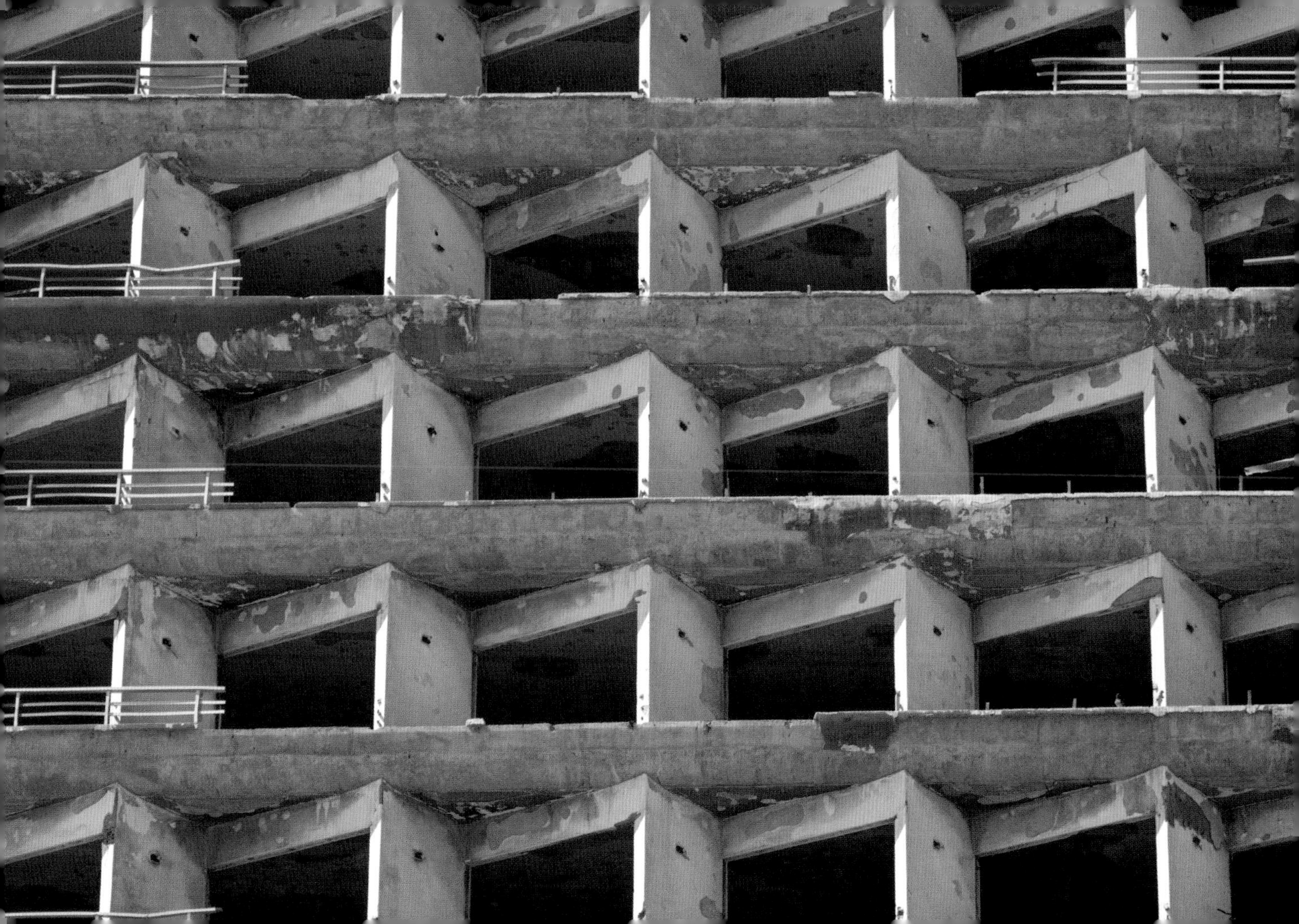

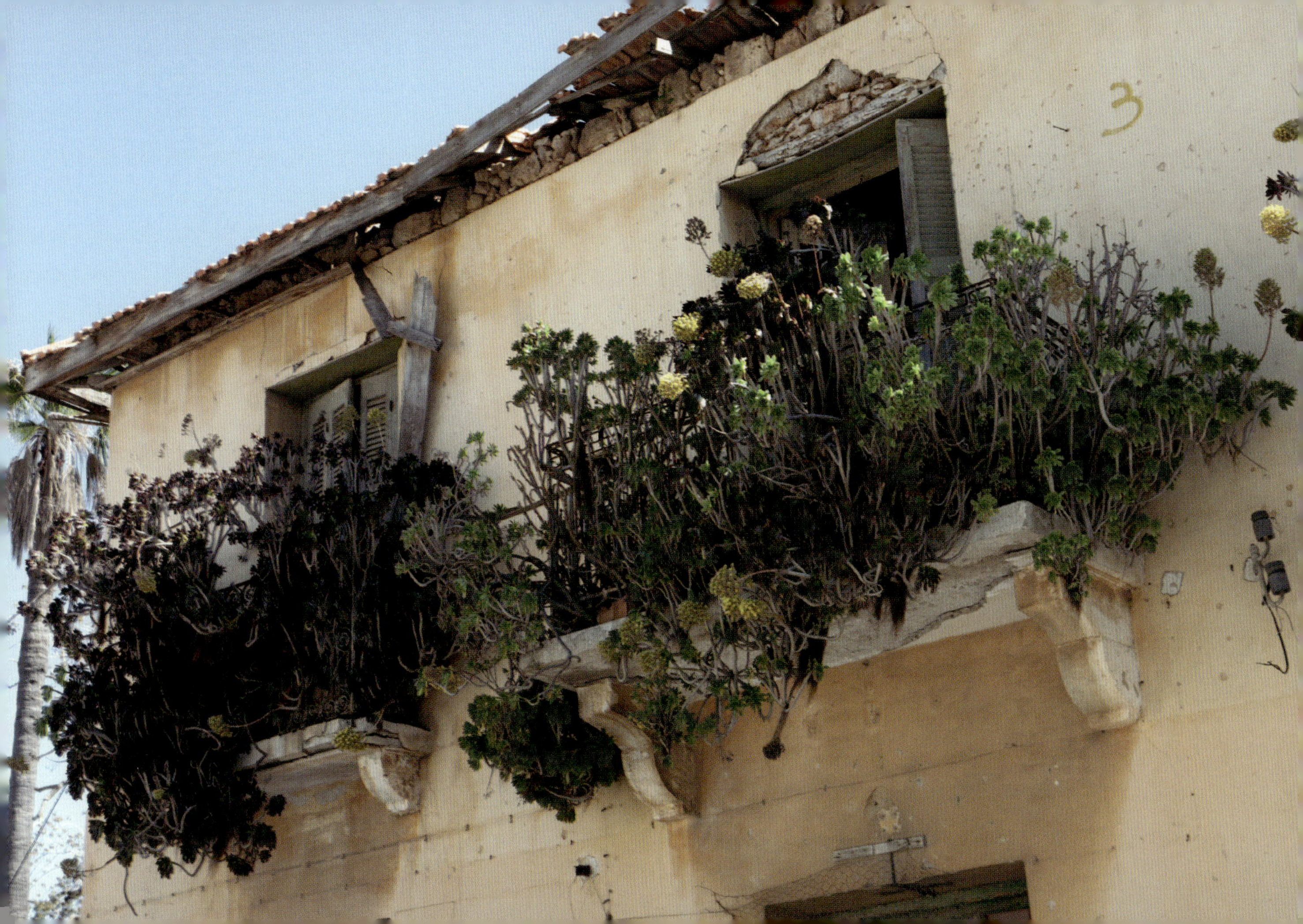

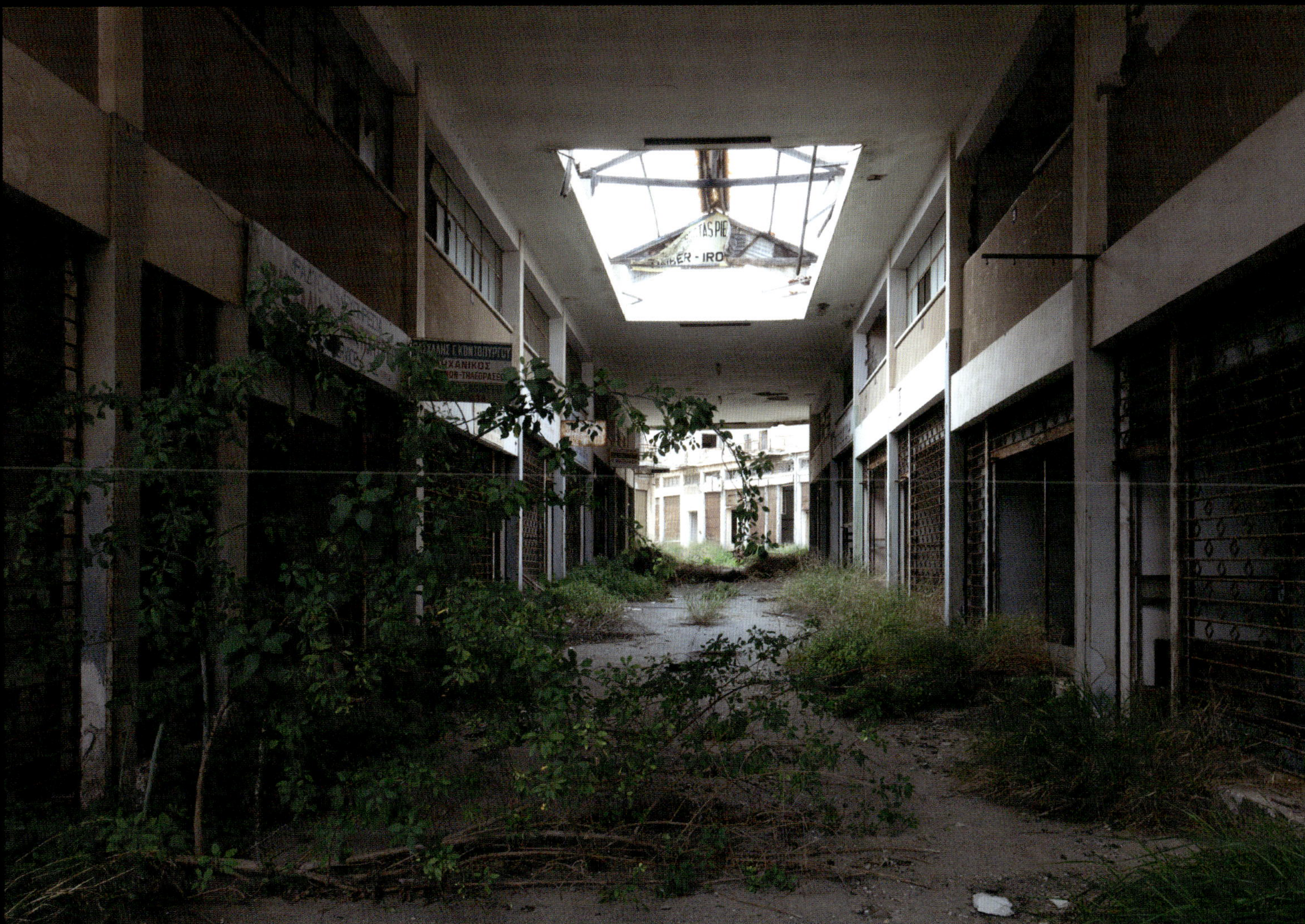

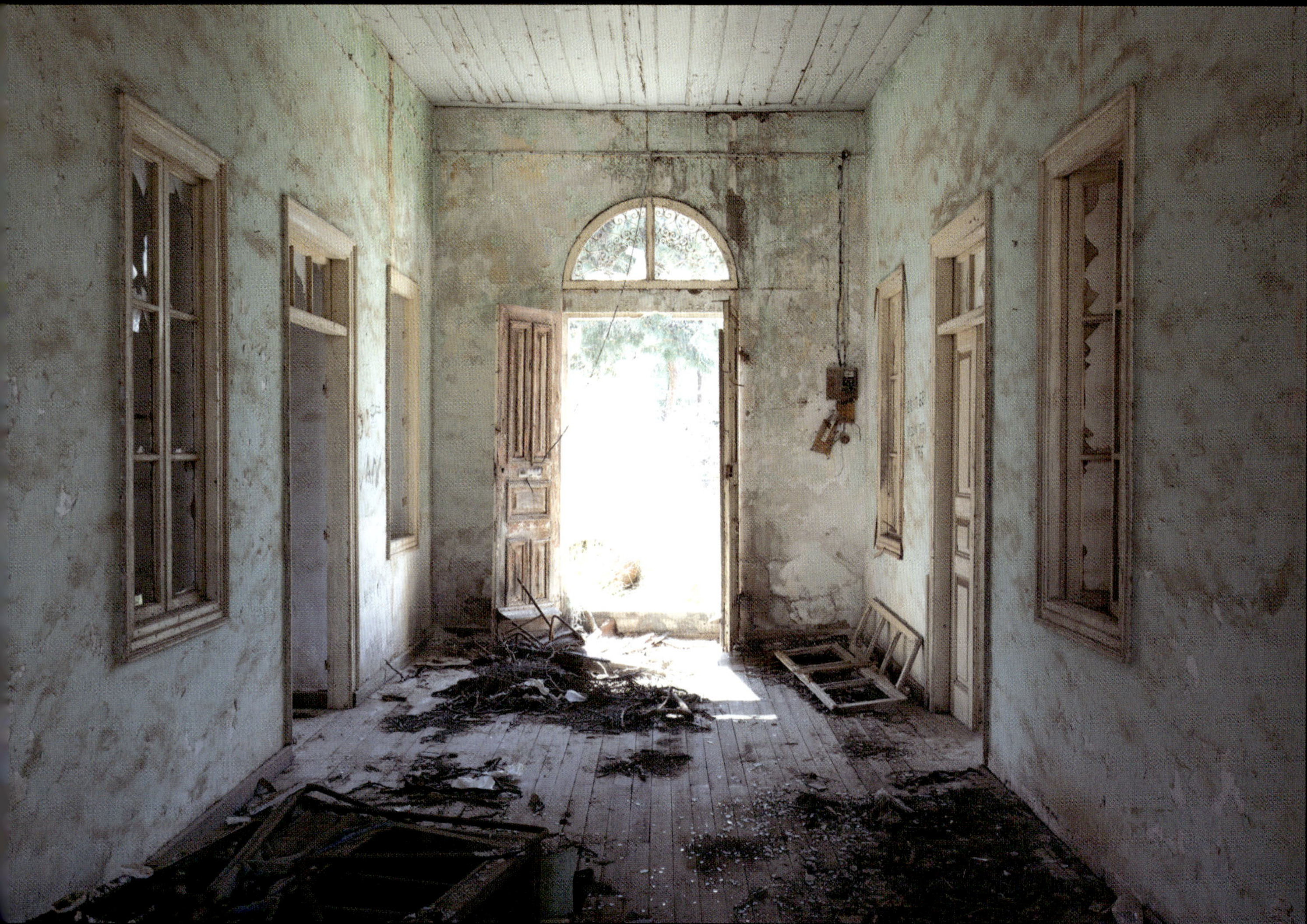

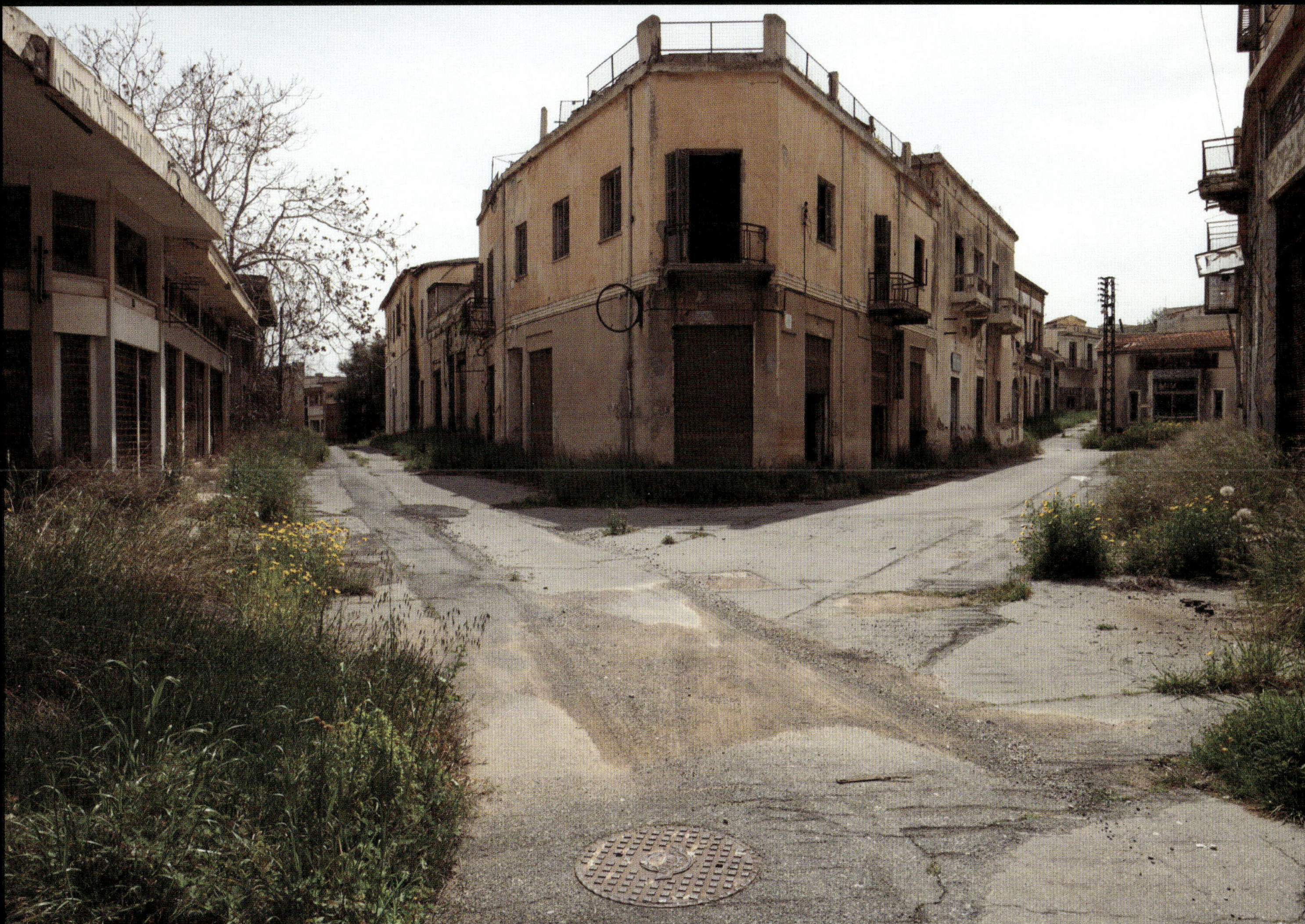

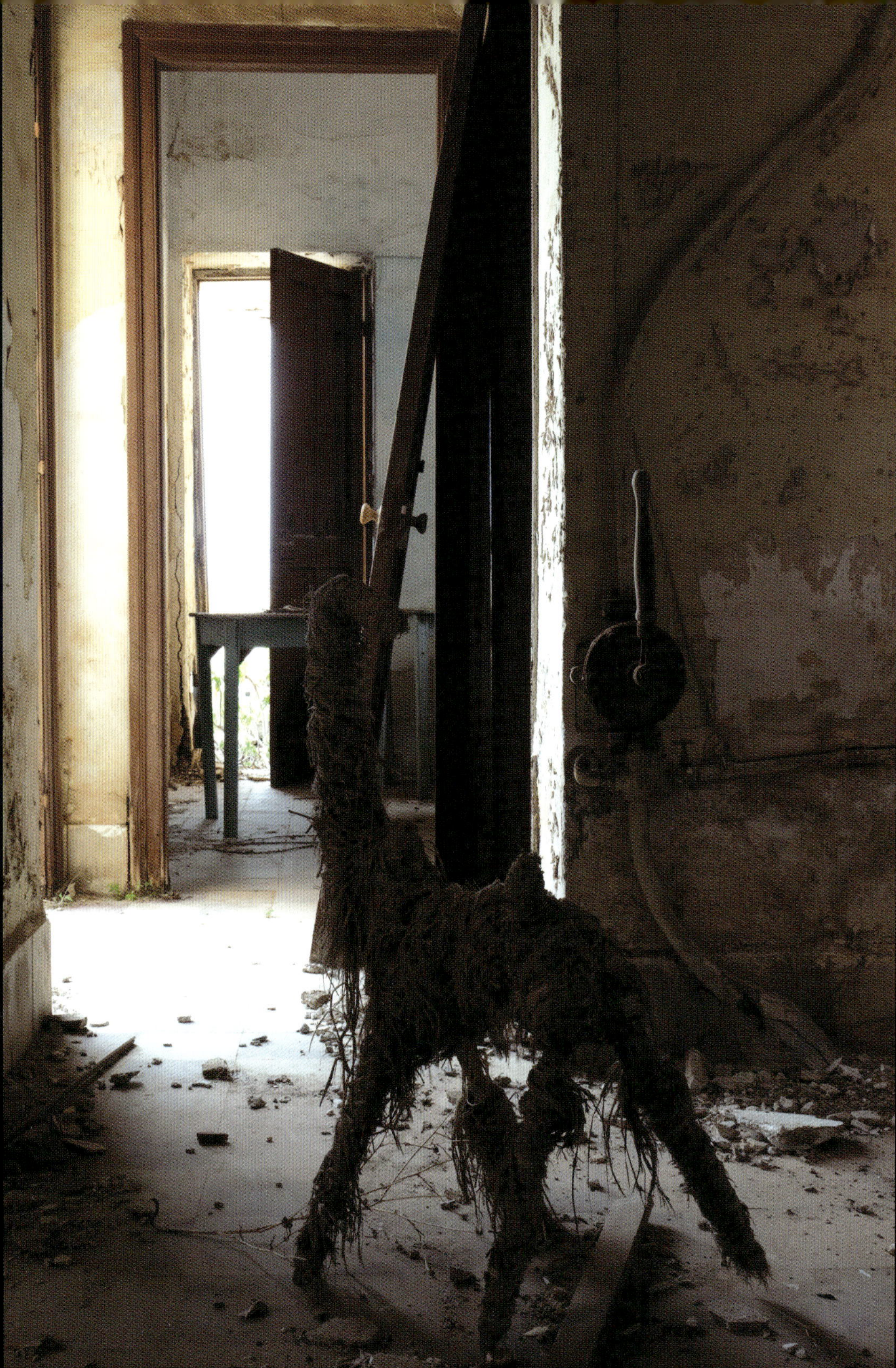

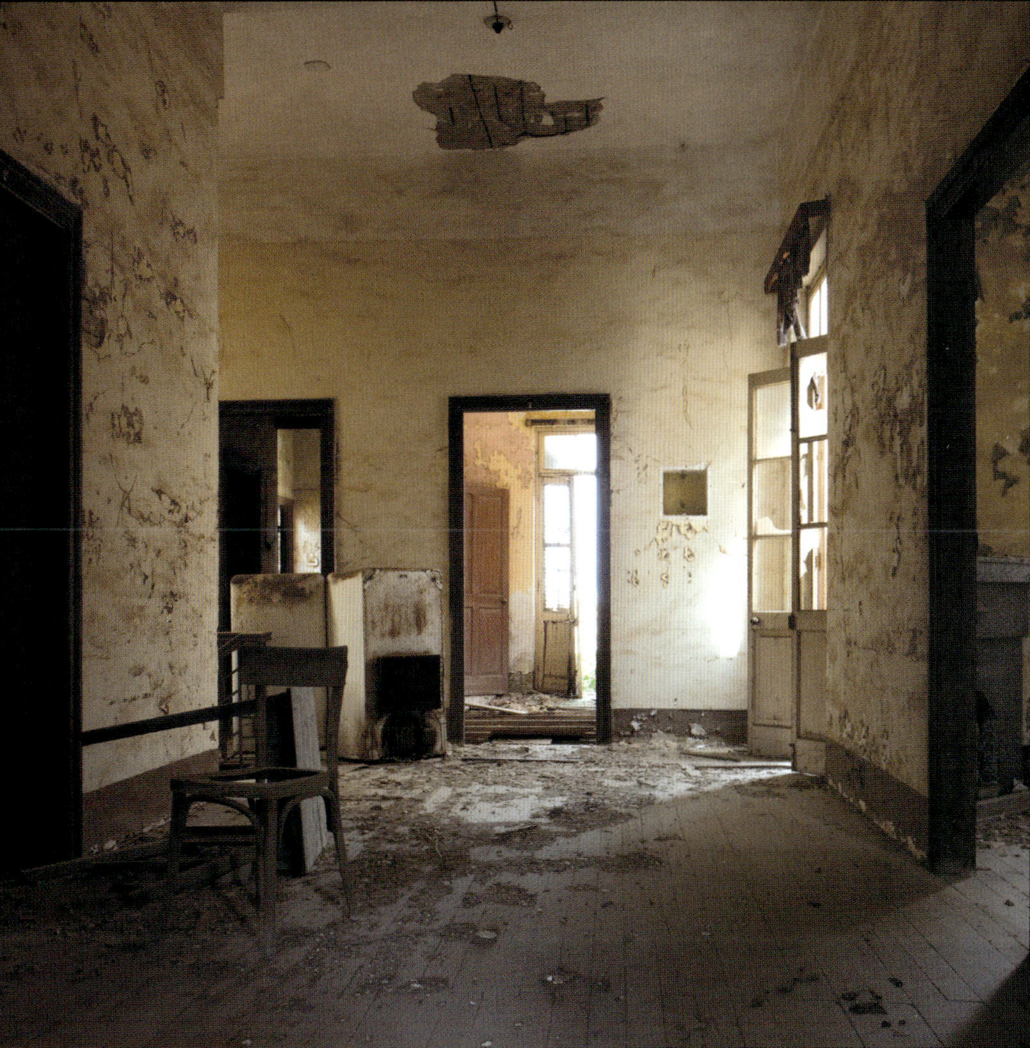

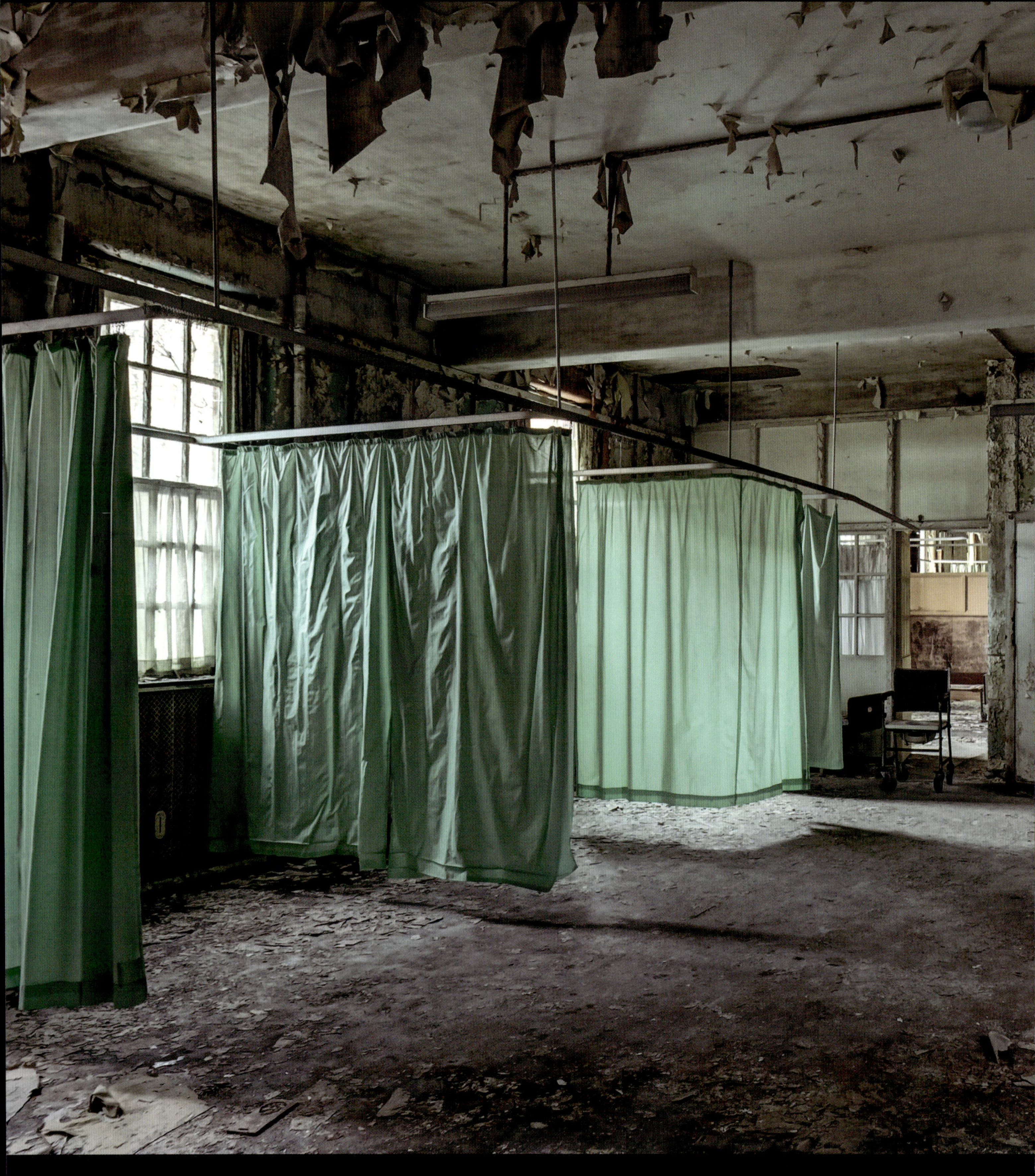

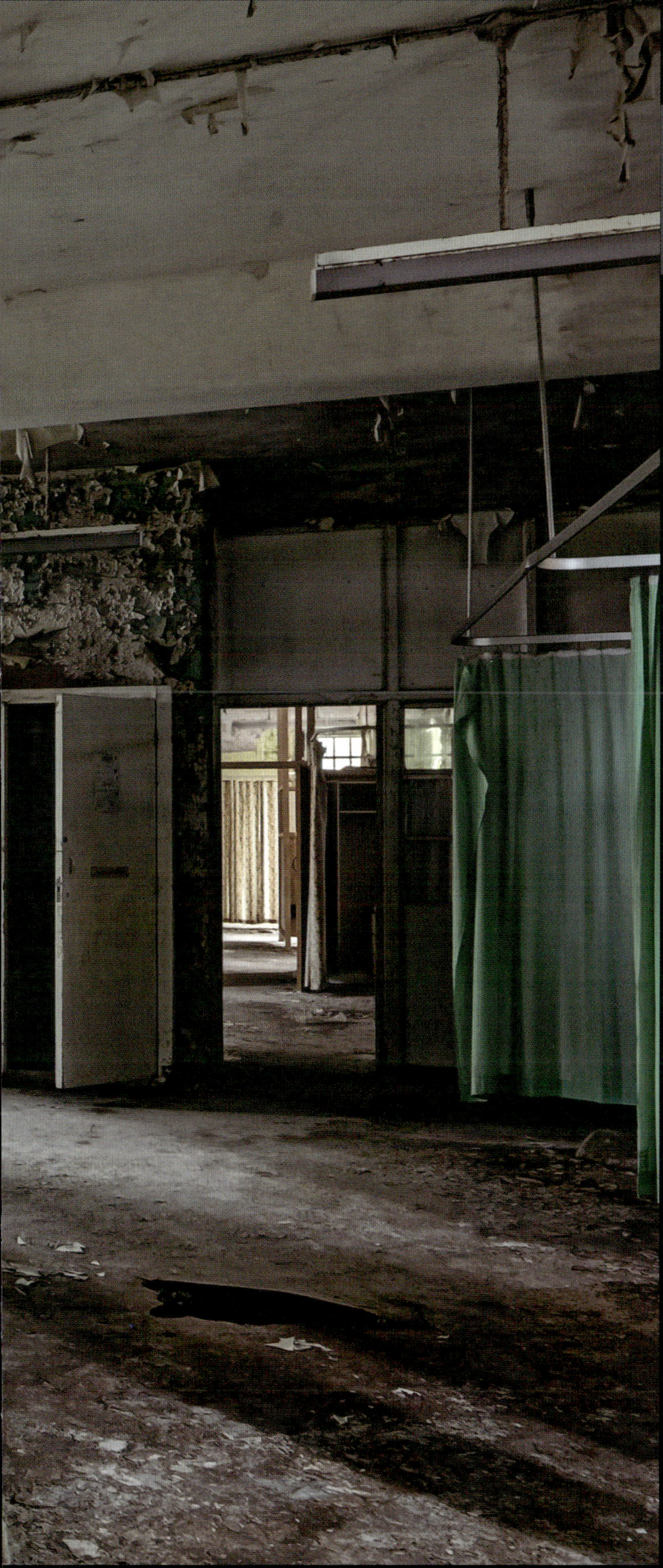

WEST PARK HOSPITAL

ENGLAND ENGLAND

FOTOS VON PHOTOS BY DAN MARBAIX

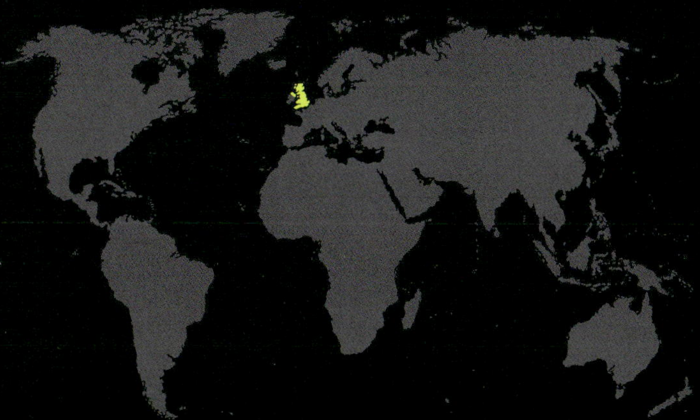

Von Charing Cross, dem Mittelpunkt Londons, etwa 30 Kilometer entfernt, liegt das seit dem 17. Jahrhundert durch seine Pferderennen bekannte Epsom. Zu Beginn des 20. Jahrhunderts verlegten jedoch die wohlhabenden Londoner ihre Rennpferdställe nach Newmarket, denn bei Epsom entstand eine der weltweit größten psychiatrischen Einrichtungen.

Der Londoner Grafschaftsrat hatte 1896 hier 1.060 Hektar Land mit Gutshaus, Wirtschaftsgebäuden, Wald, Gärten und Farmen gekauft und geplant, sechs große Kliniken für je 2.000 Patienten auf diesem Areal zu errichten. Gebaut wurden in den folgenden drei Jahrzehnten fünf. Das West Park Hospital war die in der Baufolge fünfte und größte Klinik des Psychiatriekomplexes und vom Gesundheitsminister am 20. Juni 1924 eröffnet worden. Der Terminus „Anstalt“ im Zusammenhang mit der Behandlung von Geisteskrankheiten war anrüchig und wurde 1930 gesetzlich abgeschafft.

Die Infrastruktur des Psychiatriekomplexes entsprach der einer Kleinstadt. Er verfügte unter anderem über eine eigene Wasserversorgung, Stromzentralen, ein Heizhaus, Farmen, eine Kapelle und einen Friedhof. Beschäftigungstherapien unterstützten die Versorgung der Patienten mit Nahrungsmitteln. Neben einer großen Wäscherei wurden Schuster-, Schneider-, Polstereiwerkstätten und Gartenmärkte betrieben. Zum Vergnügen luden Cafés und der Ballsaal von West Park Hospital ein, in dem auch die Bevölkerung der Umgebung tanzen ging.

Das Zentrum von West Park Hospital markierte ein 36 Meter hoher Wasserturm. Ein weitverzweigtes Netz aus hölzernen, überdachten und befensterten Korridoren führte zu den in Gruppen zusammengefassten 45 Stationen. Innerhalb der zweigeschossigen Gebäude aus rotem Backstein kamen häufig glasierte Ziegel zum Einsatz; das sparte die Kosten für den Verputz und erleichterte das Einhalten der Hygienebestimmungen.

Im November 1925 waren 1.720 Patienten eingewiesen; sie standen unter der ärztlichen Betreuung von sechs Doktoren und einem medizinischen Leiter.

Das West Park Hospital beherbergte Patienten aller Altersgruppen und aller Grade sogenannter nervlicher und geistiger Erkrankungen. Eine Liste von 1907 zur Kategorisierung von Krankheitsursachen führte noch „Masturbation“ und „sexuelle Ausschweifungen“ an; „moralische Mängel“ wurden zur „geistigen Instabilität“ gezählt. Die Chiffre „O.“ bedeutete „bei Einweisung nicht wahnsinnig“. – Die Insulin-Koma-Therapie, der Elektroschock, die Schlafkur, der Schlafentzug oder das prolongierte Bad, in dem Patienten sich bis zu zwei Wochen in warmem Wasser aufhalten mussten, wurden ab den Fünfzigerjahren von modernen Psychopharmaka und anderen Therapien abgelöst.

Ab den Achtzigerjahren ging die Patientenzahl zurück; psychisch Kranke wurden stärker in die Gesellschaft eingegliedert. Nach einem langen Abwicklungsprozess war West Park Hospital – als letzte der fünf Kliniken des Komplexes – 2004 geräumt. Ab 2010 begann der Teilabriss und die Neubebauung. Freiwillige besuchen nun auf dem verwaisten Terrain die Gummizelle. In der ehemaligen Kinderstation blättert die Farbe von den Wänden und mit ihr Sonne, Regenbogen, Sterne, Donald Duck und Micky Maus.

Epsom, known since the 17th century for its horse races, is 30 kilometers from Charing Cross, in the center of London. However, at the beginning of the 20th century, wealthy Londoners moved their racing horse barns to Newmarket because one of the world's largest psychiatric institutions was built near Epsom.

The London county council bought 1,060 hectares of land here in 1896 with a farm house, farm buildings, forest, gardens and farms and planned to construct six large clinics for 2,000 patients each on this area. In the following three decades, five of them were built. The West Park Hospital was the fifth in the construction series and largest clinic of the psychiatric hospital cluster. It was opened by the minister of health on June 20, 1924. The term, "asylum" in connection with the treatment of the mentally ill was objectionable and discontinued by law in 1930.

The infrastructure of the cluster was that of a small town. Besides other things, it had its own water supply, power stations, a boiler house, farms, a chapel and a cemetery. Occupational therapy helped to supply the patients with food. Besides a large laundry service, there were workshops for cobblers, tailors and upholsterers. For entertainment, cafes and the ballroom of the West Park Hospital beckoned, where residents from the surrounding area also went to dance.

The center of the West Park Hospital was marked by a 36 meter high water tower. An extensive network of wooden, covered and windowed corridors led to 45 stations grouped together. Inside the two storied building made of red brick, glazed tiles were often used as that saved the cost of plaster and made it easier to maintain a level of hygiene.

In November 1925, 1,720 patients were admitted under the medical care of six doctors and one medical director. The West Park Hospital housed patients of all ages and all degrees of so called nervous and mental illnesses. A list from 1907 categorizing causes of illness included "masturbation" and "sexual debauchery", and "lack of morals" also counted as "mental instability". The code "O" signified "not insane when admitted". Insulin coma therapy, electric shock, sleeping cure, sleep deprivation or prolonged baths, where patients had to stay in warm water for up to two weeks were all replaced by modern psychiatric pharmaceuticals and other therapies in the 1950s.

In the 1980s the number of patients declined as the mentally ill were introduced more and more back into society. After a long phase-out process, the West Park Hospital was cleared out in 2004 as the last of the five clinics in the complex. Partial demolition and new construction began in 2010. Today, volunteers visit the padded cells in the deserted terrain. In the former children's ward, the paint is peeling off the walls and along with it the suns, rainbows, stars, Donald Duck and Mickey Mouse.

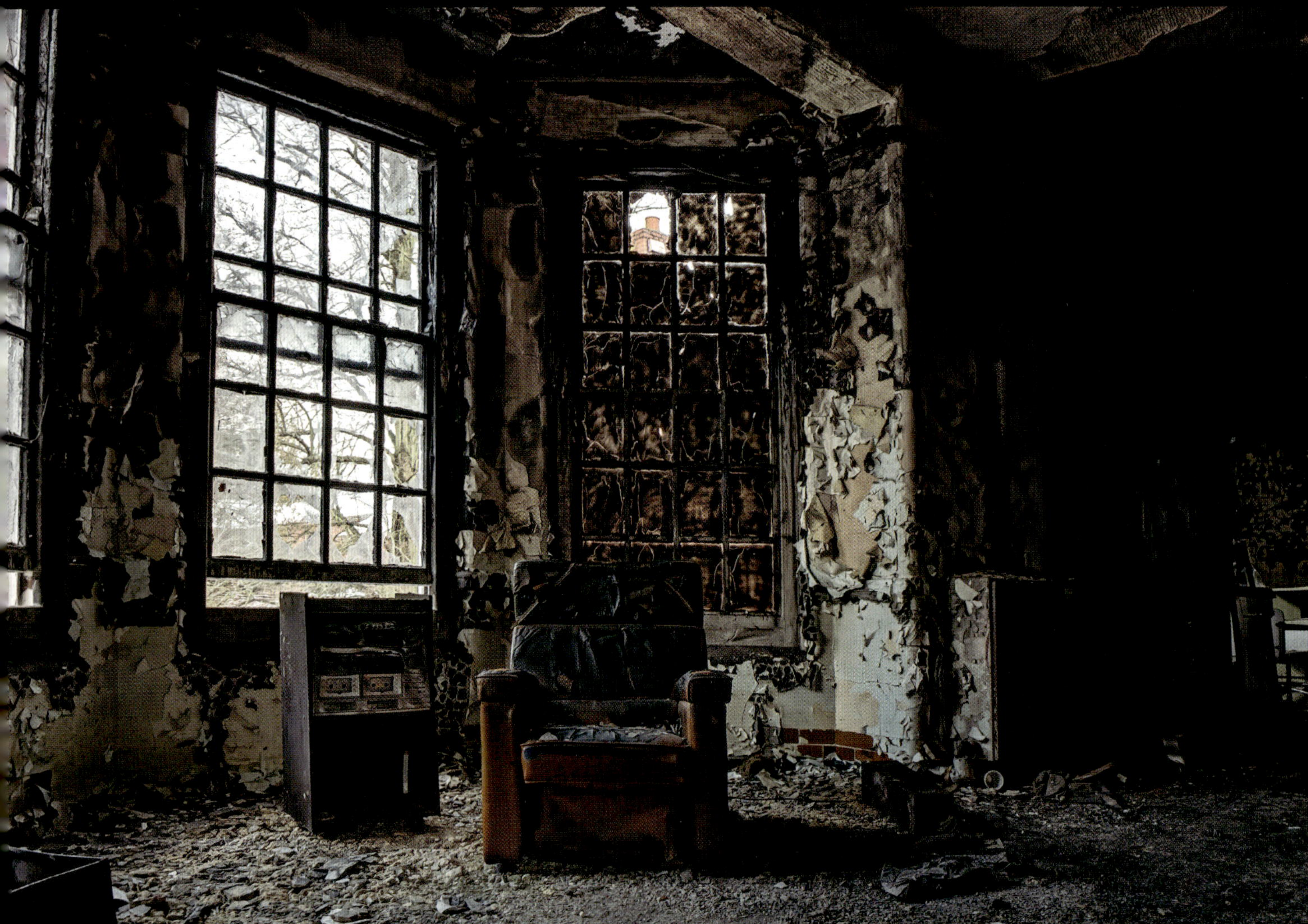

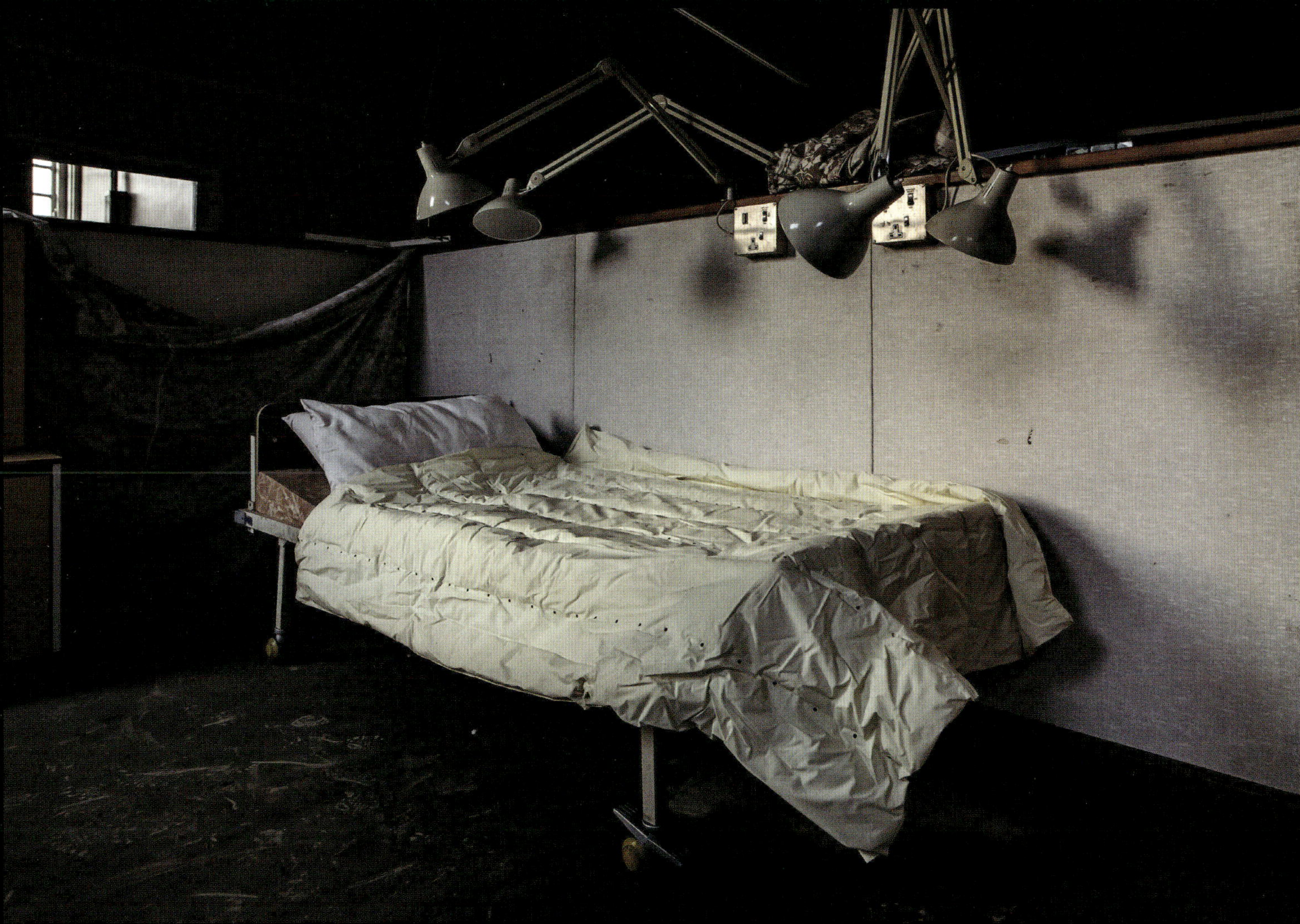

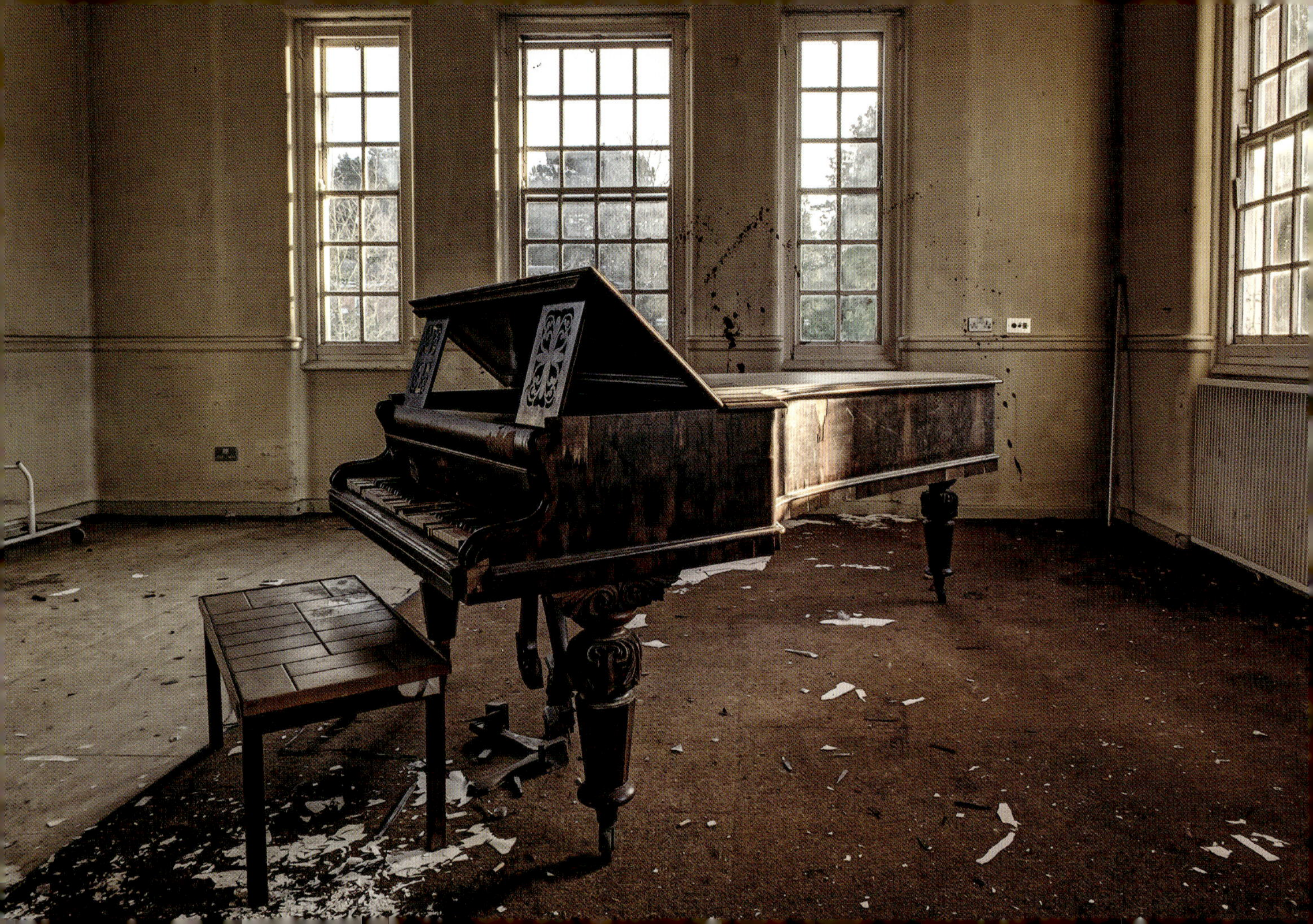

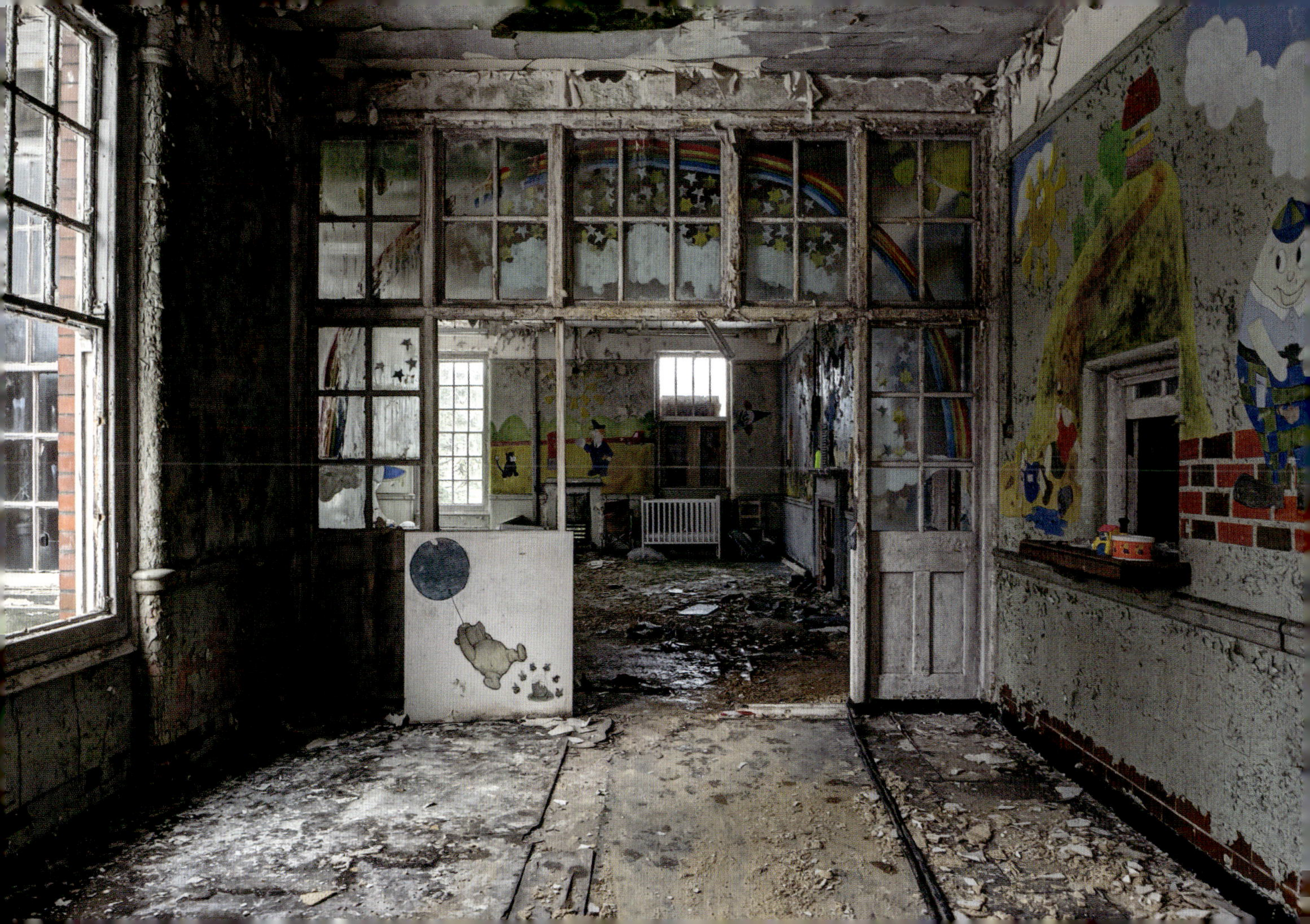

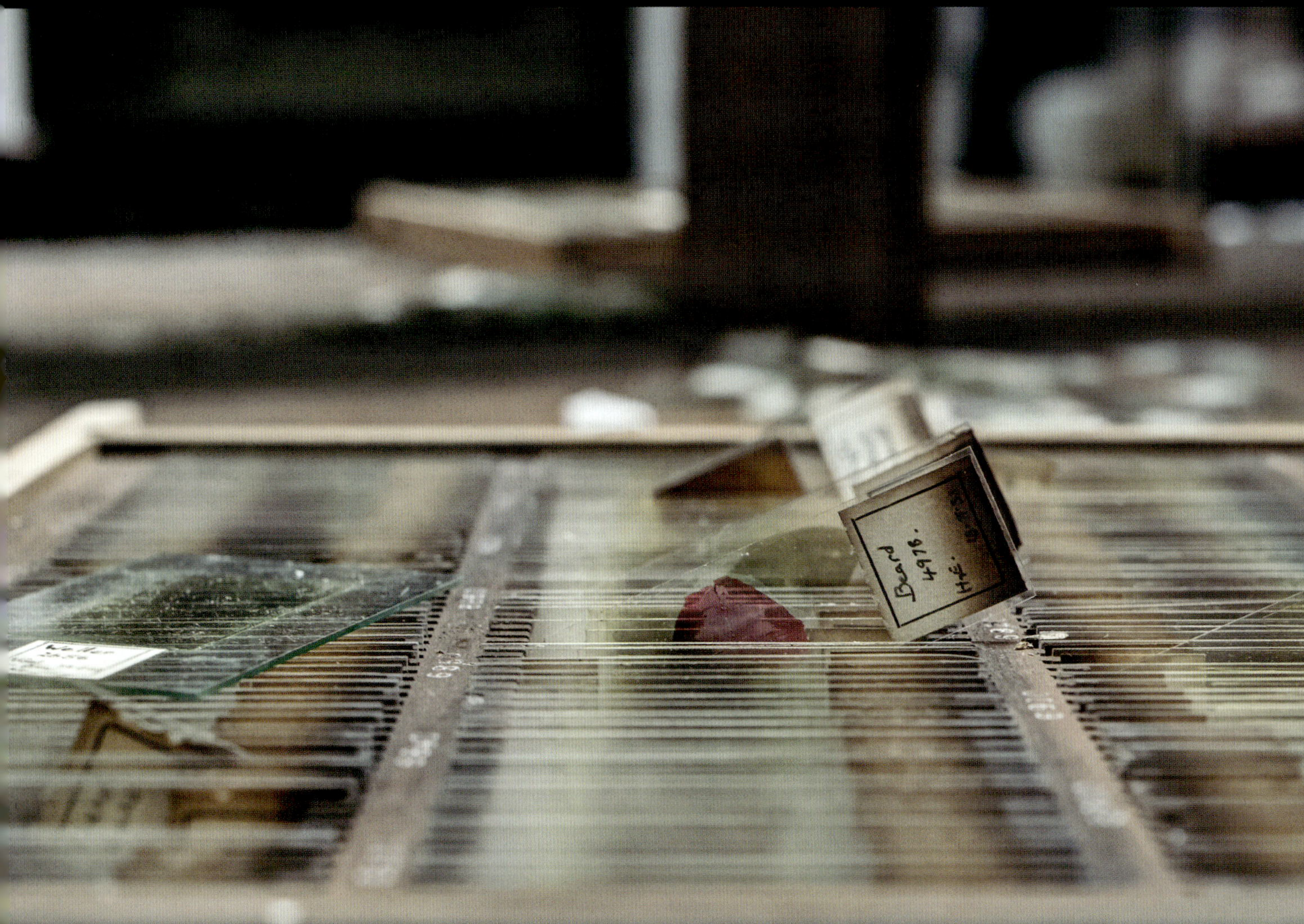
Beard
4978.
H+E.

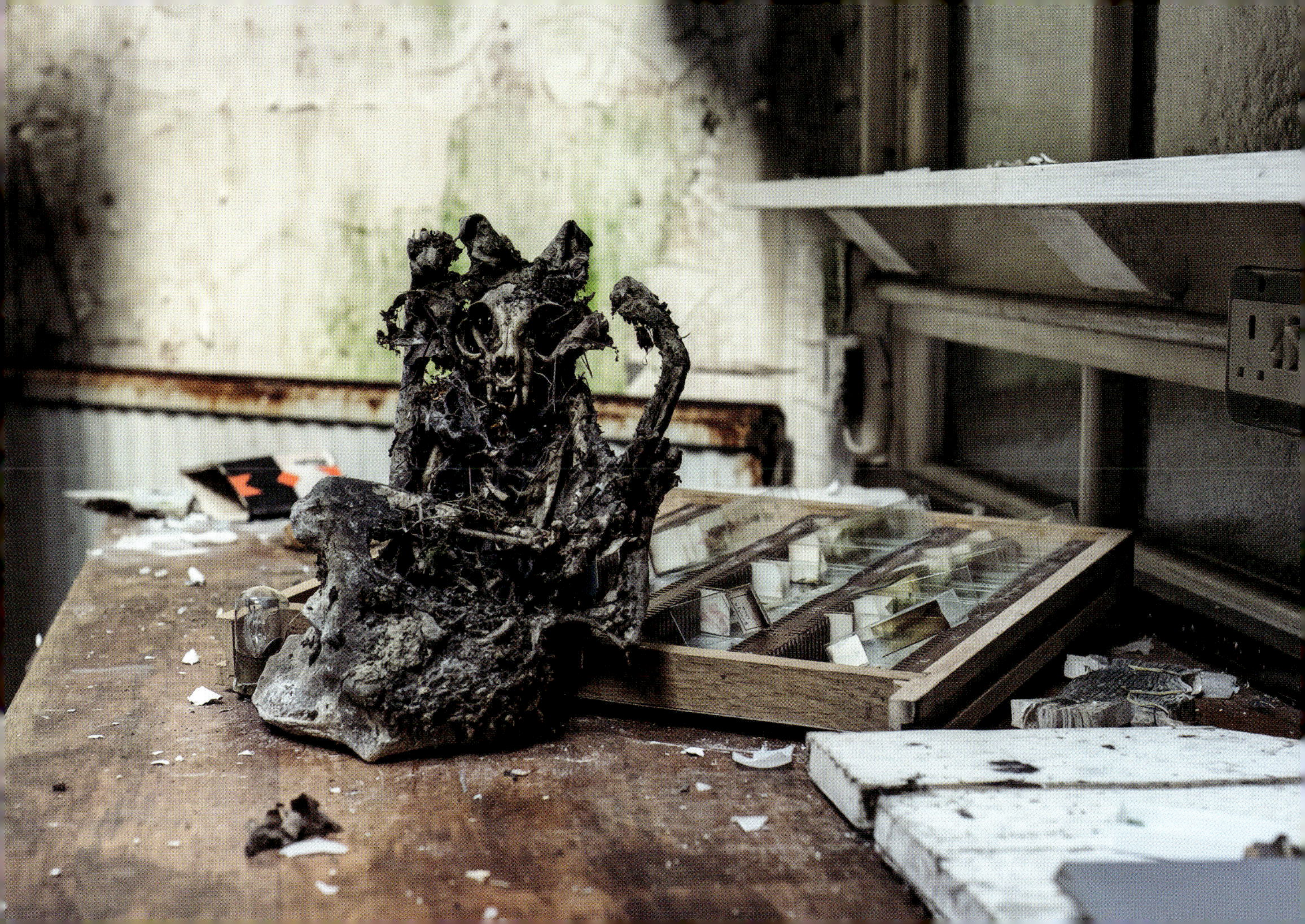

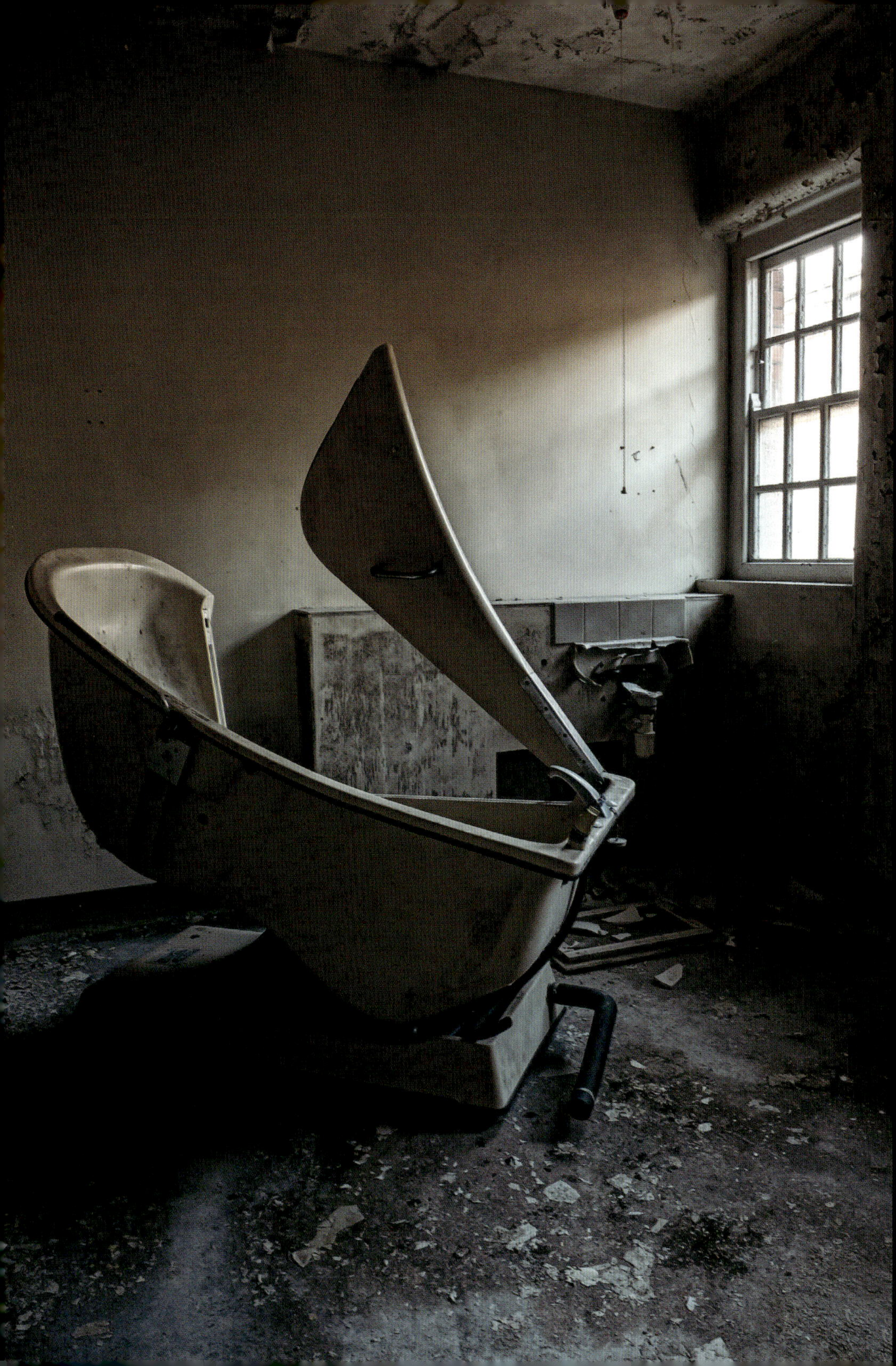

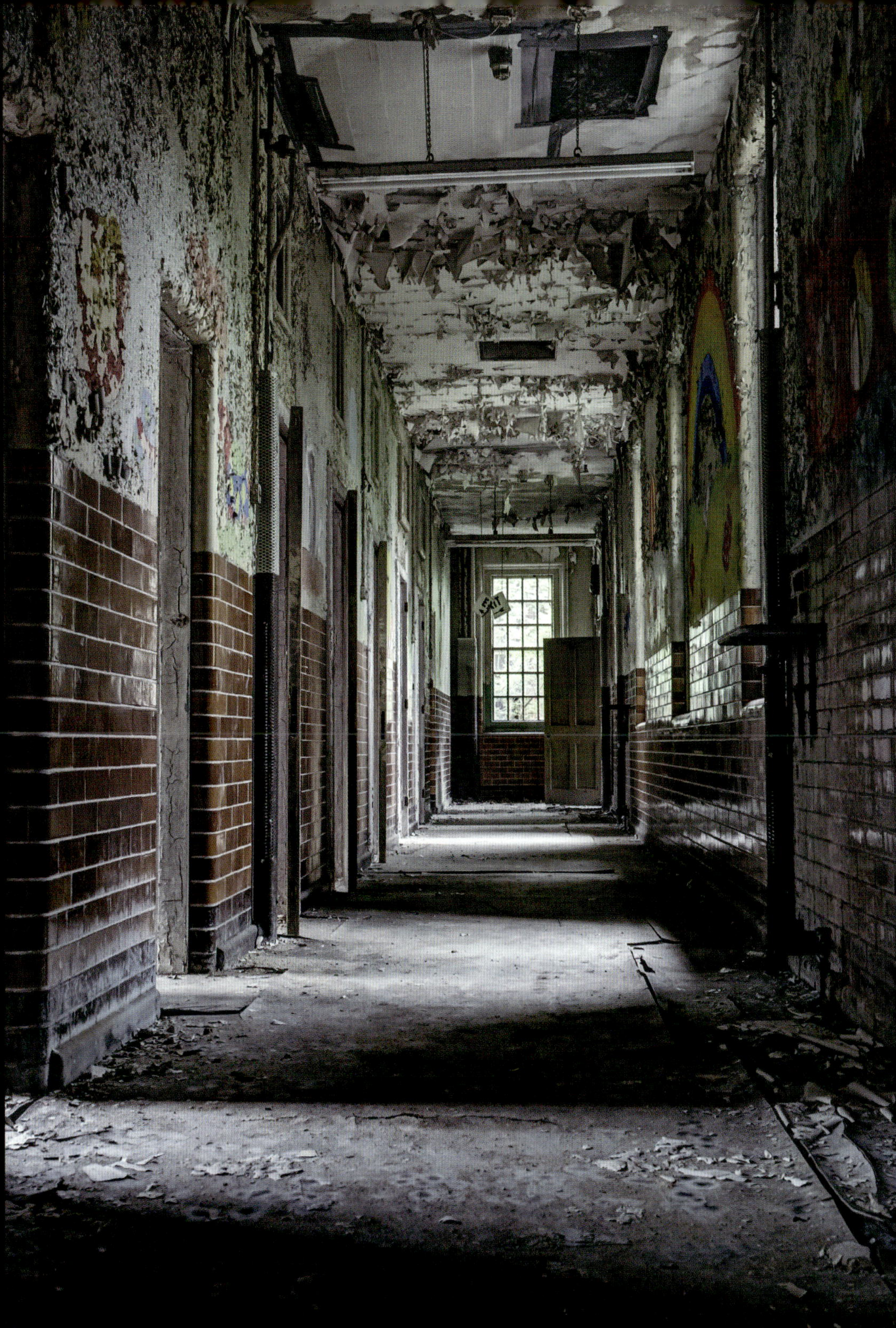

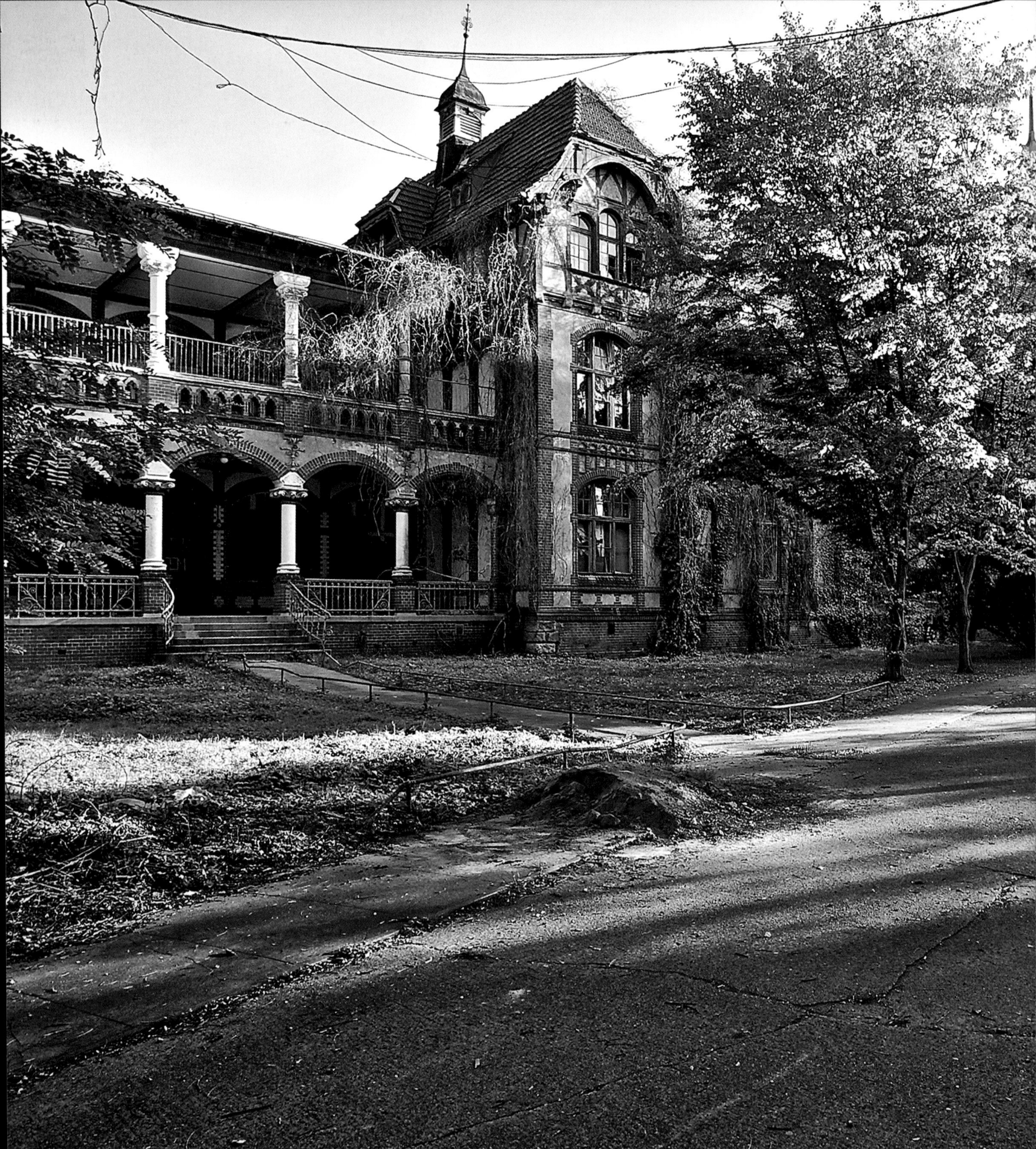

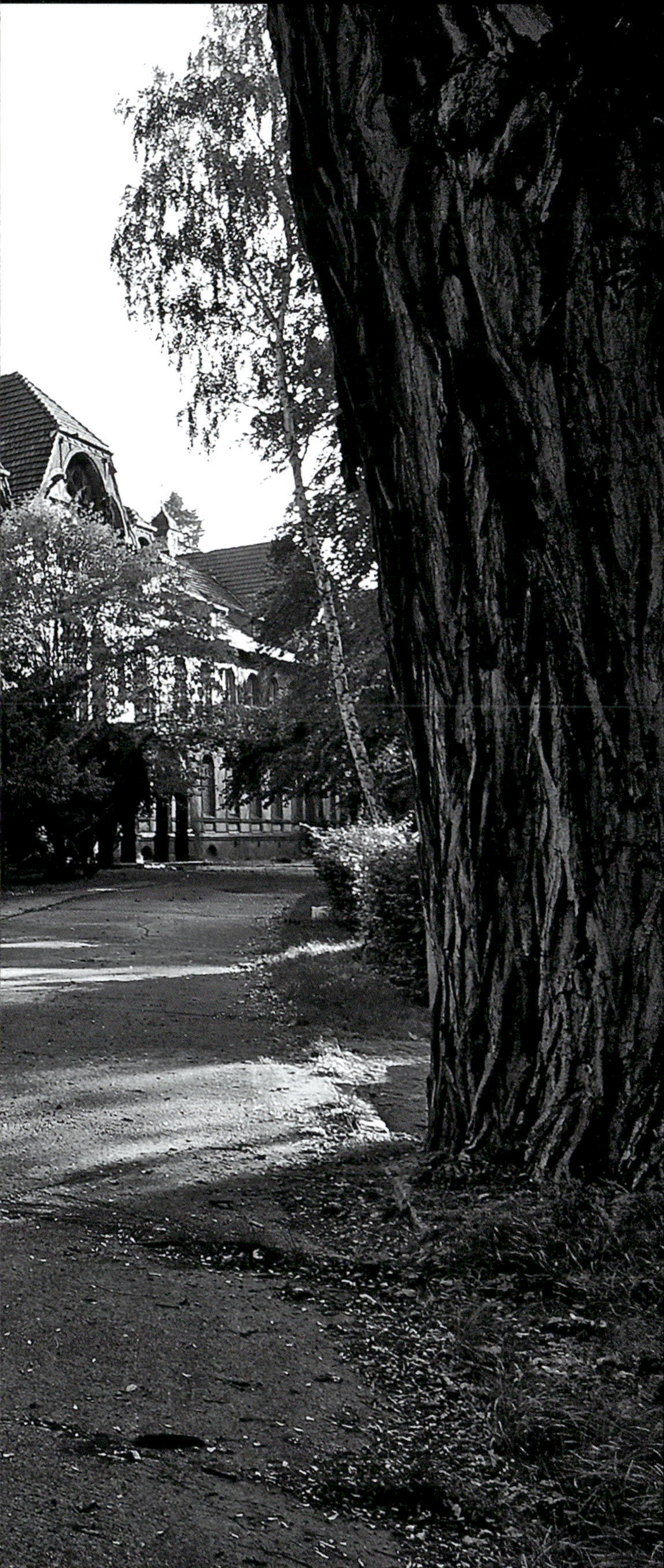

BEELITZ-HEILSTÄTTEN

DEUTSCHLAND GERMANY

FOTOS VON PHOTOS BY MARC MIELZARJEWICZ

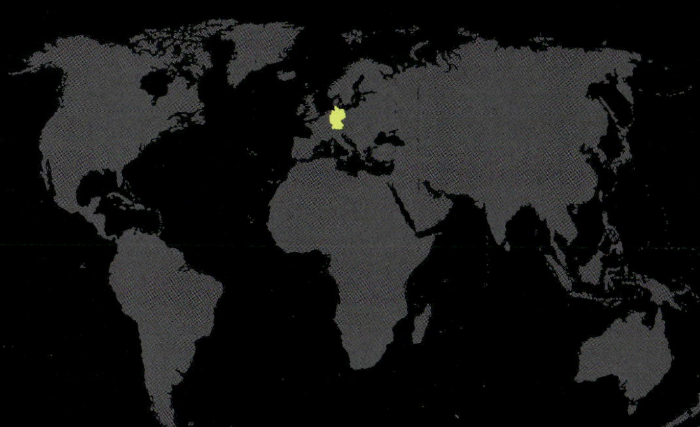

Im Beelitzer Fichtenwald ist die Luft heute wie vor 100 Jahren besser als in Berlin. Der Satz „Du kriegst die Motten" ist währenddessen der Alltagssprache abhandengekommen. Er bezog sich auf den Zustand der mit Tuberkulose infizierten Lunge, die mit einem von Motten zerfressenen Kleidungsstück verglichen wurde. Um jener Krankheit, die sich 1900 vor allem durch mangelnde Hygiene und missliche Wohnbedingungen in den Großstädten rasant ausbreitete, etwas entgegenzusetzen, errichtete die Landesversicherungsanstalt Berlin für die Arbeiter und Angestellten der Hauptstadt von 1898 bis 1930 die Arbeiter-Lungen-Heilstätten Beelitz. Auf einer Fläche von 200 Hektar, mit 60 Gebäuden, war sie eine der größten und modernsten Lungenheilstätten jener Zeit, 56 Kilometer vom Berliner Alexanderplatz entfernt. Kein Davos – jedoch gegenüber dem Leben in Mietskasernen und Hinterhöfen im von Industrieabgasen und Hausbrand geplagten Berlin ein luxuriöser Aufenthaltsort mit 1.200 Betten im Jahr 1908.

Strenge Hygienevorschriften, durch hohe Fenster besonnte Räume und die Heiterkeit verströmenden, schmückenden Details der Gebäude – Herzen am Geländer, Vögelchen auf Ästen an einem Türportal, farbige Glasfenster und Bodenmosaike –, die nach Fichten duftende Luft beim Spaziergang oder während der sechsstündigen Liegekur im Freien, regelmäßige Mahlzeiten: Dies alles sollte zur Genesung der Patienten beitragen. Robert Koch hatte zwar schon 1882 den Tuberkulose-Erreger beschrieben, 1905 den Nobelpreis für Medizin für seine Entdeckung erhalten, doch eine wirksame medikamentöse Behandlung durch Antibiotika erfolgte erst in den Vierzigerjahren.

Gefilterte, befeuchtete und im Winter erwärmte Außenluft wurde durch Frischlufthäuschen, die sich im Abstand von 80 Metern auf dem Areal verteilten, über unterirdische Kanäle zu den Innenräumen geführt. Bei schlechtem Wetter nutzten die Patienten die Wandel- und Liegehallen, welche sich im Zentrum der streng nach Geschlechtern aufgeteilten Pavillon-Anlagen befanden. 1930 wurde das Chirurgiegebäude fertiggestellt. Es war mit modernster Medizintechnik ausgerüstet und bot neben drei OP-Räumen einen Hörsaal, eine Lichttherapie, ein Röntgeninstitut, Labors und eine Apotheke.

Die Größe des Ensembles verlangte eine autonome Infrastruktur: Neben den Wirtschaftsgebäuden entstand eines der ersten Kraftwerke mit Kraft-Wärme-Kopplung weltweit, was die Ofenheizung verzichtbar machte. Zur Beköstigung trugen eine eigene Bäckerei und Fleischerei bei, und die Briefe der Patienten konnten auf dem eigenen Postamt aufgegeben werden.

Mit dem Ersten Weltkrieg begann die militärische Nutzung der Heilstätten als Lazarett und Militärlungenheilanstalt. In den wenigen Friedensjahren bis zum Zweiten Weltkrieg blühte der zivile Heilstättenbetrieb wieder auf – mit Einschränkungen während der Wirtschaftskrise und Inflation in den Jahren 1923/1924. Ab 1945 nutzte die Sowjetarmee die Anlage als Militärkrankenhaus. Seit ihrem Abzug 1994 vollständig verlassen, eroberten Wildpflanzen das Territorium und machten es zu einem verwunschenen Ort. Zwar wurden einige Gebäude der unter Denkmalschutz gestellten Anlage restauriert, doch der größte Teil der Beelitzer Heilstätten liegt in tiefem Schlaf und wartet auf das Erwachen.

The air in the Beelitz spruce forest is better today than in Berlin, as it was 100 hundred years ago. Now, the expression "you'll get moths" has been lost from everyday language. It referred to the condition of lungs infected with tuberculosis that resembled a piece of clothing that had been eaten away by moths. Because of this illness that had spread rapidly in the large cities mainly due to poor hygiene and inadequate living conditions, the Berlin state insurance institution built the Arbeiter-Lungen-Heilstätten Beelitz (Beelitz Workers-Lung-Sanatorium) for workers and employees of the capital city between 1898 and 1930. On an area of 200 hectares with 60 buildings, it was the largest and most modern lung sanatorium of its time, 56 kilometers from Berlin's Alexander Square. Not exactly Davos, Switzerland, however when compared to life in rented barracks and backyards, plagued with the industrial exhaust and house fires in Berlin, it was a luxurious place to stay with 1,200 beds in the year 1908.

Strict hygiene regulations, sun-filled rooms with high windows, the cheerfulness of the flowing, decorative details of the buildings – hearts on the railings, little birds on branches over doorways, colorful stained glass windows and floor mosaics – the air scented like spruce during a walk or during the six hour reclining cure outdoors, regular meals: All of this was to contribute to the recovery of the patients. Robert Koch had indeed already described the tuberculosis pathogen in 1882 and won the Nobel Prize for medicine for his discovery in 1905, but effective medical treatment with antibiotics was only discovered in the 1940s.

Outside air that was filtered, humidified and warmed in the winter was fed via underground channels to the interior rooms through fresh air huts that were distributed around the area at distances of 80 meters. During bad weather, the patients used walking and lying halls found in the center of the pavilion system that were strictly separated by gender. In 1930 the surgery building was completed. It was equipped with the most modern medical technology and besides three operating theatres, it had a lecture hall, light therapy, an X-ray institute, laboratories and a pharmacy.

The size of the ensemble required an autonomous infrastructure: As well as the administration buildings, there was one of the first power plants power in the world with combined heating and power making furnace heating unnecessary. For catering, it had its own bakery and butcher, and patients' letters could be dropped off at its own post office.

In the First World War, the military used the sanatorium as a military hospital and military lung sanatorium. During the few years of peace before the Second World War, the civil sanatorium business prospered, except for reductions during the Great Depression and inflation in the years, 1923–1924. From 1945, the Soviet army used the facility as a military hospital. Since their withdrawal in 1994, it has been completely abandoned. Wild plants have taken over the territory and turned it into an enchanted place. Although some of the buildings have been restored as historic monuments, most of the Beelitz Sanatorium lies in a deep sleep and waits to be woken.

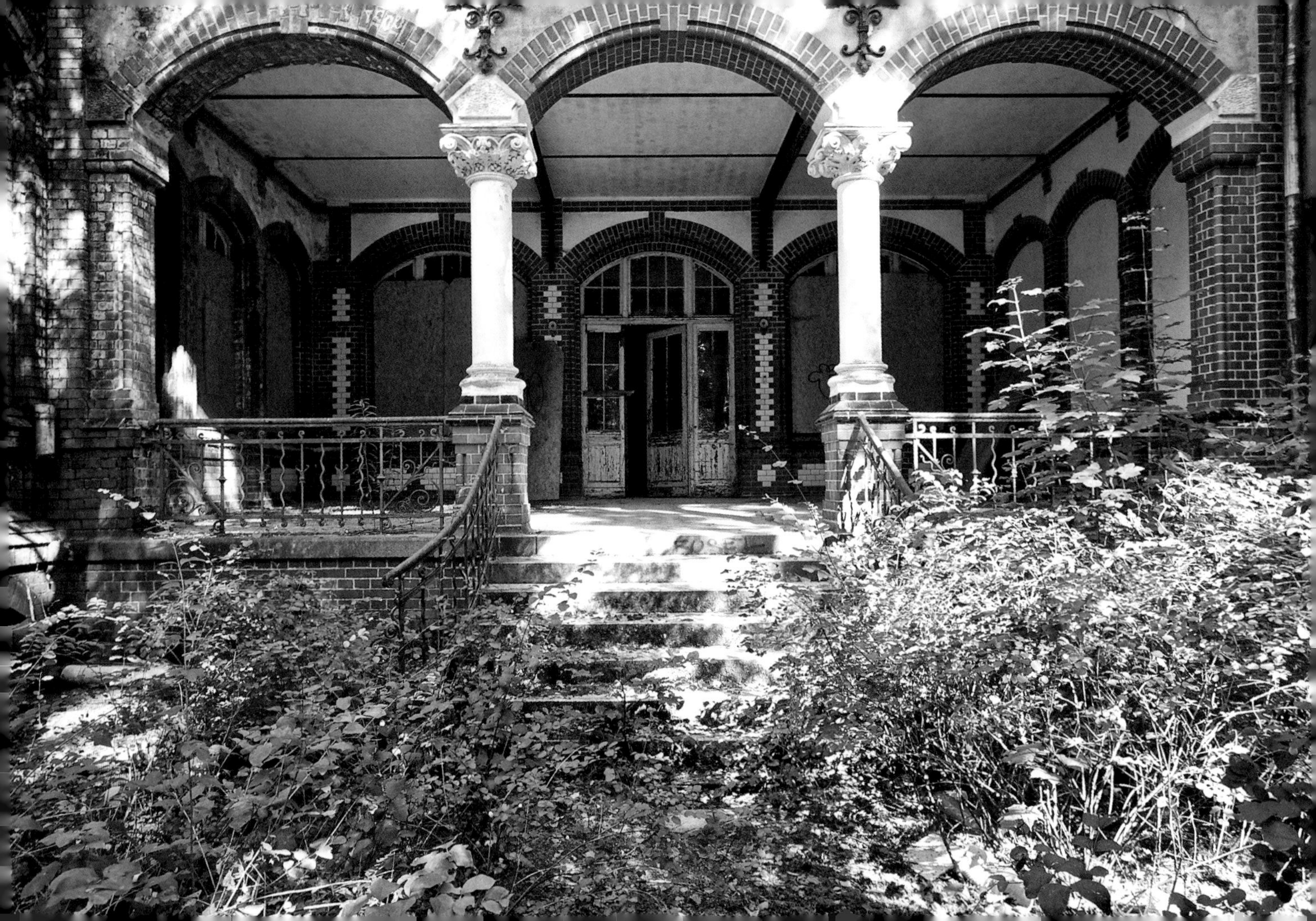

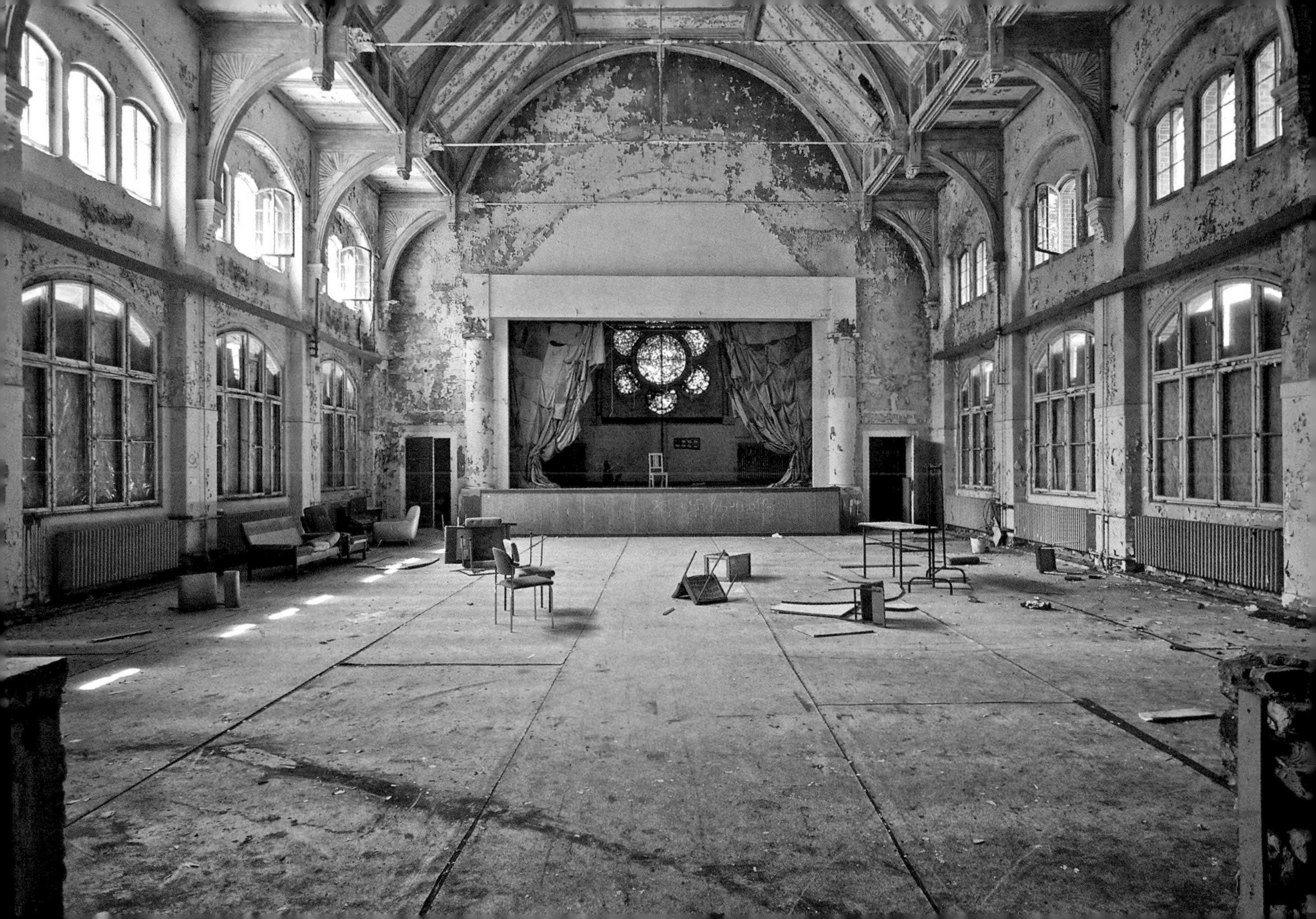

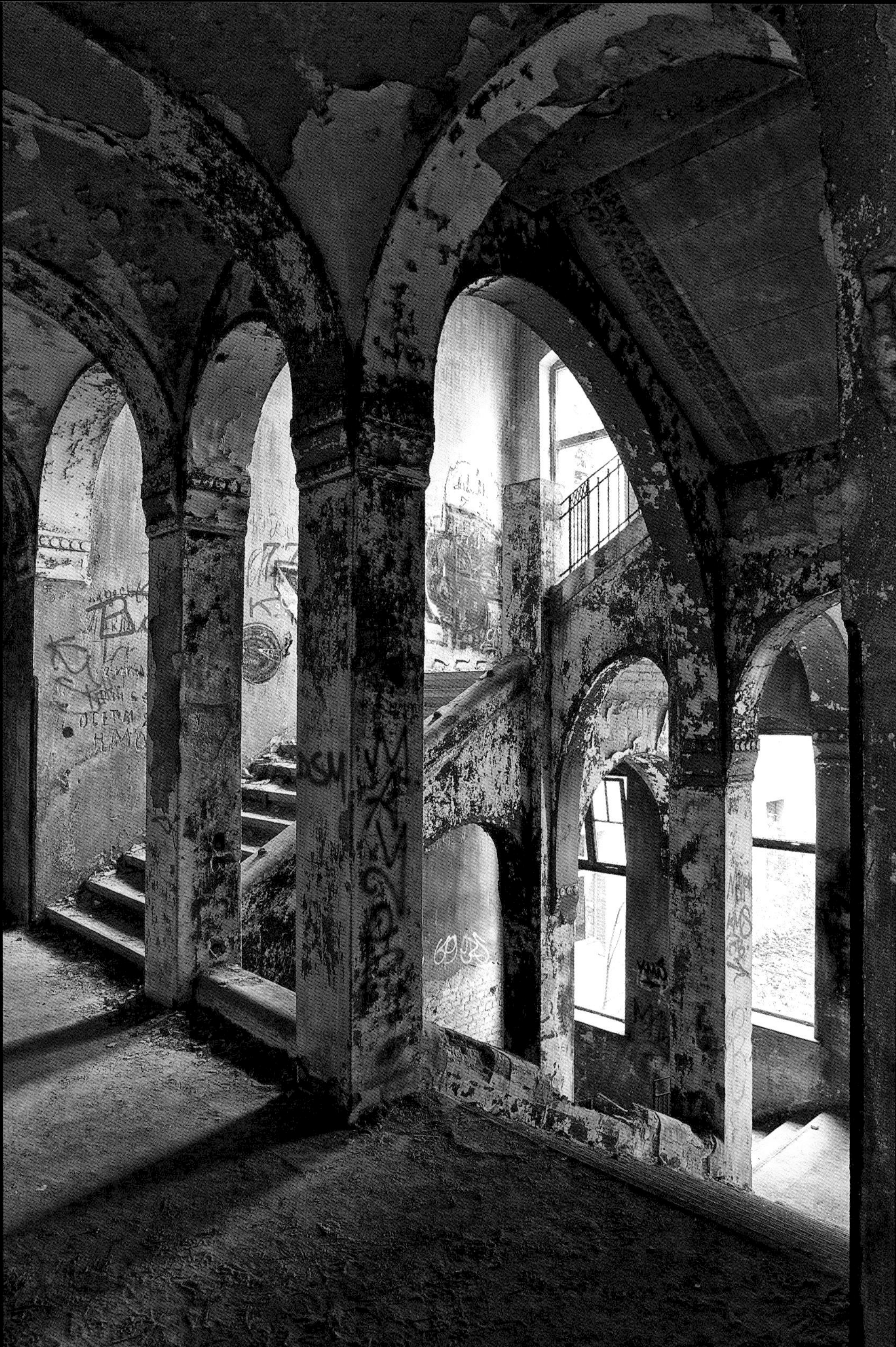

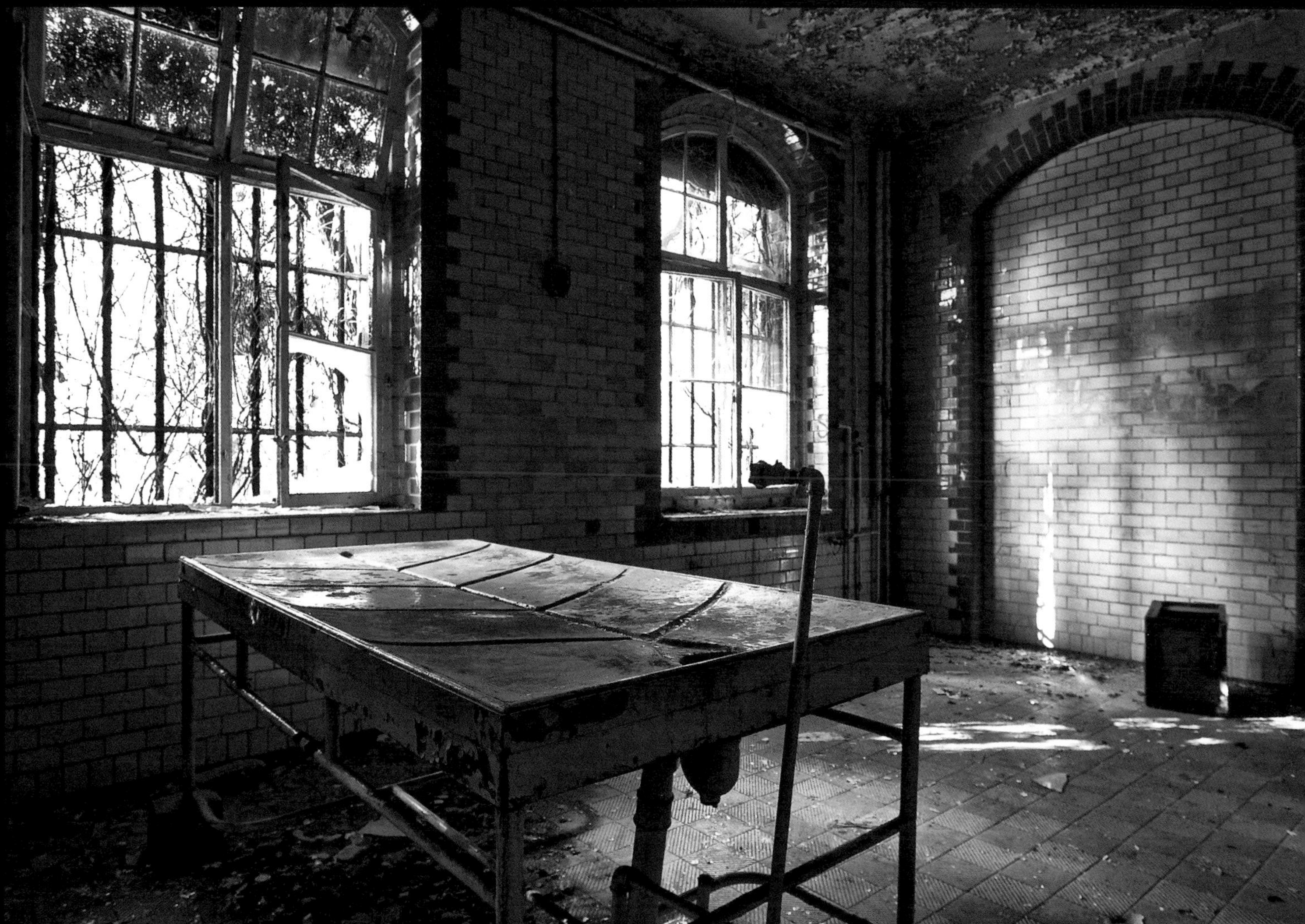

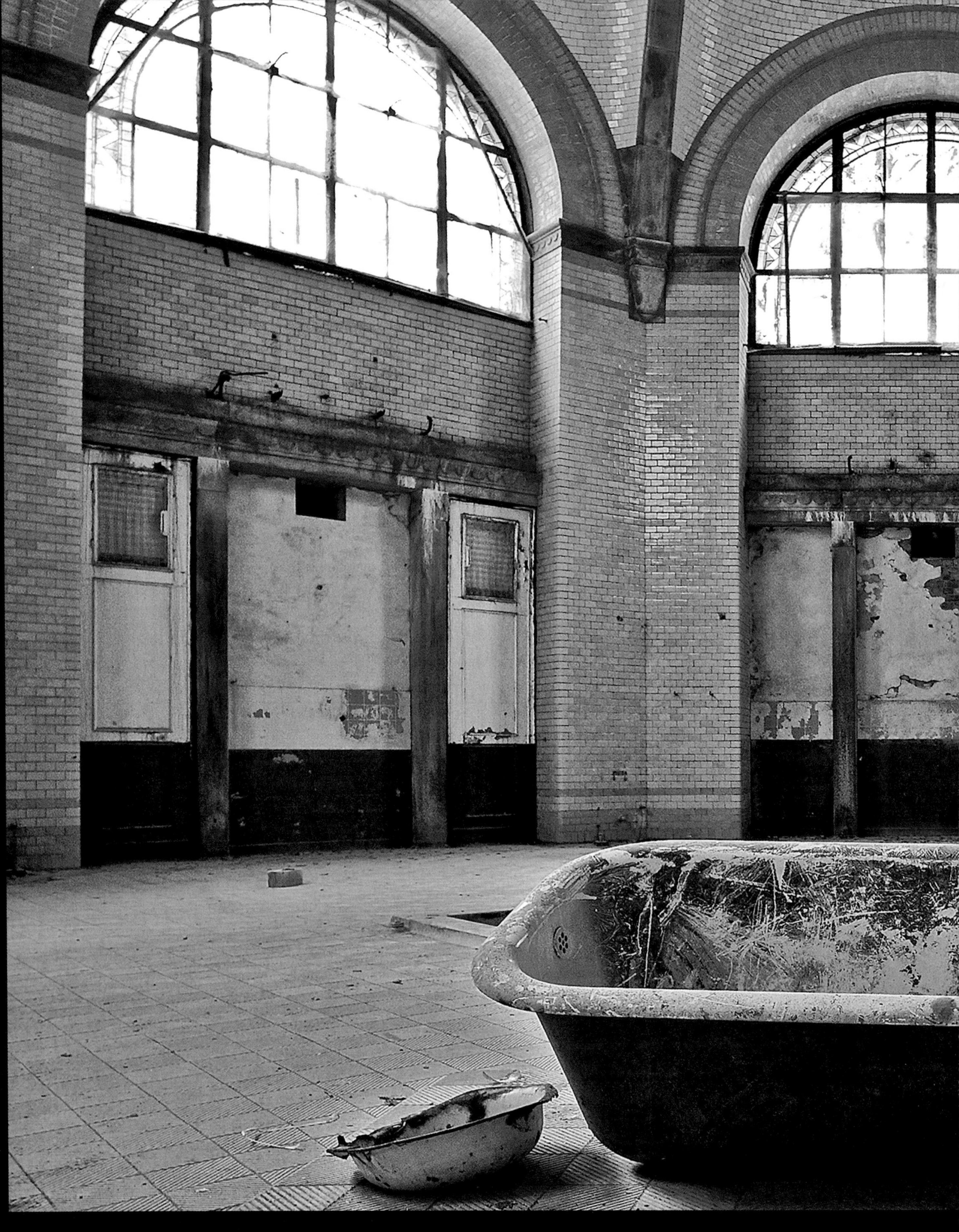

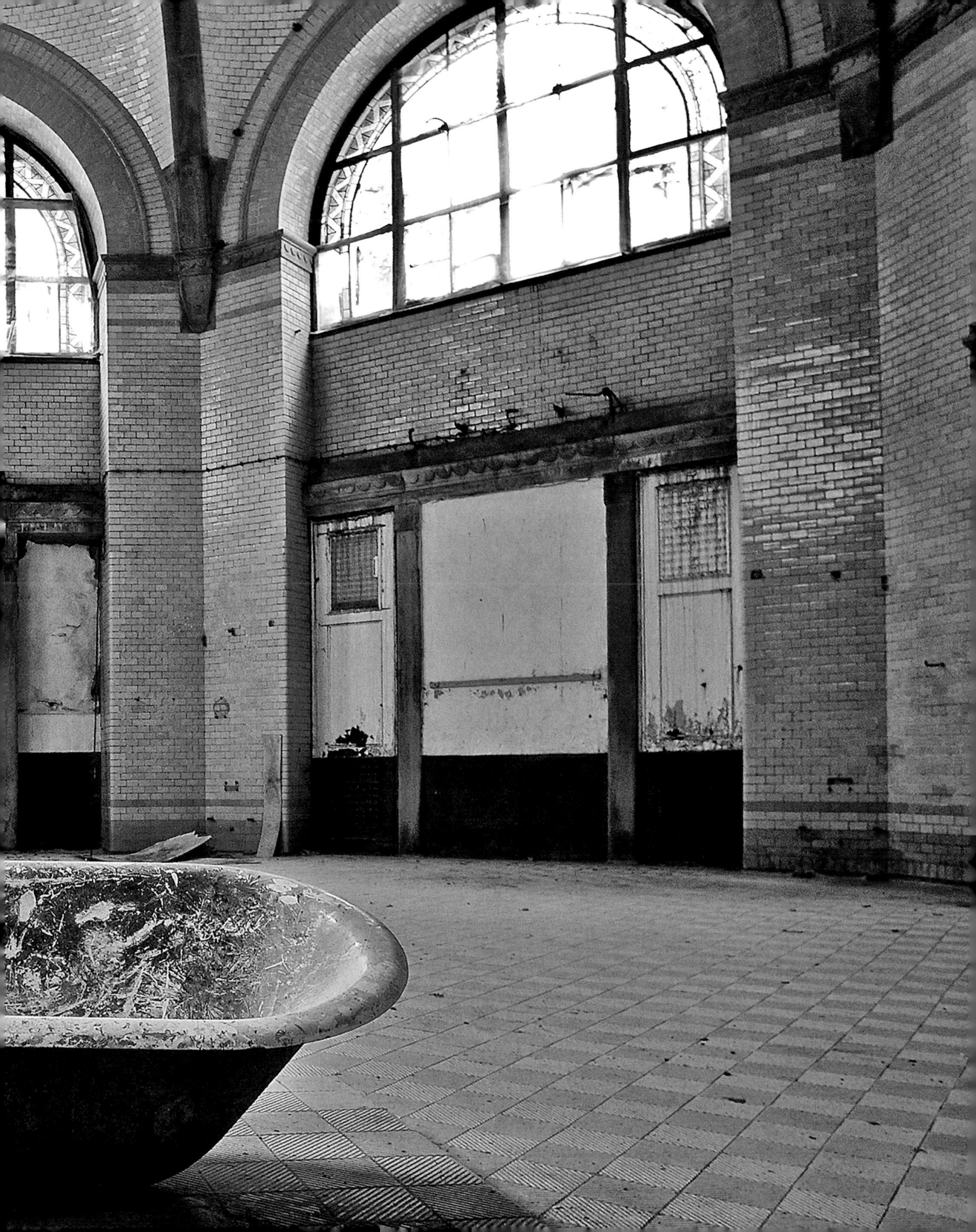

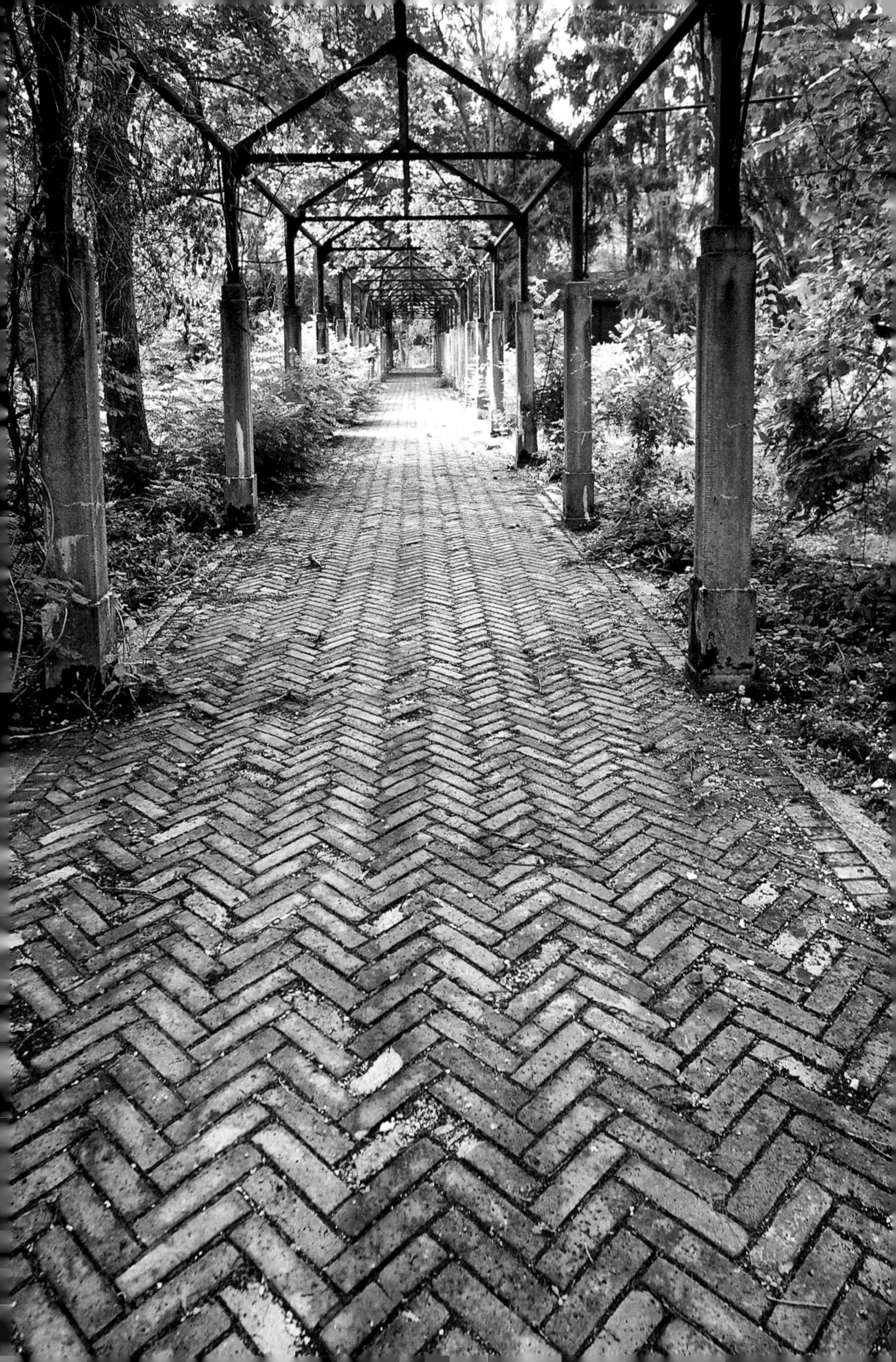

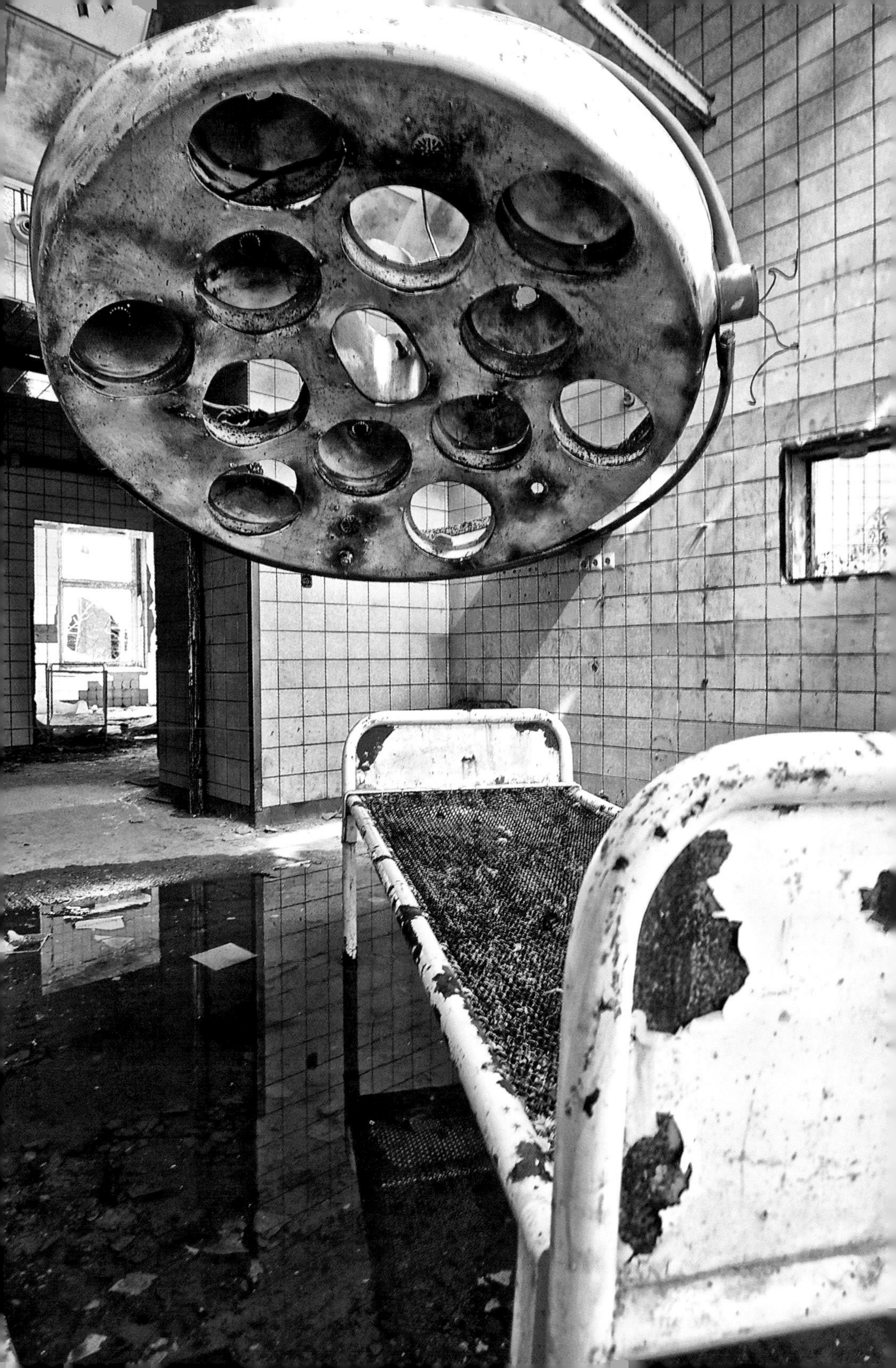

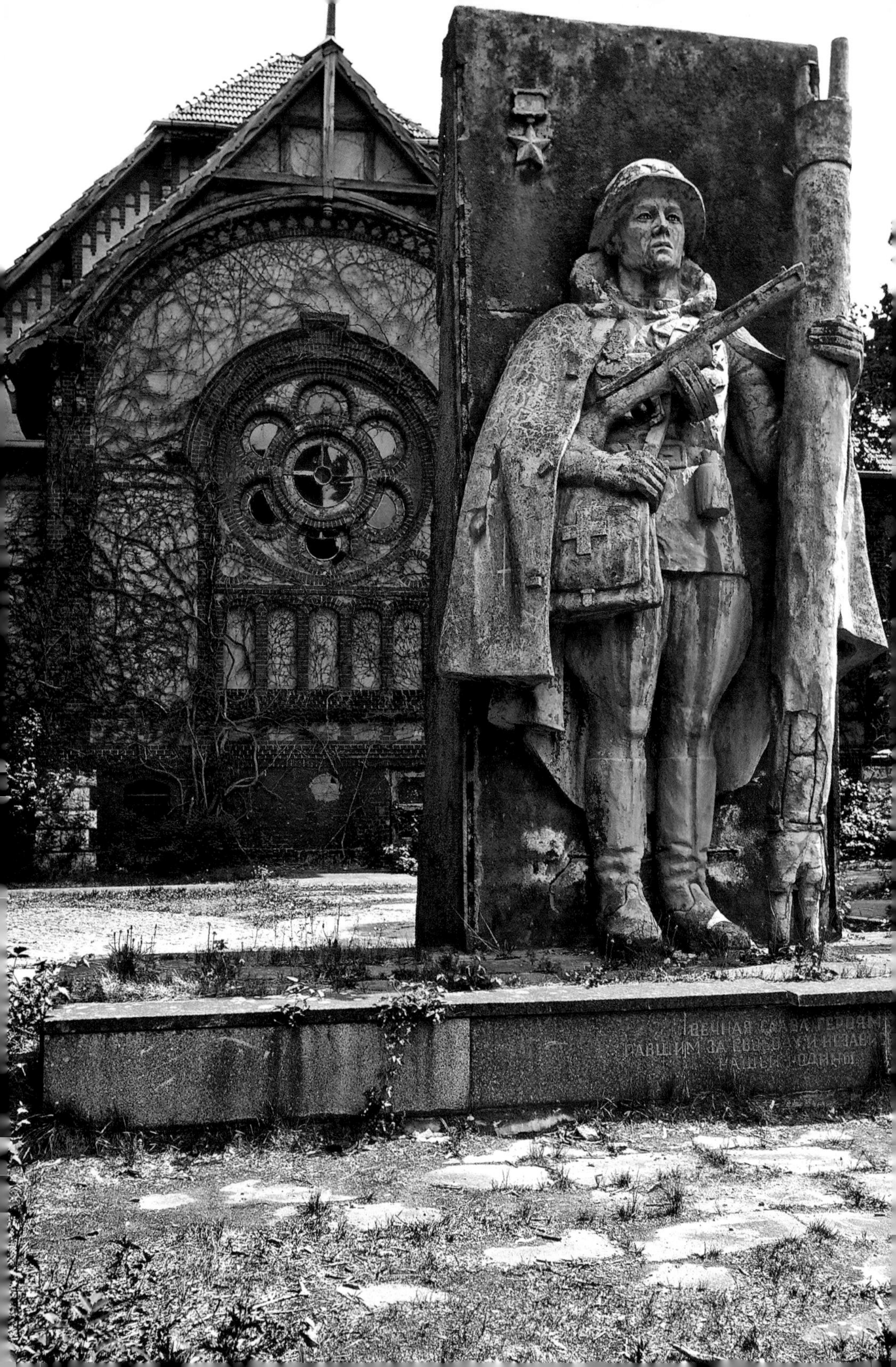
ВЕЧНАЯ
ПАВШИМ ЗА
НАШЕЙ

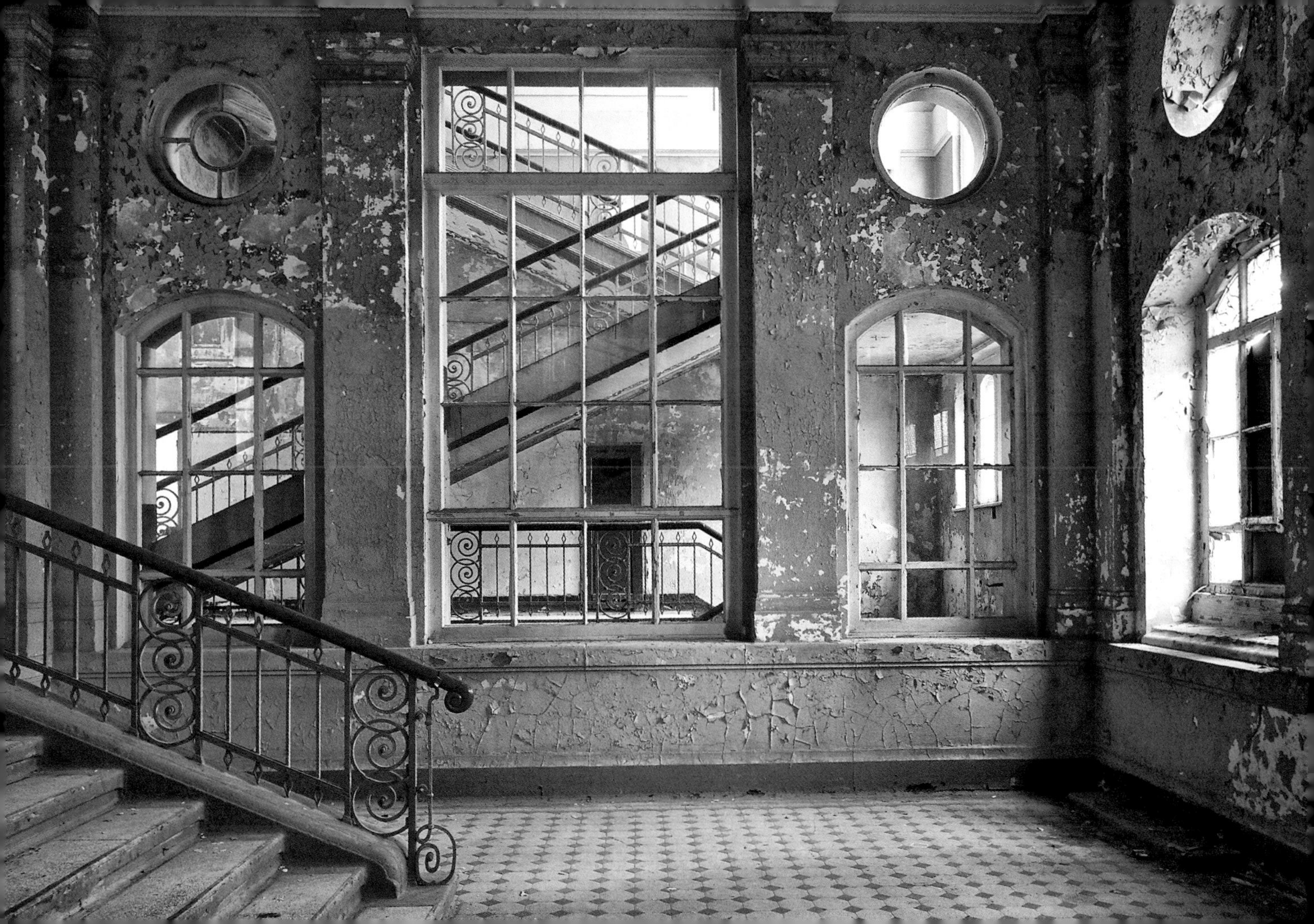

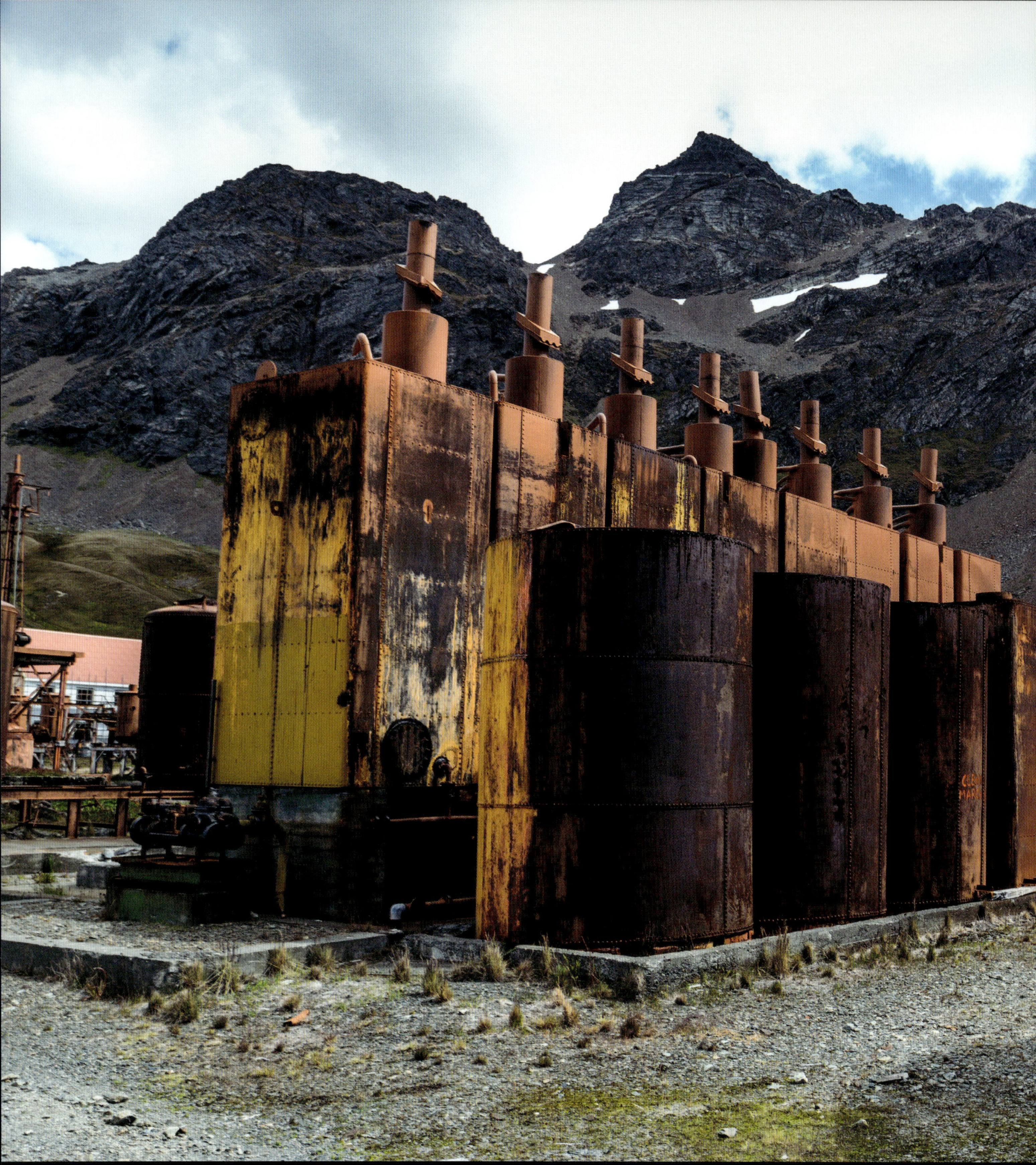

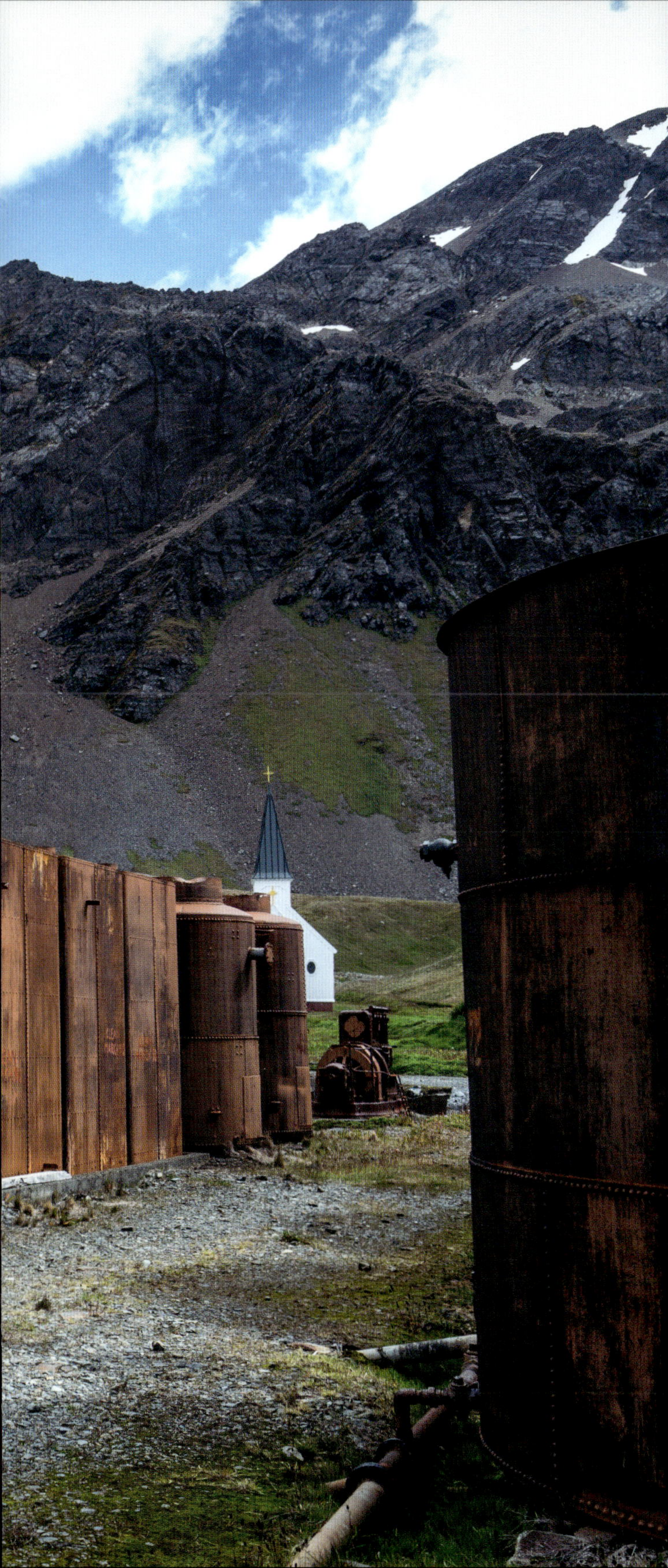

GRYTVIKEN

SÜDGEORGIEN SOUTH GEORGIA

FOTOS VON PHOTOS BY ROB SALL

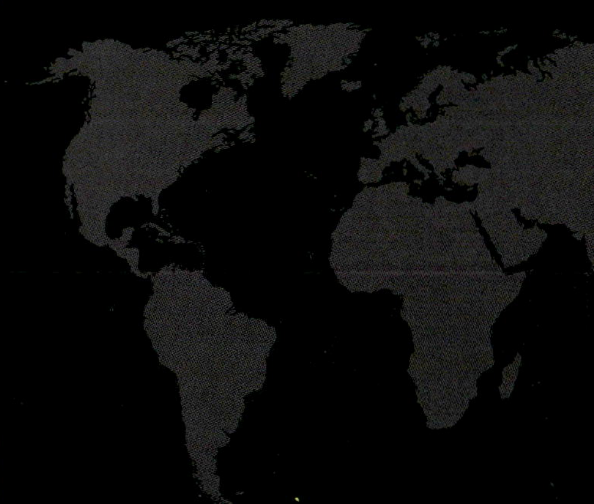

Wild blüht der Rost auf Grytvikens Metalloberflächen. Von den Rohrleitungen, Trankesseln und -kochern der einstigen Walfangstation, ihren Rauchabzügen, Pumpen und Motoren beständig sich lösende Eisenbrösel offenbaren sein unbändiges Wirken. Übrig bleibt eine bräunliche Spreu auf Südgeorgiens steinigem Boden, die sich bei kräftigem Regen in gewundenen Rinnsalen sammelt und fortgewaschen wird. Hier zwischen dem 50. und 60. Grad südlicher Breite, im Gebiet der „Wütenden Fünfziger", wühlt ein von den Schiffsmannschaften gefürchteter Westwind die See auf. Es entstehen Wellen von 30 Meter Höhe, und manche davon sollen um die ganze Erde gelangen, ohne dass sie auf Land treffen. Von der Antarktis treiben blau schimmernde Eisberge durch den Südatlantik wie vor sich hinträumende Riesen und bilden eine schwer vorhersagbare Gefahr für den Seeverkehr.

Von Juni bis August, dem Winter auf der Südhalbkugel, toben Schneestürme. Oder es verhüllt dichter Nebel tagelang die Sicht. Wenn er sich schließlich auflöst, gibt er weit vor der Küste Argentiniens, fast 2.000 Kilometer vor Kap Horn, die Insel Südgeorgien bzw. South Georgia frei. Ihre Entfernung zum geografischen Südpol beträgt etwa 4.000 Kilometer. Mit einer Fläche von 3.756 Quadratkilometern ist sie das größte Eiland der nach ihr benannten Inselgruppe, zu der unter anderem auch die Welcome-, die Pickersgill- und die Willisinseln gehören. Sie erstreckt sich über eine Länge von 160 Kilometern und ihre breiteste Stelle misst 30 Kilometer. Zusammen mit den Südlichen Sandwichinseln und den Falklandinseln gehört sie zum britischen Überseegebiet.

Die Station Grytviken wurde an ihrer Ostküste errichtet. Der Name leitet sich von der Bucht ab, an der sie erbaut wurde. Ihr Aussehen erinnert an einen Kessel, worauf das norwegische Wort „Gryte" hinweist. Die bis 2.900 Meter hohen Berge Südgeorgiens schützen den Siedlungsplatz vor dem Westwind. Das gesamte Jahr über bleiben große Teile des gebirgigen Landesinneren von Schnee und Eis bedeckt. Erreicht der Sommer von Dezember bis Februar die Insel, steigen die Temperaturen selten über zehn Grad Celsius. Die Wassertemperaturen liegen zwischen sechs bis drei Grad. Grytviken gleicht einem natürlichen Kühlschrank. Und der norwegische Kapitän Carl Anton Larsen fand, dass es einen „der feinsten Häfen" besaß. Ideale Voraussetzungen für seine Geschäftsidee: Wale dort zu fangen, wo es noch niemand versucht hatte.

Im April 1904 trug er die Compañia Argentina de Pesca in das Unternehmensregister von Buenos Aires ein und noch im gleichen Jahr begann man in Grytviken mit der Arbeit. Es wird berichtet, dass zu Weihnachten das erste Fass Waltran abgefüllt war. Im darauffolgenden Jahr füllte man 7.000 Fässer und im dritten Jahr schon 27.000 Fässer mit Tran. Die erzielten hohen Gewinne überraschten auch Larsens Anteilseigner. Angezogen von diesem Erfolg entstanden auf Südgeorgien weitere Walfangstationen. Allein in der Jagdsaison von 1930 bis 1931 wurden über 40.000 Wale getötet. In der Antarktis schien der Buckelwal beinahe ausgerottet zu sein, da begann der Preis für Waltran zu sinken. Die Stationen auf Südgeorgien mussten eine nach der anderen schließen. 1962 übernahmen japanische Geschäftsleute Grytviken, verkauften es jedoch 1965 wieder. Dass der Ort aufgegeben wurde, erlebte sein Gründer Carl Anton Larsen nicht. Bei der Erkundung neuer Jagdgebiete war er 1924 in der Antarktis gestorben.

Rust thrives wildly on the metal surfaces at Grytviken. Constantly detaching bits of iron reveal its irrepressible effect on pipelines, whale oil kettles and boilers, and the chimneys, pumps and motors of the one-time whaling station. Brown chaff remains on South Georgia's stony ground that collects in winding rivulets and is washed away during heavy rainfall. Here, between 50 and 60 degrees latitude south in the area known as the "furious fifties", one of the west winds feared by sailing crews churns up the sea. Waves develop up to a height of 30 meters and some of them travel around the entire world without touching land. Blue shimmering icebergs from the Antarctic work their way through the South Atlantic like sleeping giants, creating a difficult to predict danger for maritime transport.
Snow storms rage in the winter in the southern hemisphere from June to August. Or thick fog obscures the view for days at a time. When it finally lifts, South Georgia Island, or alternatively South Georgia, becomes free, far from the coast of Argentina almost 2,000 kilometers from Cape Horn. The distance to the geographic South Pole is about 4,000 kilometers. With an area of 3,756 square kilometers, it is the largest island of the island group named after it, including among others Welcome Island, Pickersgill Islands and Willis Islands. It covers a length of 160 kilometers and its widest point measures 30 kilometers. It is part of the British overseas territories together with the South Sandwich Islands and Falklands Islands.
The Grytviken station was built on its east coast. The name comes from the bay on which it is built. Its appearance resembles a kettle, hence the Norwegian word "gryte". The high mountains of South Georgia that reach up to 2,900 meters protect the settlement from the west wind. The whole year long, large areas of the hilly interior remain covered in snow and ice. When summer reaches the island from December to February, the temperature rarely rises above ten degrees Celsius. The water temperature stays between three and six degrees. Grytviken is comparable to a natural refrigerator. And the Norwegian captain Carl Anton Larsen found that it had one of "the finest harbors". Ideal conditions for his business idea to hunt whales where nobody had yet tried.
In April 1904, he registered the Compañia Argentina de Pesca in the company register of Buenos Aires and work began in Grytviken the same year. It is reported that the first barrel of whale oil was filled that Christmas. In the following year, 7,000 barrels were filled and 27,000 in the third year. The high earnings even surprised Larsen's shareholders. This success attracted more whaling stations that were built on South Georgia. In the hunting season alone from 1930 to 1931, more than 40,000 whales were killed. It appeared that the humpback whale was almost extinct in Antarctica and the price for whale oil began to drop. The stations on South Georgia were forced to close one after the other. In 1962, Japanese businessmen took over Grytviken, but sold it again in 1965. Its founder, Carl Anton Larsen, did not experience the abandoning of the location. He died in 1924 in Antarctica exploring new hunting areas.

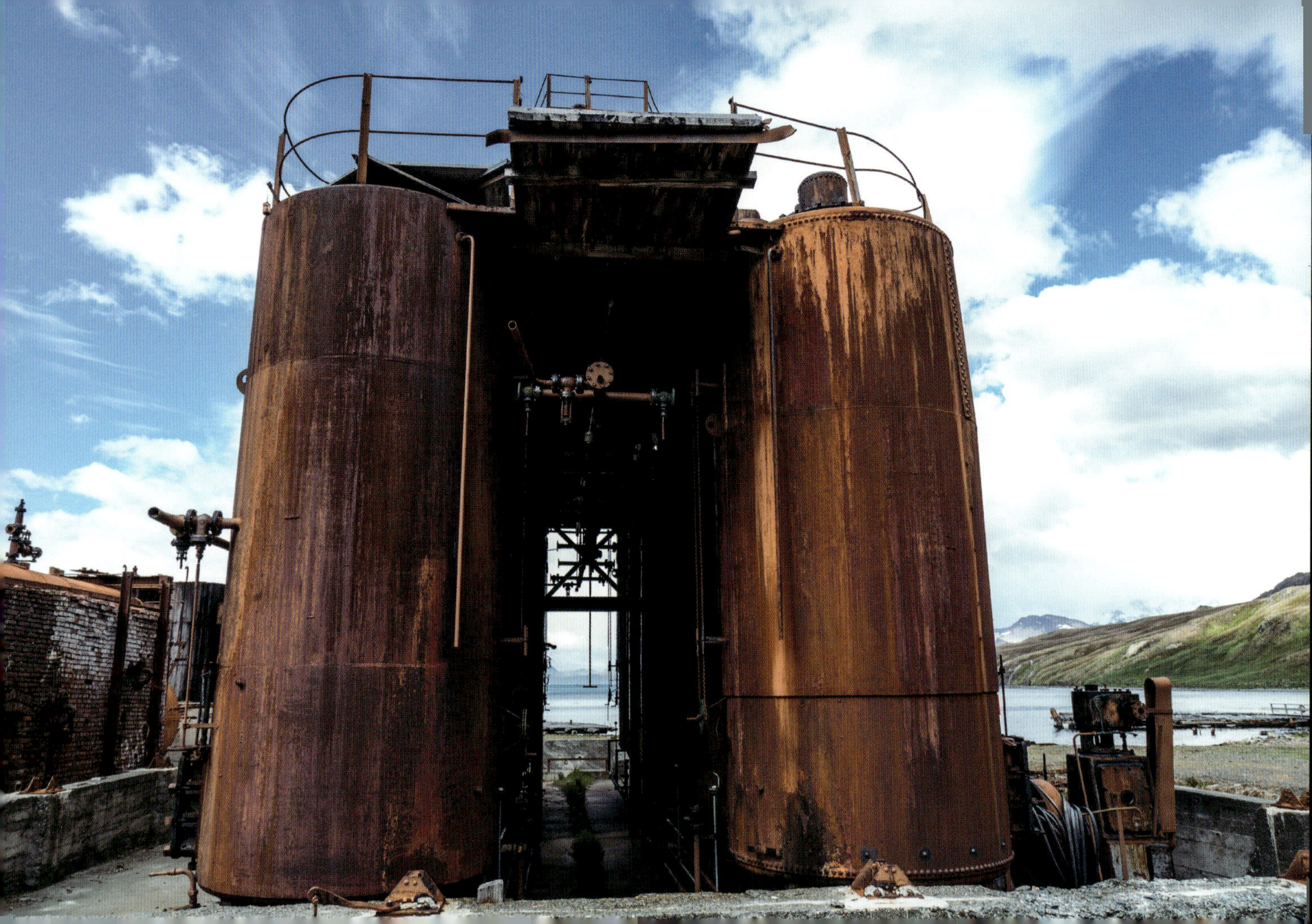

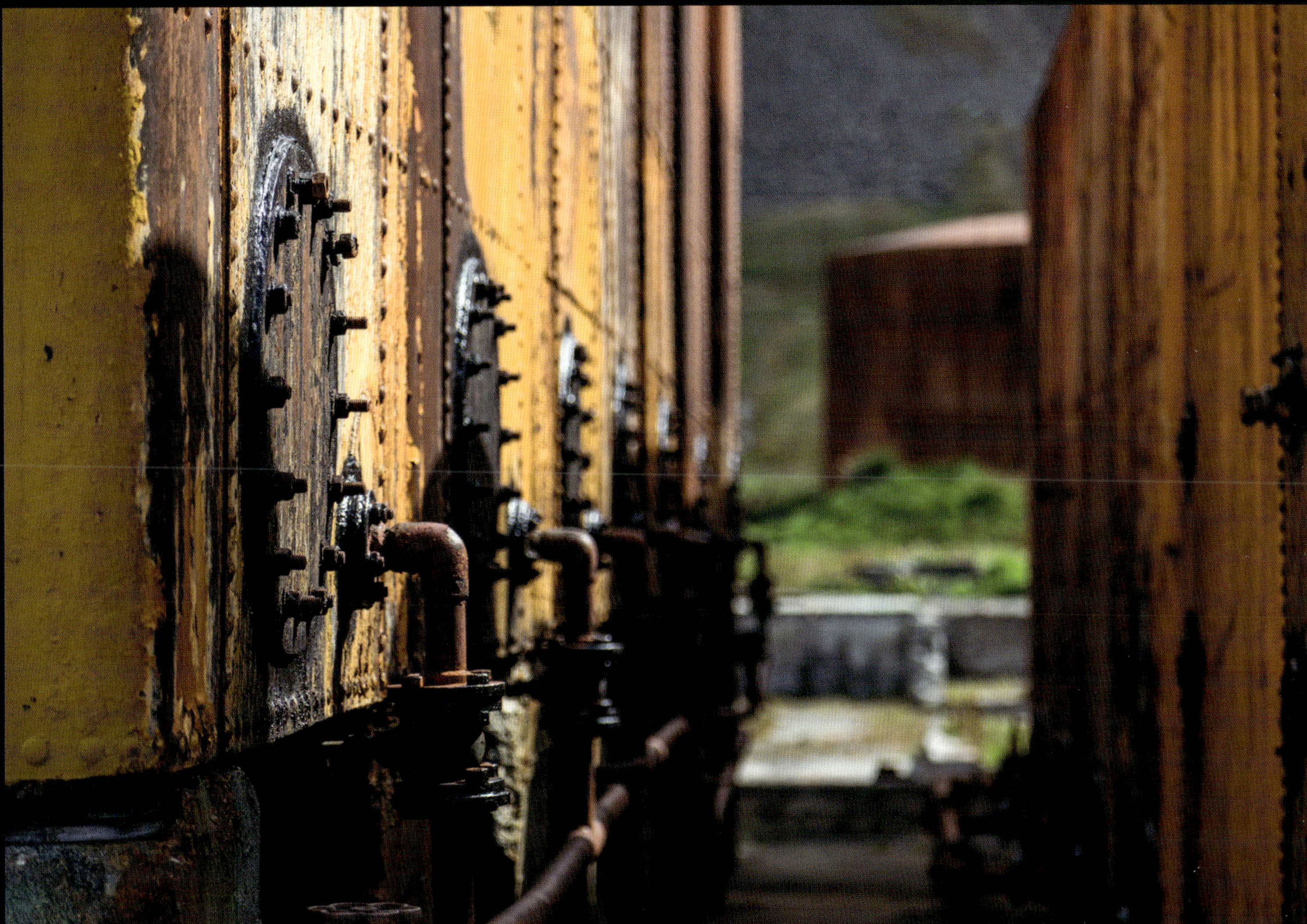

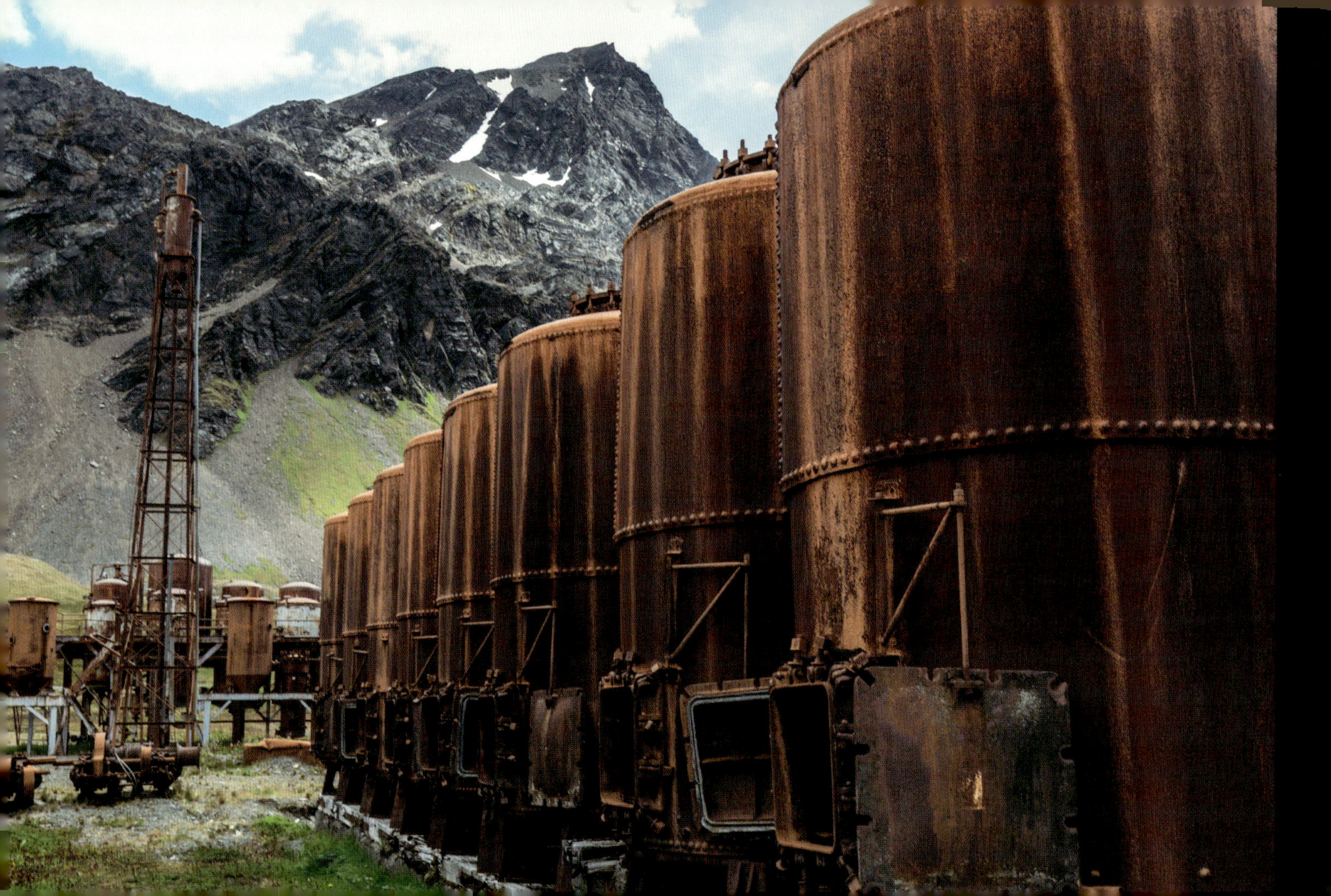

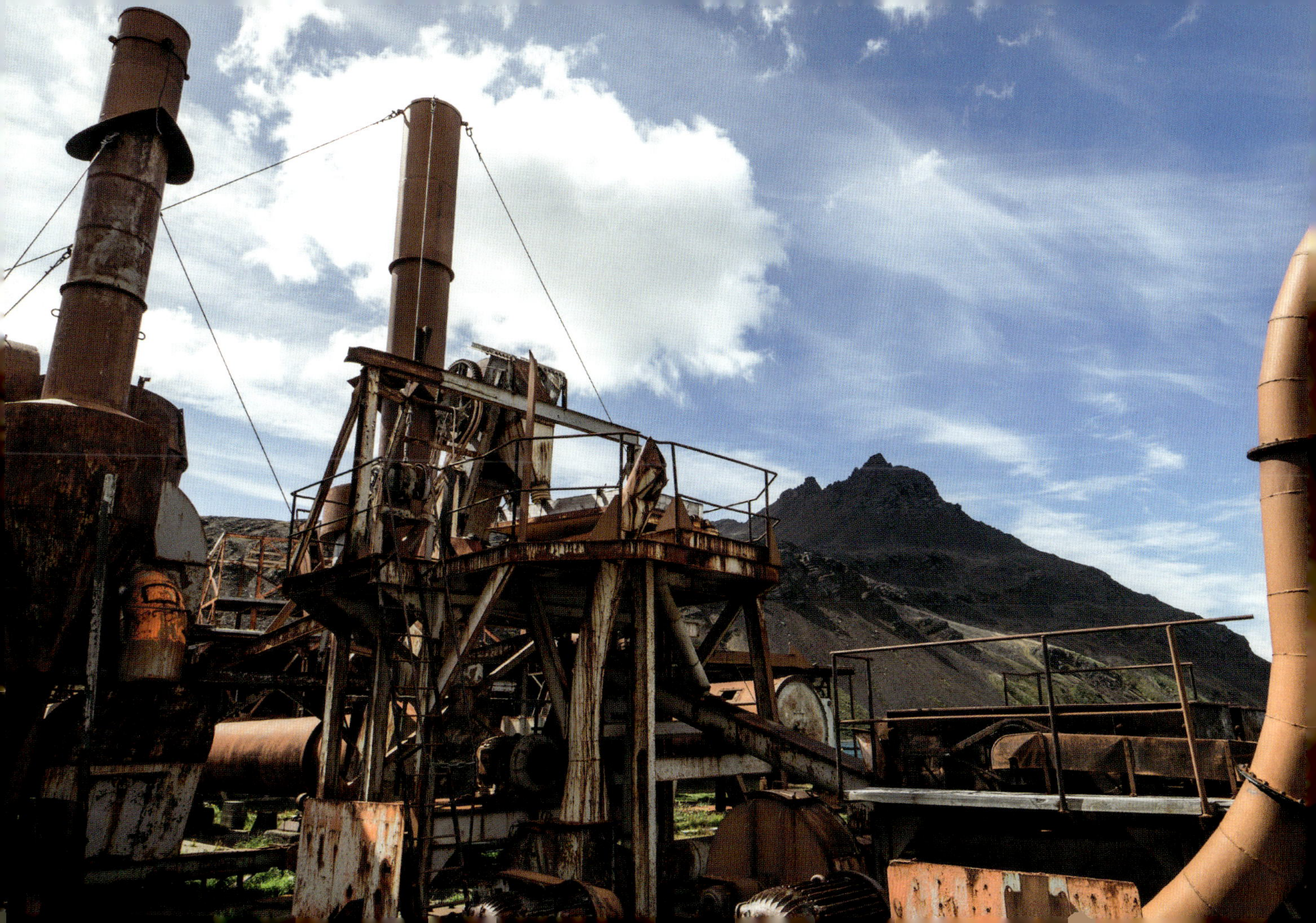

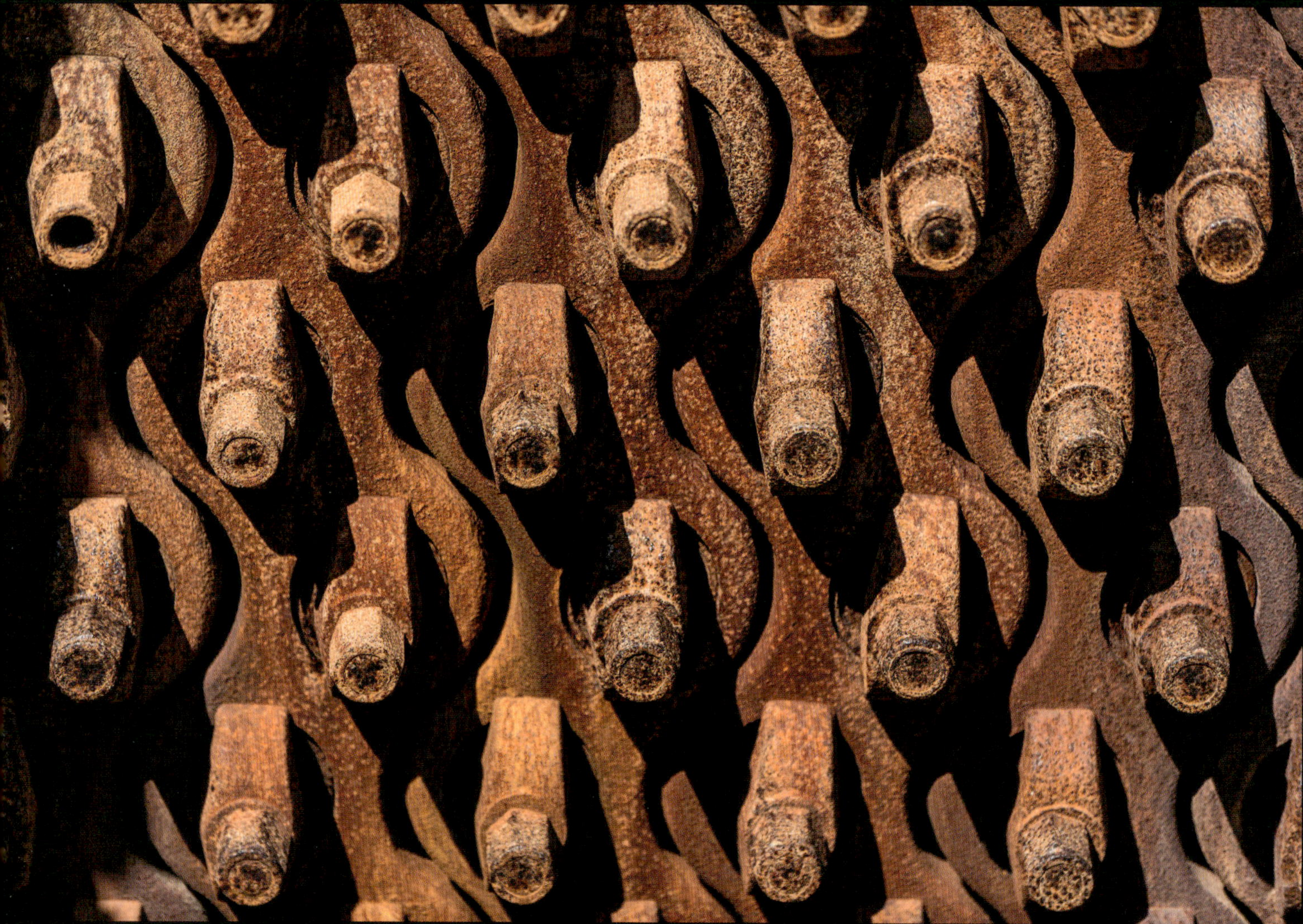

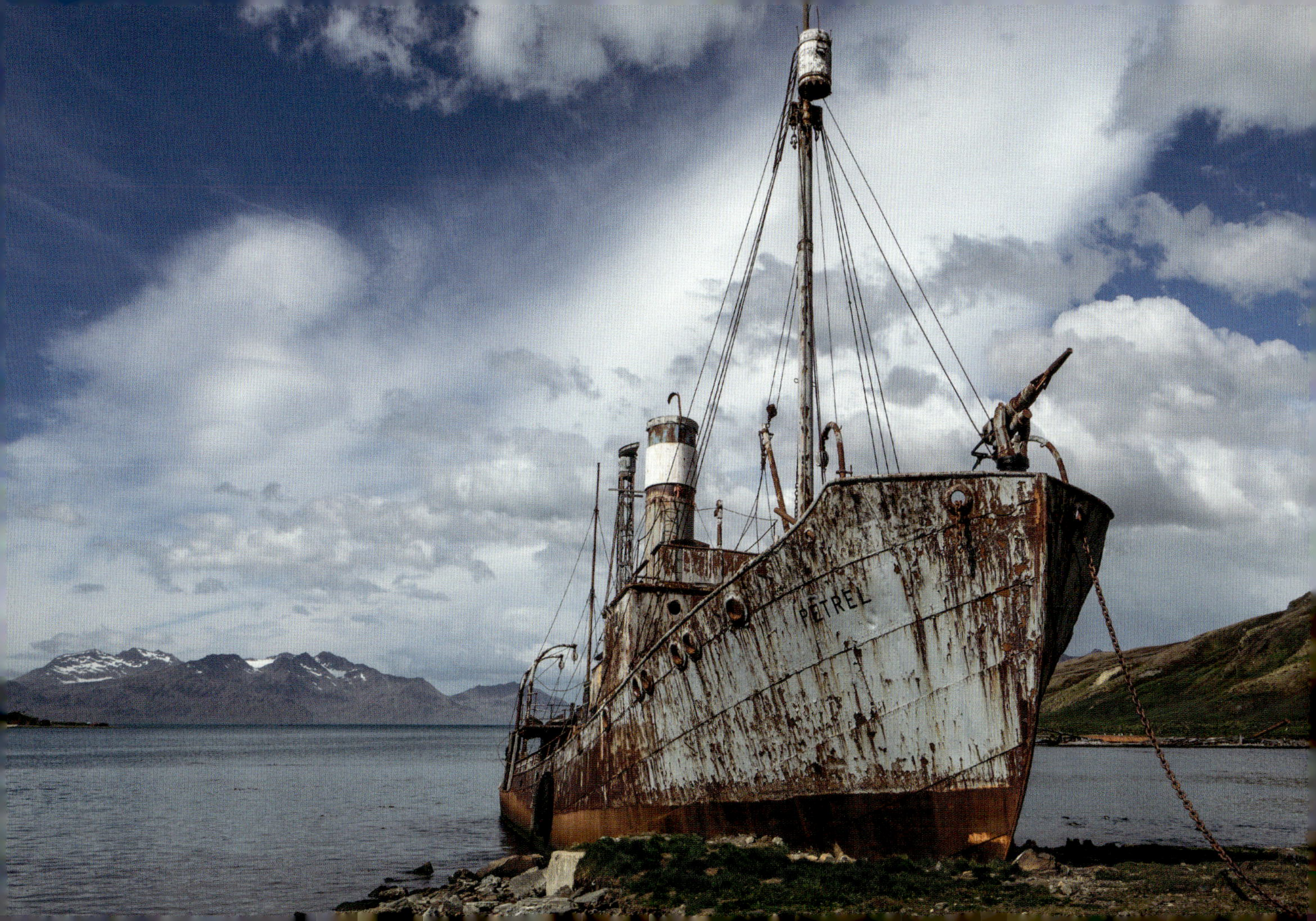
PETREL

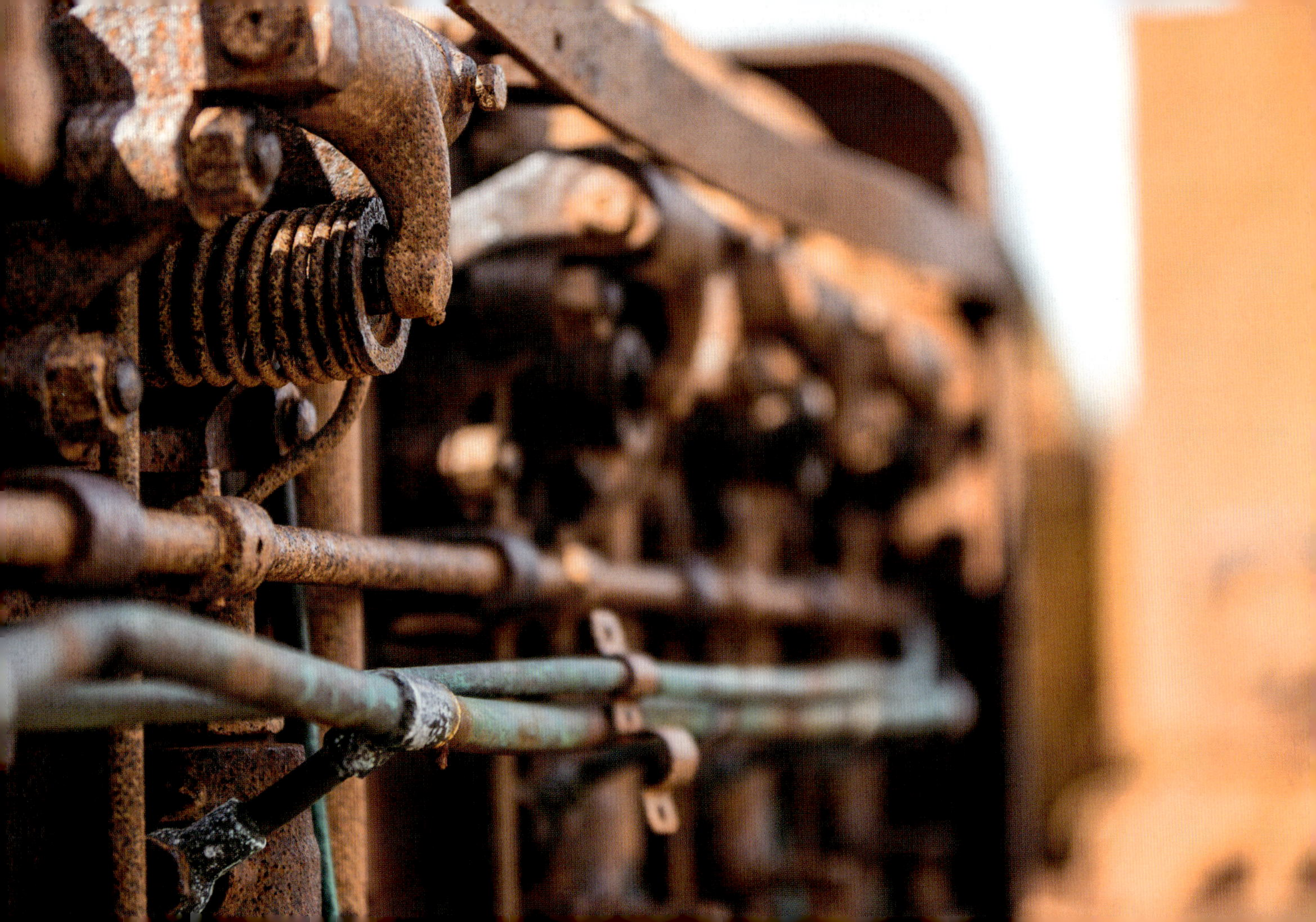

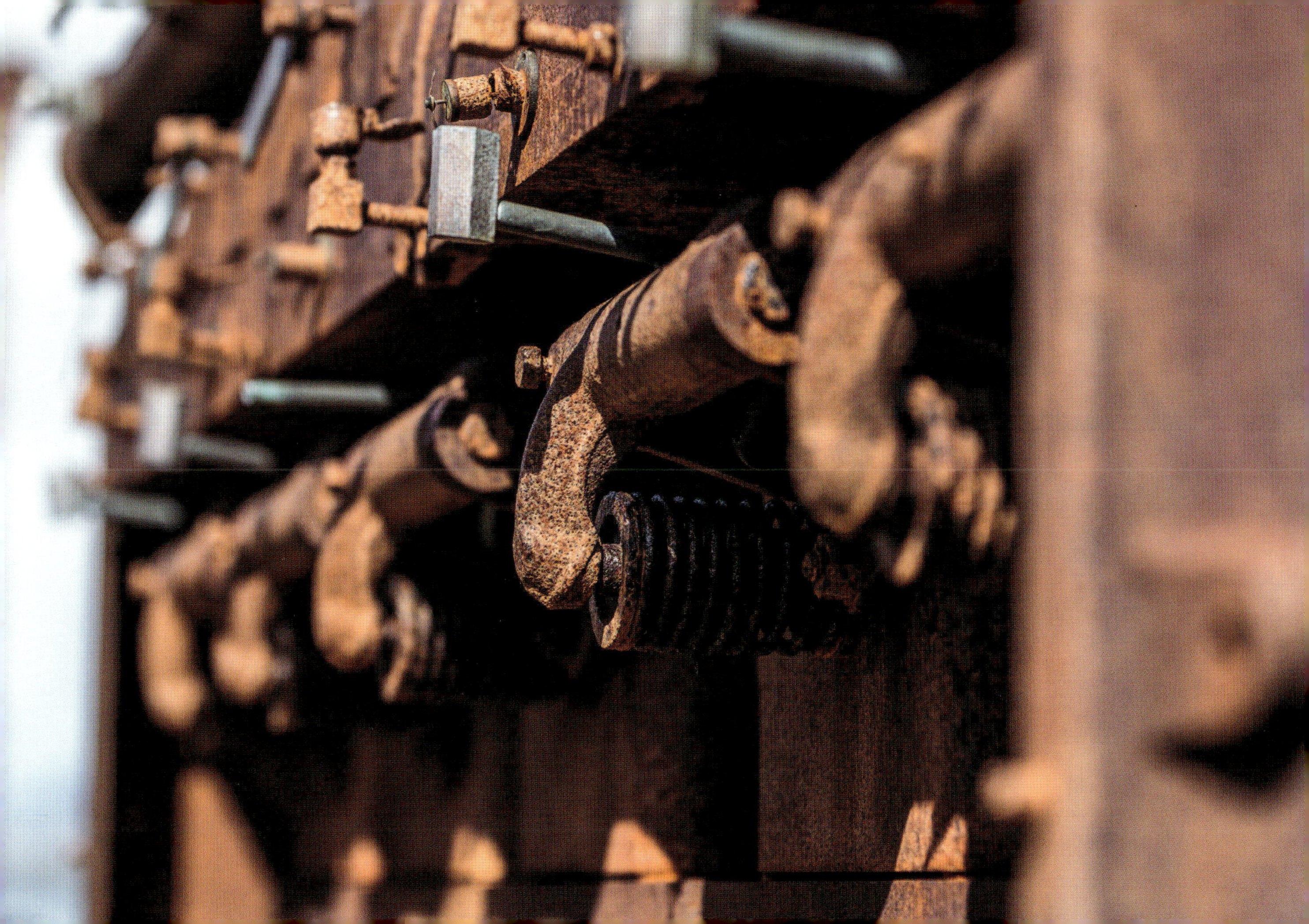

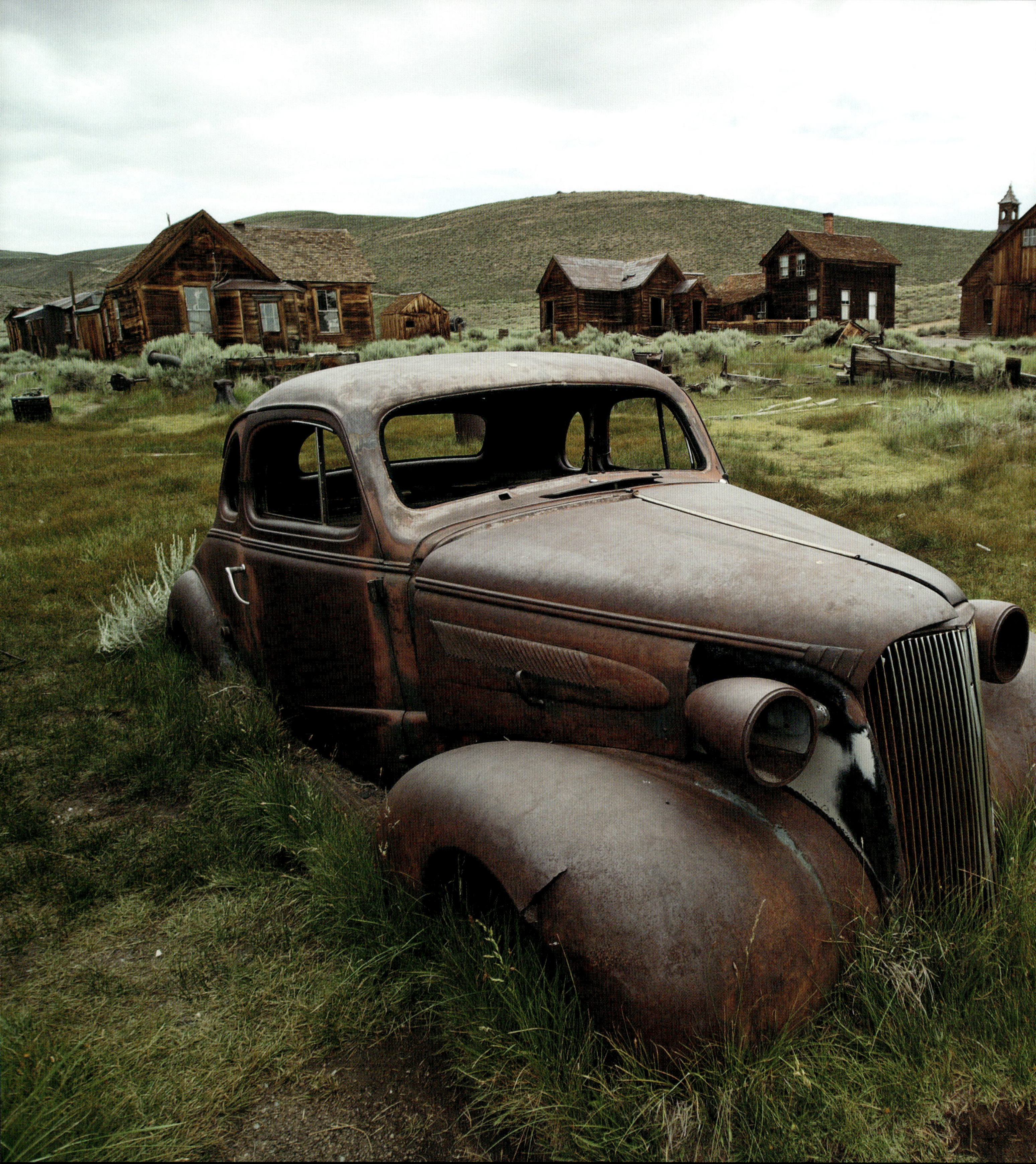

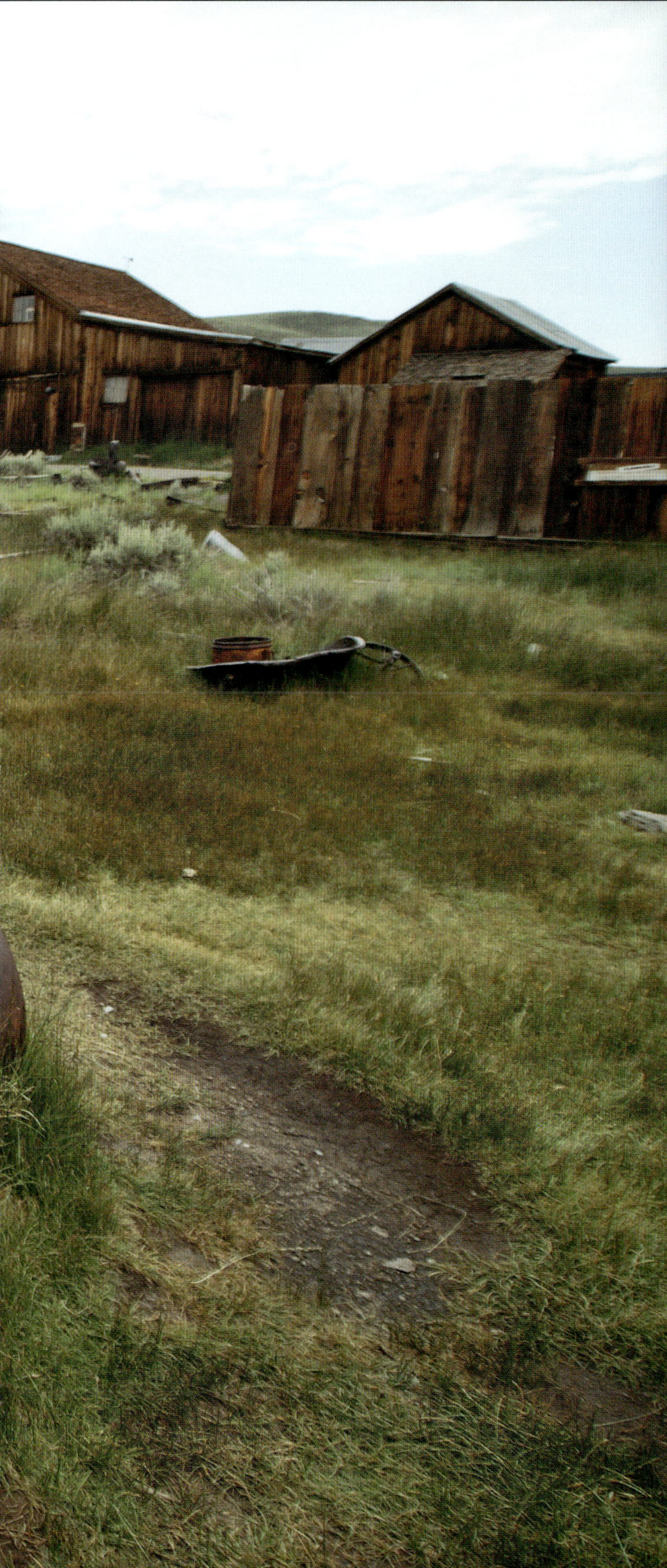

BODIE

VEREINIGTE STAATEN UNITED STATES

FOTOS VON PHOTOS BY DANIEL TER-NEDDEN

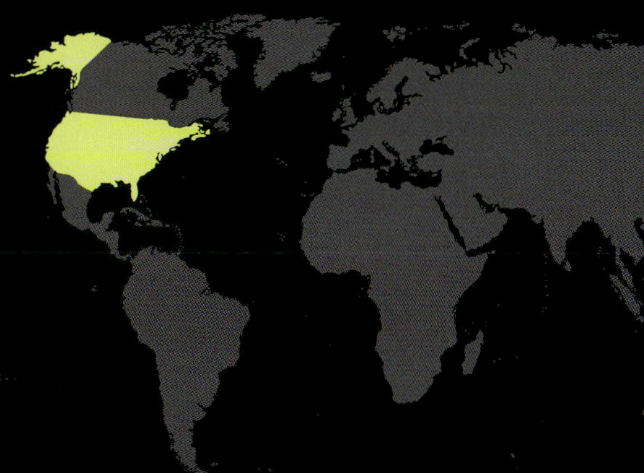

Staub fällt auf Staub, bildet üppigere Schichten, schwillt und beginnt sich zu bewegen, rinnt und kräuselt sich, wo Zugluft ihn erreichen kann. Fast meint man es hören zu können, sein sachtes Treiben. Er hat die übrig gebliebenen Holzhäuser, ihre Wohn- und Geschäftsräume, Möbel, Musikinstrumente, Waren, Regale und Auslagen, Tresen, Saloonausstattungen, Bierflaschen, Billardtische und Schaukelstühle in Besitz genommen, nachdem die letzten Bewohner in den Vierzigerjahren ihre einst so berühmte und berüchtigte Stadt verlassen hatten. Nach draußen gelangt, in die Hochebene der östlichen Sierra Nevada, vermischt er sich mit dem herumwirbelnden Sand und streift über das hin, was nicht schnell genug fortkam, wie etwa das Chevrolet Coupé gleich am Eingang des Ortes.

„Auf Wiedersehen, lieber Gott, morgen fahren wir nach Bodie." Das schrieb vor 130 Jahren ein Kind in sein Tagebuch. Es hatte Angst vor dieser Stadt im Wilden Westen mit den ständigen Schießereien und Selbstmorden, 60 Saloons, Spielhöllen und 15 Bordellen, den Glückssuchern, Spielern, immer angetrunkenen Goldgräbern, Huren und Dieben. Das Böse schien damals einzig aus Bodie zu kommen. Und amerikaweit unterstützte die Presse diesen Eindruck, da er ihre Verkaufszahlen enorm steigerte. Seitdem hier in der Bunker Hill Mine ab 1877 eine reiche Gold- und Silberader ausgebeutet wurde und sich die Nachrichten über die fantastischen Gewinne verbreiteten, war der kleine Siedlungsflecken wie verwandelt. 1878 gab es bereits 22 Minen. Die Einwohnerzahl wuchs auf 8.000 an und es entstanden etwa 2.000 Gebäude. Zugleich ereignete sich die erste größere Schießerei mit tödlichem Ausgang.

Nur drei Jahre später erhielt Bodie den Anschluss an das Eisenbahnnetz. Auch auf die Frage, warum – ausgerechnet in dieser Stadt – man mit Gewalt so erfolgreich sein konnte, fand die Lokalpresse eine Antwort: „Es muss an der Höhe liegen." Kaum ein Täter wurde jedenfalls verurteilt. Die Menschen erinnerten sich 1879 an jenen ersten Goldsucher, dem die Stadt ihren Namen verdankte: Wakeman S. Bodey. Allein für den Vornamen gibt es bis heute drei Versionen – Wakeman, William oder Waterman. Vermutet wird, dass er aus dem Bundesstaat New York nach Kalifornien kam. Wie alle seine Nachfolger war er auf der Suche nach so viel Gold, dass es sein Leben verändern konnte, und er fand 1859, was er suchte. Im Winter des gleichen Jahres brach er zusammen und erfror. Seine Gefährten begruben ihn bei der Fundstätte und nannten ihr Lager nach ihm. Das war die Gründung der späteren Stadt.

Die Einwohner von Bodie ließen das Grab suchen, nahmen die Gebeine heraus und betteten sie auf den städtischen Friedhof um. Wohin genau, das scheint verloren gegangen zu sein. Im Jahr 1883 war dann der Taumel vorbei. Wer konnte, zog nach Colorado weiter, um dort das Glück zu finden. Aus der einst so verruchten Goldgräbersiedlung war mit einem Mal eine ruhige Kleinstadt geworden. Drei Jahre später wohnten hier noch 1.500 Menschen. Die Stromversorgung gab der verbliebenen Minenindustrie einen positiven Impuls, aber der Goldrausch war vorüber. In einem großen Feuer verging dann 1932 fast der gesamte Ort. Bis zu diesem Zeitpunkt fand man hier Gold und Silber mit einem Wert von 34 Millionen Dollar. Längst ist Bodie nun ein Museum. Es hat sich zur Aufgabe gemacht, die Ursprünglichkeit seines Angebots zu bewahren und die Kraft von Wetter, Wind und Staub nicht zu leugnen.

Dust settles on dust, creates elaborate layers, swells and begins to move, run and flow where drafts can reach it. You can almost hear its soft movements. It took over the remaining wooden houses, their living and business rooms, furniture, music instruments, goods, shelves and wares, counters, saloon interiors, beer bottles, billiard tables and rocking chairs after the last residents left their once so famous and notorious town in the 1940s. Outside on the high plateau of the eastern Sierra Nevada, the dust mixes with the swirling sand, blowing over everything that wasn't fast enough to get away, perhaps like the Chevrolet coupe at the entrance of the town.

"Good-bye dear God, tomorrow we're going to Bodie", wrote a child in a journal 130 years ago. The child was afraid of this city in the Wild West with the constant shootings and suicides, 60 saloons, gambling houses and 15 brothels, the fortune seekers, gamblers and drunken prospectors, whores and thieves. At that time, it seemed that evil was the only thing to only come out of Bodie. Across America the press supported this impression, because it increased their sales figures enormously. After a rich gold and silver vein was exploited in the Bunker Hill Mine in 1877 and the news about the fantastic profit had spread, the little settlement transformed. By 1878 there were already 22 mines. The number of residents reached 8,000 and there were about 2,000 buildings. At that time, the first big shooting took place with deadly results.

Only three years later, Bodie was connected to the railway network. Also, the question about why in this city of all places, a person could be so successful with violence, was answered in the local newspaper: "It must be the elevation". Almost no perpetrators were ever charged. People remembered one of the first prospectors in 1879, from whom the city got its name: Wakeman S. Bodey. To this day there are three versions of his first name: Wakeman, William or Waterman. It is assumed that he came from the state of New York to California. Like all those who came after him, he was looking for so much gold so that he could change his life, and in 1859 he found what he was looking for. He collapsed and froze to death in the winter of the same year. His companions buried him at the claim and named their camp after him. That was the founding of the future city.

The residents of Bodie found the grave, exhumed the body, and buried it in the city cemetery. It appears that the exact location has been lost. By the year 1883, the frenzy had passed. Anyone who was able moved to Colorado to find their fortune there. All at once, the one-time so disreputable prospector settlement became a quiet small town. Three years later only 1,500 people lived here. The electricity supply gave the remaining mining industry a positive impulse, but the gold rush was finished. Then, in 1932 almost the entire place vanished in a huge fire. By that point in time, the gold and silver that had been found there amounted to 34 million dollars. Now, Bodie has been a museum for a long time. It has the task of preserving its origins and to not deny the power of the weather, wind and dust.

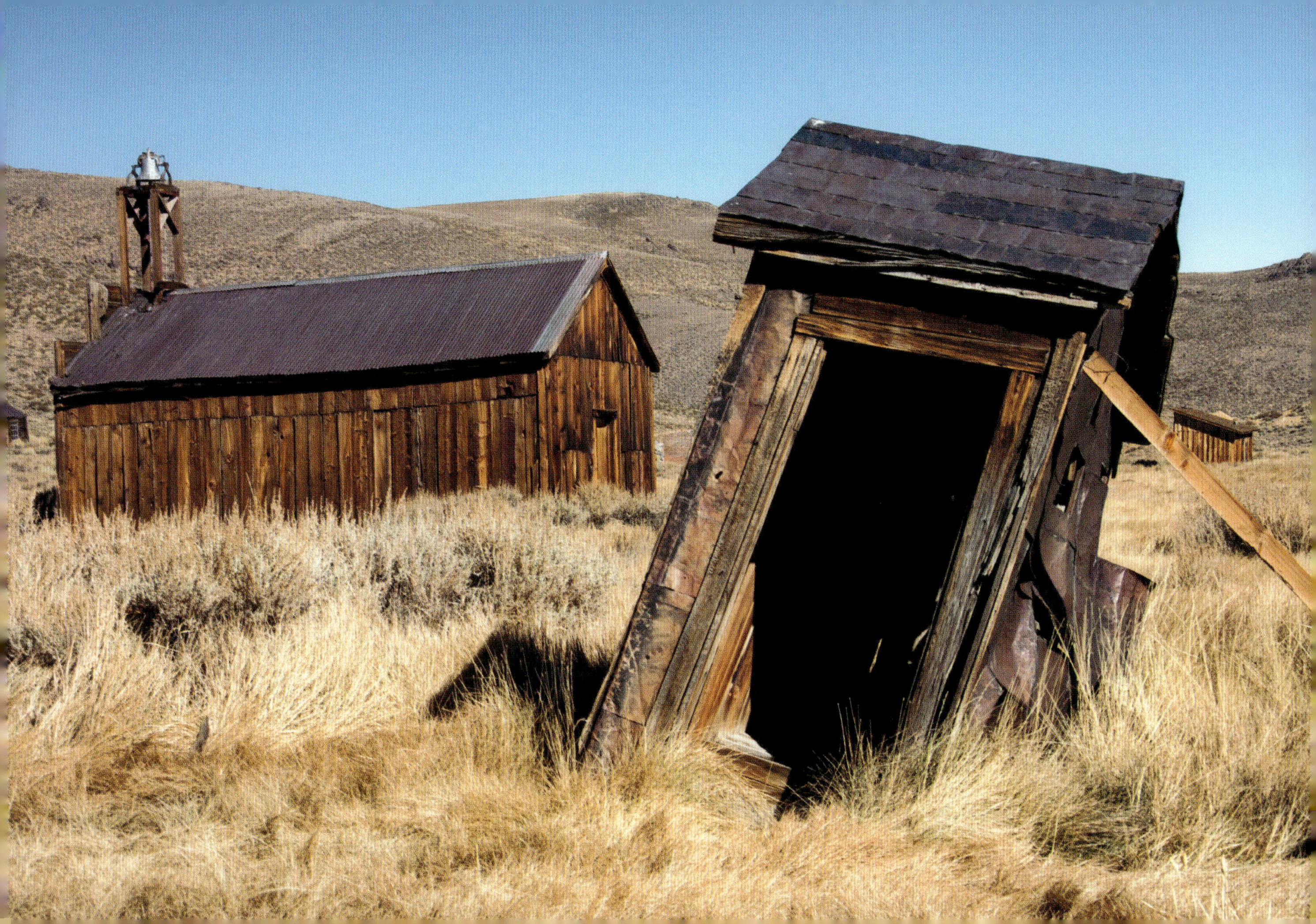

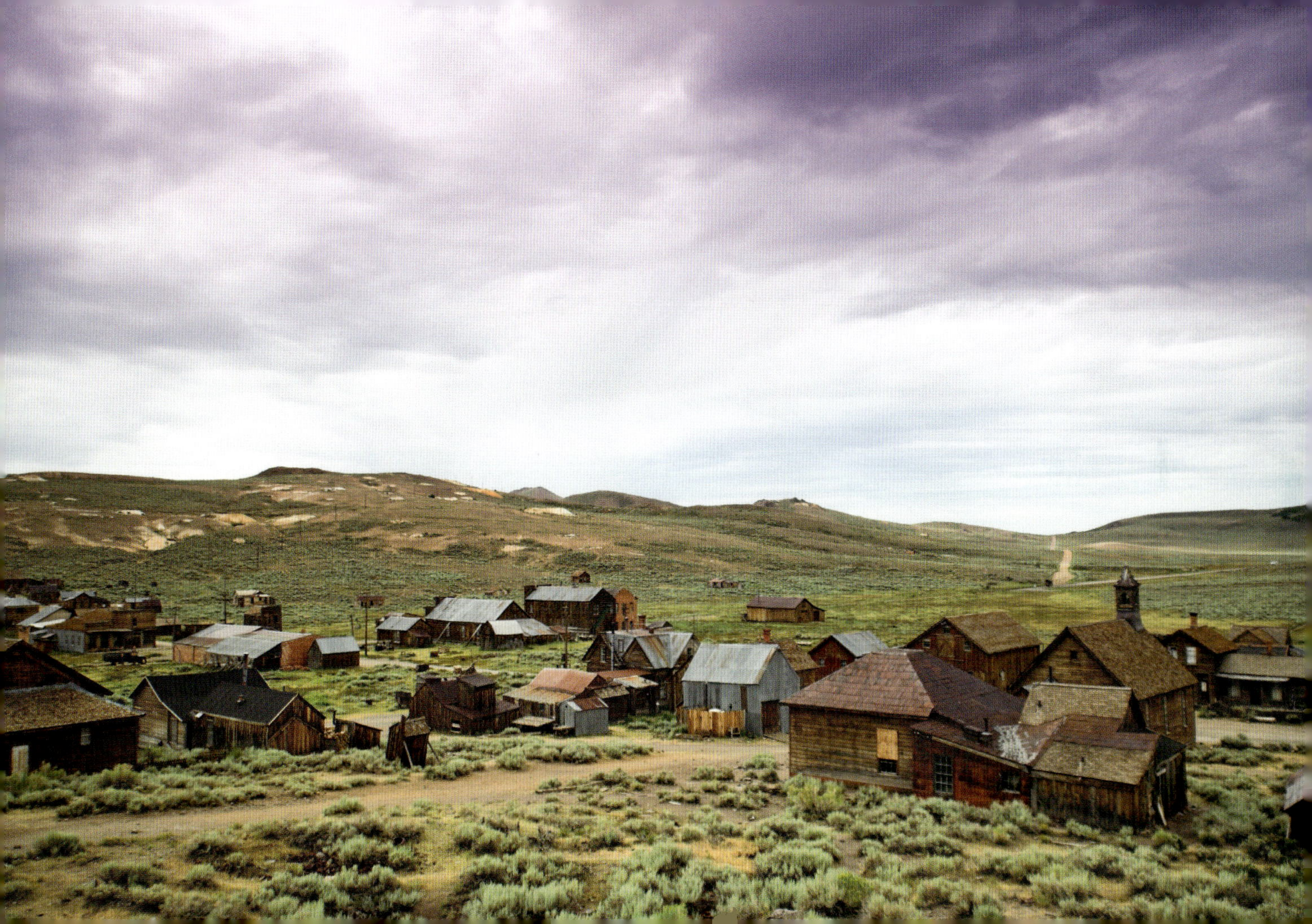

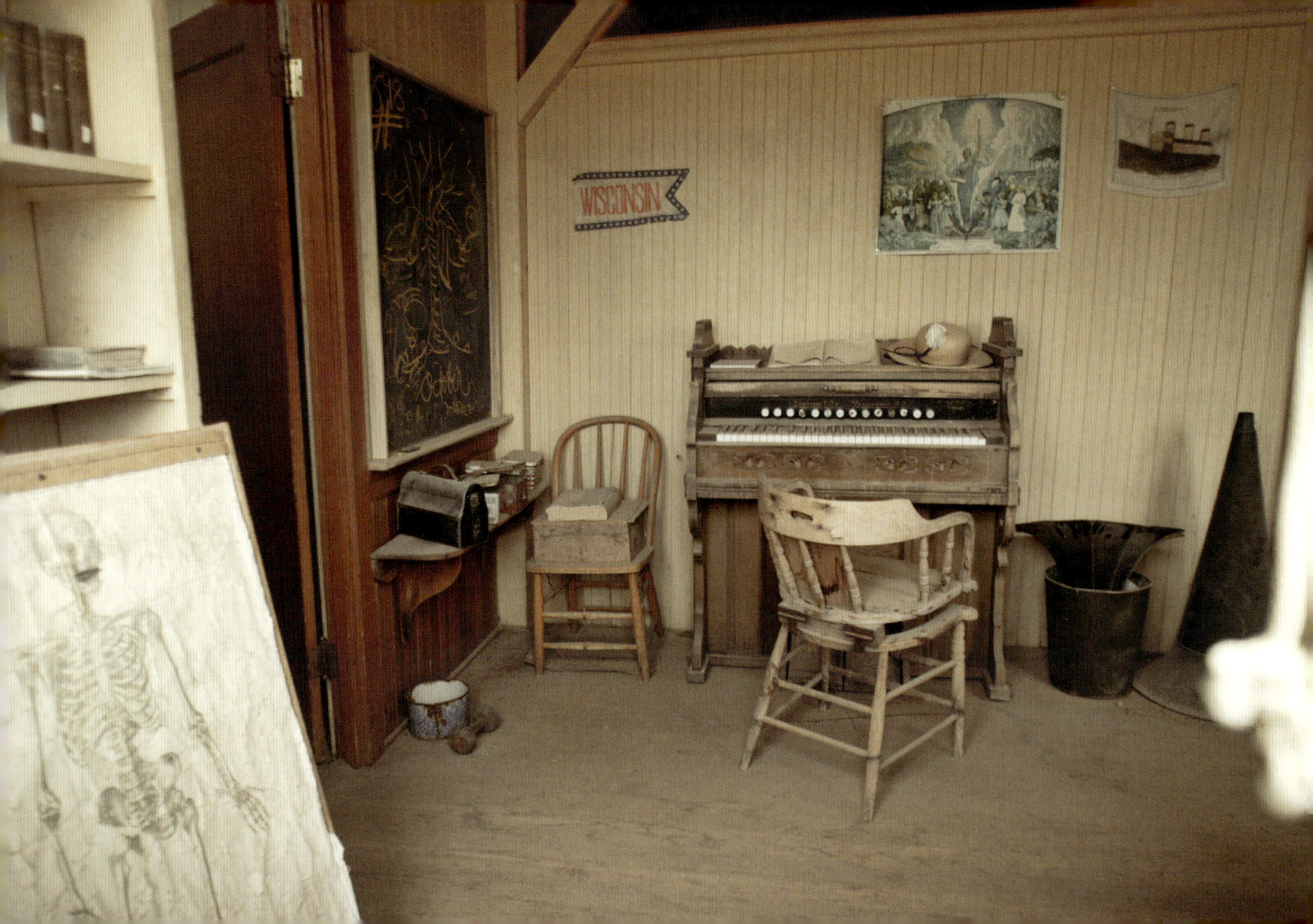
WISCONSIN

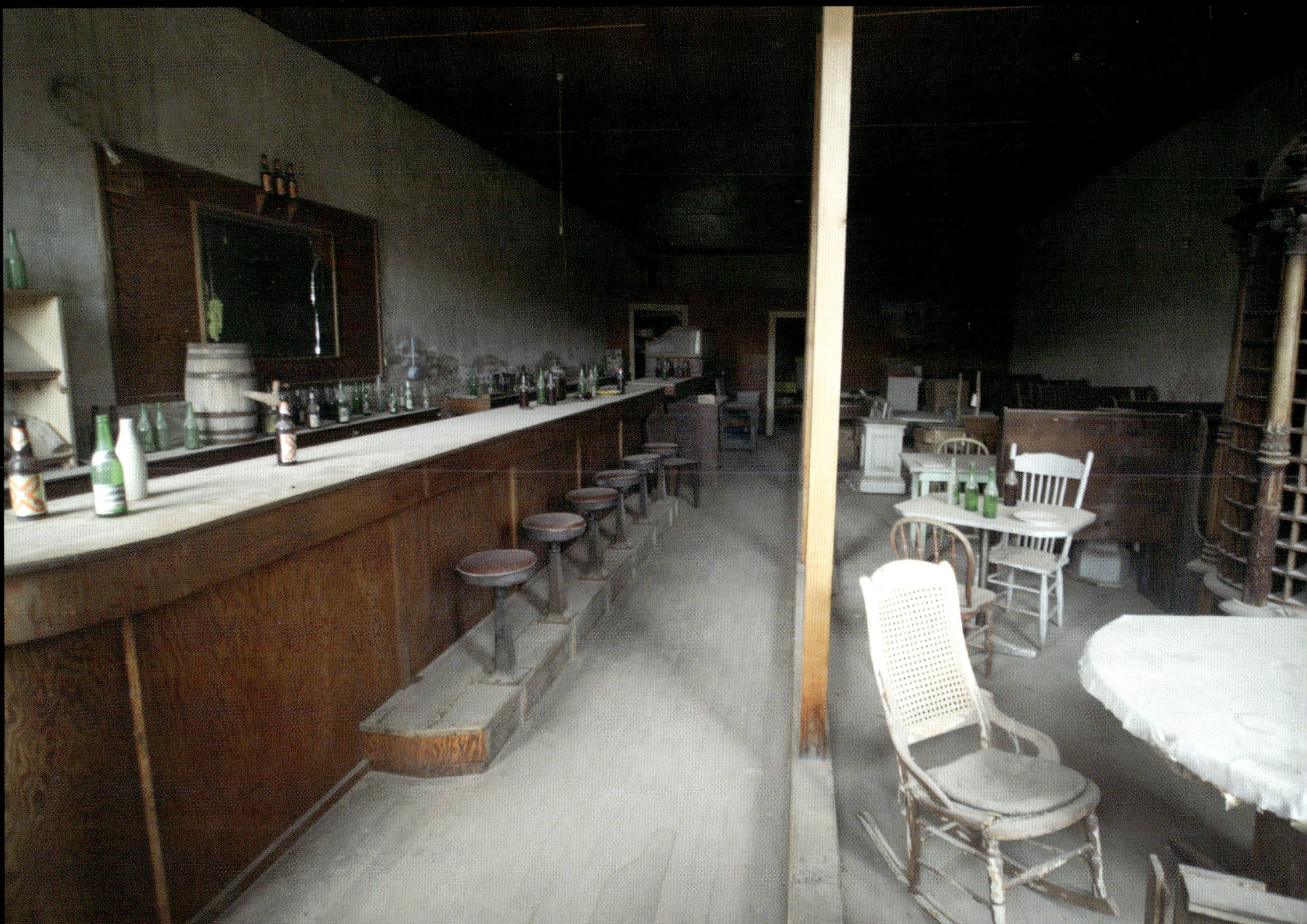

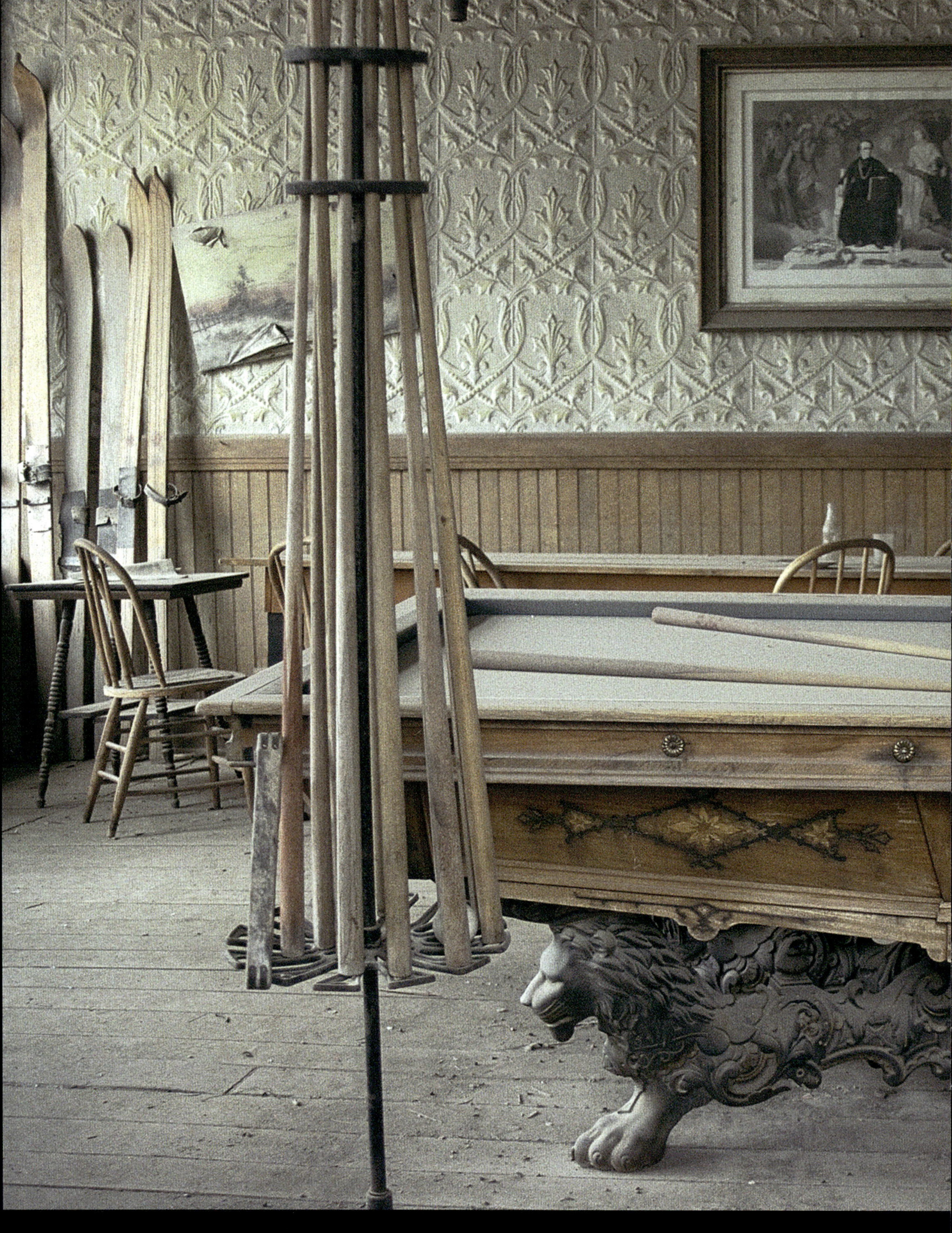

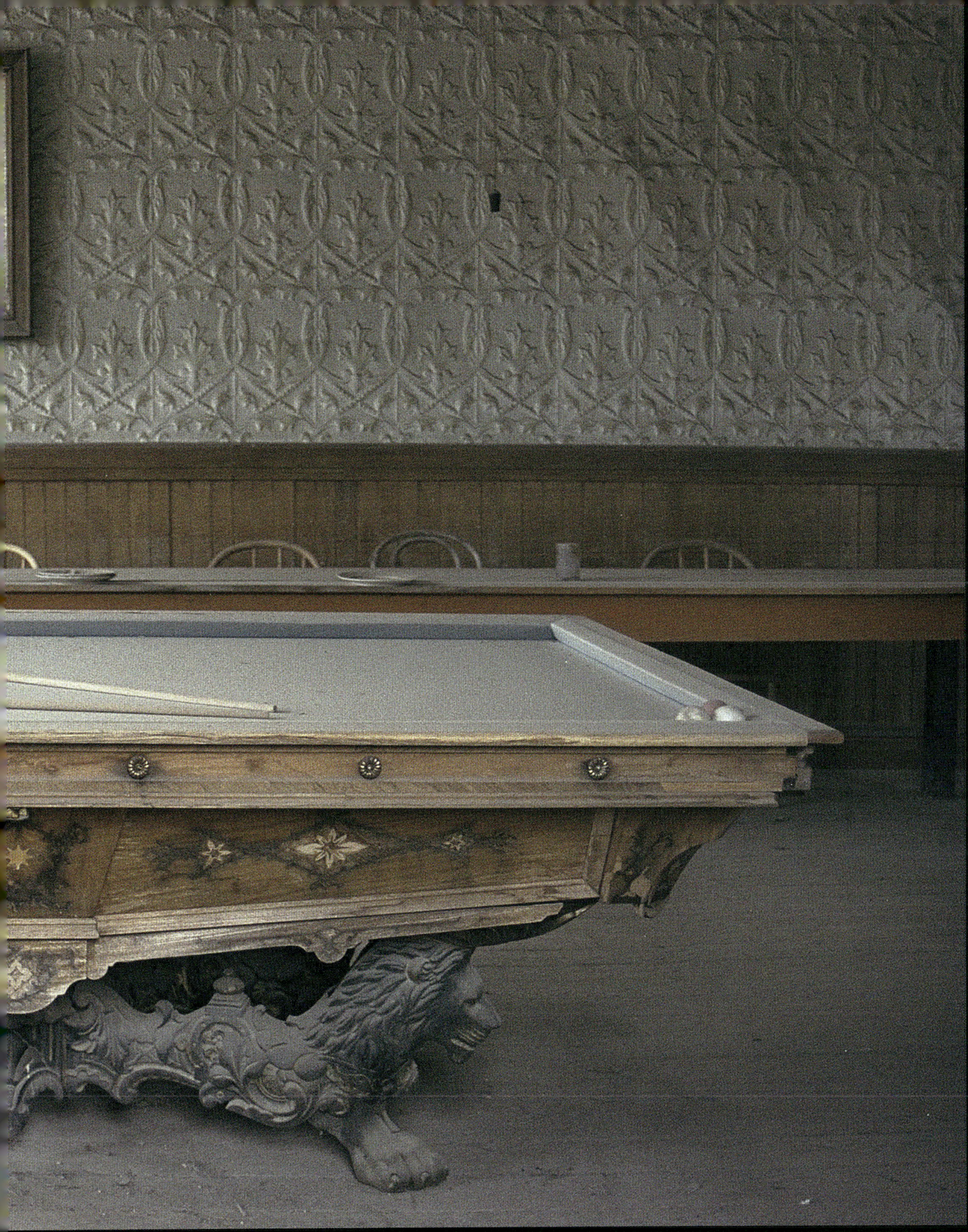

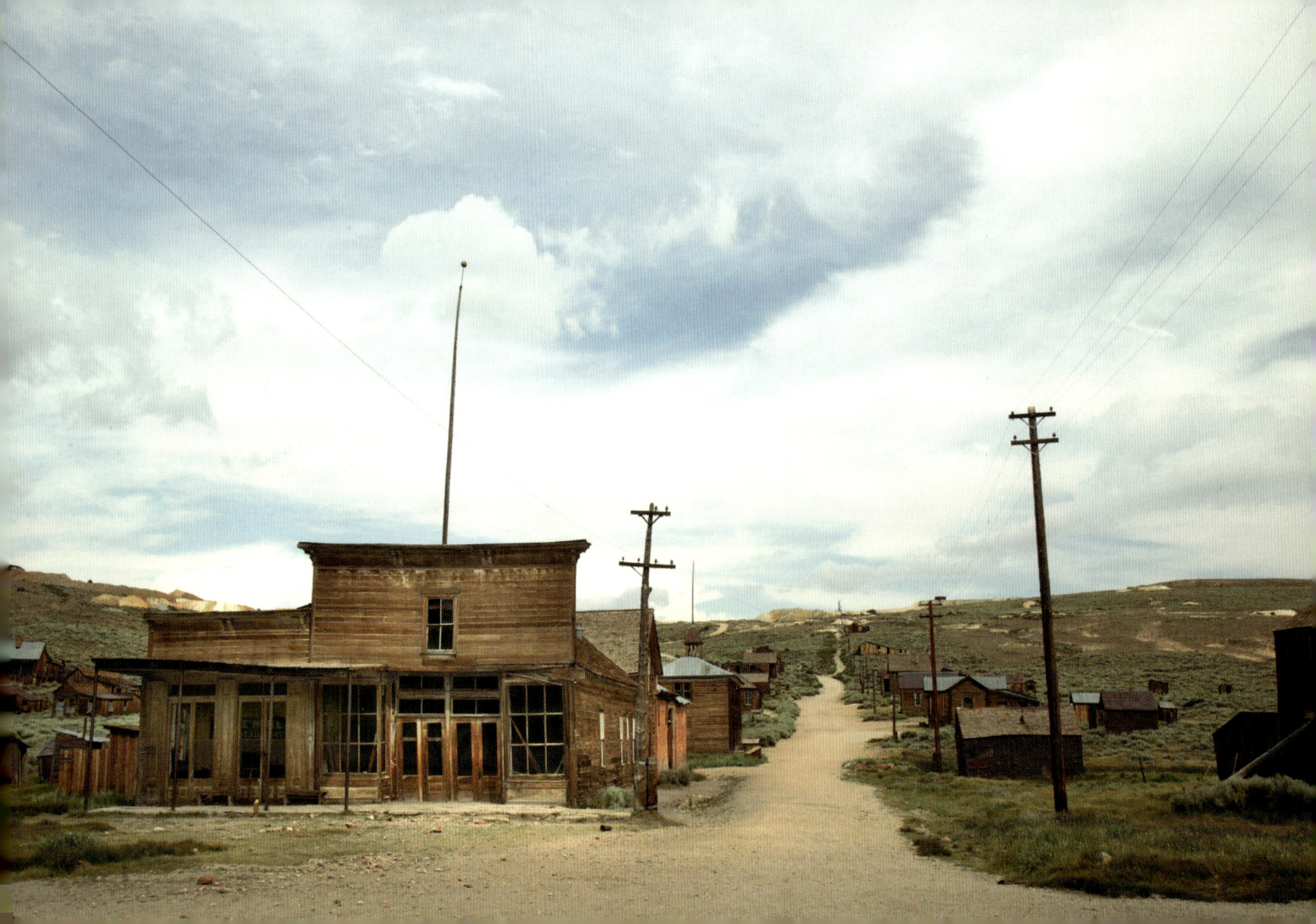

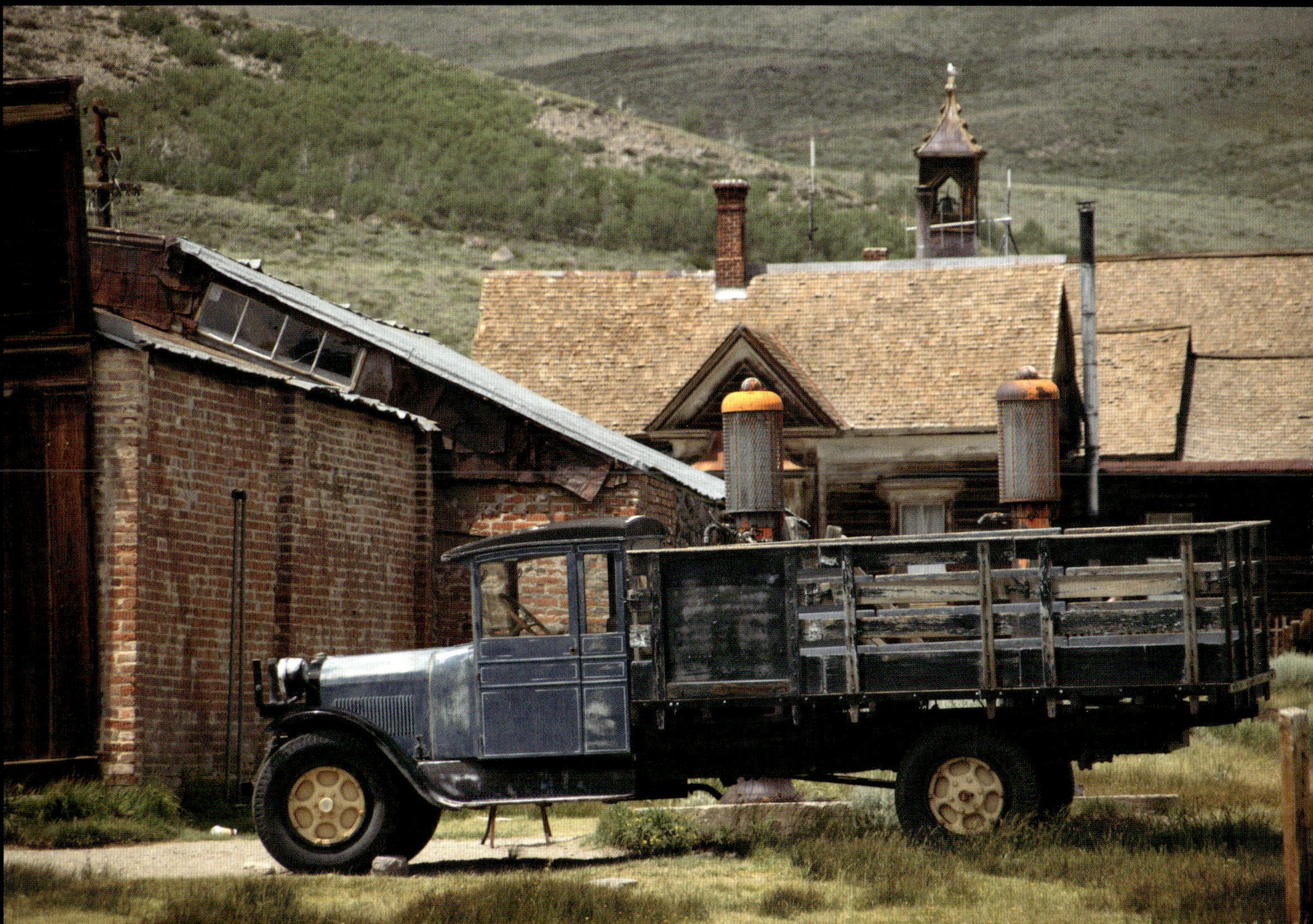

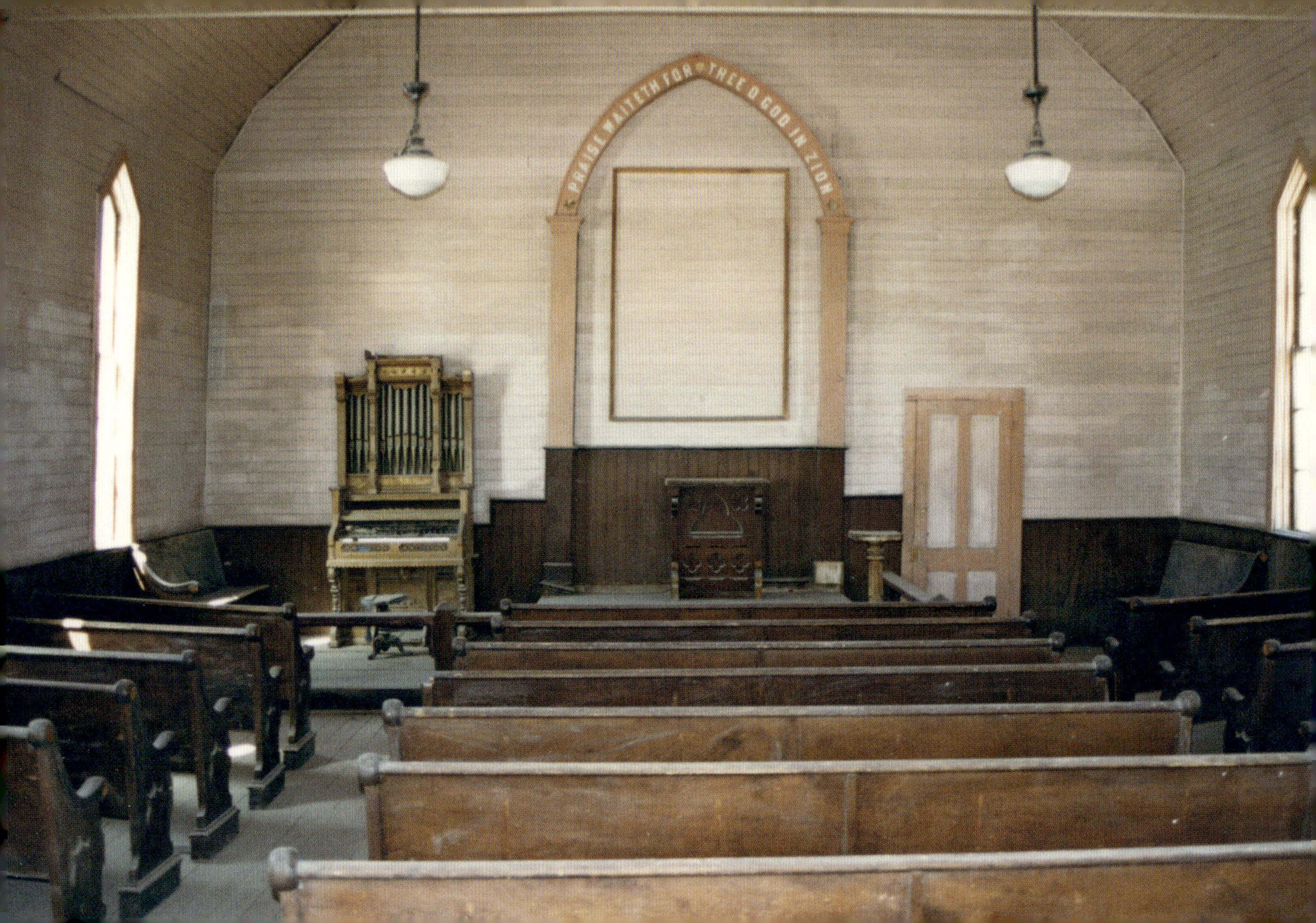
PRAISE WAITETH FOR THEE O GOD IN ZION

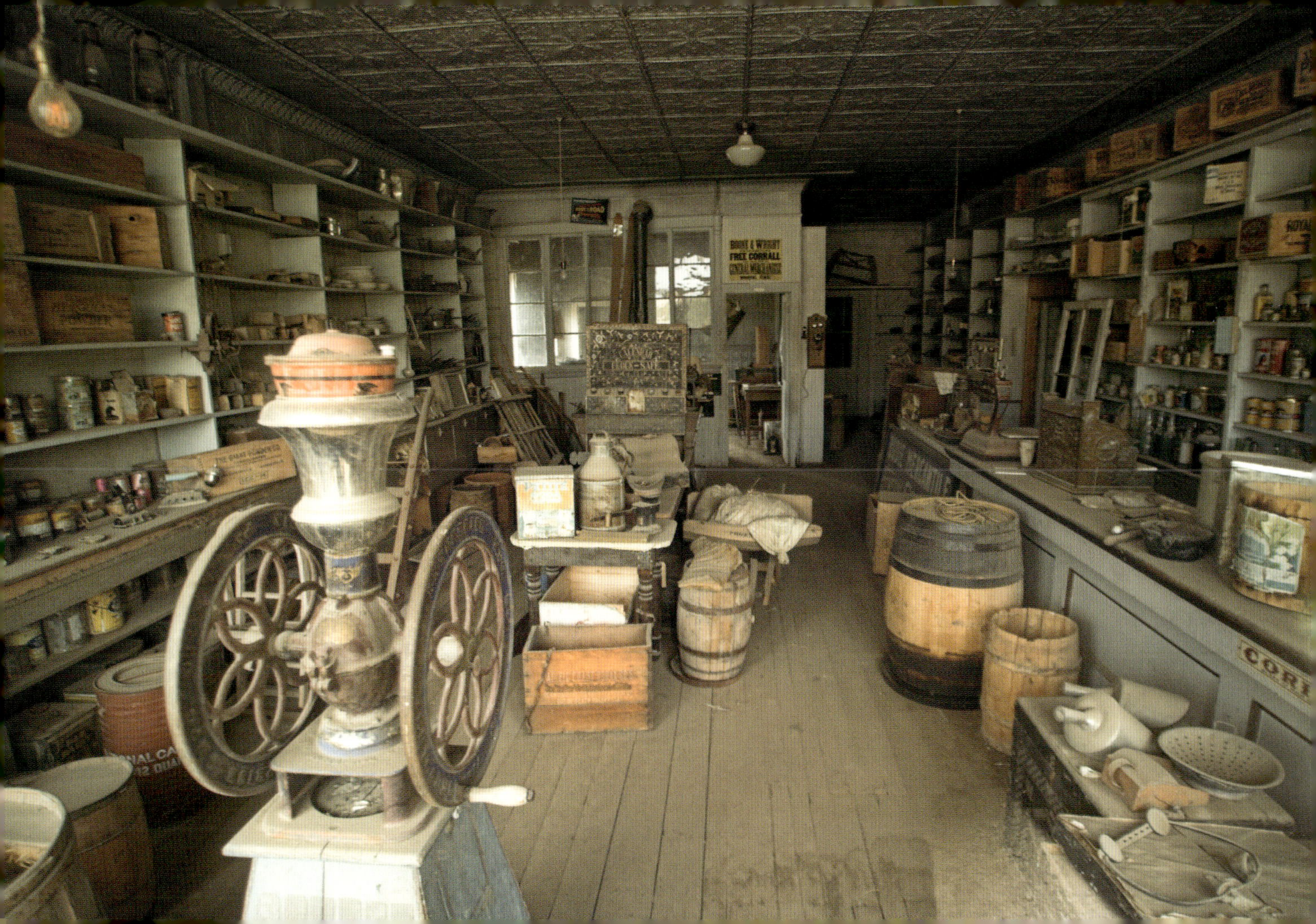
BOONE & WRIGHT
FREE CORRALL

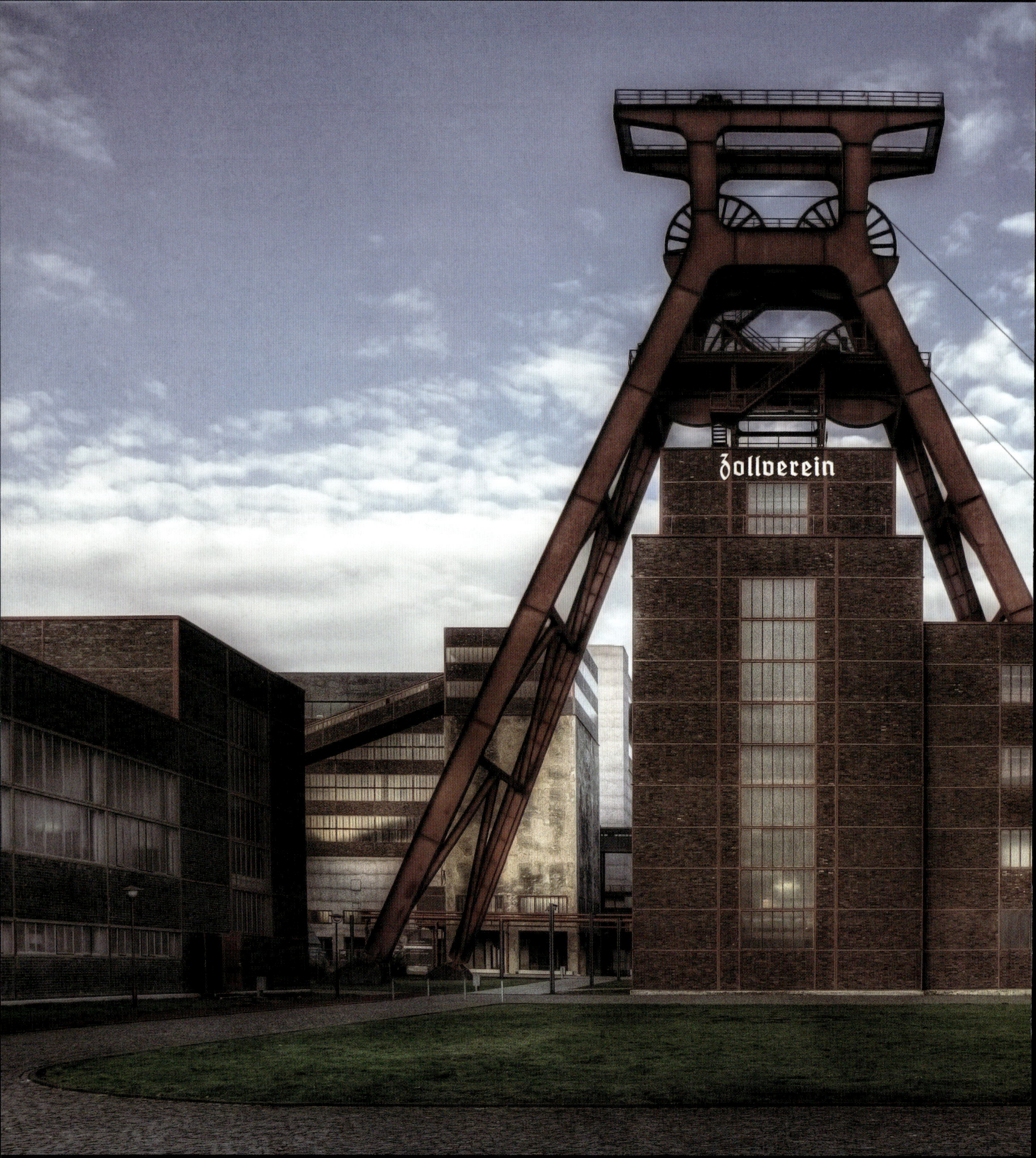
Zollverein

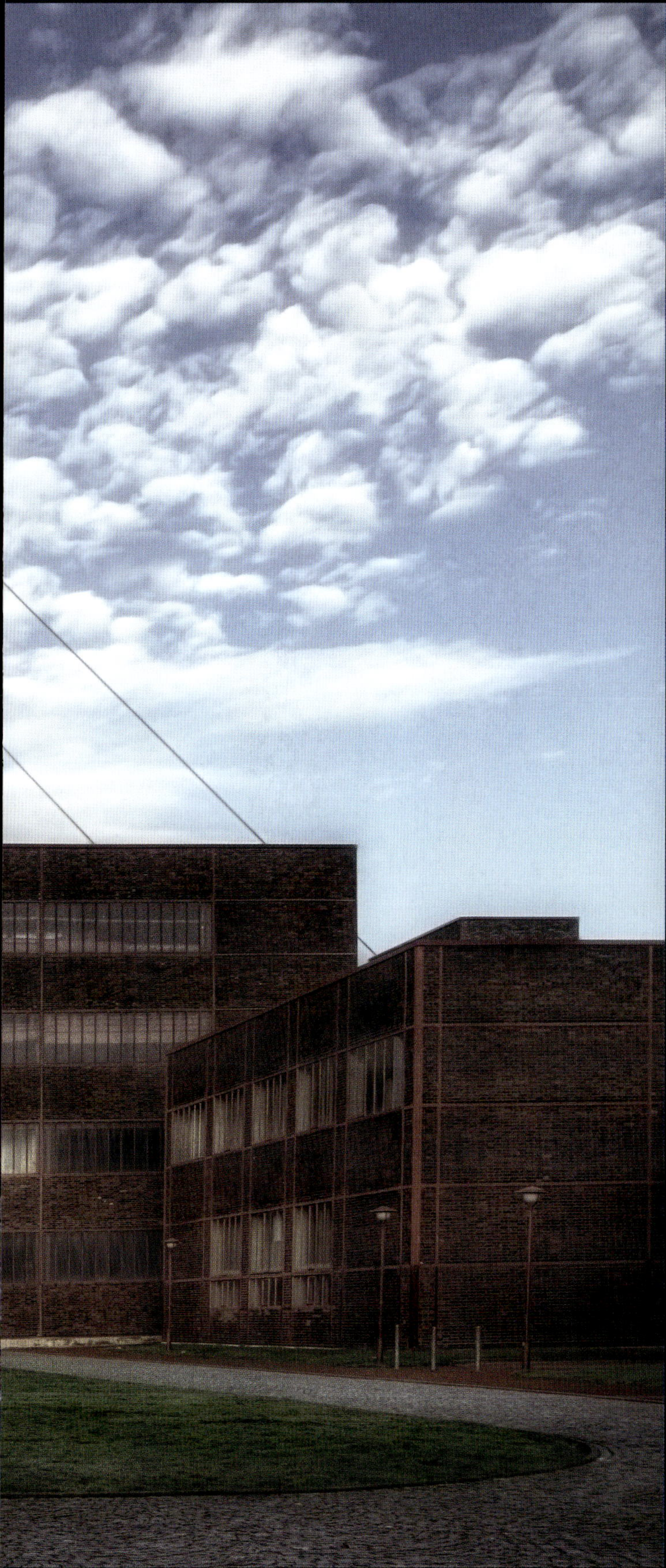

ZECHE ZOLLVER

DEUTSCHLAND GERMANY

FOTOS VON PHOTOS BY PETER UNTERMAIERHOFER

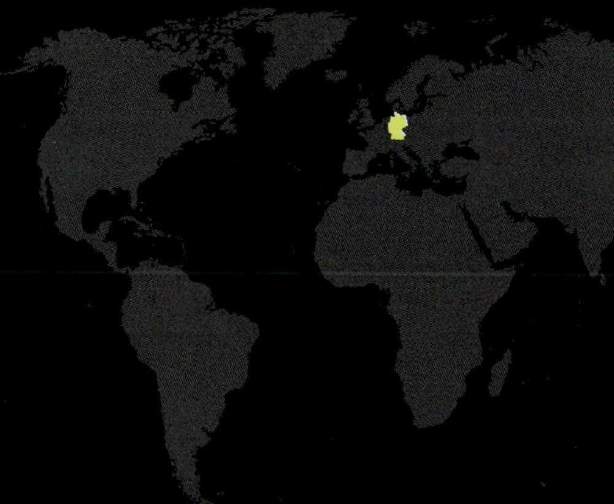

Die zu Beginn der Dreißigerjahre erweiterte Zeche Zollverein in Essen galt als eine der modernsten Anlagen der Welt. Man war damals überzeugt, dass sie die schönste im Revier sei und das auch bleiben würde. Die Ansprüche an Zweckgebundenheit und Form der Erbauer von Schacht XII, der Architekten Fritz Schupp und Martin Kremmer, bildeten zugleich die Grundlage für die enorme Produktivität des Bergwerkbetriebs. Beide teilten die Auffassungen des Bauhauses über Funktionalität und Sachlichkeit moderner Industriearchitektur. Das 1931 in der Nähe des Haupteingangs Gelsenkirchener Straße erbaute Doppelbock-Fördergerüst wurde lange Zeit als gelungenes Beispiel für den Bau späterer Fördereinrichtungen angesehen. Es war aber weit mehr als nur ein stählerner Werkturm. Die Konstruktion glich einem an den Blickhorizont gesetzten, riesigen Signet. Über den Backsteinwänden und den im Sonnenlicht aufblitzenden Glasflächen der Schachtanlage stand es wie ein Herkunftszeichen, dessen herber Reiz vom Leben der Region Zeugnis gab.

Als das im Gebiet von Katernberg entdeckte Steinkohleflöz nach dem 1833 ins Leben gerufenen Deutschen Zollverein benannt wurde, war das der Entstehungsmoment für die gleichnamige Zeche. Der Unternehmer Franz Haniel gründete sie als „bergrechtliche Gewerkschaft“ im Jahr 1847. Er war Teilhaber der Hüttengewerkschaft und Handlung Jacobi, Haniel und Huyssen, der späteren Gutehoffnungshütte (Aktienverein für Bergbau und Hüttenbetrieb in Oberhausen), und beabsichtigte, das neue Bergwerk mit der Eisenhütte und der Maschinenfabrik in Sterkrade zusammenzuschließen. Allerdings stimmten die Miteigentümer seinem Plan nicht zu, sonst wäre die erste Hüttenzeche des Ruhrgebiets entstanden. Haniel ließ 1851 im 130 Meter tiefen Schacht I mit dem Steinkohlenabbau beginnen. Im Jahr darauf nahm Schacht II den Betrieb auf. Eine leistungsfähigere Kokerei ersetzte 1866 mehrere Meileröfen, die seit 1857 Koks erzeugten. Noch vor der Jahrhundertwende erreichte die Zeche Zollverein mit über einer Million Tonnen Kohle die höchste Jahresproduktion im Deutschen Kaiserreich. Kontinuierlich wuchs das Bergbauunternehmen weiter. Erst in den Zwanzigerjahren gab die Familie Haniel die Geschäftsführung aus den Händen.

Im Jahr 1928 wurde beschlossen, den Schacht XII zu bauen, der mit einer Tageskapazität von 12.000 Tonnen die Fördermenge der elf älteren Schächte übernehmen konnte. Bis 1937 stieg die Steinkohlenförderung auf 3,6 Millionen Tonnen im Jahr an und die 54 Öfen der damaligen Kokerei stellten zur selben Zeit etwa 200.000 Tonnen Koks her. Die von Architekt Fritz Schupp entworfene Zentralkokerei übernahm 1961 die Kohleveredlung. In den Siebzigerjahren auf 304 Öfen erweitert, verwandelte sie jeden Tag 10.000 Tonnen Steinkohle in 8.600 Tonnen Koks. Mit der Umstellung auf Erdöl begann auch in Deutschland der Niedergang der einheimischen Kohleindustrie. Die Bergleute kämpften für den Erhalt ihrer Zeche, konnten die Stilllegung im Dezember 1986 aber nicht verhindern.

Im Juni 1993 wurde die Kokerei geschlossen. Das Land Nordrhein-Westfalen erwarb vom letzten Eigentümer, der Ruhrkohle AG, das Gelände des Zollvereins und stellte es unter Denkmalschutz. Mit der Sanierung begann eine langjährige Metamorphose, die von besonderem Erfolg gekrönt war. Man nahm im Dezember 2001 die Zeche und die Kokerei in die Liste des Kultur- und Naturerbes der Welt auf. Beide sind heute Teil eines für seine Kunst- und Kulturveranstaltungen viel besuchten Erlebnisraums mitten im Ruhrgebiet.

The Zollverein Coal Mine Industrial Complex in Essen, which was expanded at the beginning of the thirties, was considered to be one of the most modern facilities in the world. People were convinced at that time that it was the most beautiful one in the district and that it would stay that way. The demands by the architects Fritz Schupp and Martin Kremmer on the specific purpose and design of Shaft XII, were also the foundation for the enormous productivity of the mining operation. The two of them shared views on the Bauhaus style with the functionality and objectivity of modern industrial architecture. The Doppelbock winding tower built in 1930 near the main entrance of Gelsenkirchener Straße became a successful model for the construction of subsequent mining facilities. It was significantly more than simply a steel framework tower. The structure was like a giant sign placed on the horizon. It stood like a mark of origin above the brick walls and glass surfaces of the mine sparkling in the sunlight, witnessing about the austere charm of life in the region.

When a hard coal seam that was discovered in the Katernberg region was named after the German Zollverein, it was the beginning of the coal mine of the same name. The entrepreneur Franz Haniel founded it in 1847 as a "bergrechtliche Gewerkschaft" (trade union under mining law). He was part owner of "Hüttengewerkschaft und Handlung Jacobi, Haniel und Huyssen", which later became the Gutehoffnungshütte ironworks (Aktienverein für Bergbau und Hüttenbetrieb in Oberhausen). He intended to merge the new mine with the ironworks and machine works in Sterkrade. However the co-owners did not agree with his plan, otherwise the first ironworks/coal mine of the Ruhr area would have been built. Haniel started mining hard coal in 1851 in the 130 meter deep shaft in. Shaft II began operation the following year. A higher performance coking plant replaced many charcoal burning furnaces in 1866 that had produced coke since 1857. Before the turn of the century, the Zollverein coal mine reached more than one million tons of coal, the highest annual production in the German empire. The mining company grew continuously and the Haniel family only gave up managing the business in the 1920s.

In 1928, it was decided to build Shaft XII, which had a daily capacity of 12,000 tons combining the output of the eleven older shafts. By 1937, hard coal output increased to 3.6 million tons per year and the 54 furnaces of the coking plant at that time produced about 200,000 tons of coke at the same time. The central coking plant designed by the architect Fritz Schupp took over coal refinement in 1961. In the 1970s, it expanded to 304 furnaces, converting 10,000 tons of hard coal into 8,600 tons of coke every day. The changeover to oil also marked the decline of the local coal industry in Germany. The miners fought to keep their coal mine but could not prevent its shutdown in December 1986. The coking plant closed in 1993. The state of North Rhine Westphalia bought the premises of the Zollverein from the last owner, Ruhrkohle AG, and put it under monumental protection. Many years of metamorphosis began with the rehabilitation, which was crowned with a great deal of success. In December 2001, the coal mine and coking plant were placed on the list of world cultural and heritage sites. Today, both of them are part of a highly frequented area because of its art and cultural events in the middle of the Ruhr district.

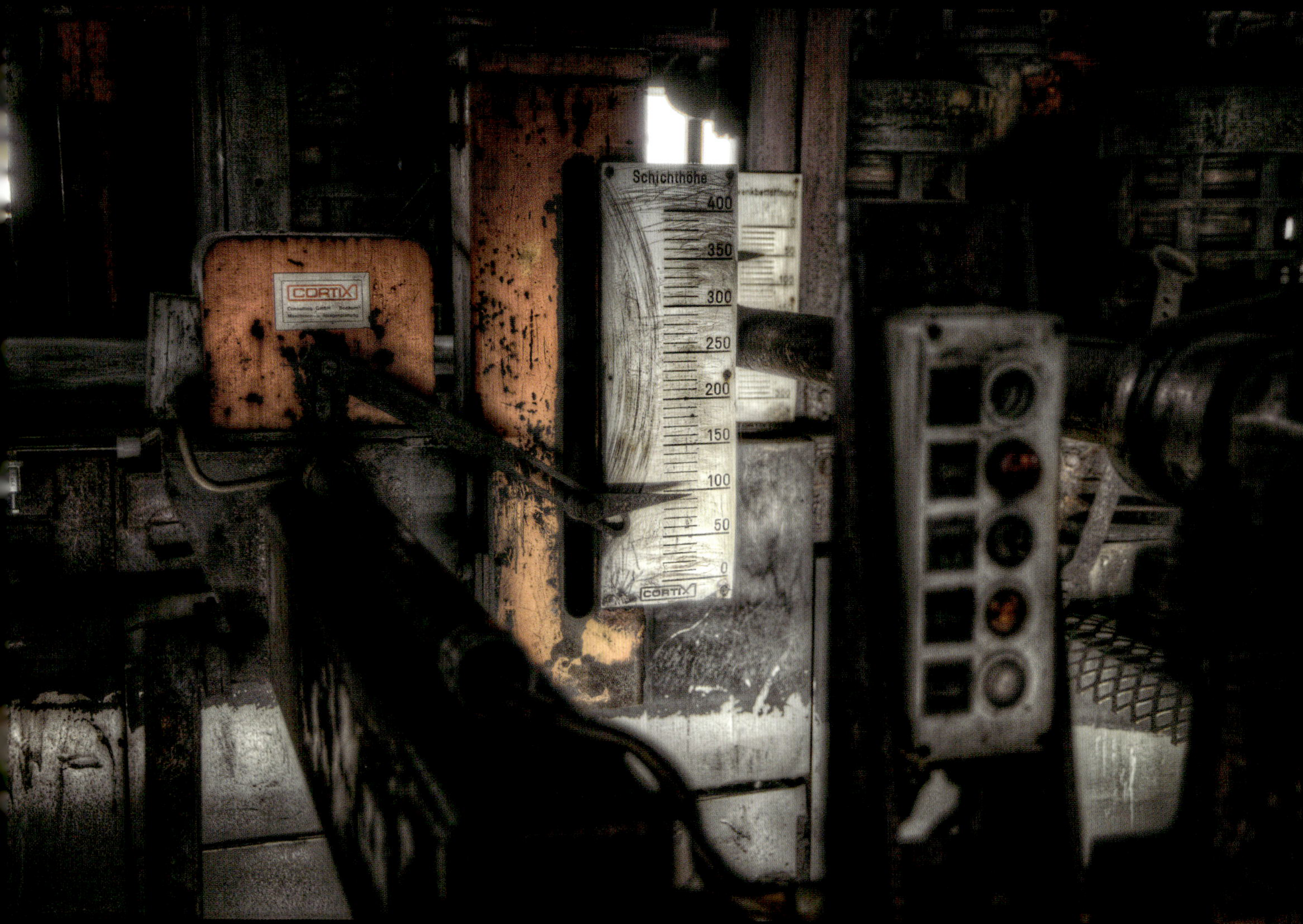
CORTIX
Schichthöhe
400
350
300
250
200
150
100
50
0
CORTIX

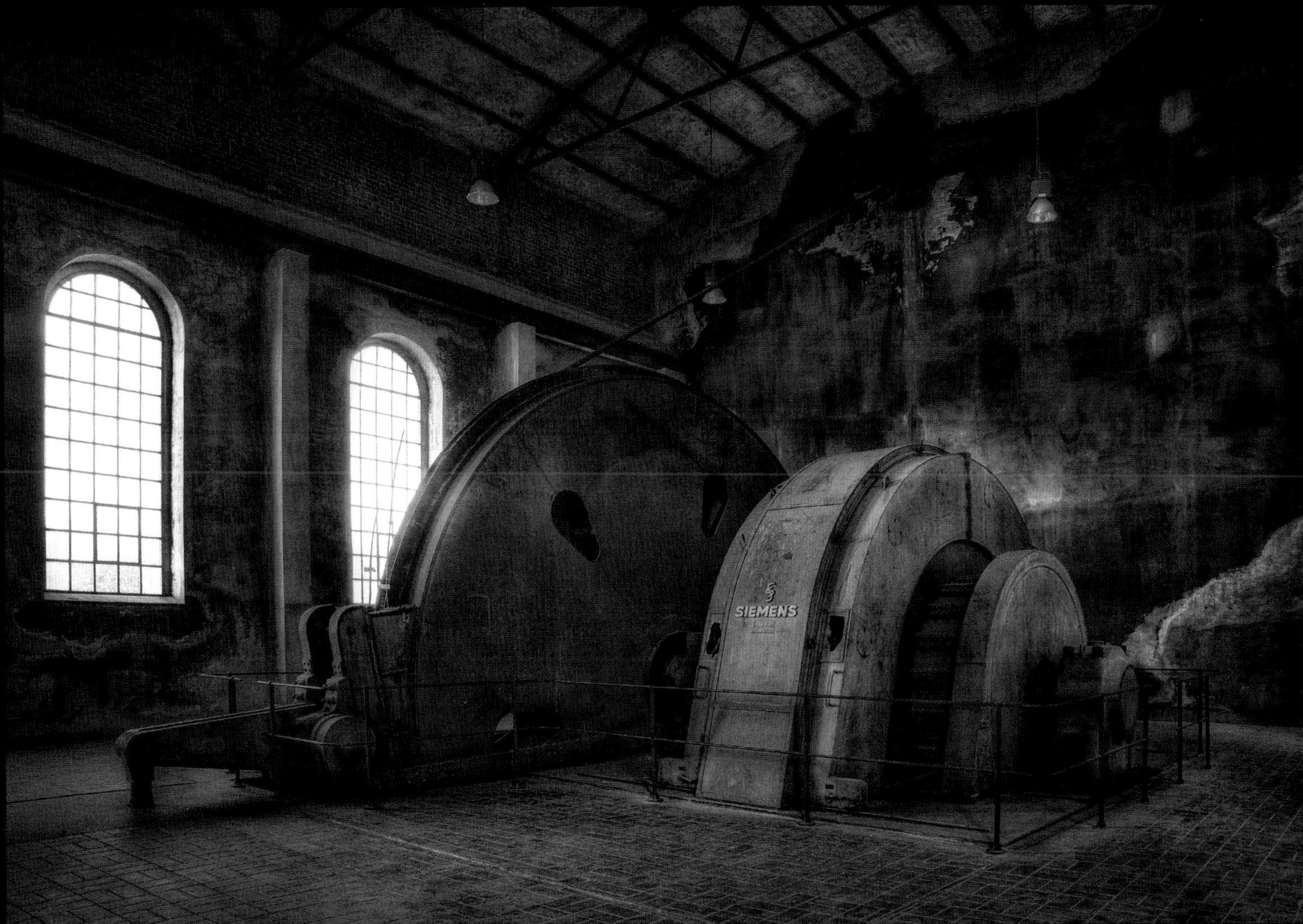
SIEMENS

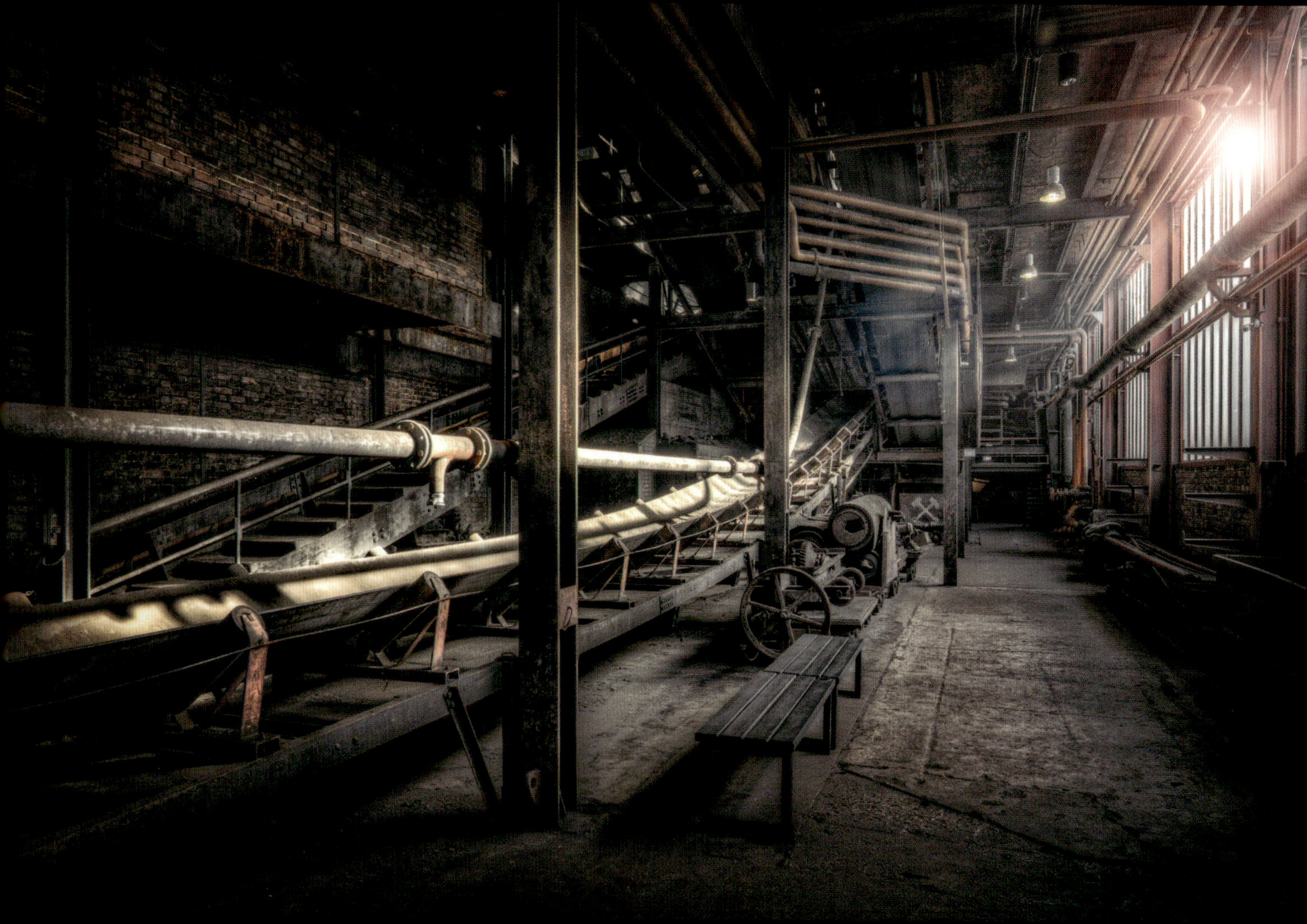

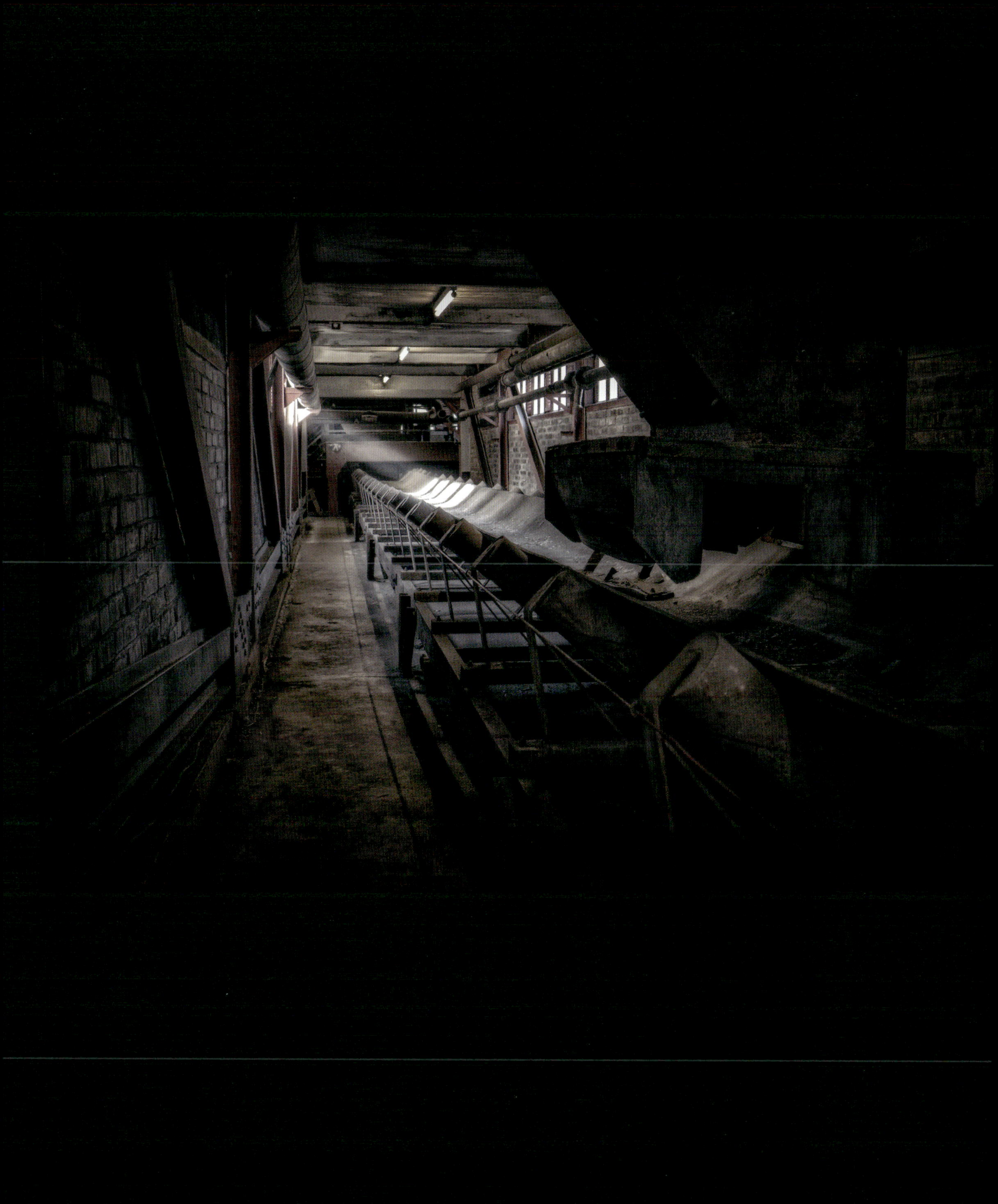

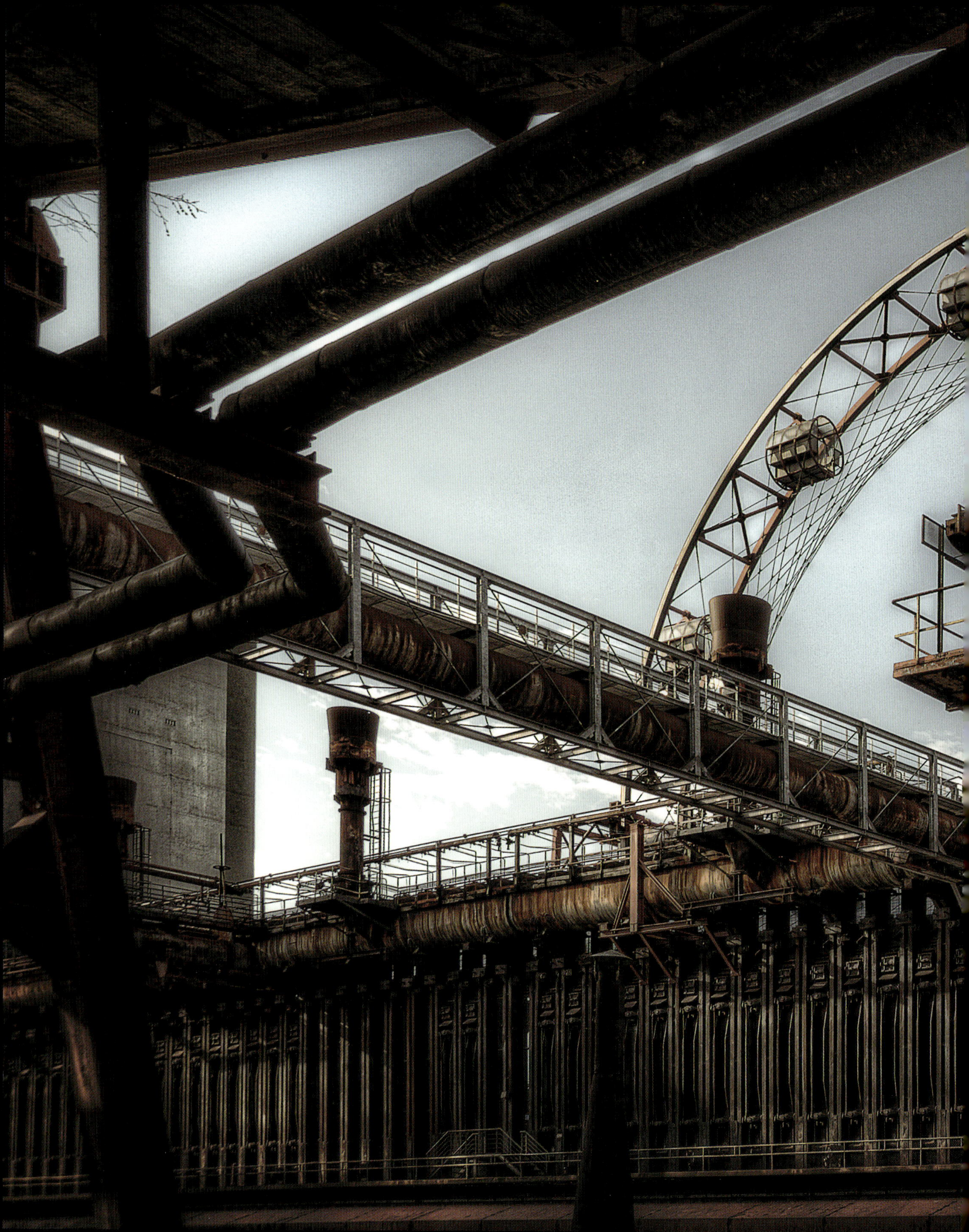

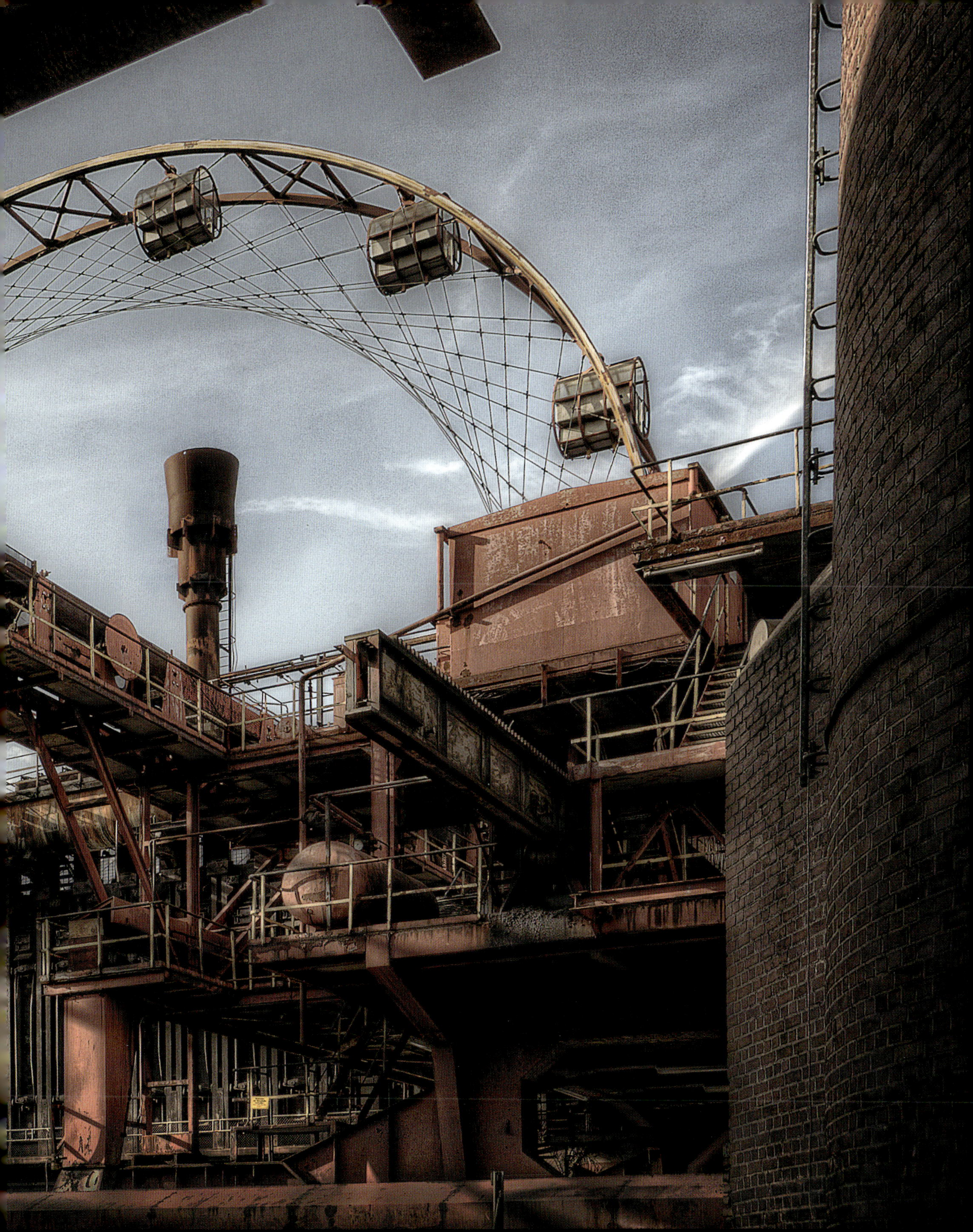

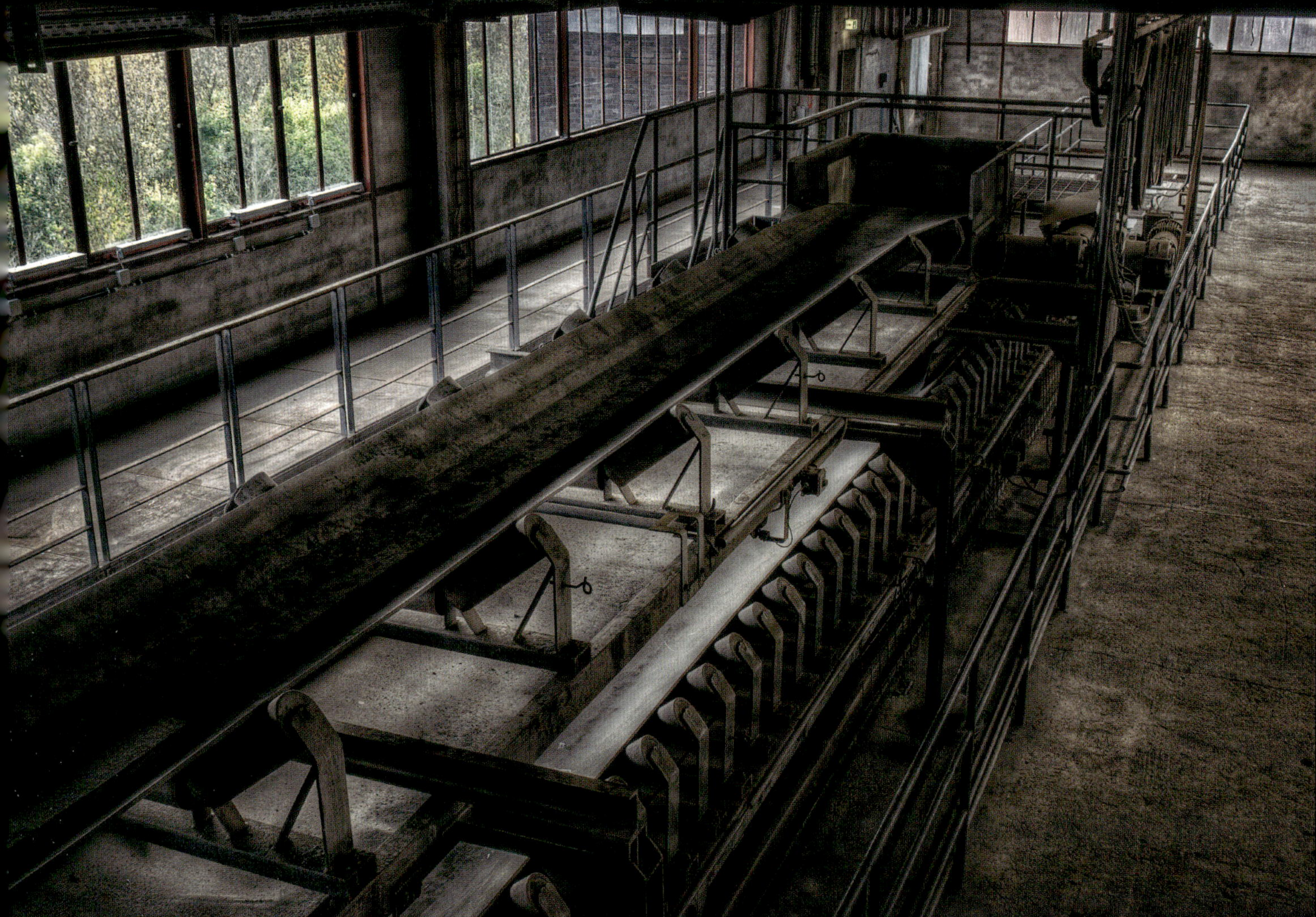

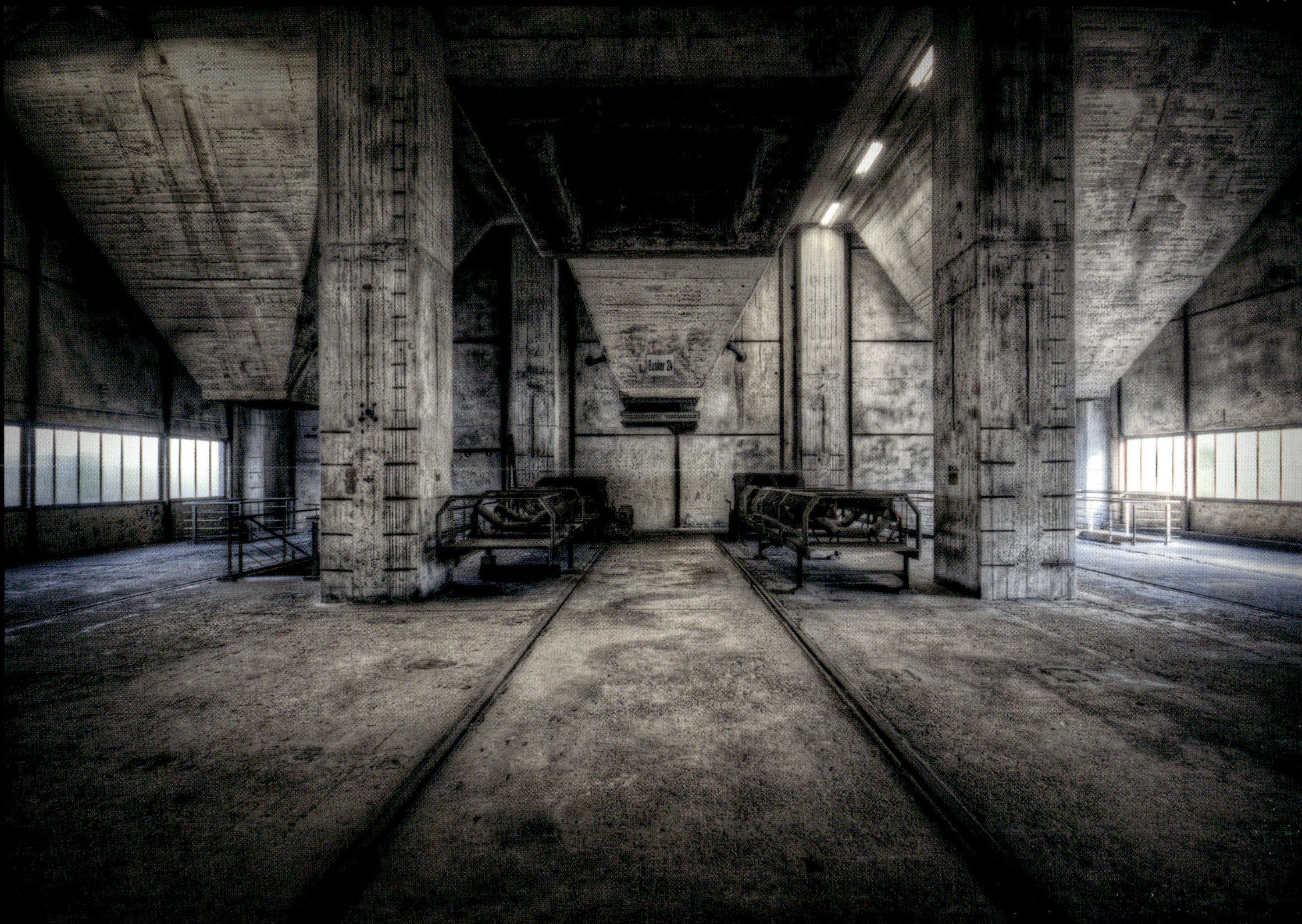
Bunker 24

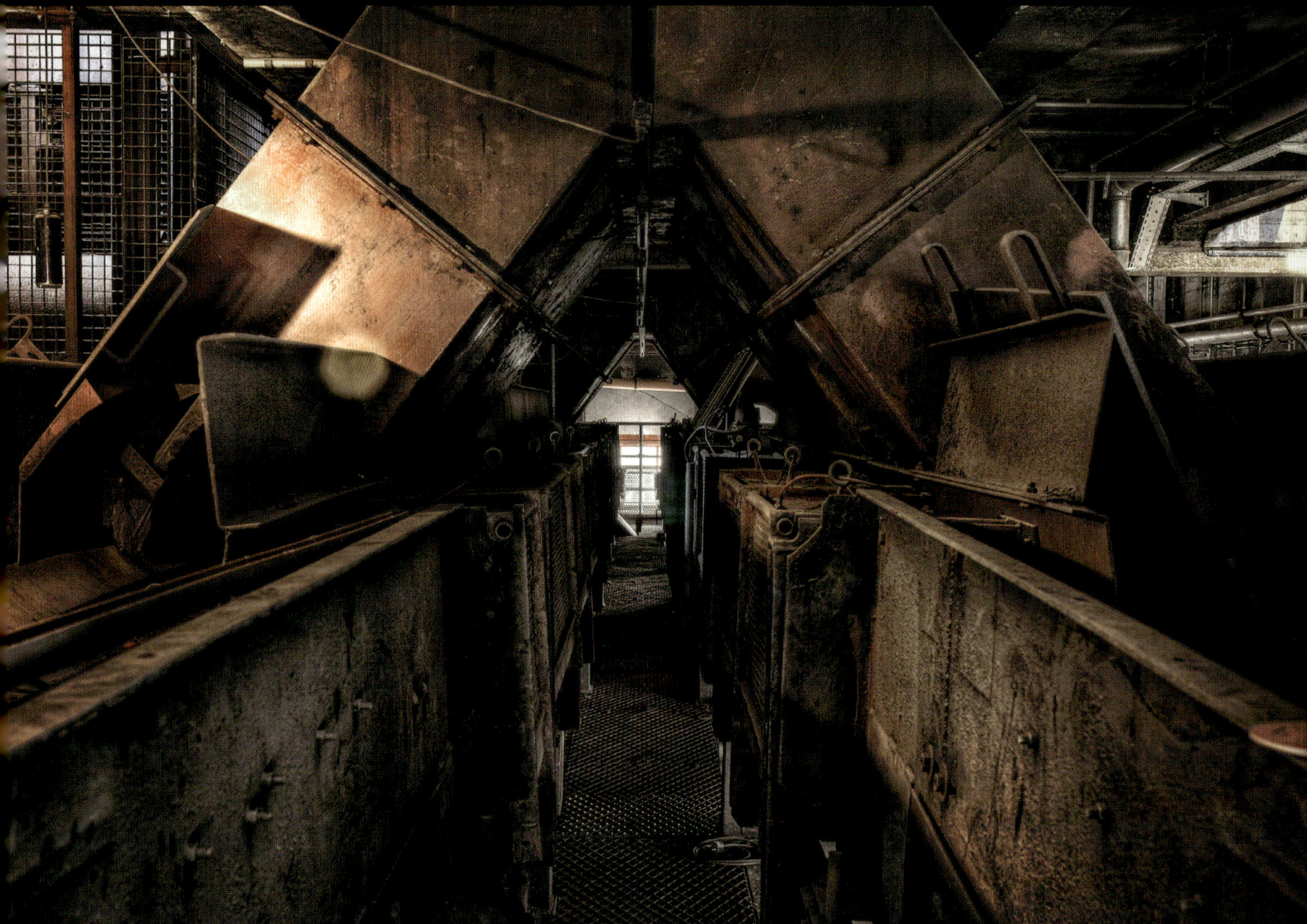

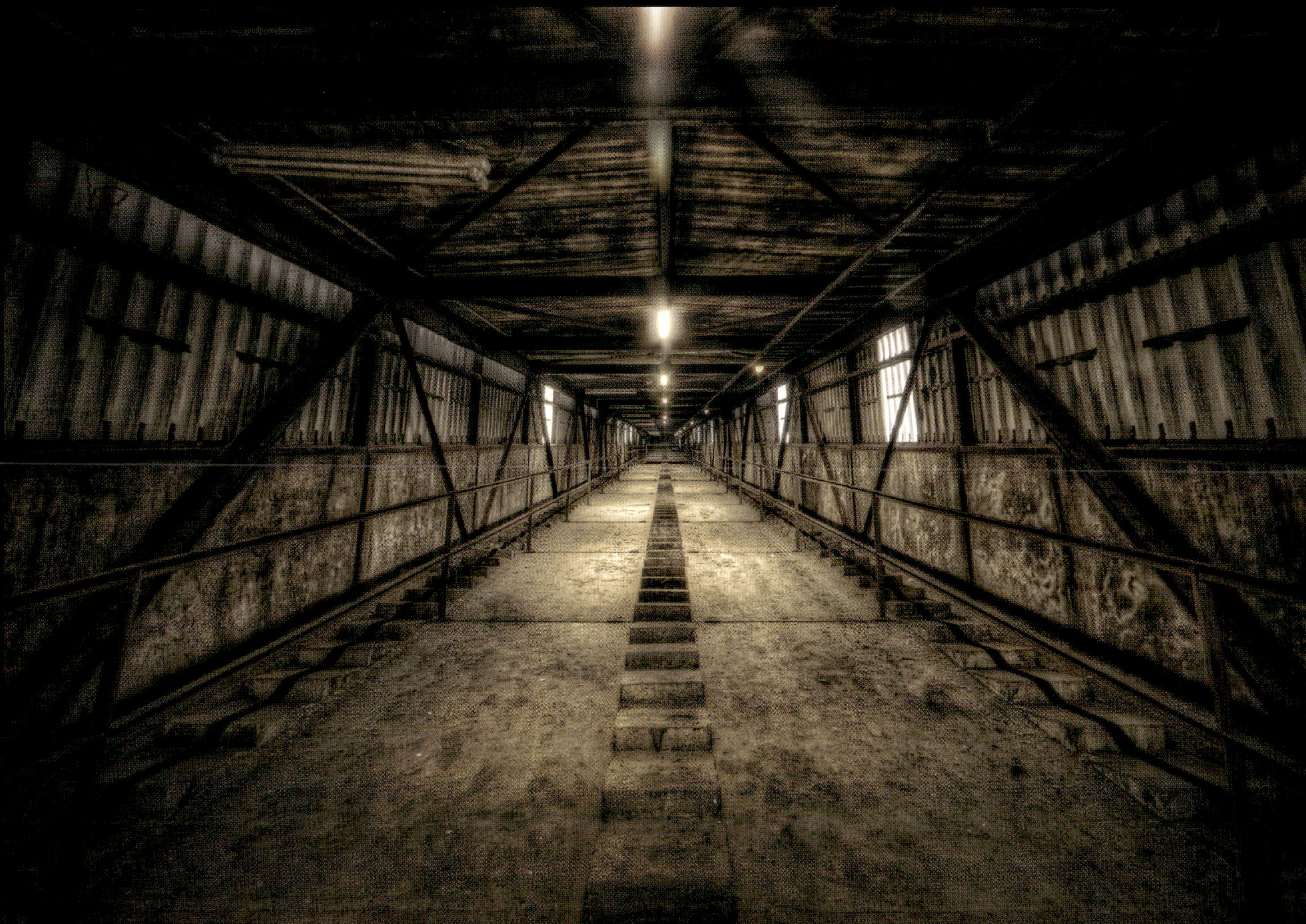

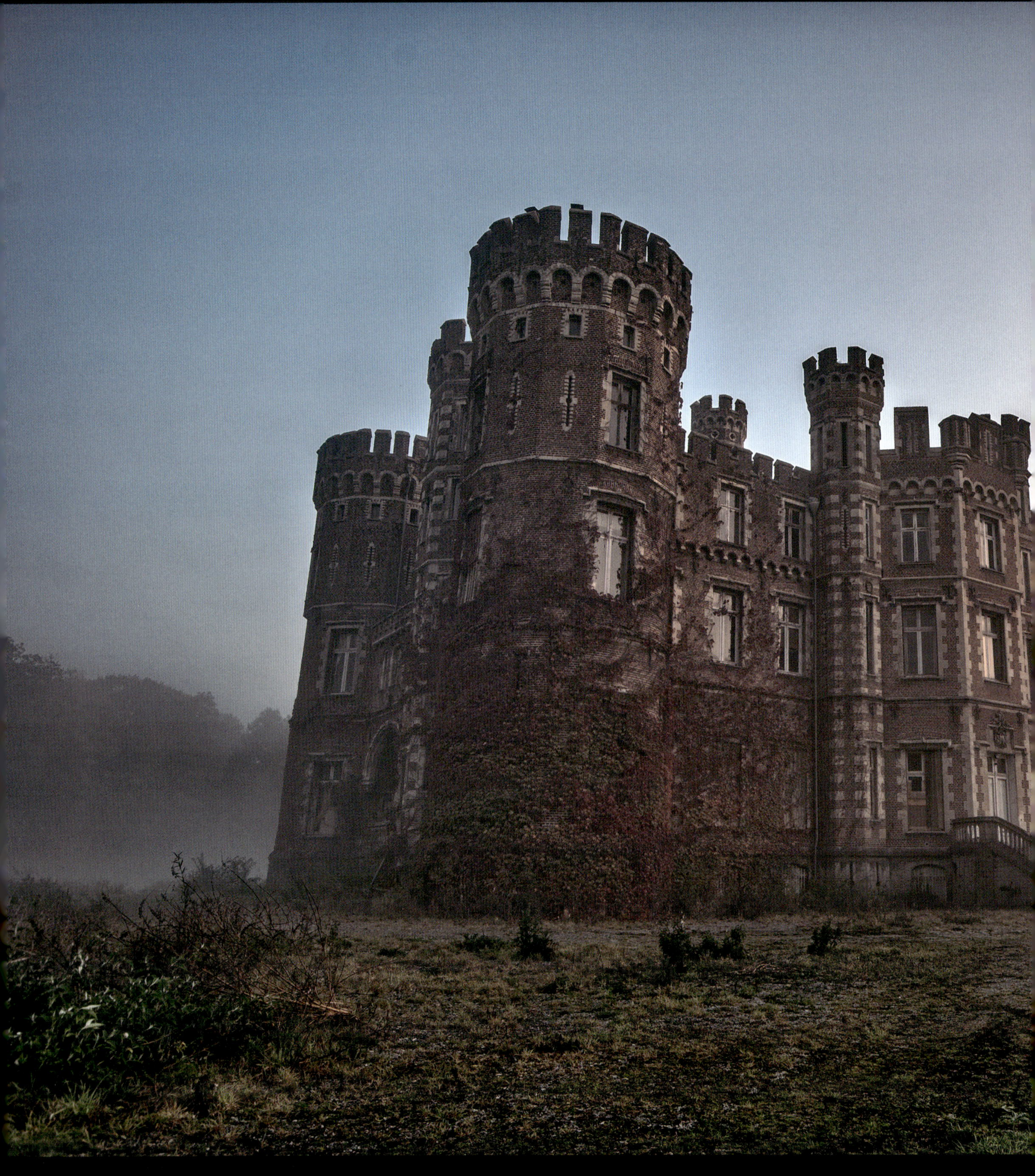

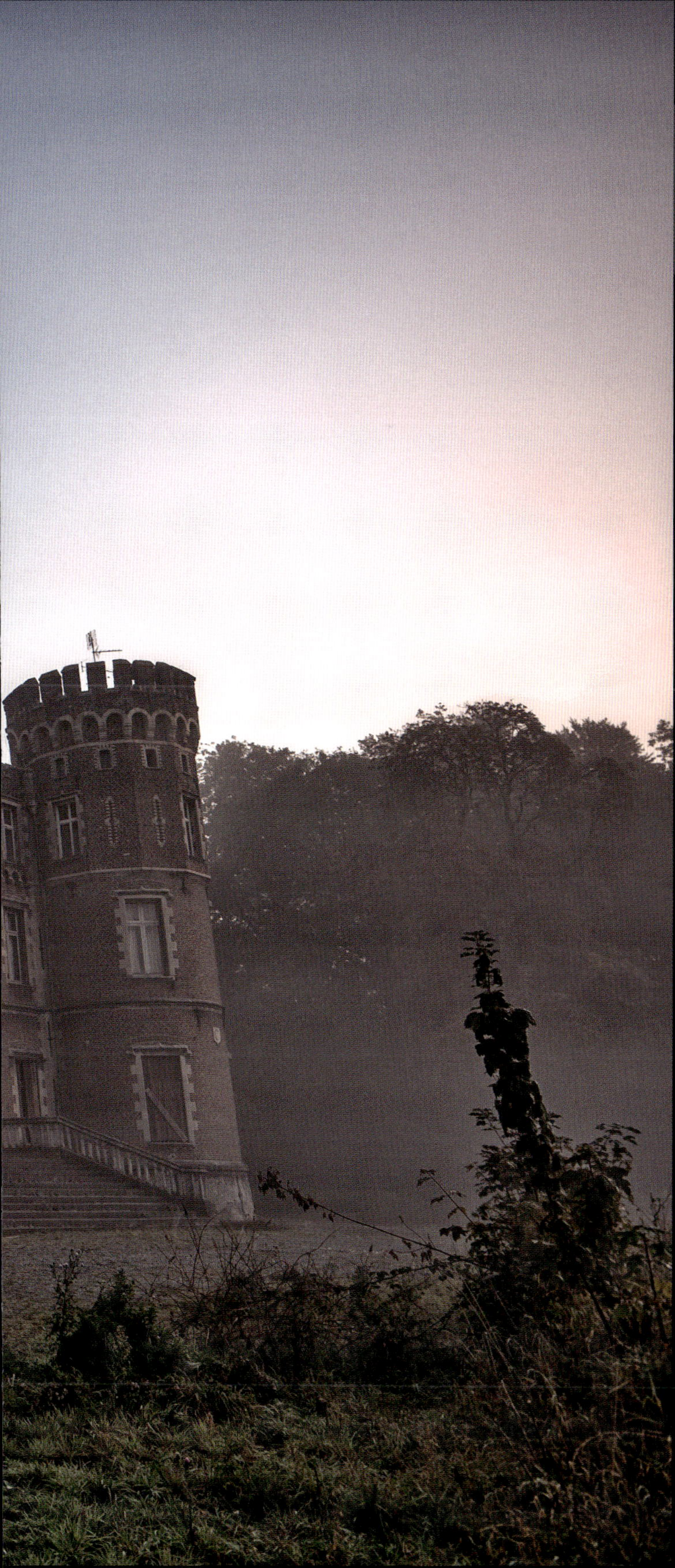

CHÂTEAU DE LA FORÊT

BELGIEN BELGIUM

FOTOS VON PHOTOS BY BRIAN J. ROMEYN

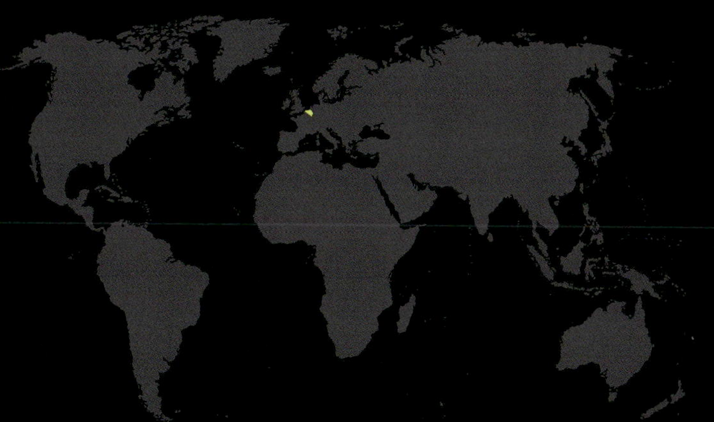

Wenn der Frühnebel tief über den Gräsern hinzieht und der heftig einsetzende Chor der Ammern, Finken, Dompfaffen, Drosseln, Kernbeißer, Stieglitze und Zeisige die Baumkronen und Sträucher im Park von Moulbaix erfüllt, nähern sich Gäste heimlich dem Schloss. Sie tragen Kameras und Taschenlampen und erinnern sich flüsternd an die Gerüchte über einen jähzornigen Mann mit Jeep und seinen Helfer auf einem Roller, an die Patrouillen der Hausmeister, die gereizte Wachsamkeit der örtlichen Polizei und daran, dass niemand willkommen sei im Château de la Forêt. Der romantische Adelssitz liegt in der Province de Hainaut – der Provinz Hennegau –, die Teil der Französischen Gemeinschaft und der Wallonischen Region Belgiens ist. Im Jahr 1860 gab der Marquis de Chasteler den Auftrag zu seiner Errichtung. Der Architekt Désiré Athois Limburg ließ sich für die Aufgabe von der englischen Spätgotik inspirieren. Er schuf, dem damals in Europa populären Historismus verpflichtet, ein Bauwerk im Neo-Tudorstil. Heute erscheint die architektonische Inszenierung von ritterlicher Wehrhaftigkeit und feudalem Beharrungswillen der Besitzer allerdings wie ein Fluch für das Anwesen.

Weder wirken seine zinnenbewehrten wuchtigen Ecktürme noch die vielen Schießscharten abschreckend. Im Gegenteil, die Erforscher und Dokumentaristen verlassener urbaner Räume fühlen sich herausgefordert. Sie sind trotz der beständigen Absicherung des Gebäudes und der Zahl seiner Wächter nicht abzuhalten. Erst einmal eingedrungen, begeistern sie sich an der großen marmornen Eingangshalle und den weitverzweigten Fluren. Sie durchstreifen die Wohnräume im Parterre, das Esszimmer und die Bibliothek und gelangen über den breiten Treppenaufgang in die Schlafzimmer des Obergeschosses mit ihrem einst so mondänen Mobiliar. Im Stich gelassenes Spielzeug fasziniert sie, genauso wie die hier und da verstreuten Kleidungsstücke, die geöffneten Schubladen oder die schweren Tapeten, welche sich unter der eigenen Last allmählich von den Wänden schälen und in die weichen Betten sinken. Die ungebetenen Besucher aus aller Welt nennen in ihren Internet-Blogs das Château de la Forêt einen der herrlichsten Orte Europas. Es verfügt über Hunderte Fenster, einen beachtlichen Kellerbereich und auf dem bewaldeten Terrain der Umgebung finden sich Überreste einer ehemaligen Burg.

Der Besitz gehört den Nachkommen des Grafen d'Ursel Aymard. Es gelingt der Erbengemeinschaft nicht, sich darüber zu einigen, und die nötige Sanierung des Schlosses im Wald muss weiter warten. Anders als die Anhänger der Urban Exploration scheinen einige Nachbarn darüber eher enttäuscht zu sein. Immerhin steht die letzte funktionstüchtige Windmühle im Hennegau, die Moulin de la Marquise, kaum einen Kilometer vom Schloss entfernt. 1614 errichtet, versetzte man sie 1752 nach Moulbaix und selbst der grüne Michelin-Reiseführer widmet ihr etwas Aufmerksamkeit. Viel berühmter ist jedoch die seit dem Mittelalter in der nahe gelegenen Stadt Ath gefeierte „Ducasse d'Ath". Es ist ein zehntägiges Spektakel am Ende des Augusts, welches die Legenden und Sagen aus der Welt der Riesen und Drachen wiederaufleben lässt und das seine Wurzeln in den kirchlichen Prozessionszügen begründet sieht. Die UNESCO erklärte das Stadtfest im Jahr 2005 zu einem Meisterwerk des mündlichen und immateriellen Erbes der Menschheit.

When the spring fog hangs heavily over the fields and the full incipient choir of buntings, finches, bullfinches, song thrushes, hawfinches, goldfinches and siskins fills the treetops and bushes in the park of Moulbaix, guests are secretively getting near to the castle. They are carrying cameras and flashlights and remember in whispers the rumors of a grouchy man with a jeep and his helper on a scooter, the caretaker's patrols, the agitated watchfulness of the local police and the fact that nobody is welcome at Chateau de la Forêt. The romantic aristocratic estate is found in Province de Hainaut, which is part of the French community and the Wallonish region of Belgium. In the year 1860, the Marquis de Chasteler commissioned its construction. The architect, Desire Athois Limburg, got his inspiration for the task from the English late Gothic style. He created something that was dutiful to popular historicism at that time in Europe, a construction in neo Tudor style. Today, it seems the architectural staging of the chivalrous truthfulness and feudal persistence of the owner is like a curse for the property.
Neither the massive pewter covered corner towers nor the many arrow slits are a deterrent. Just the opposite is true; explorers and documentary makers of abandoned urban space feel challenged. They cannot be kept away despite vigilant protection of the building and the number of guards. Once they get in, they are thrilled by the large marble entrance hall and the far reaching corridors. They pass through the living rooms on the ground floor, the dining room and the library and reach the bedrooms with their once so sophisticated furnishings on the upper floor via the wide staircase. Neglected toys fascinate them, as do the pieces of clothing strewn here and there, the open drawers or the heavy wallpaper that is slowly peeling off the walls from its own weight and sinking into the soft beds.
The uninvited visitors from all over the world call the Chateau de la Forêt one of the most magnificent places in Europe in their Internet blogs. It has hundreds of windows, an impressive cellar and there are the remains of a former castle on the forested terrain of the surroundings.
The property belongs to the descendants of the dukes of Ursel Aymard. It was not possible for the community of heirs to come to an agreement and the necessary renovation of the castle in the forest still has to wait. In contrast to the fans of urban exploration, some neighbors appear to be more disappointed about it. After all, the last functioning windmill in Hainaut, the Moulin de la Marquise, is not quite one kilometer from the castle. Built in 1614, it was moved in 1752 to Moulbaix and even the green Michelin travel guide gives it some attention. However, much more famous since the Middle Ages is the acclaimed "Ducasse d'Ath" in the nearby town of Ath. It is a ten day spectacle at the end of August that brings the legends and myths from the world of giants and dragons to life again and has its origins in church processions. UNESCO designated the city festival a masterpiece of Oral and Intangible Heritage of Humanity in 2005.

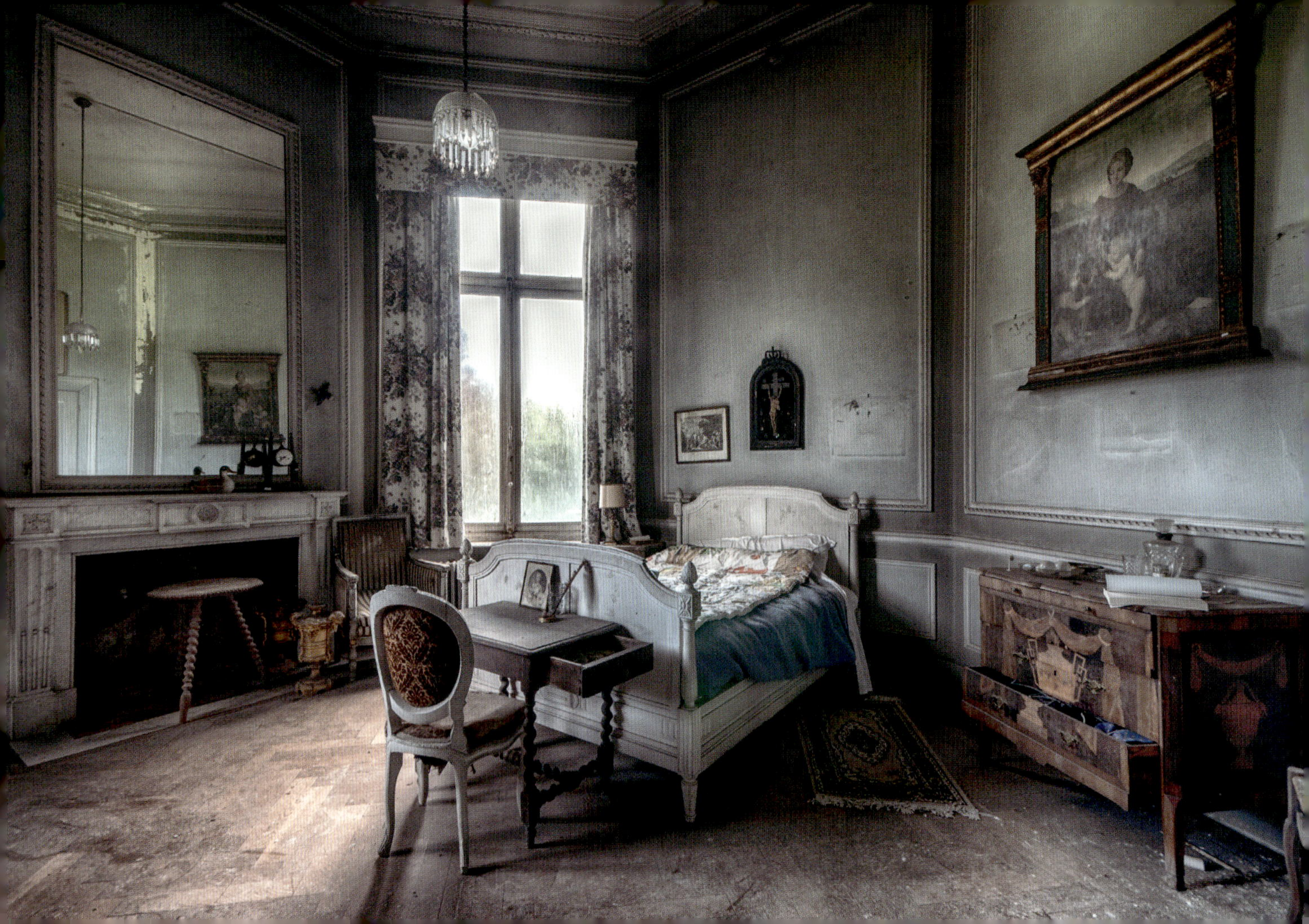

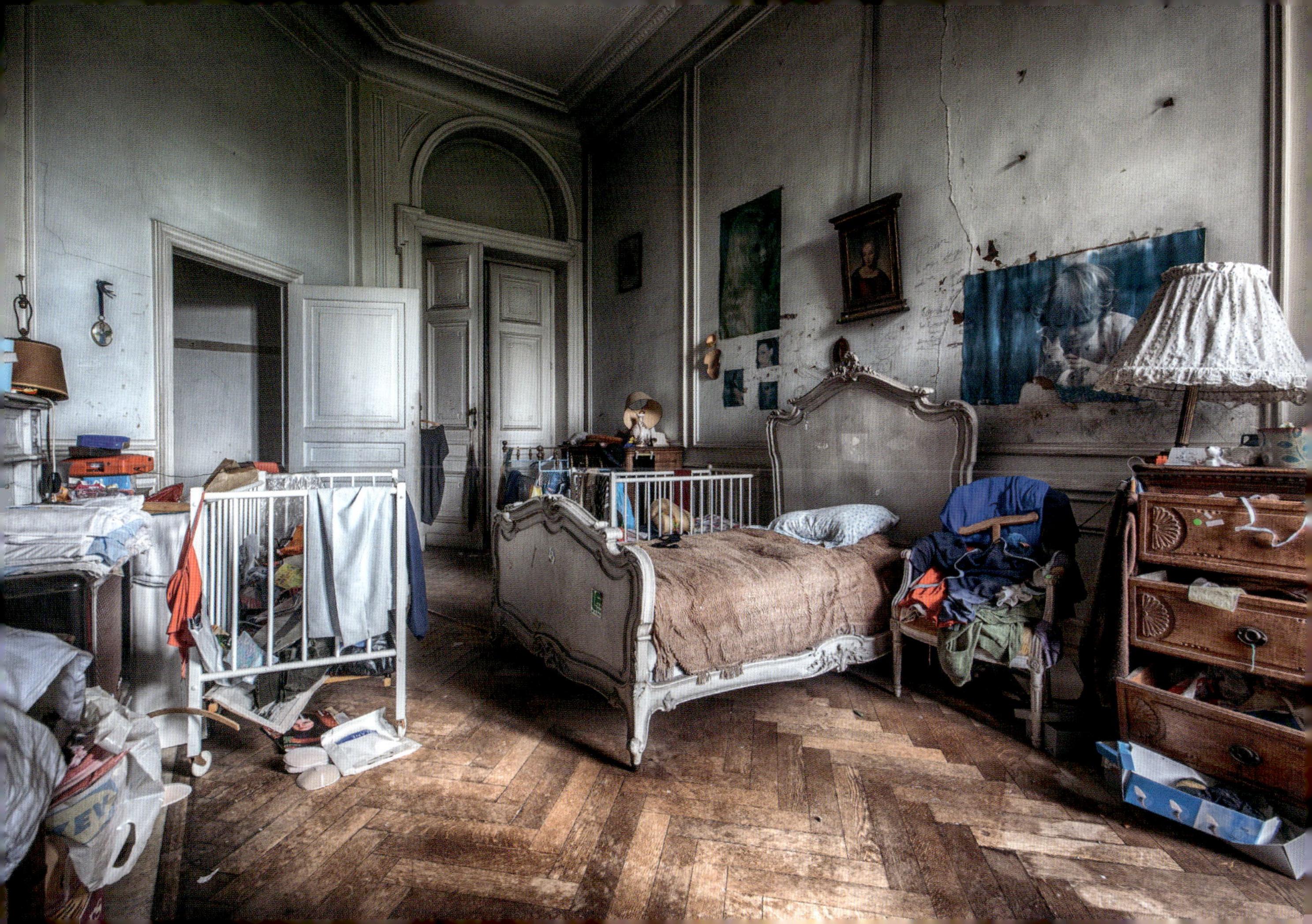

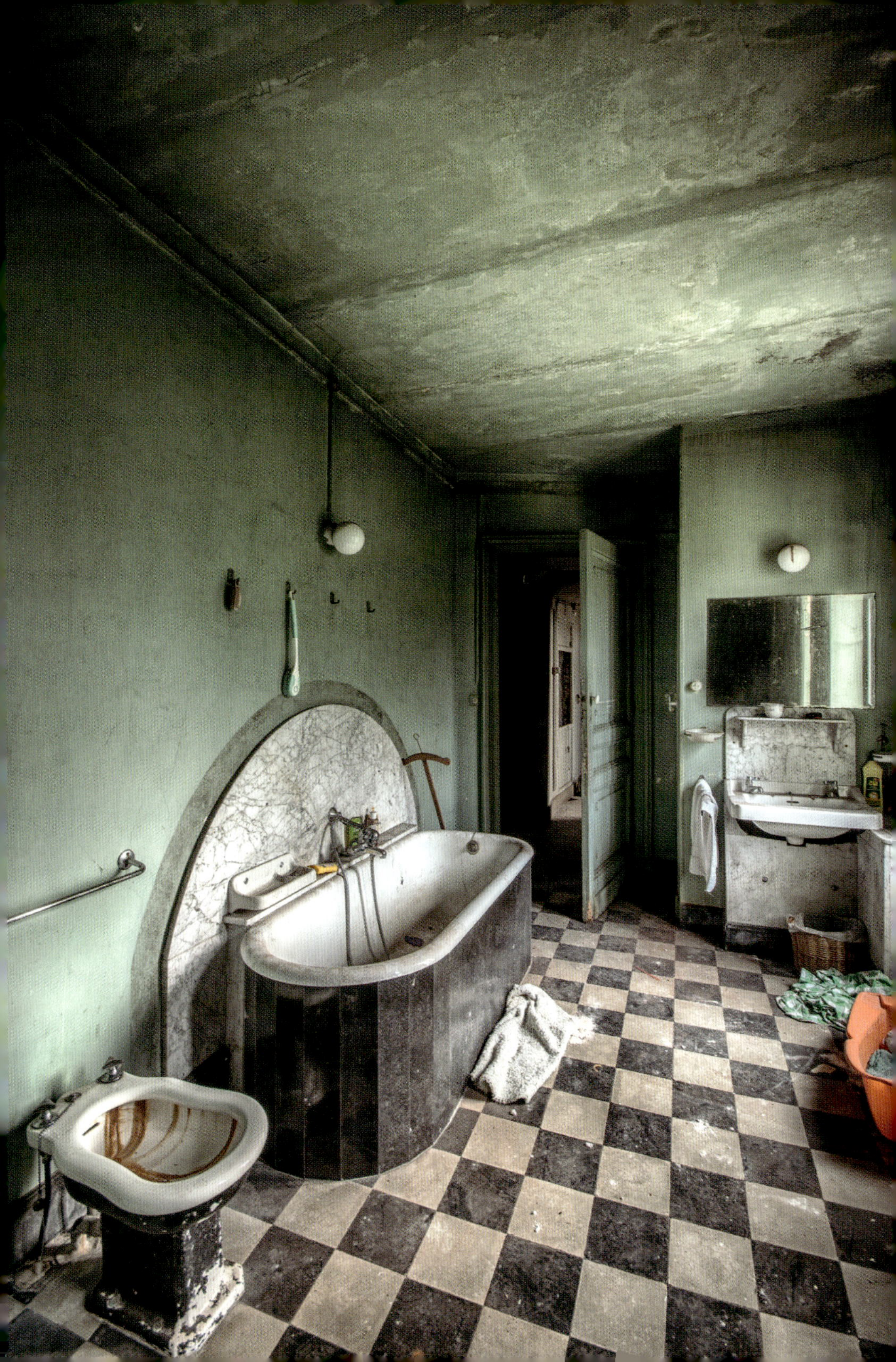

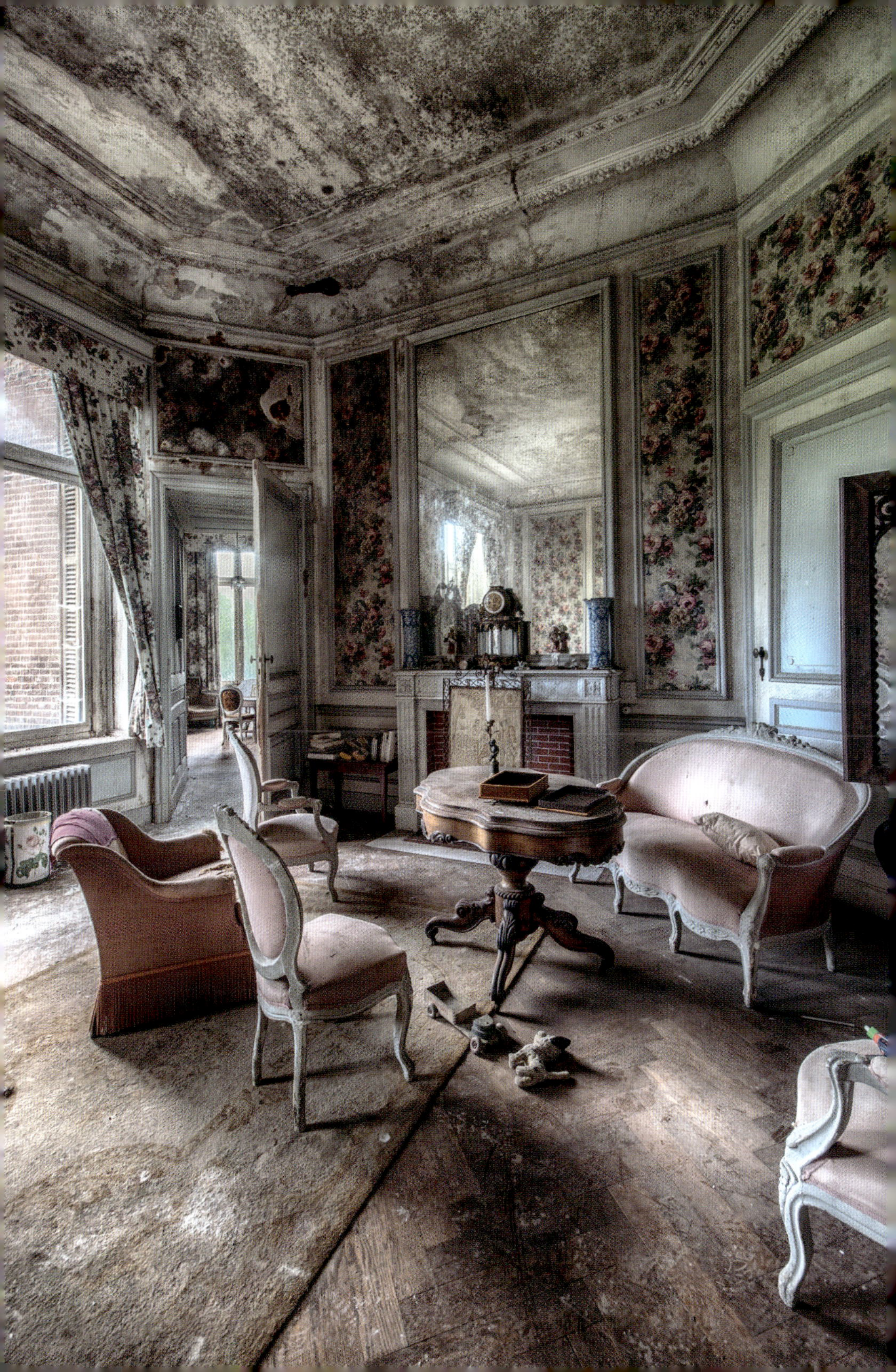

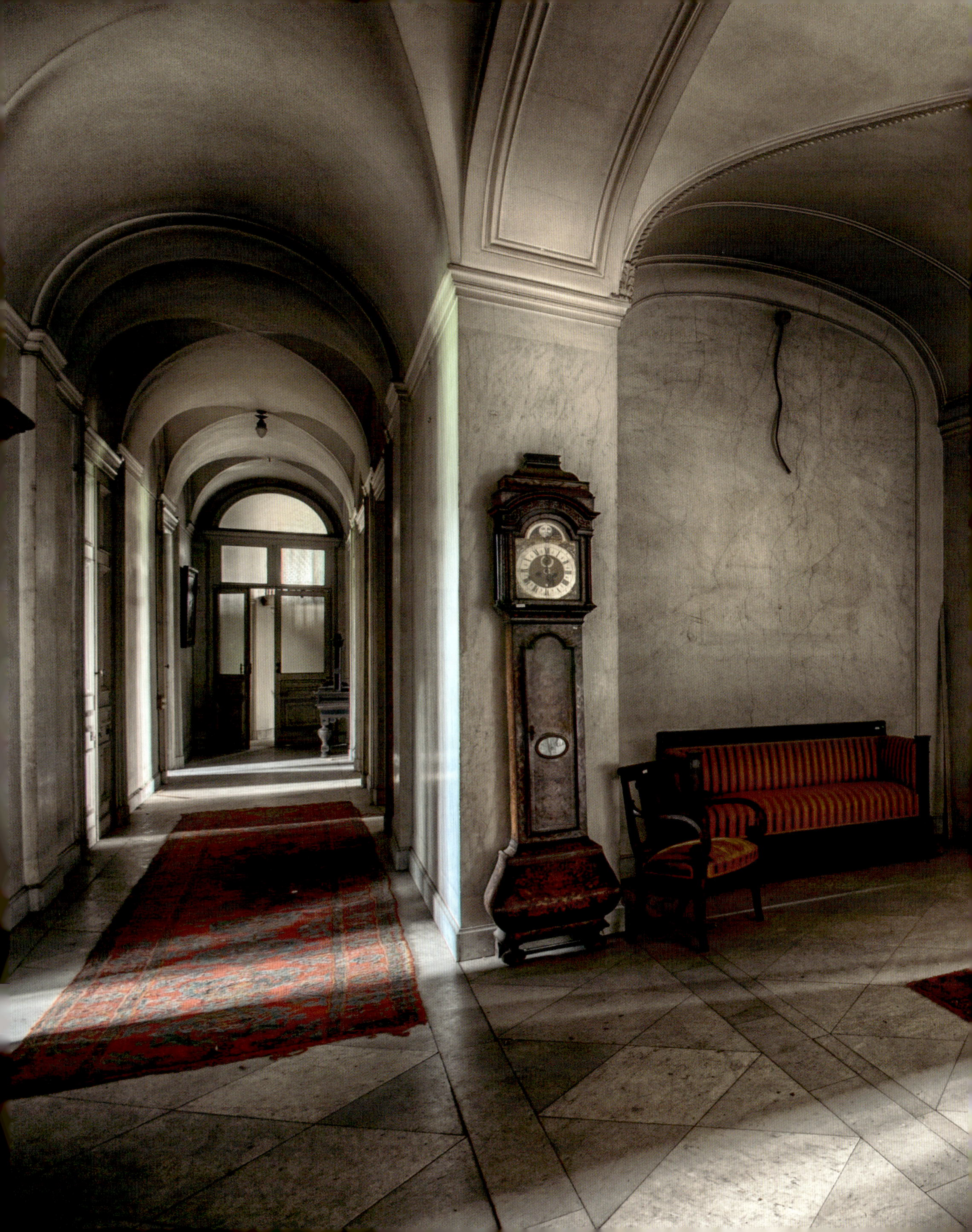

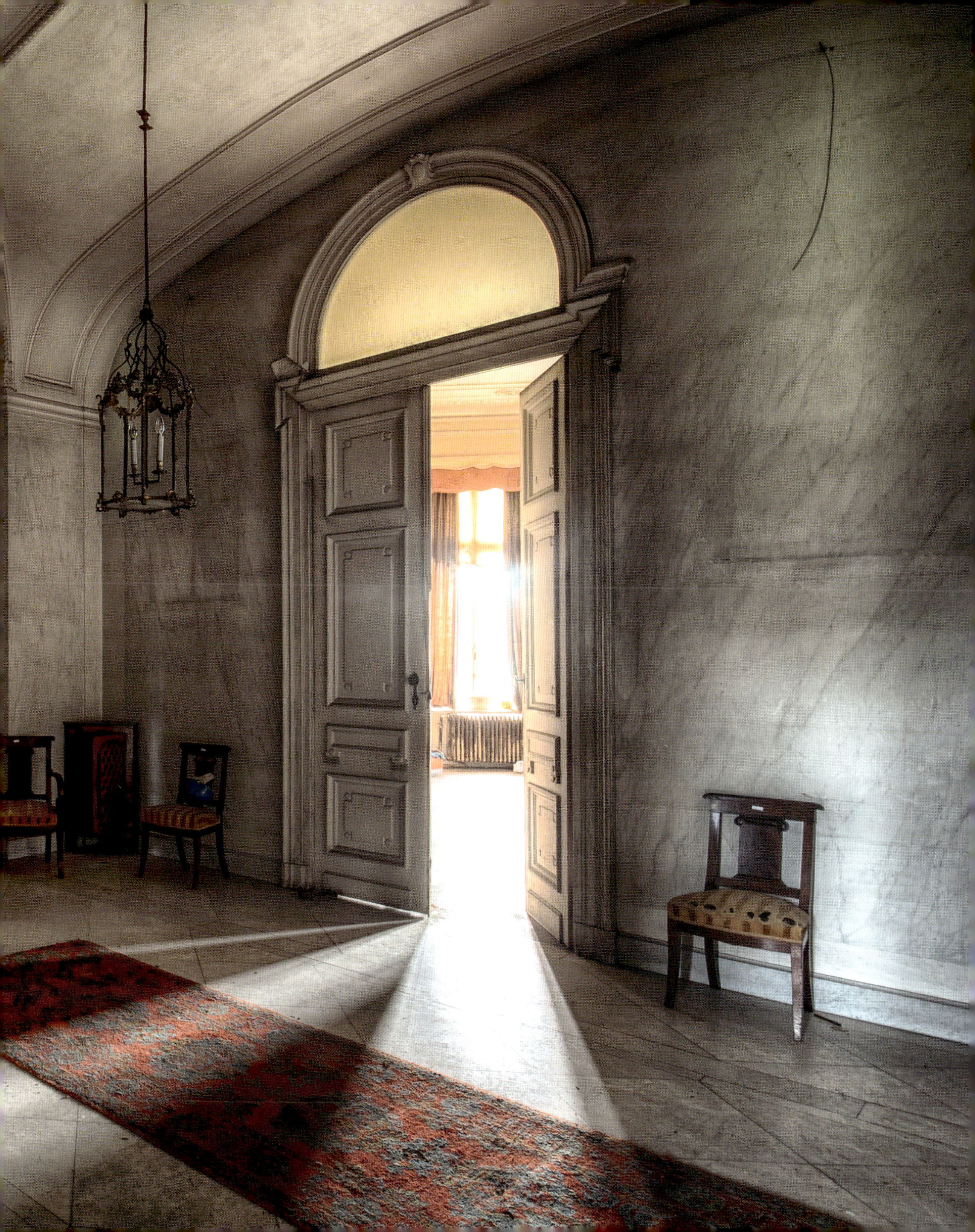

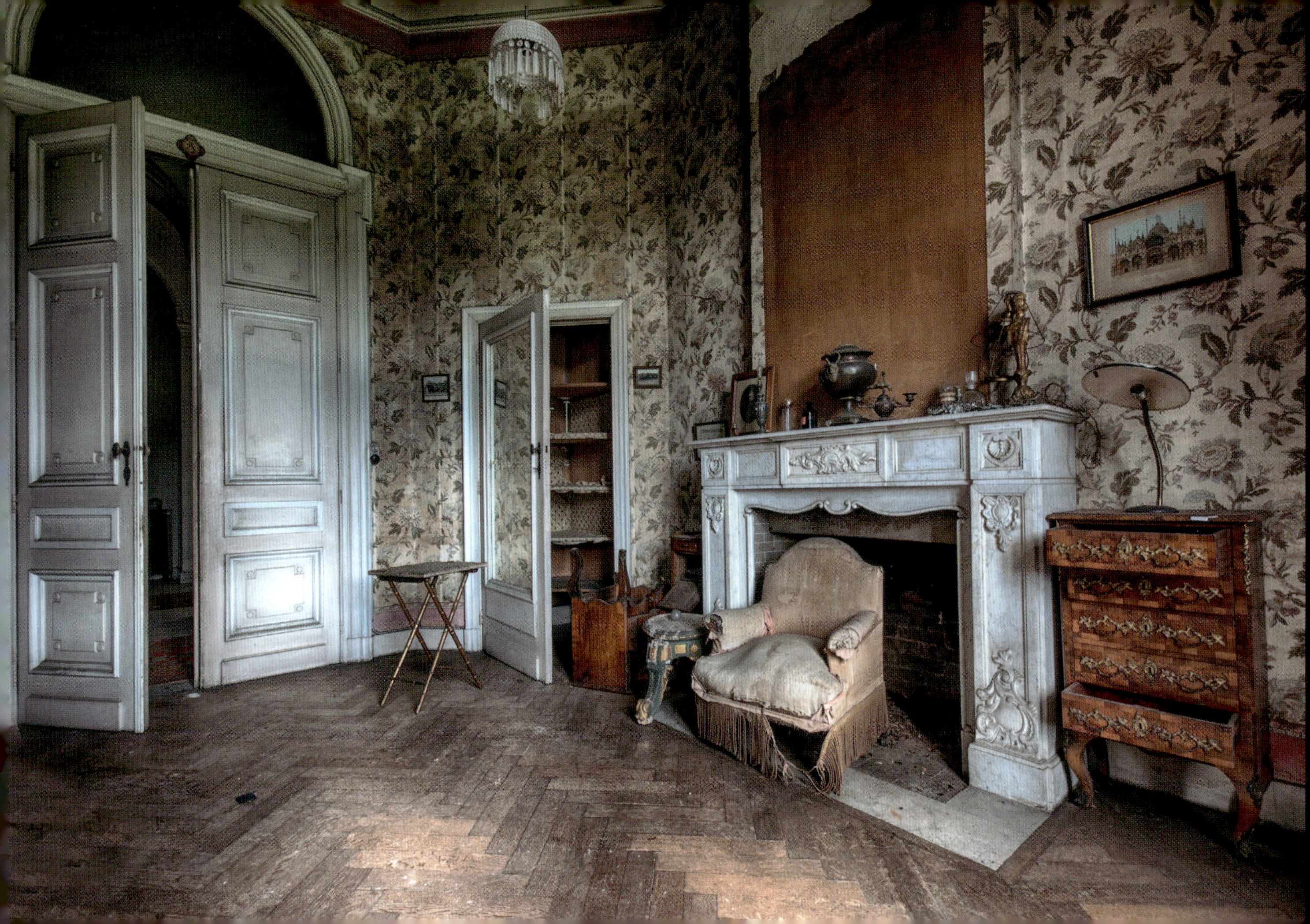

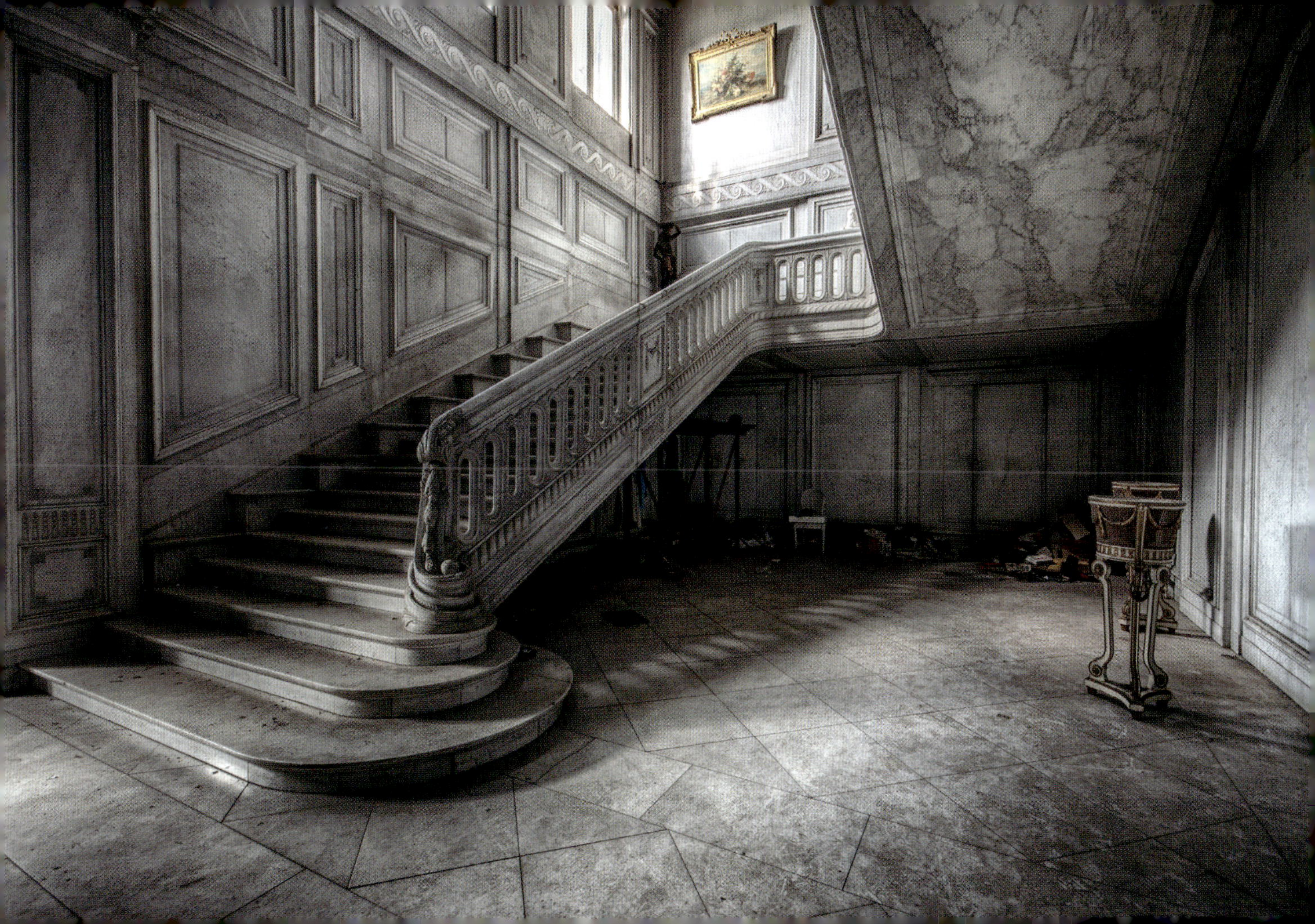

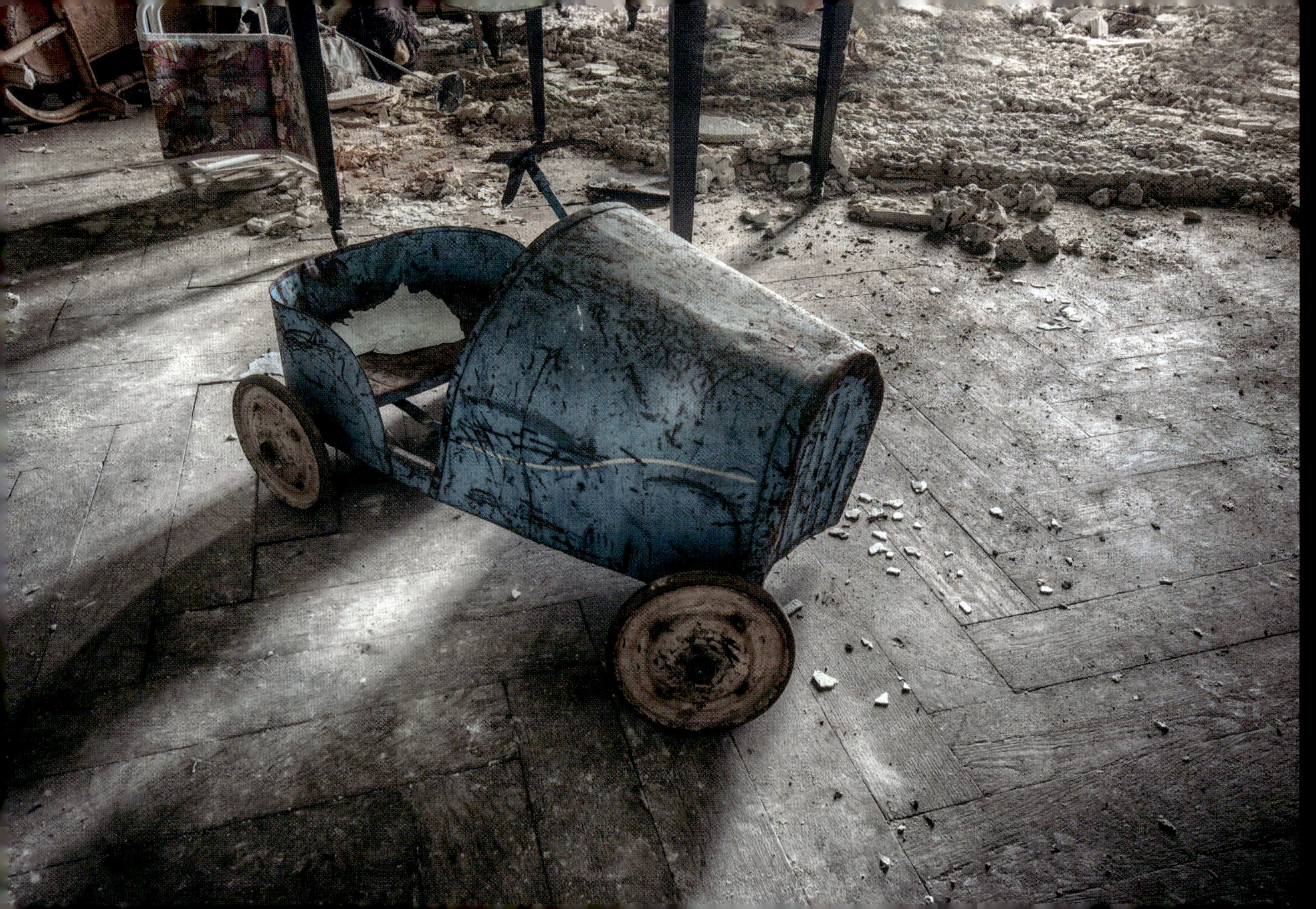

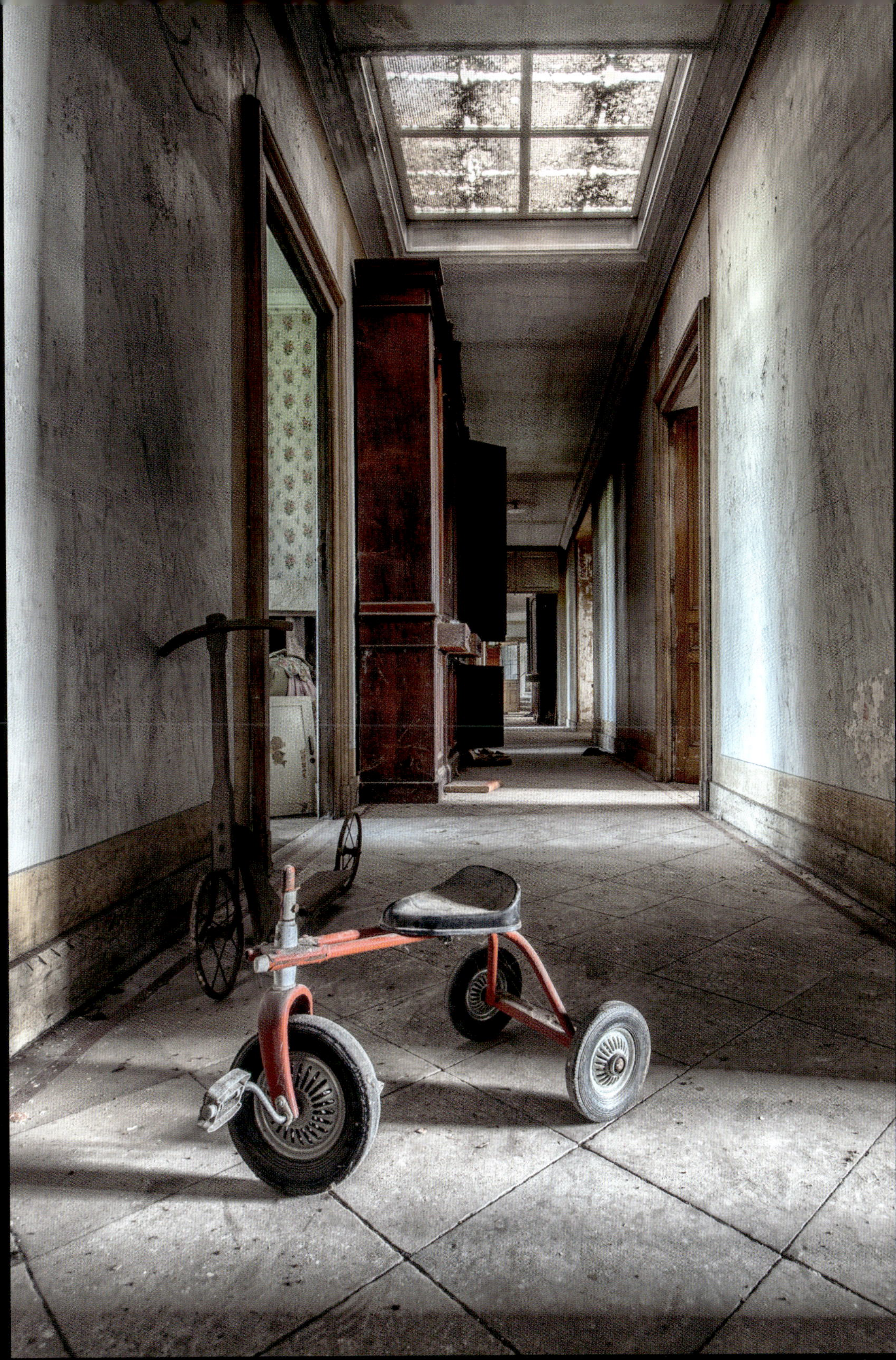

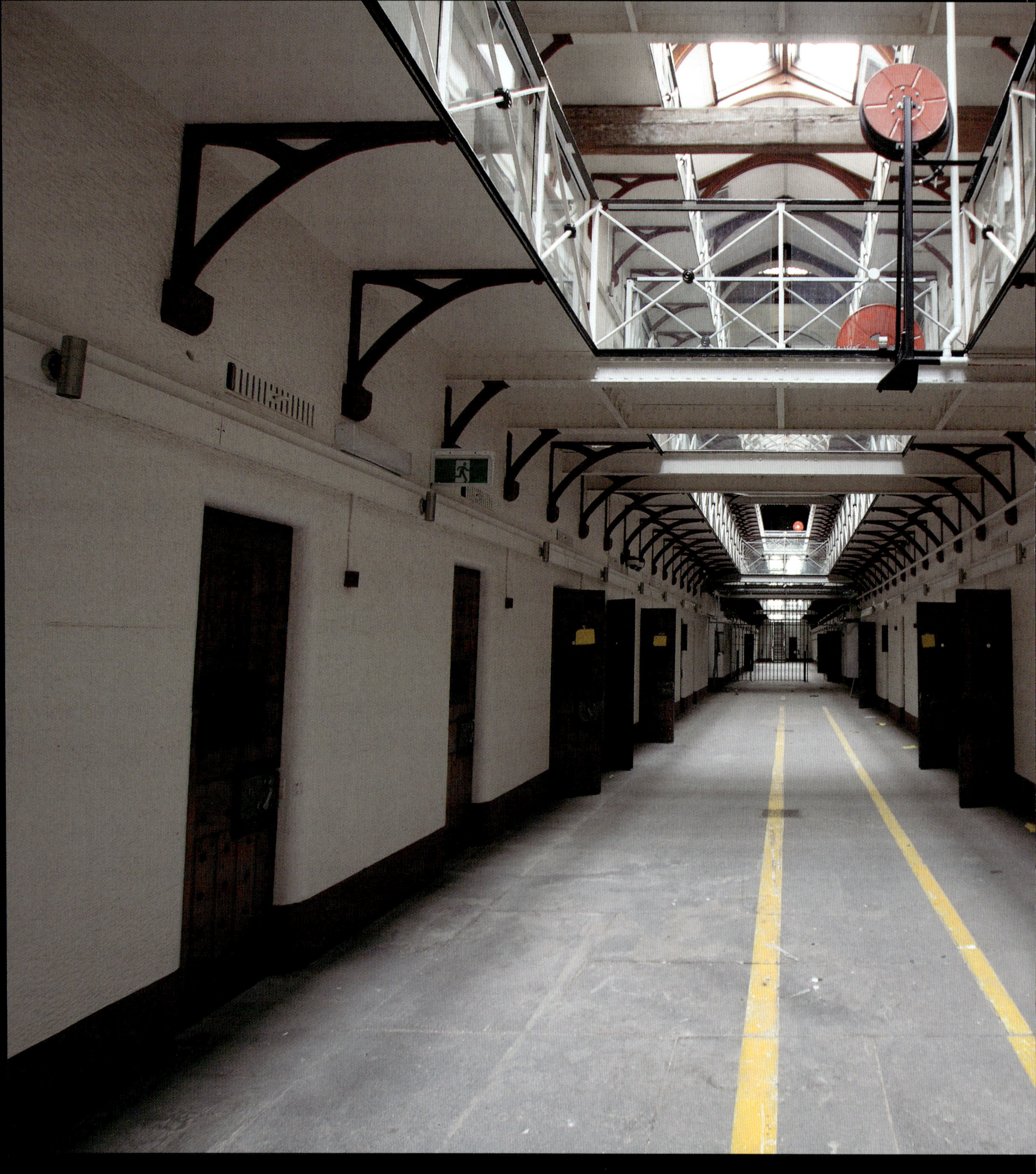

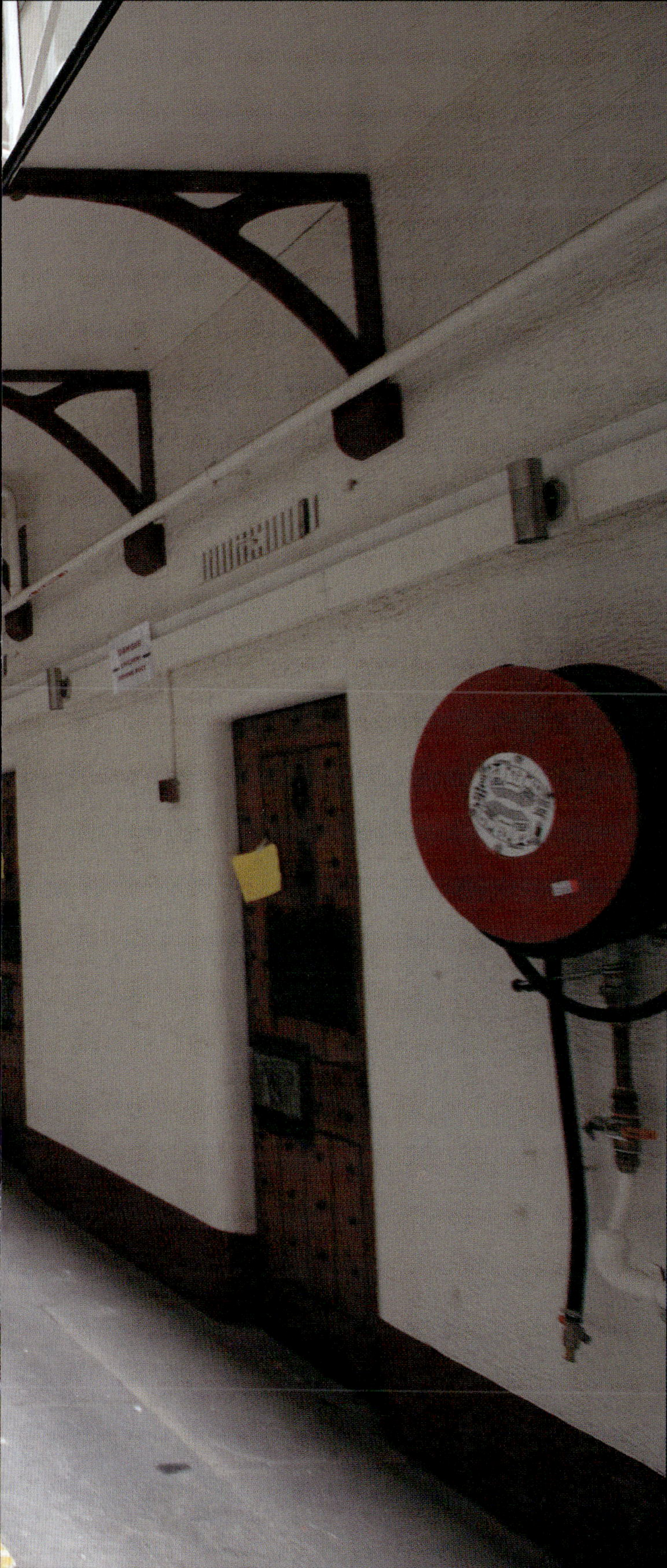

HM PRISON PENTRIDGE

AUSTRALIEN AUSTRALIA

FOTOS VON PHOTOS BY MATTHEW BOYER

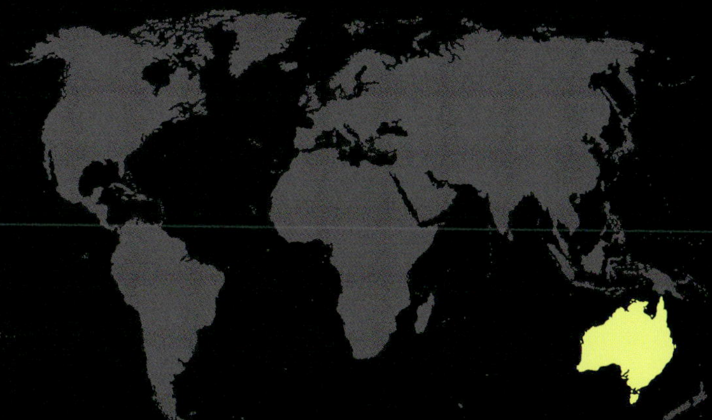

Als James Cook auf seiner ersten Südseereise 1770 mit seinem Schiff „Endeavour" die Ostküste des australischen Kontinents – damals Neuholland – erreichte, fand er eine so üppige Pflanzenwelt vor, dass er der Bucht den Namen Botany Bay gab. Seine Mannschaft staunte über die riesigen Hasen, die von den Ureinwohnern Kängurus genannt wurden. Der Entdecker kartografierte das Gebiet und beanspruchte es als New South Wales für die britische Krone. Die Bestimmung zur englischen Strafkolonie erlebte Cook nicht mehr; er verlor 1779 im Kampf gegen Ureinwohner auf Hawaii sein Leben.

Nach achtmonatiger Reise auf See, begleitet von zwei Kriegs- und drei Frachtschiffen, gingen im Januar 1788, die Sonne schien unbarmherzig, die ersten sechs Gefangenenschiffe an der australischen Ostküste vor Anker. Etwa tausend Menschen waren auf den Südkontinent verbracht worden, um eine englische Kolonie zu gründen, darunter 778 Sträflinge. Die mitgeführten Pflanzen gingen ein, die Siedler litten Hunger. Doch erhielten sie Unterstützung von den australischen Ureinwohnern, den Aborigines.

In die Strafkolonien zu geraten, war in jener Zeit einfach, denn neben Mördern gelangten auch Urkundenfälscher, Falschmünzer und Diebe in die englischen Verbannungsorte. So sollte Elisabeth Bason wegen des Diebstahls von sechs Meter Kattun gehängt werden, entging aber durch die Verschickung in die Strafkolonie der Todesstrafe. Und John Hill wurde für sieben Jahre nach Australien verbannt, weil er ein Taschentuch, das einen Wert von sechs Penny besaß, gestohlen hatte. Bis 1857 waren ungefähr 134.000 Gefangene aus England – Männer, Frauen und Kinder – nach Australien verschifft worden. Ein Gesetz von 1857 beendete, wenigstens formal, die Abschiebungspraxis.

1851 wurde nahe Melbourne, im Bundesstaat Victoria, Gold gefunden. Nirgendwo auf der Erde schürfte man in den darauffolgenden Jahren mehr Gold. Die Zahl der freien Siedler stieg rasant an. Das HM – ein Kürzel für „Her Majesty": Ihrer Majestät – Prison Pentridge in Coburg, einem Stadtteil von Melbourne, nahm 1851 den Betrieb auf. Sein Spitzname „Bluestone College" leitete sich von den Bluestone-Steinbrüchen des Umlands ab, in denen Häftlinge zum Einsatz kamen. Die Gefangenen waren auf zehn Abteilungen verteilt. 1980 kam die elfte hinzu: Jika Jika, ein Hochsicherheitstrakt. Garantiert ausbruchssicher. Doch schon 1983 gelang vier Häftlingen die Flucht; ein Feuer und der Tod von fünf Gefangenen 1987 besiegelten das Ende von Jika Jika.

Heute blühen vor den Festungsmauern des am 1. Mai 1997 geschlossenen Gefängnisses rote Rosen. Die meisten Gebäude wurden abgerissen. Für 25 Dollar werden Interessierte eine Stunde lang durch die Untersuchungshaft-Abteilung, ihre Zellen und schließlich zum Galgen geführt. Die letzte Hinrichtung fand 1967 statt. In den Gängen vor den Zellentüren breiten nun regelmäßig Händler ihre Produkte aus: Gewürze, frische Paprika, handgemachte Pralinen überlagern die Erinnerung an die einstigen Insassen. Der Rosengarten, der sich an die Untersuchungshaft anschließt, ist ein beliebter Ort für Hochzeitszeremonien, private Cocktailpartys und Weihnachtsfeiern. Zum unterhaltsamen Diner im noblen Restaurant hinter Mauern und Stacheldraht bucht man einen redegewandten ehemaligen Strafgefangenen. Wer die Aufenthalte in diesem Ambiente als zu kurz empfindet, kann sich wie der Bankräuber Graeme Alford, der sieben Jahre lang inhaftiert war, seine Zelle kaufen im HM Prison Pentridge.

When James Cook reached the east coast of the Australian continent (called New Holland at that time) in 1770 on board his ship "Endeavour" on his first voyage to the South Seas, he found such a bountiful world of plants that he gave the bay the name, Botany Bay. His crew was amazed by the huge rabbits called kangaroos by the native people. The explorer mapped the area and claimed it for the British monarchy as New South Wales. Cook did not experience its designation as an English penal colony; he lost his life in 1779 in a battle against the natives on Hawaii.

After an eight-month voyage at sea accompanied by two warships and three cargo ships, the first six prisoner ships laid anchor in January 1788 off the Australian east coast under an unmerciful sun. About one thousand people, including 778 prisoners, had been brought to the southern continent to found an English colony. The plants brought with them died and the settlers hungered. However, they were helped by the Australian natives, the Aborigines.

Getting into the prison colony was easy at that time because besides murderers, forgers, counterfeiters and thieves also landed in the English place of exile. Elisabeth Bason was to be hanged for stealing six meters of calico fabric, but she escaped the death penalty by being sent to the prison colony. And John Hill was exiled to Australia for seven years because he had stolen

of Melbourne, began operations in 1851. Its nickname, "Bluestone College" came from the bluestone quarries of the surrounding land where the prisoners were put to work. The prisoners were divided into ten sections. In 1980, the eleventh was added: Jika Jika, a high security wing. Guaranteed escape proof. However, four prisoners escaped as soon thereafter as 1983. A fire and the death of five prisoners in 1987 sealed the fate of Jika Jika.

Today, red roses bloom in front of the fortified walls of the prison that closed on May 1, 1997. Most of the buildings were demolished. For 25 dollars, anyone who is interested can go for an hour through the remand department, the cells and finally the gallows. The last execution took place in 1967. Today, merchants regularly display their products in the hallways in front of the cell doors. Spices, fresh paprika, and homemade pralines cover up the memory of the former inmates. The rose garden that connects to the remand center is a popular place for wedding ceremonies, private cocktail parties and Christmas parties. To have an entertaining dinner in an exquisite restaurant behind walls and barbed wire, you book an eloquent, former convict. If you feel that the stay in this ambiance is too short, you can buy your own cell in the HM Prison Pentridge, as did bank robber Graeme Alford who was imprisoned there for seven years.

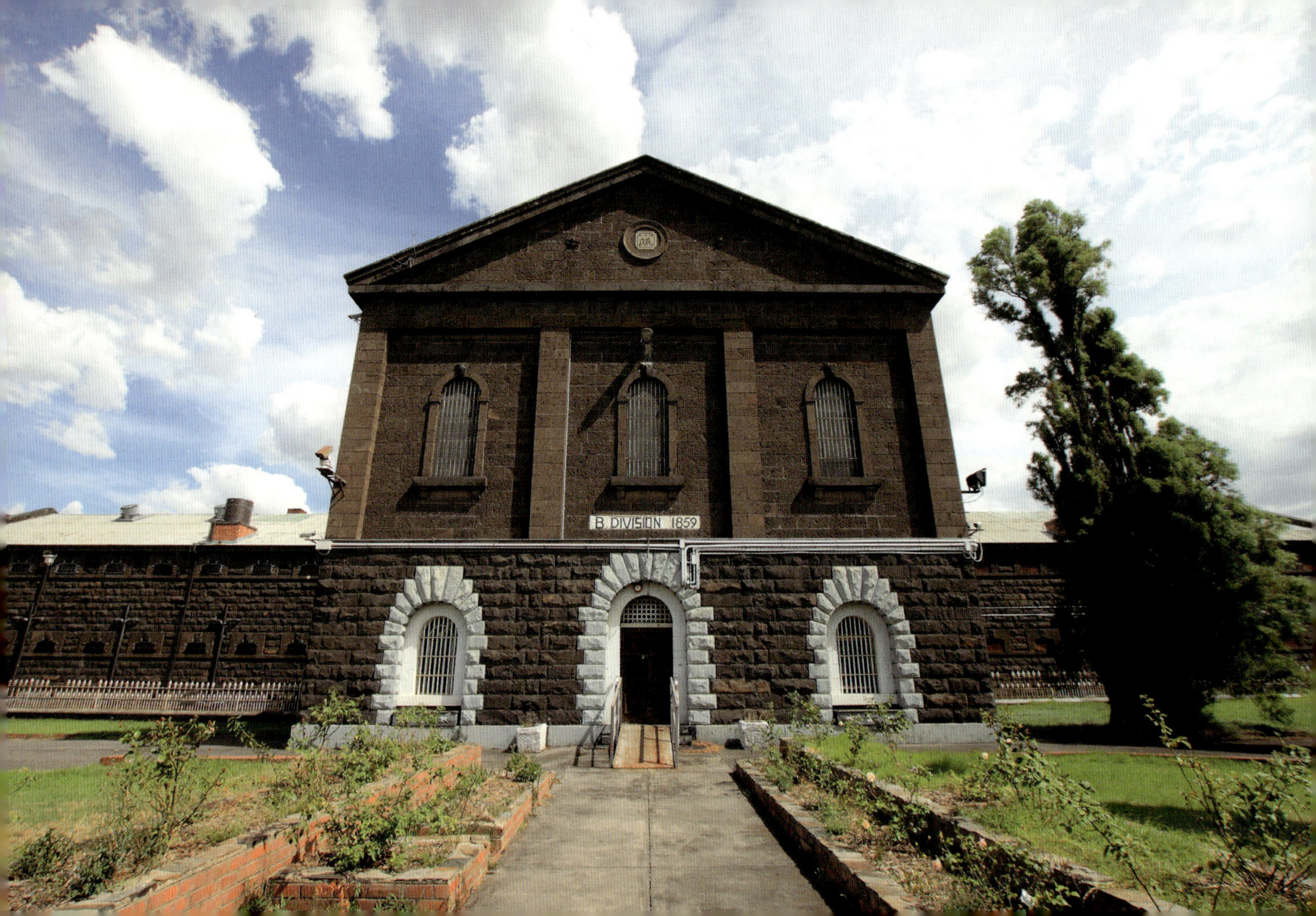
B DIVISION 1859

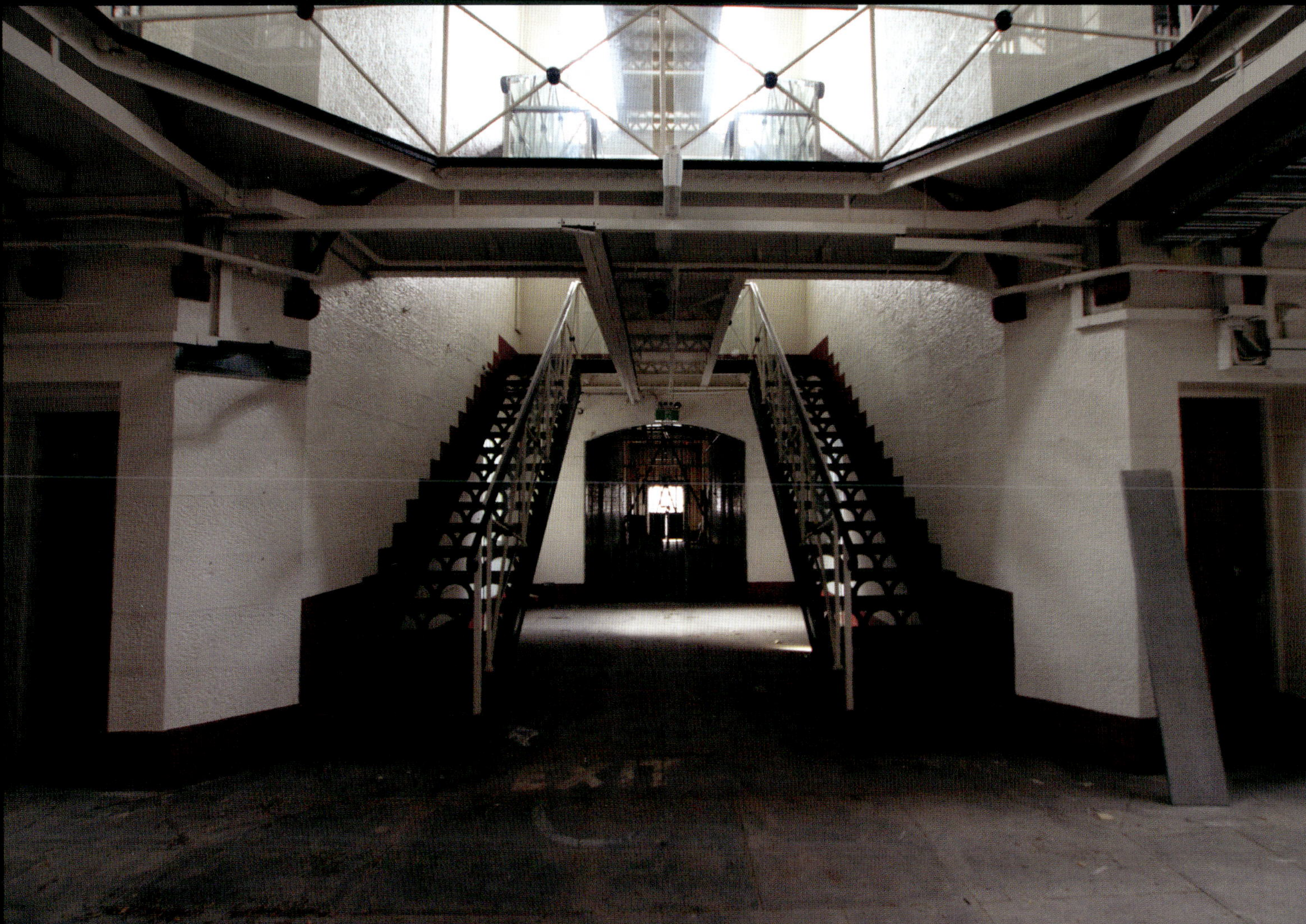

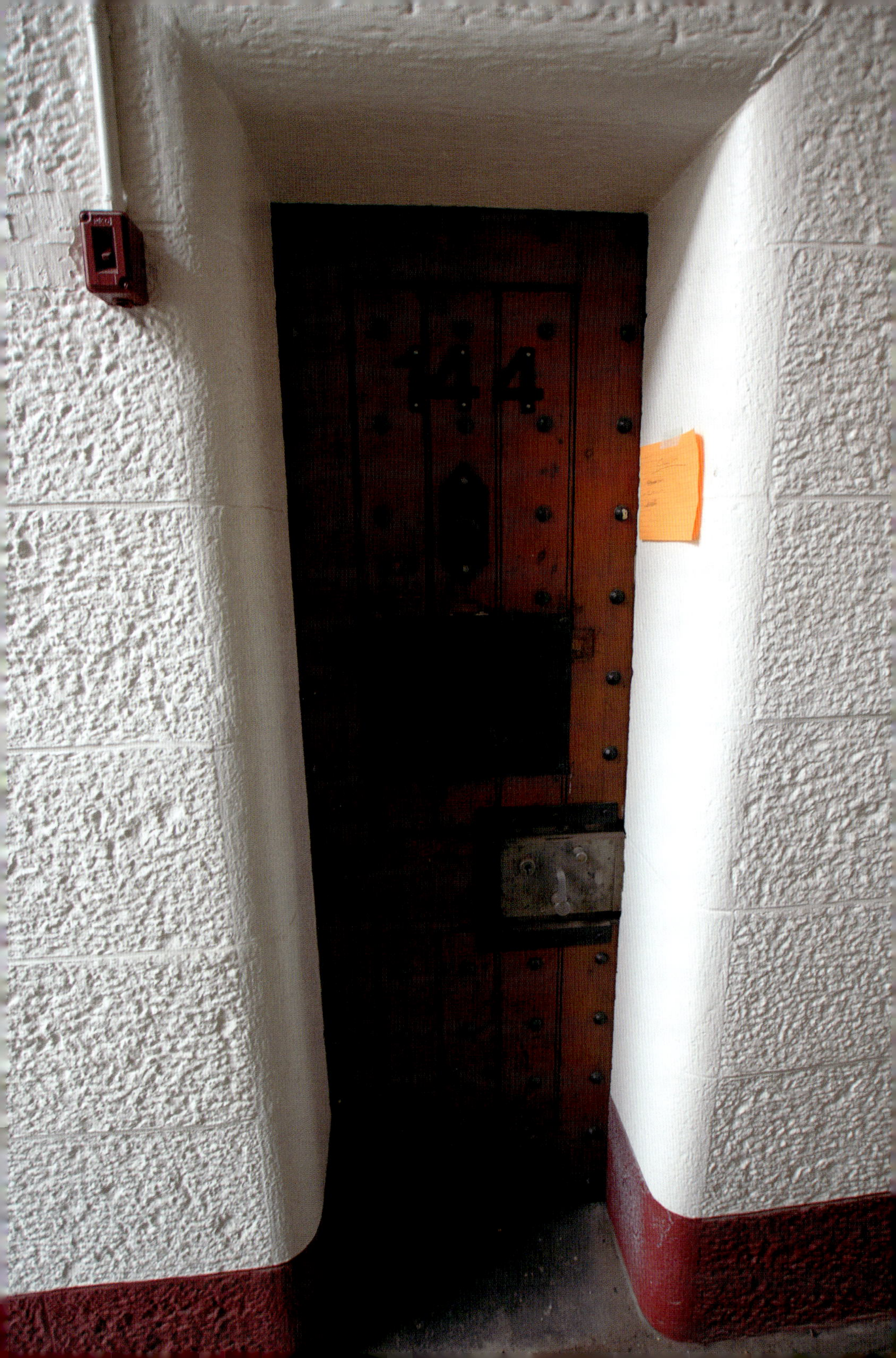
144

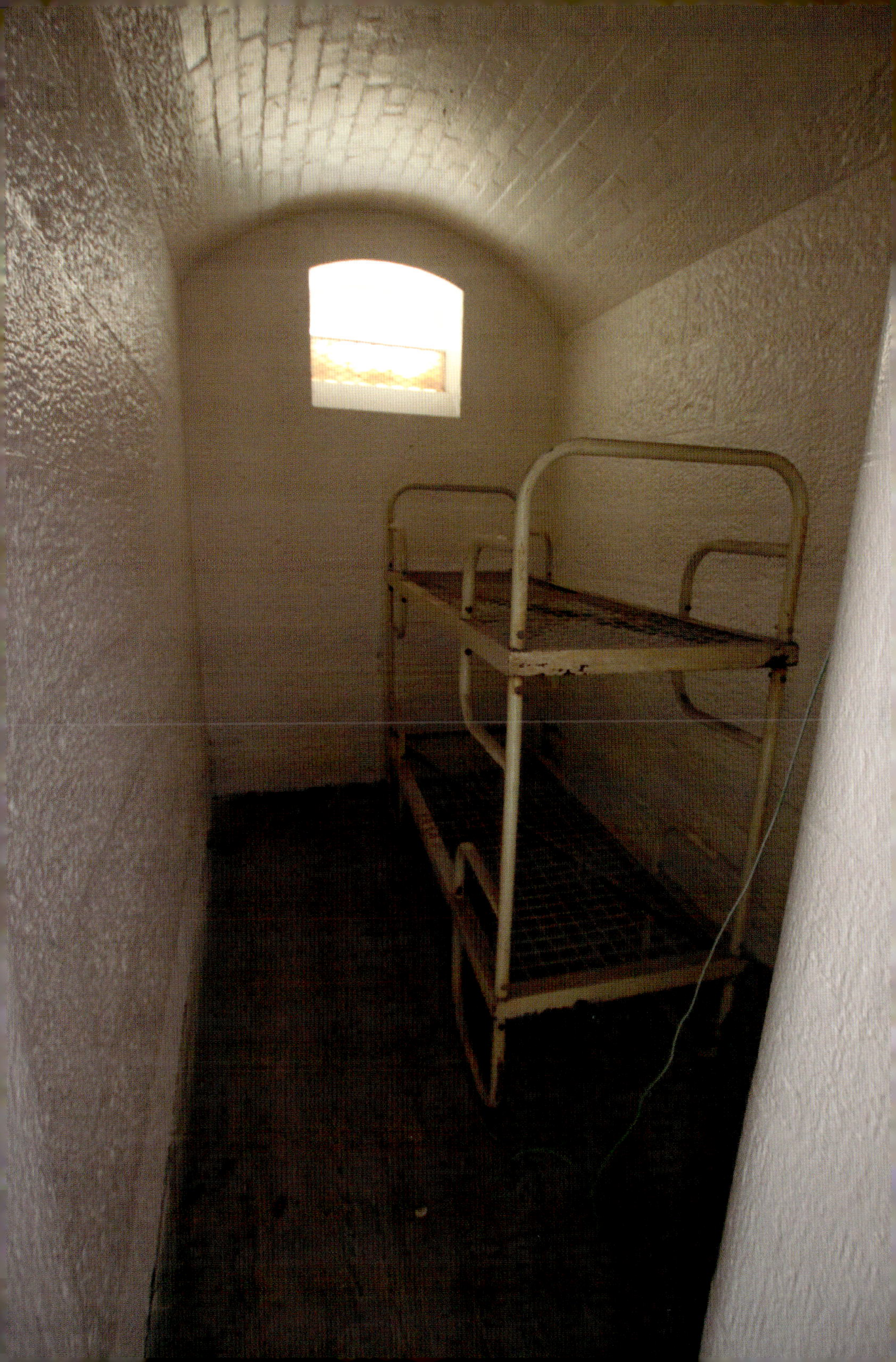

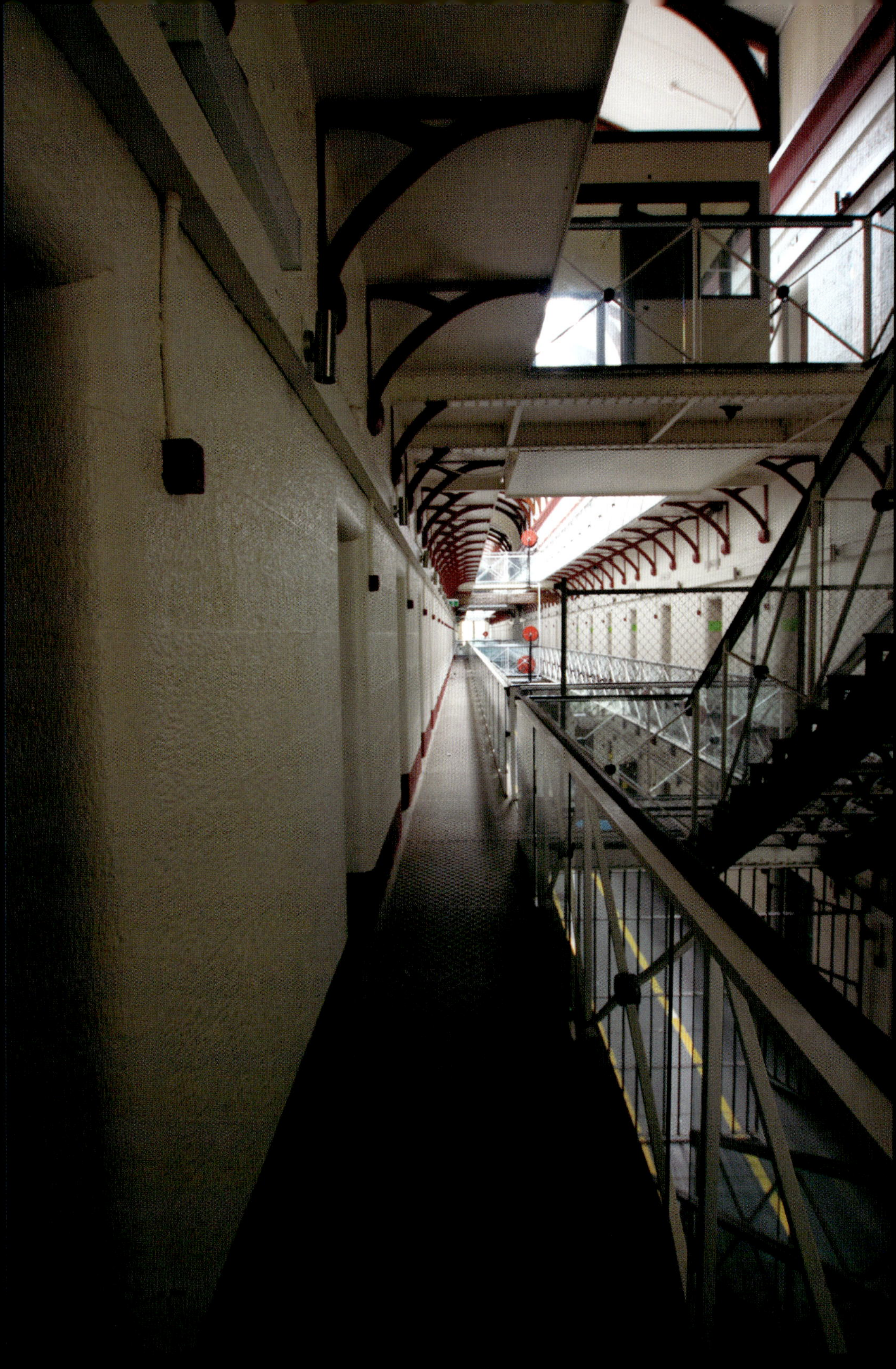

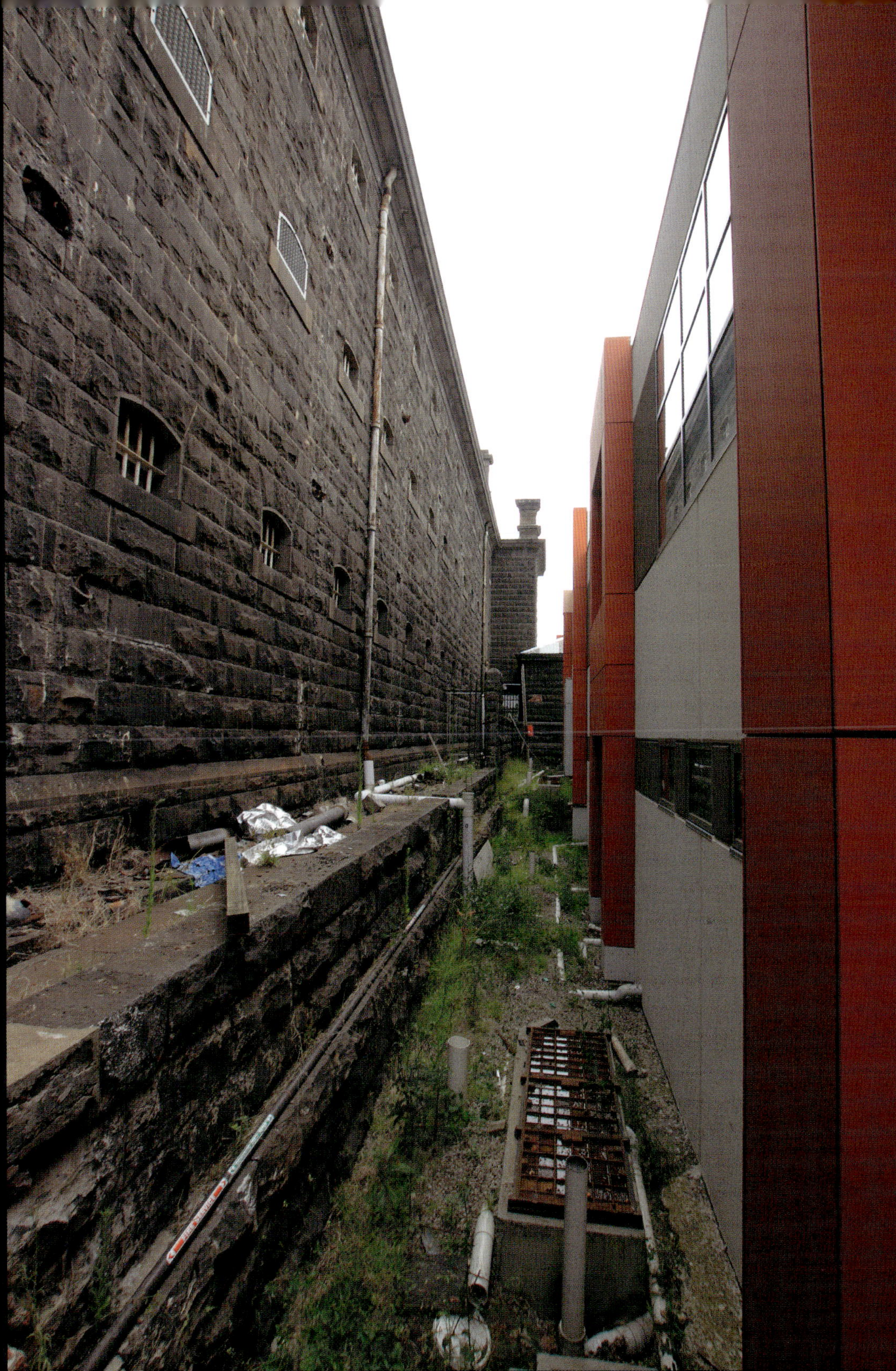

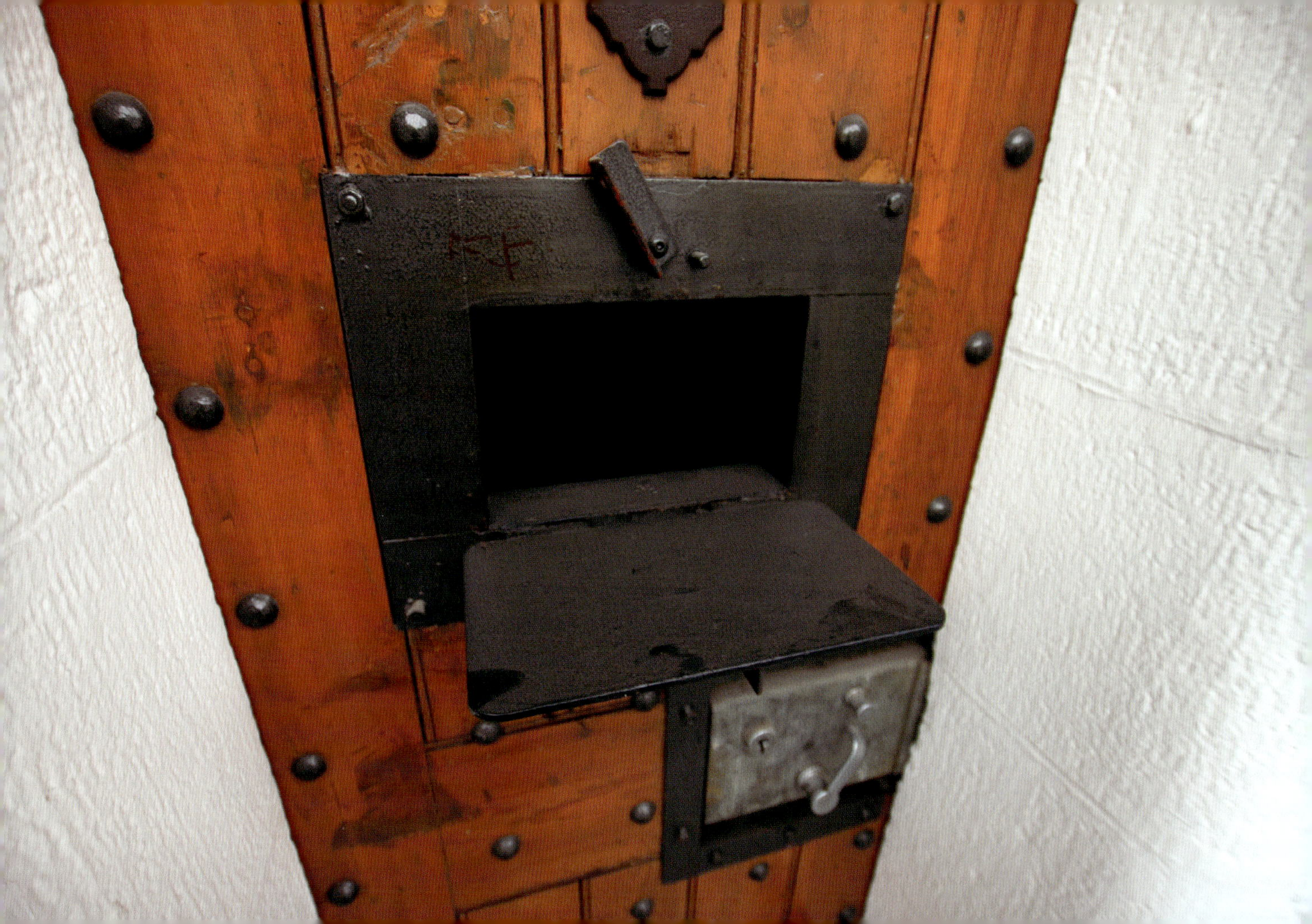

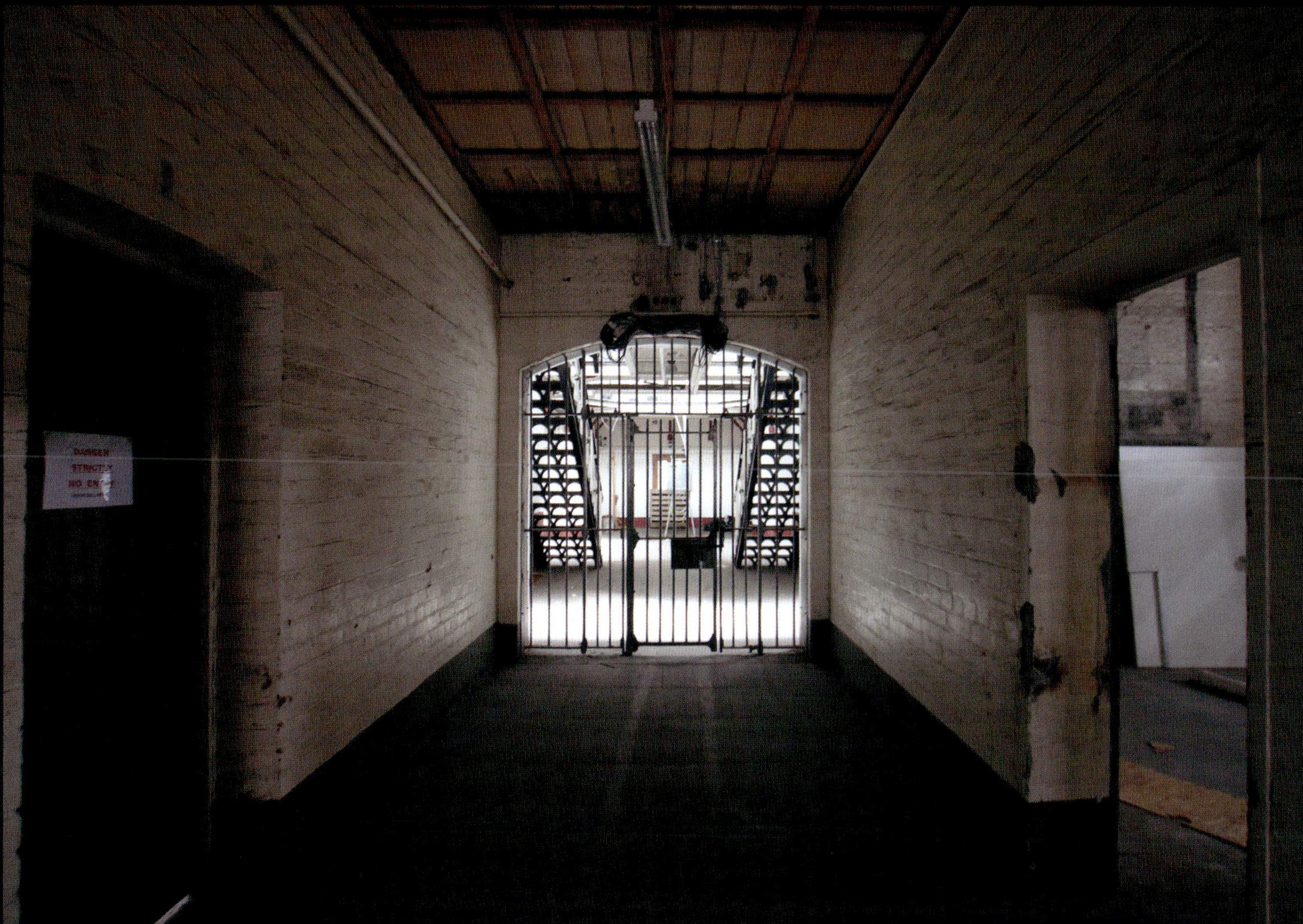
DANGER
STRICTLY

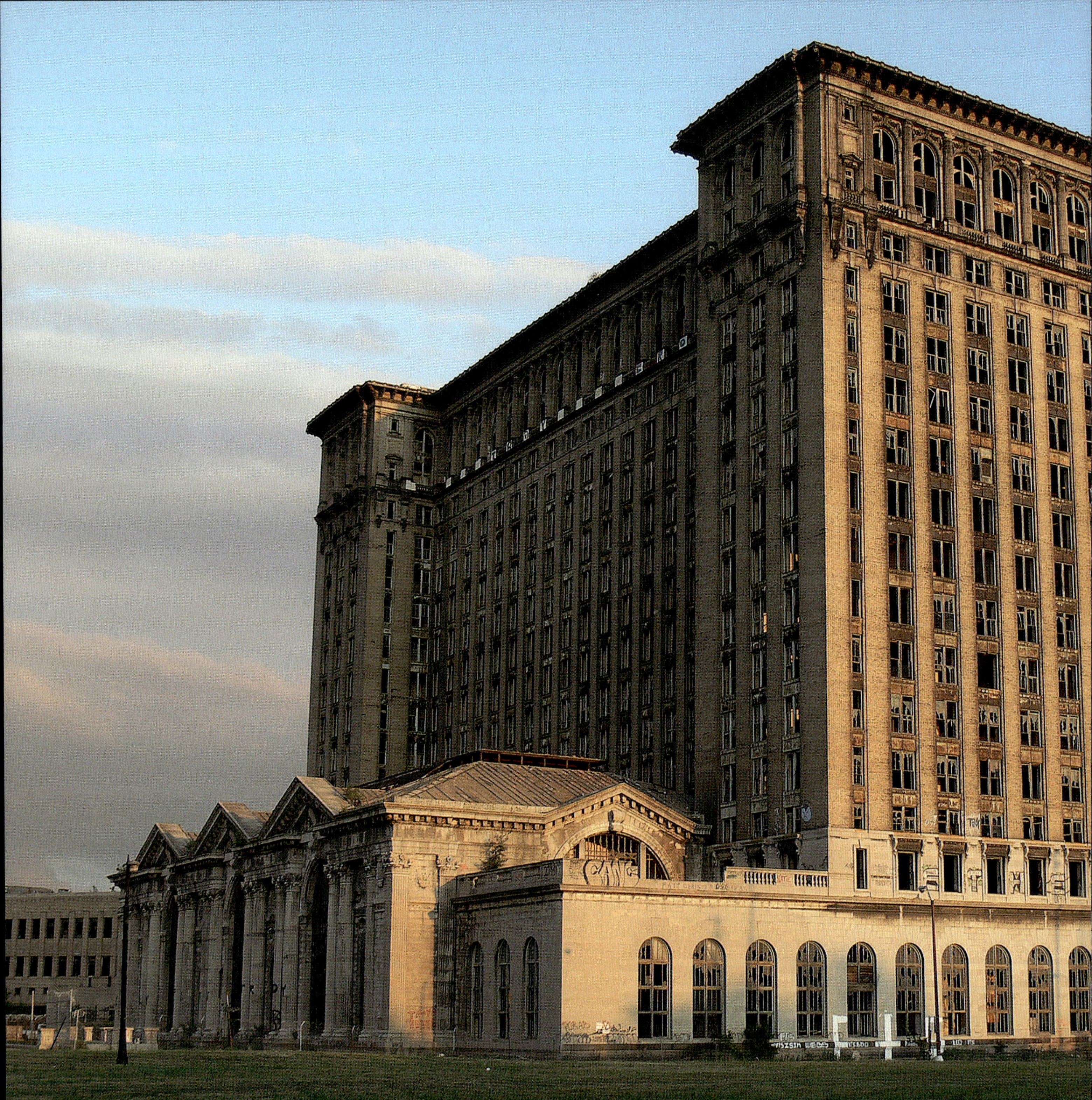

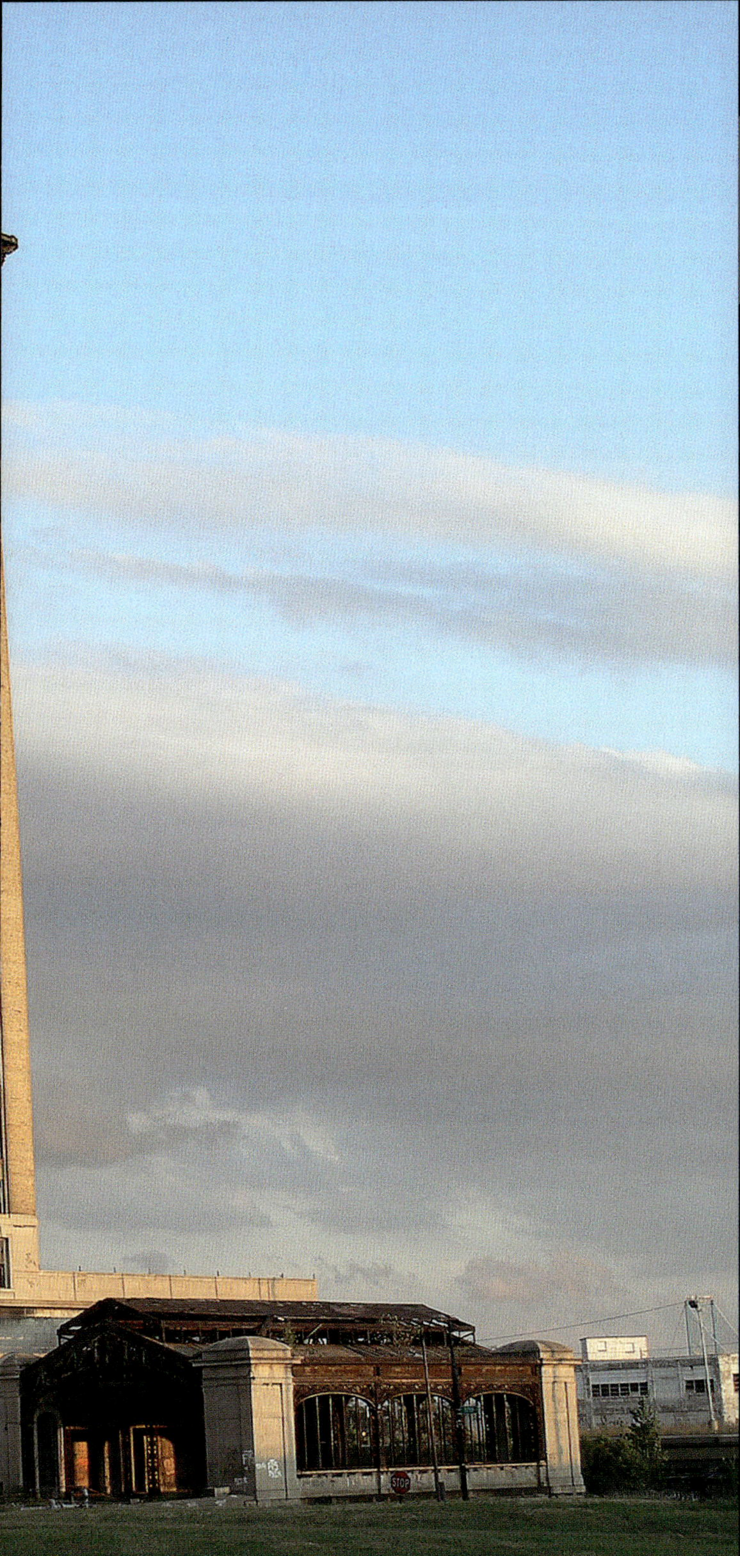

DETROIT

VEREINIGTE STAATEN UNITED STATES

FOTOS VON PHOTOS BY DEREK FARR

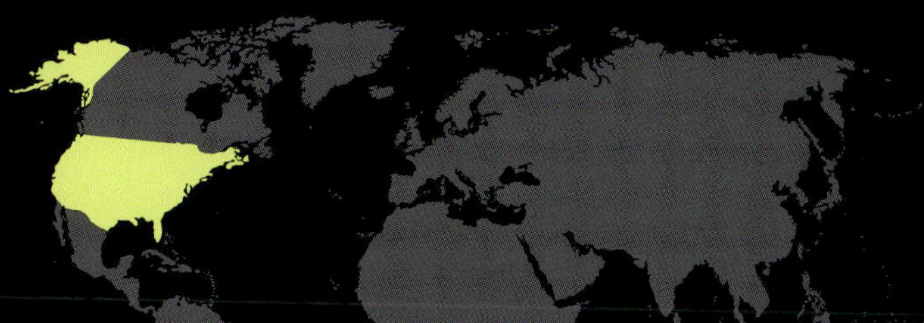

Einst war sie der Mittelpunkt der automobilen Welt. Sie galt als Star der aufblühenden industriellen Moderne und wuchs so unermüdlich, wie die an sie geknüpften Hoffnungen. Chromverzierte Fahrzeuge, die mit hochglänzenden Lacken und raffinierten Details jeden beeindruckten, durchquerten die bis Downtown, in ihr kühnes Herz am Detroit River, weisenden Straßenfluchten. Parfümiert von Benzin, von bläulich-rauchigen Abgasnoten und dem Duft erhitzter Motorenöle, begriff man die Stadt als schöne Gefährtin eines vollkommen neuen Bedürfnisses: dem Wunsch nach globaler Mobilität. Es war die Geburtsstunde des Mythos Auto. Und Zeit war Geld. – Nur wenige hatten davon so präzise Vorstellungen, wie ein großer Architekt Detroits: Albert Kahn. Funktionaler, kostengünstiger und schneller als seine Konkurrenten bauen zu können, machte ihn weit über die Grenzen der USA hinaus bekannt. Im Zweiten Weltkrieg ehrte man ihn, den Sohn eines aus Deutschland in die Vereinigten Staaten übersiedelten Rabbiners, für seine Arbeit schließlich mit hohen Auszeichnungen.

Kahn errichtete für die im 20. Jahrhundert rigoros expandierende Automobilindustrie Hunderte Bauwerke in und bei Detroit und verlieh auch der Silhouette seiner Stadt maßgeblich Gestalt. Seit ihrer Gründung als Ville d'Étroit, der „Stadt an der Meerenge", durch den französischen Kapitän Antoine de la Mothe Cadillac im Juli 1701, entwickelte sich die Ortschaft an der kanadischen Grenze zu einer prosperierenden Handelssiedlung. Öfter wurde zwischen den wechselnden Machthabern darum gekämpft, sie zu beherrschen. Trotz großer Umbrüche in der Fahrzeugbranche und einem tief greifenden, daraus folgenden Wandel in der Stadtentwicklung ist Detroit die größte Metropole des amerikanischen Bundesstaats Michigan. Hier legte 1907 Albert Kahn mit dem Bau einer Fabrik für Packard Motors den Grundstein seines beruflichen Erfolgs. Er setzte auf den günstigen Preis und die Verwendungsvielfalt von Stahlbetonkonstruktionen, denen eine hohe ästhetische Wirkung jedoch nicht abzusprechen war, und beeindruckte so seinen nächsten großen Auftraggeber.

Für Henry Ford schuf der Architekt in Highland Park eine Produktionsanlage, die 70.000 Arbeitern Platz bot. Auf vier taghellen Werketagen wurden massenhaft Autos hergestellt. Die Fertigung am Fließband ließ das Ford-Modell T zum meistgekauften Personenkraftfahrzeug der Welt werden. Es hielt diesen Rekord bis 1972, erst dann wurde es durch den VW Käfer abgelöst. Highland Park stand am Beginn der modernen Zeit mit ihren unerschöpflich scheinenden Effizienzanforderungen. 1927 nahm im neu erbauten River-Rouge-Komplex die Ford-Produktion den Betrieb auf. Von Albert Kahn für 90.000 Mitarbeiter konzipiert, galt dieser Betrieb damals als die weltweit größte Werkanlage. Im Laufe der Zwanzigerjahre von ihm fertiggestellt, hielt das General Motors Building, heute Cadillac Place genannt, als größtes Bürogebäude seiner Zeit einen weiteren Rekord der Baugeschichte. Und Kahns 135 Meter hohes, im Art-déco-Stil reich geschmücktes Fisher Building blieb 80 Jahre lang das bewunderte Wahrzeichen der Stadt am Detroit River.

Vom Sog des früheren Reichtums ist Detroit nicht viel geblieben. Die durch enorme Investitionen rasch ausgedehnte Metropole bildet sich immer stärker zurück. Sie wurde inzwischen von über 60 Prozent ihrer Bevölkerung verlassen. Ganze Stadtgebiete sind dem Verfall preisgegeben. Und Wildnis erobert die aufgegebenen Flächen, auch wenn in Detroit bis heute die größte Automesse Amerikas stattfindet.

It was once the center of the automobile world. It was known as the star of the blossoming modern industrial era and grew as untiringly as did the hopes pinned to it. Chrome decorated vehicles with high gloss paint and refined details that impressed everyone crisscrossed the streets pointing to the downtown in the city's bold heart on the Detroit River. Perfumed by gasoline, blue smoky exhaust and the scent of hot motor oil, the city was understood to be the beautiful companion of a completely new need: the need for global mobility. It was the moment of birth of the legend of the automobile. And time was money. Only a few people had as detailed ideas as Detroit's great architect, Albert Kahn. Being able to build in a way that was more functional, more cost-effective and faster than his competitors made him known beyond the borders of the USA. The son of a rabbi from Germany who had emigrated to the United States, he was ultimately honored in the Second World War with prestigious awards for his work.

For the rigorously expanding automobile industry in the 20th century, Kahn built hundreds of buildings in and near Detroit and gave the silhouette of his city its definitive shape. Since its founding in July 1701 as Ville d'Etroit, the "city on the strait" by the French captain Antoine de la Mothe Cadillac, the town on the Canadian border developed into a prosperous business settlement. Often there was a battle to control it by the changing rulers. In spite of the collapse of the motor vehicle industry and the consequent far-reaching change in the city's development, Detroit is still the largest metropolis in the American state of Michigan. It was here that Albert Kahn laid the foundation of his career success with the construction of a factory for Packard Motors in 1907. He relied on a low price and the wide range of uses of reinforced concrete construction, which had no aesthetic appeal to speak of but it impressed his next large customer. The architect designed a manufacturing plant for Henry Ford in Highland Park that provided 70,000 jobs. Automobiles were manufactured on a massive scale on four factory story's that were as bright as day. Manufacturing on an assembly line resulted in the Ford Model T becoming the best-selling passenger car in the world. It held this record until 1972 when it was overtaken by the VW Beetle. At the beginning of modern times, Highland Park stood out with its apparently inexhaustible performance standard. In 1927, Ford production opened in the newly built River Rouge complex. Designed by Albert Kahn for 90,000 employees, this plant was the largest factory facility in the world at that time. Completed by him in the 1920s, the General Motors building, today Cadillac Place, was the largest office building of its time, holding another record in construction history. And Kahn's Fisher building, 135 meters high and richly decorated in the art deco style, remained the admired landmark of the city on the Detroit river for 80 years.

Not much remains in the wake of Detroit's earlier wealth. The metropolis that expanded quickly due to enormous investments is regressing more and more. In the meantime, more than 60 percent of the former population has left. Entire neighborhoods have fallen into disrepair. And the wilderness is taking over abandoned areas, even though the largest car show in America still takes place in Detroit today.

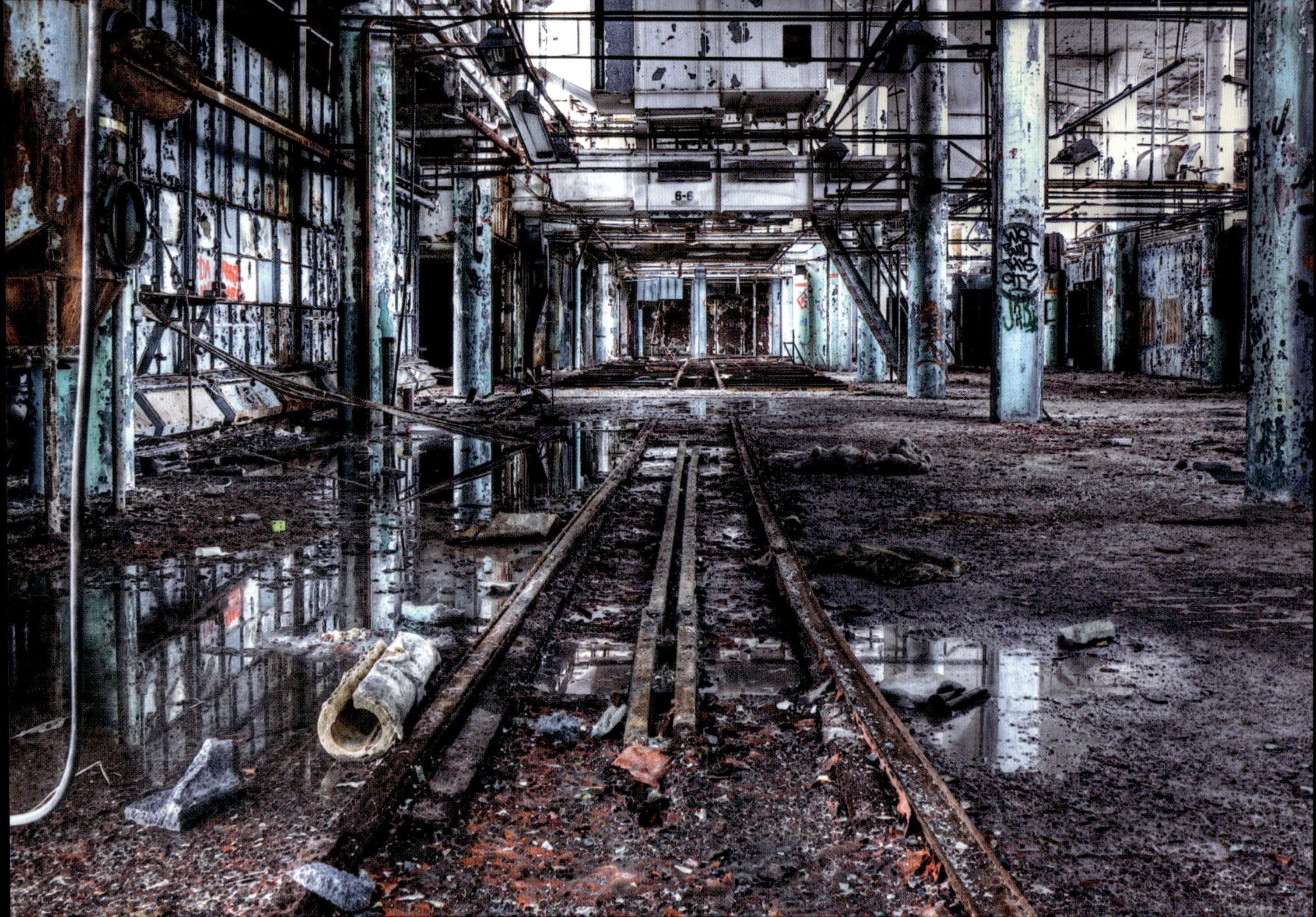
6-6

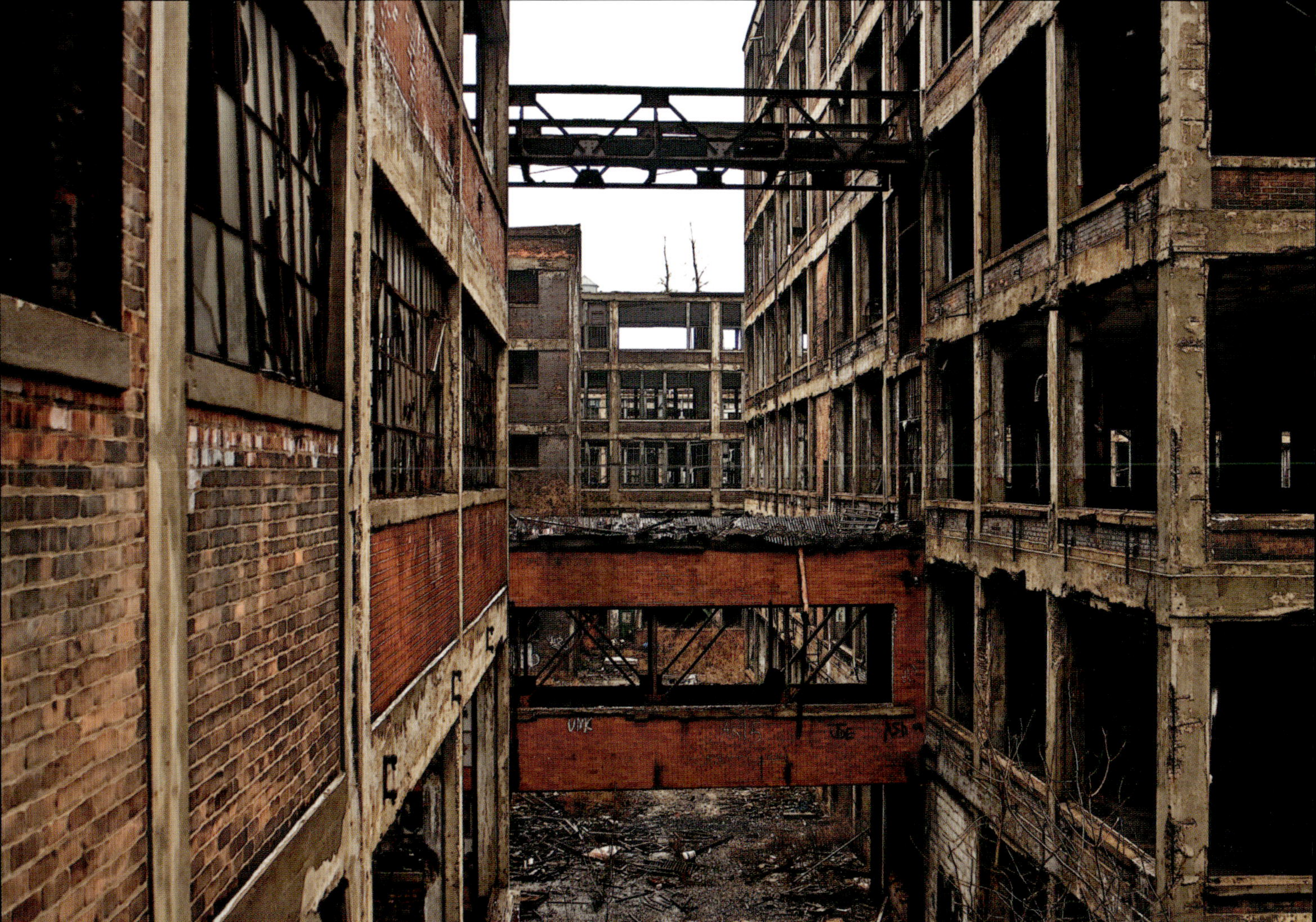

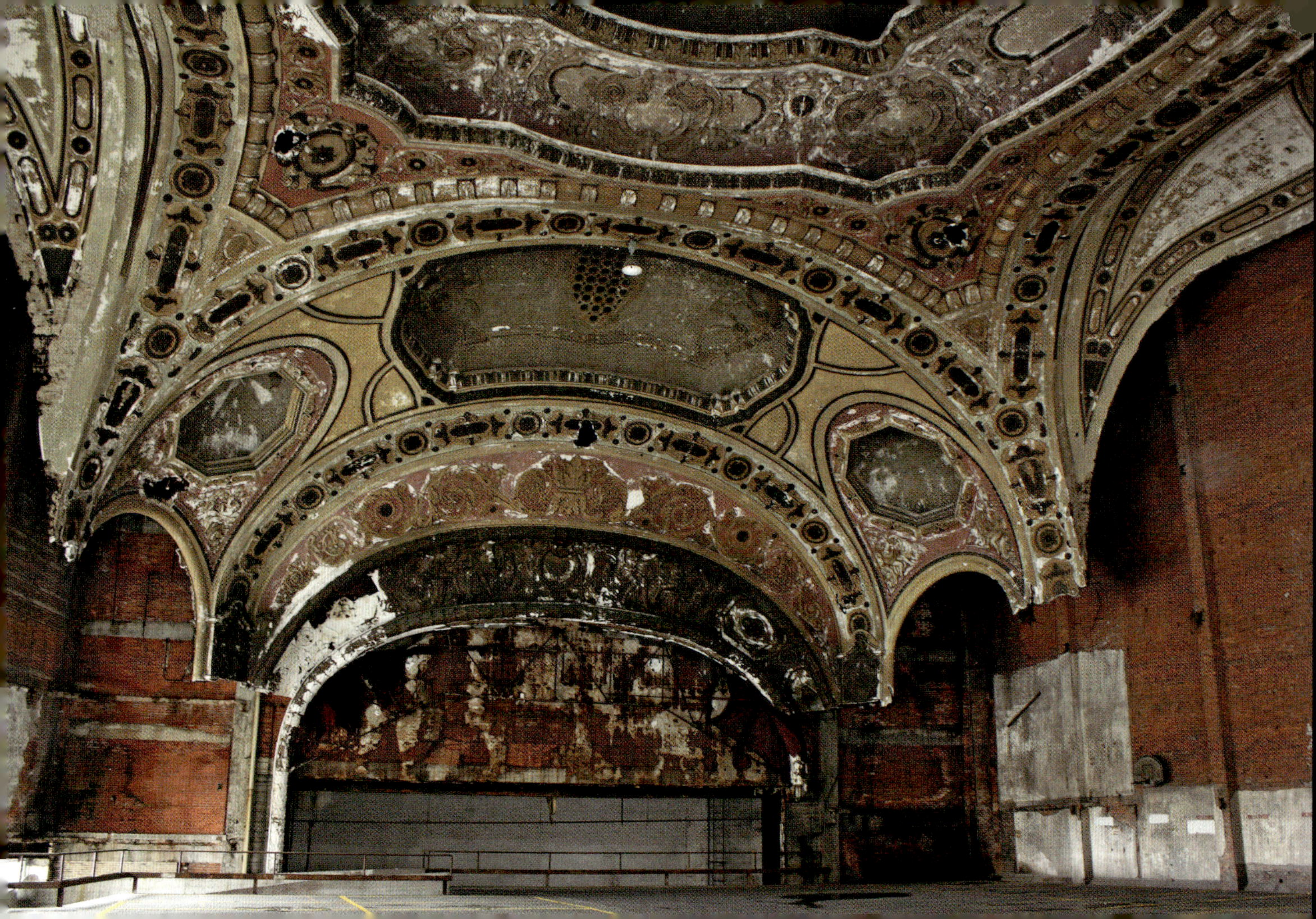

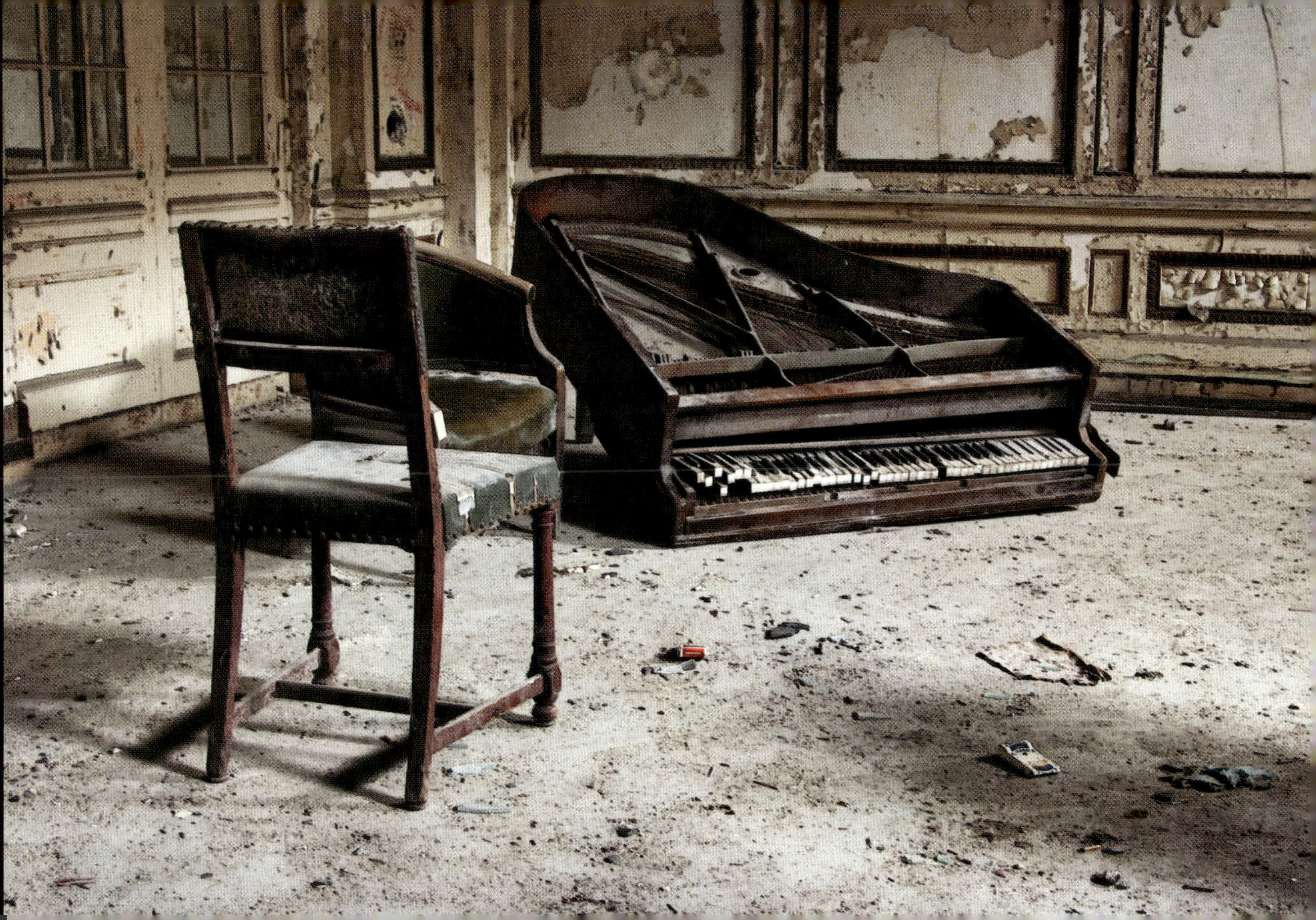

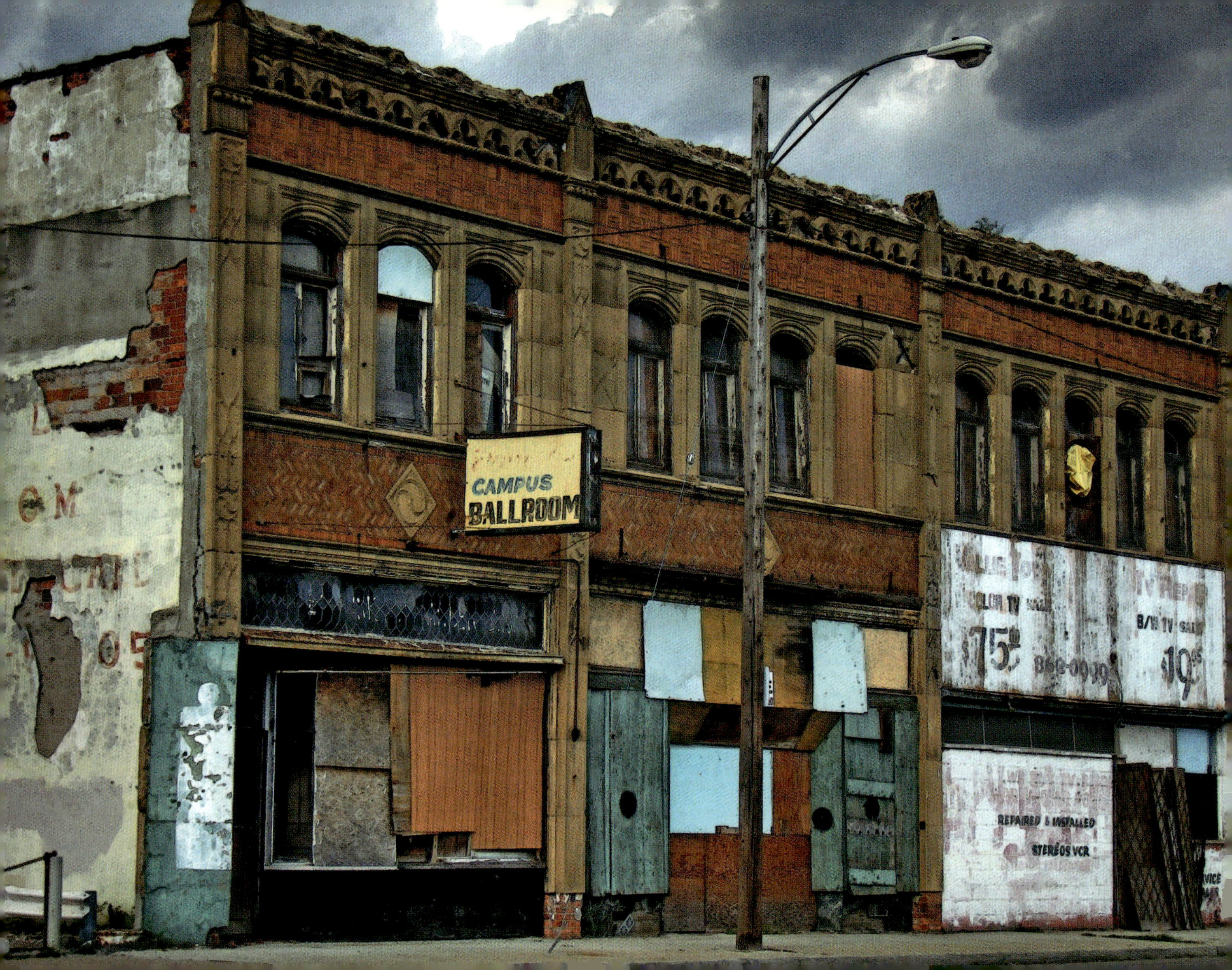
CAMPUS
BALLROOM
REPAIRED & INSTALLED
STEREOS VCR

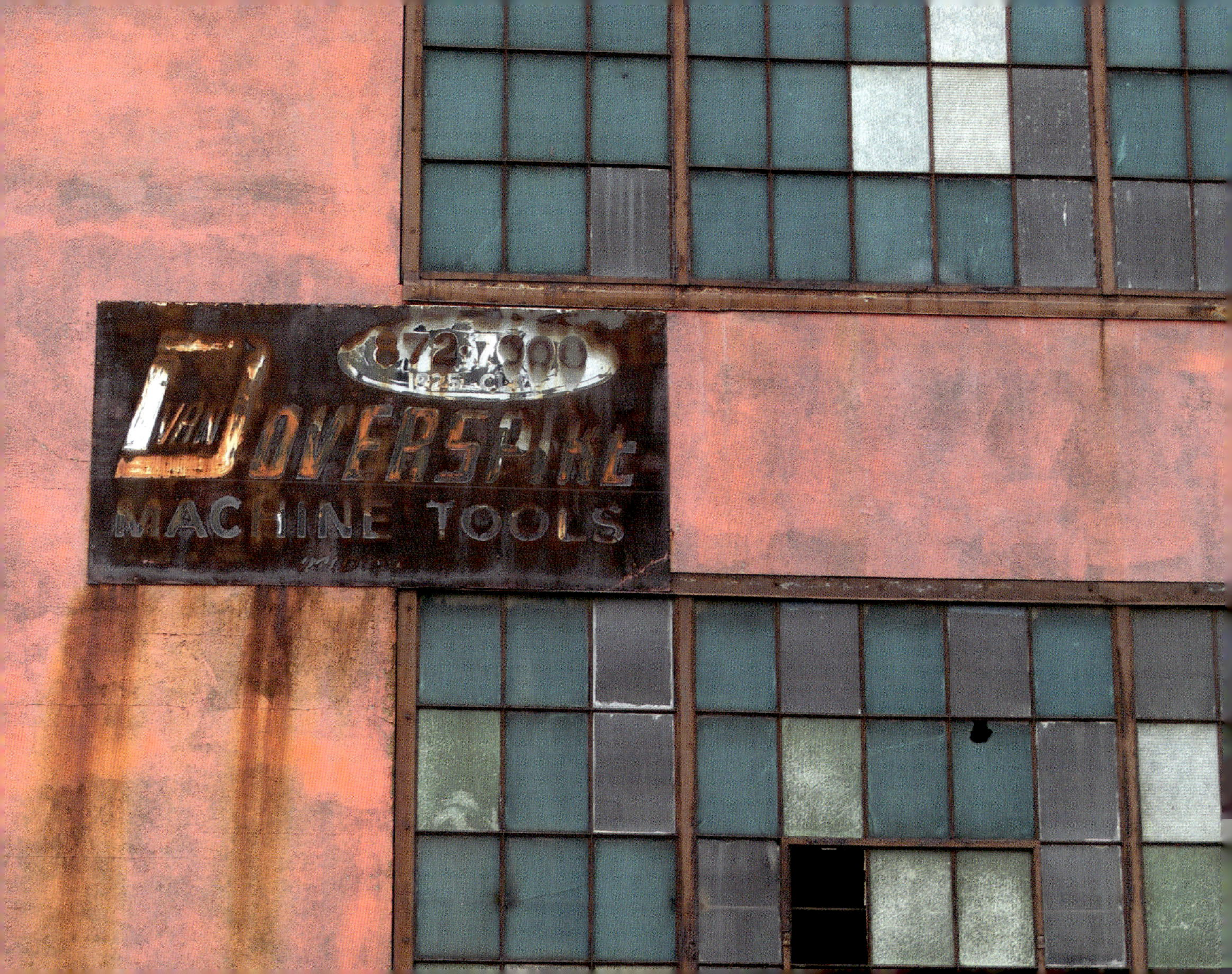
872-7000
VAN DOVERSPIKE
MACHINE TOOLS

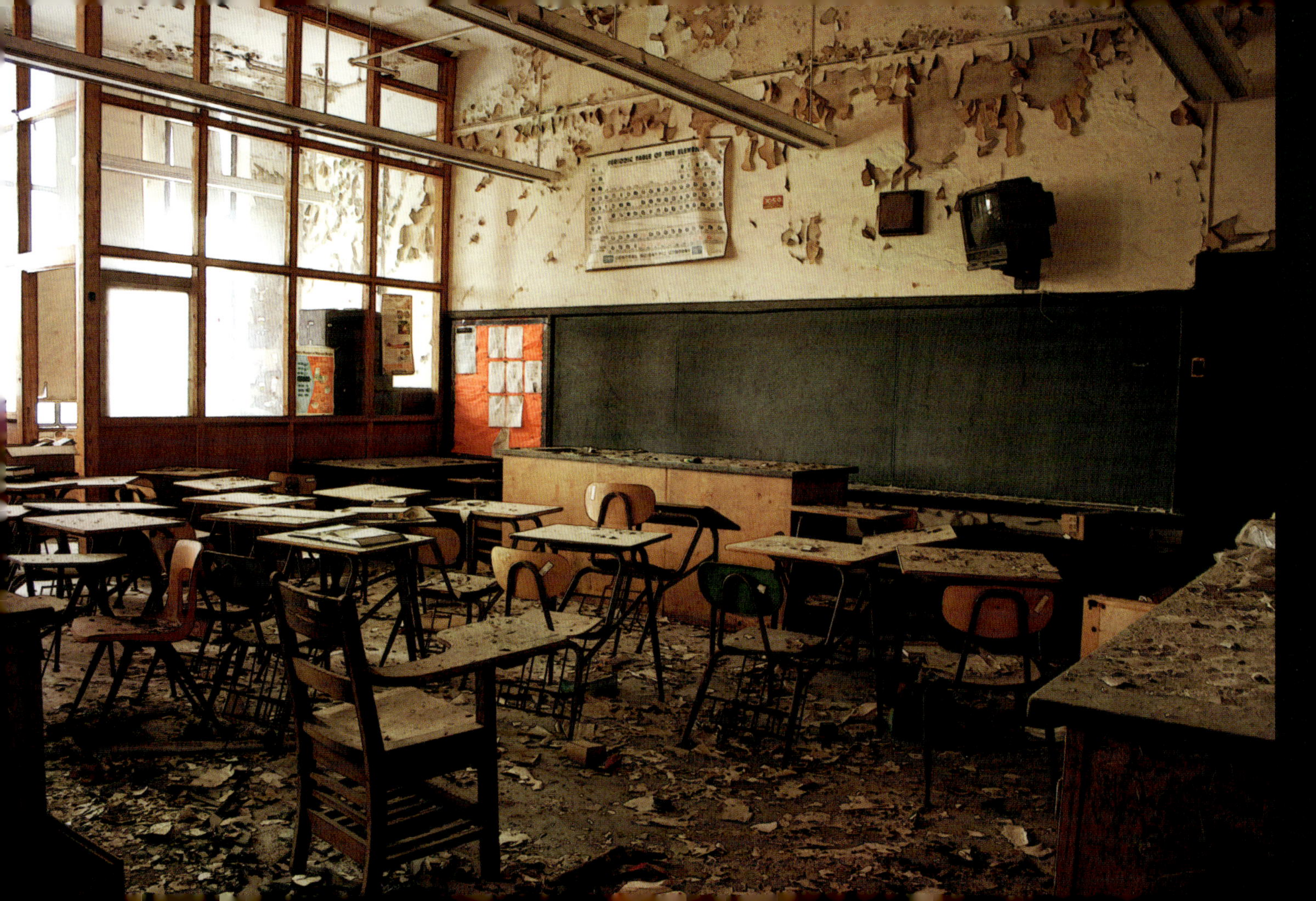

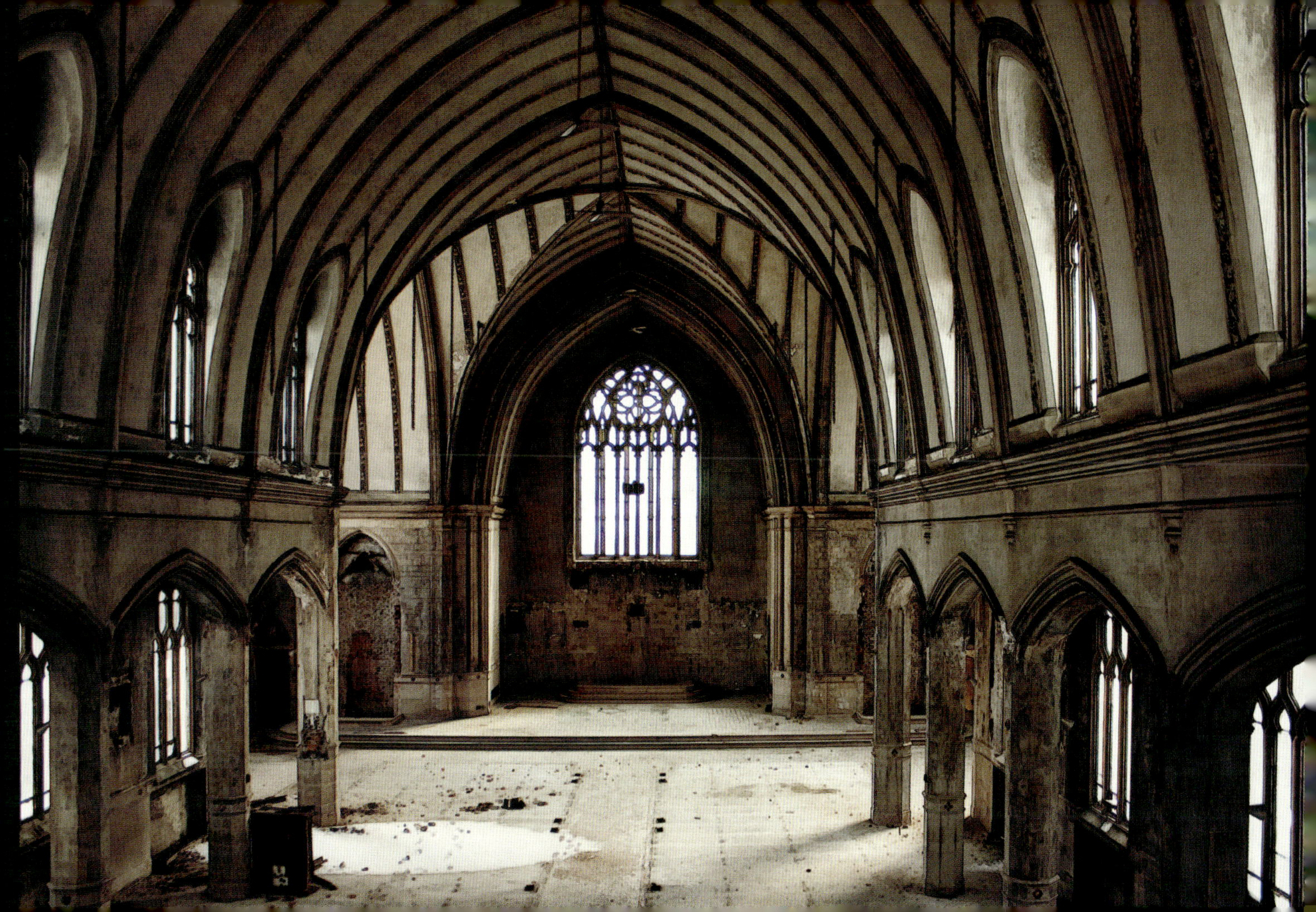

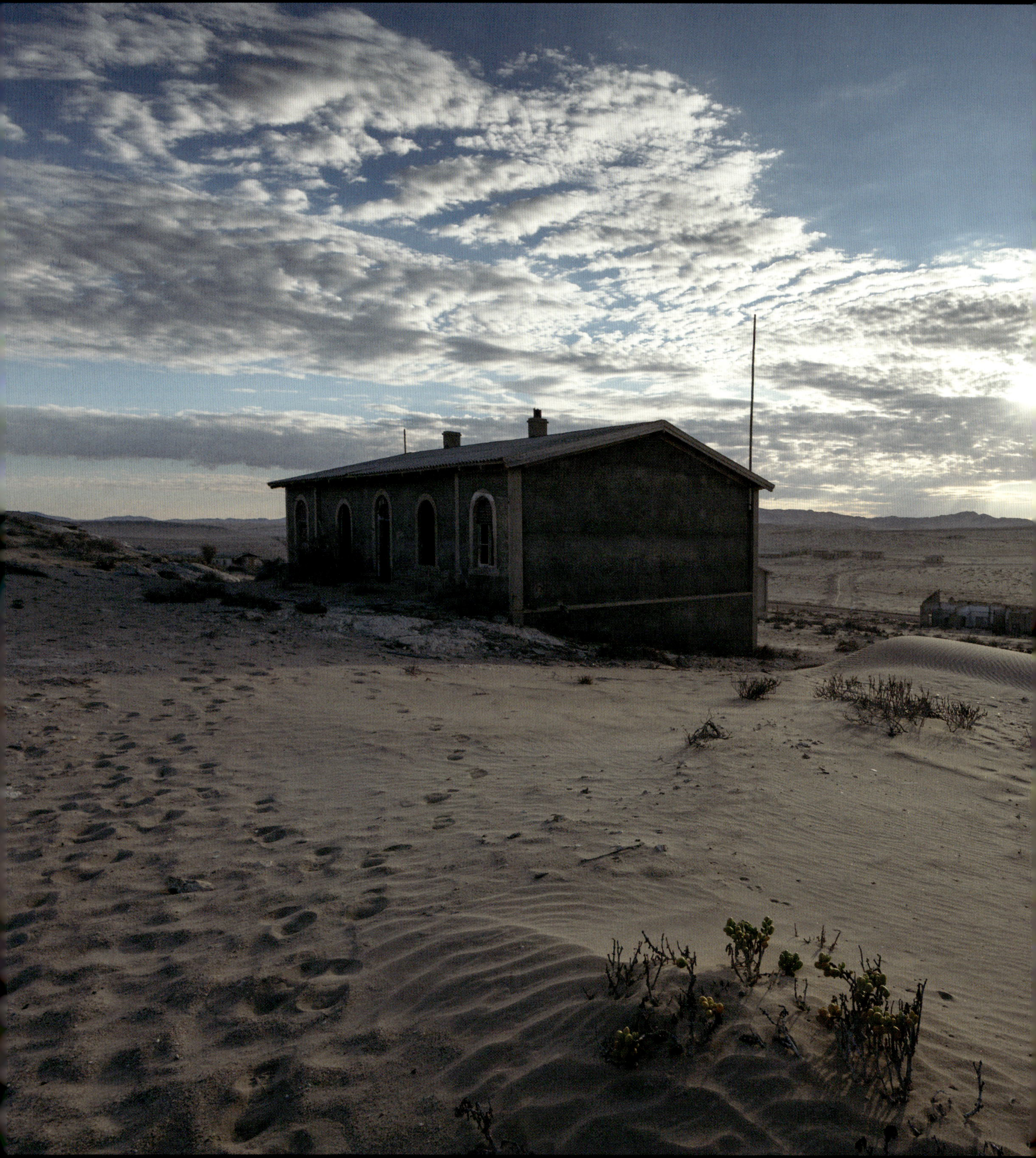

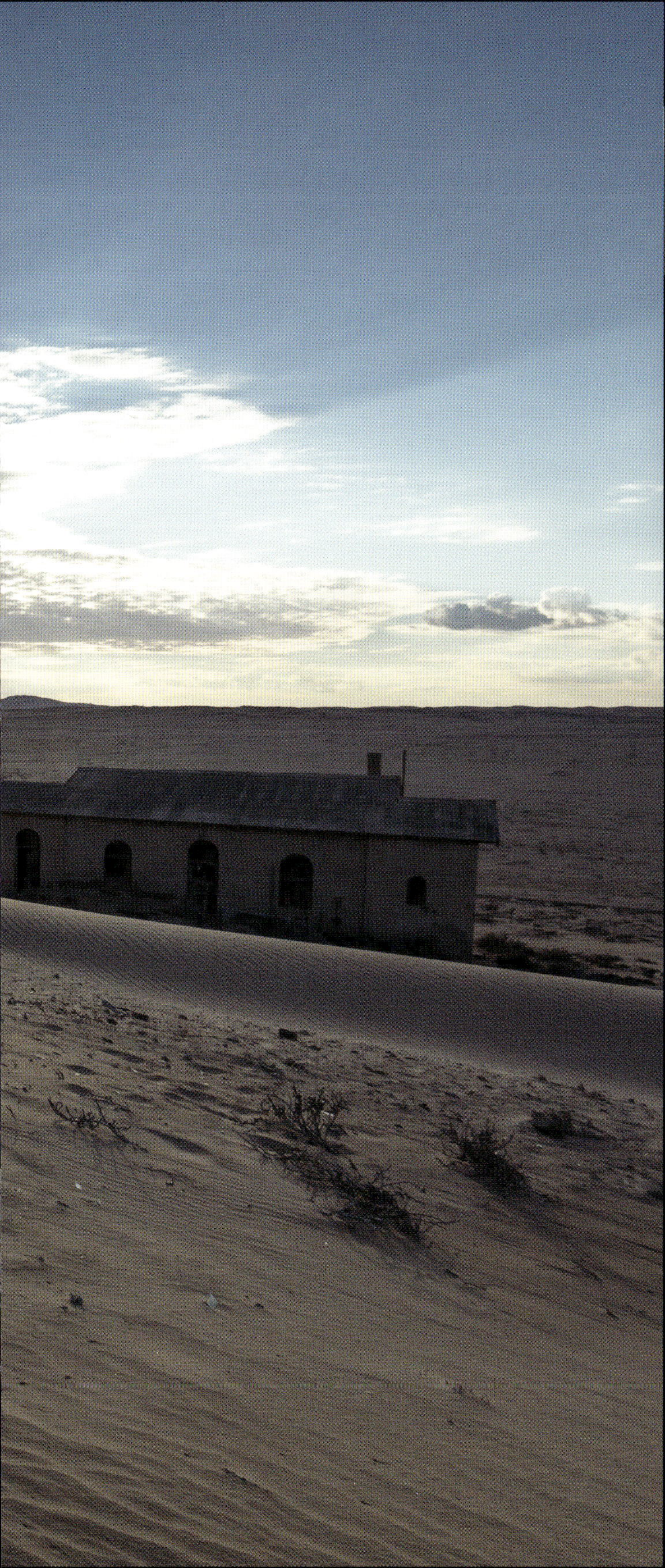

KOLMANNSKUPPE

NAMIBIA NAMIBIA

FOTOS VON PHOTOS BY KRIS DELCOURTE

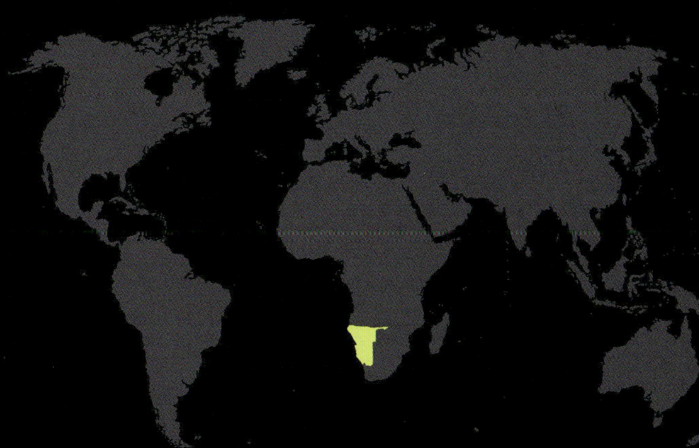

Wohin man auch blickte: Sand. Die älteste Wüste der Erde, die Namib, was „leerer Platz" oder „Ort, wo nichts ist" bedeutet. Der deutsche Bahnangestellte August Stauch hatte seinem Vorgesetzten nachgegeben und war 1907 in die Kolonie Deutsch-Südwestafrika gereist. Der Thüringer litt an Asthma, das er in wärmerem Klima zu kurieren hoffte. Vom Thüringer Wald kam er in die Ortschaft Grasplatz – letztere hatte sich Stauch anders vorgestellt. Eine Wüste hatte er nicht erwartet vorzufinden. Auch das Kommende sollte seine Vorstellungskraft überbieten, ja: sprengen – und ihn für alles entschädigen. Als Bahnmeister wachte Stauch über eine Teilstrecke der Lüderitz-Eisenbahn zwischen Lüderitzbucht und der Siedlung Aus. Er hatte dafür zu sorgen, dass die Schienen nicht unter Treibsand verschwanden. Eine Sisyphusarbeit, dazu der scharfe Wind – eigentlich war alles zum Ersticken.
Am 14. April 1908 aber, am Ort Grasplatz, wo eigentlich kein Grashalm wuchs, zeigte ihm der afrikanische Hilfsarbeiter Zacharias Lewala einen „schönen Stein". An seinem Uhrglas prüfte Stauch die Härte, der Stein ritzte es an. Ein befreundeter Bergwerksingenieur aus Lüderitz bestätigte ihm, dass es sich um einen Diamanten handelte. Stauch steckte sofort seinen Claim ab, gab die Anstellung bei der Bahn auf und spezialisierte sich ganz auf das Diamantengeschäft. Nahe Grasplatz gründete er Kolmannskuppe, das sich in den folgenden Jahren zum reichsten Ort des Kontinents entwickeln sollte. Geschichten wie diese, dass Diamanten täglich in Marmeladengläsern dem Minenbesitzer ausgehändigt wurden und dass Stauch selbst im Sitzen, mit den Händen nur durch den Sand streichend, gleich 37 Diamanten fand, hatten Folgen. Hunderte Schatzsucher eroberten das Territorium. Bereits im September 1908 erklärte die deutsche Reichsregierung einen 100 mal 300 Kilometer umfassenden Küstenabschnitt zum „Sperrgebiet", um sich die Schürfrechte zu sichern. Es entstanden mehrere Ortschaften.
In Kolmannskuppe wohnten bald 400 Deutsche und 800 afrikanische Arbeiter. Licht, von einem Elektrizitätswerk erzeugt, beschien exklusive Jugendstilvillen und auch schmucklosere steinerne Häuser. Die afrikanischen Arbeiter waren in Holzbaracken untergebracht. Im ortseigenen Krankenhaus stand ein Röntgenapparat. Schiffe transportierten Baumaterialien, modernste Technik und Einrichtungsgegenstände aus dem Kaiserreich in die Wüstenregion. Selbst für europäische Verhältnisse luxuriöse Gegenstände wie Grammofone, Badewannen, Kühlaggregate, Toiletten mit Wasserspülung, Sportgeräte vermittelten den Siedlern Heimat. Das Trinkwasser brachten Tankschiffe aus Kapstadt. Die Kinder besuchten eine Volksschule im Ort. Zum Zeitvertreib sammelte man sich zu Turnfesten, vergnügte sich im Schwimmbad, ging ins Theater oder in den Kegelverein „Gut Holz". Abends floss der Champagner im Casino oder in der Hafenstadt Lüderitz, und es wird berichtet, dass die Bardamen mit Diamanten bezahlt wurden.
Nach dem Ersten Weltkrieg übernahm das britische Kolonialreich Deutsch-Südwestafrika. Kolmannskuppe blieb jedoch von Deutschen weiter bewohnt. 1930 endete hier der Diamantenabbau. Der Millionär August Stauch starb 1947 als armer Mann, die Weltwirtschaftskrise hatte sein Vermögen vernichtet. Seit den Fünfzigerjahren liegt der Ort verlassen da. Wind treibt Sandschleier vor sich her und löscht die Spuren der Besucher in der einstigen Diamantenstadt. Um die verlassenen Häuser schmiegt sich Sand und in der Mittagssonne glaubt man, etwas darin aufblitzen zu sehen.

Everywhere you look: Sand. The oldest desert in the world, the Namib means, "empty place" or "place where nothing is". The German railway employee, August Stauch gave in to his superiors and travelled in 1907 to the colony in German Southwest Africa. The man from Thuringia suffered from asthma, which he hoped to cure in the warmer climate. He went from the Thuringian forest to the town of Grasplatz, different from what Stauch had imagined. He hadn't expected to find a desert. Also, that which was to come exceeded his imagination – well, it blew it away – and compensated him for everything. As railway manager, Stauch watched over a segment of the Lüderitz railway between Lüderitzbucht and the settlement of Aus. Therefore, he had to make sure that the tracks did not disappear under drifting sand. It was a never ending job because of the strong wind, and actually everything was suffocating.

On April 14, 1908 at the town of Grasplatz, where actually no blade of grass grew, an African laborer, Zacharias Lewala, showed him a "beautiful stone". Stauch tested its hardness on his watch glass, and the stone scratched it. A mining engineer friend from Lüderitz confirmed to him that it was a diamond. Stauch registered his claim immediately, gave up his position with the railway and specialized completely in the diamond business. Near to Grasplatz, he founded Kolmanskop, which became the richest place on the continent in the following years. Stories like these, that diamonds are handed to mine owners in jam jars every day and that Stauch himself found 37 diamonds while he was seated stroking his hand through the sand, had consequences. Hundreds of treasure seekers streamed into the territory. By September 1908, the German government declared a 100 by 300 kilometer coastal area as a "restricted zone" in order to secure the mining rights for itself. Many towns sprung up.

Soon almost 400 Germans and 800 African workers lived in Kolmanskop. Light provided by a power plant illuminated exclusive art nouveau villas and also less tasteful stone houses. The African workers were housed in wooden barracks. There was an x-ray machine in the town's own hospital. Ships transported building materials, the latest technology and interior furnishings from the German empire to the desert region. Even by European standards, luxury items like gramophones, bathtubs, cooling units, toilets with flushing water and sports equipment brought the settlers a sense of being at home. Drinking water was brought by tankers from Cape Town. The children attended a public school in the town. To pass the time, people gathered at sports competitions, enjoyed themselves in the swimming pool, went to the theatre or to the "Good Wood" bowling alley. In the evenings, champagne flowed in the casino or in the port town of Lüderitz, and they say that the barmaids were paid with diamonds.

After the First World War, the British colonial empire took over German Southwest Africa. Kolmanskop, however continued to be populated by Germans. In 1930 diamond mining ended there. The millionaire, August Stauch died in 1947 as a poor man; the worldwide economic depression had destroyed his fortune. The town has been abandoned since the 1950s. Wind blows veils of sand, covering the tracks of the visitors to the former diamond town. Sand nestles up against the abandoned buildings and in the midday sun, you think you can see something sparkling in it.

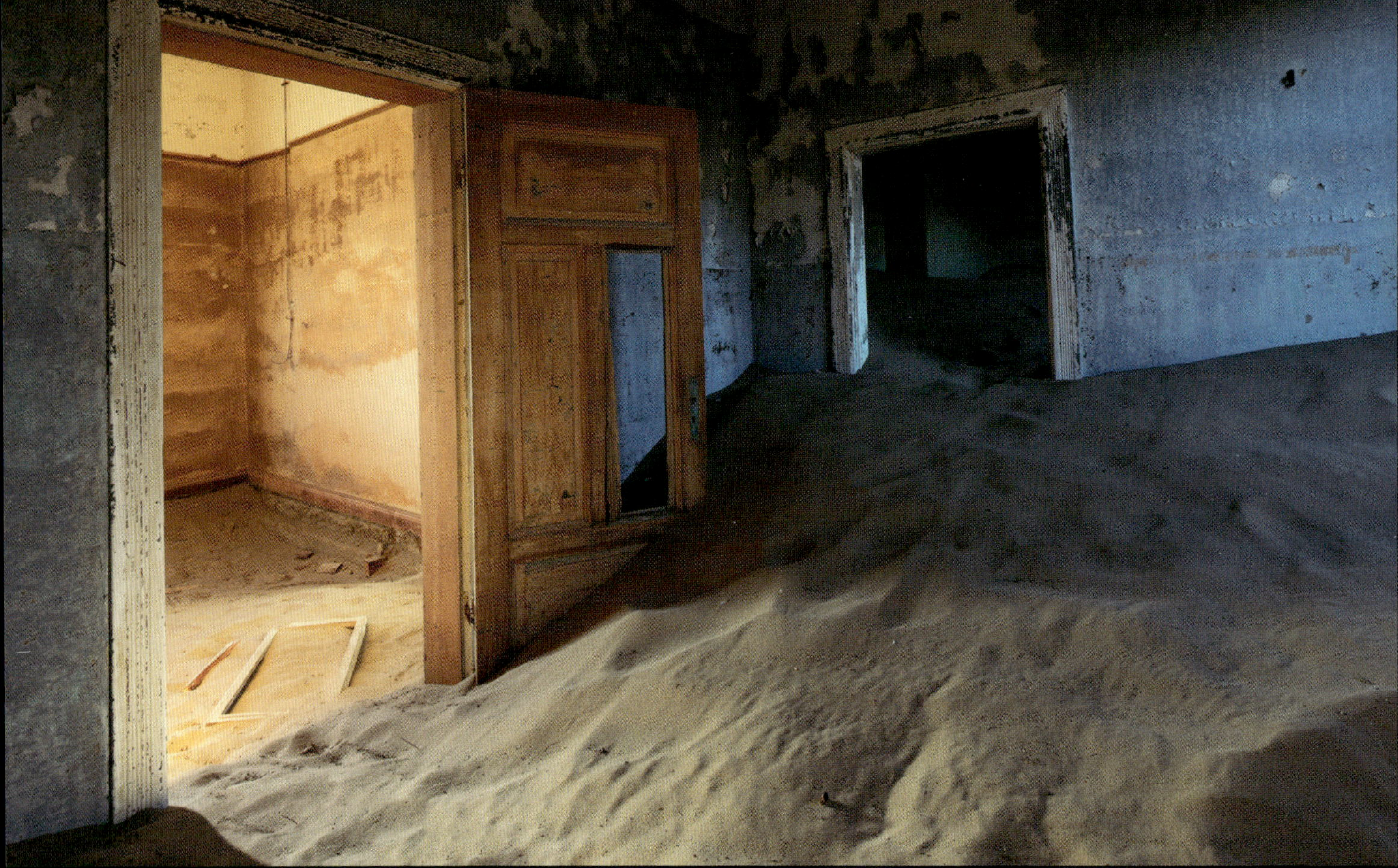

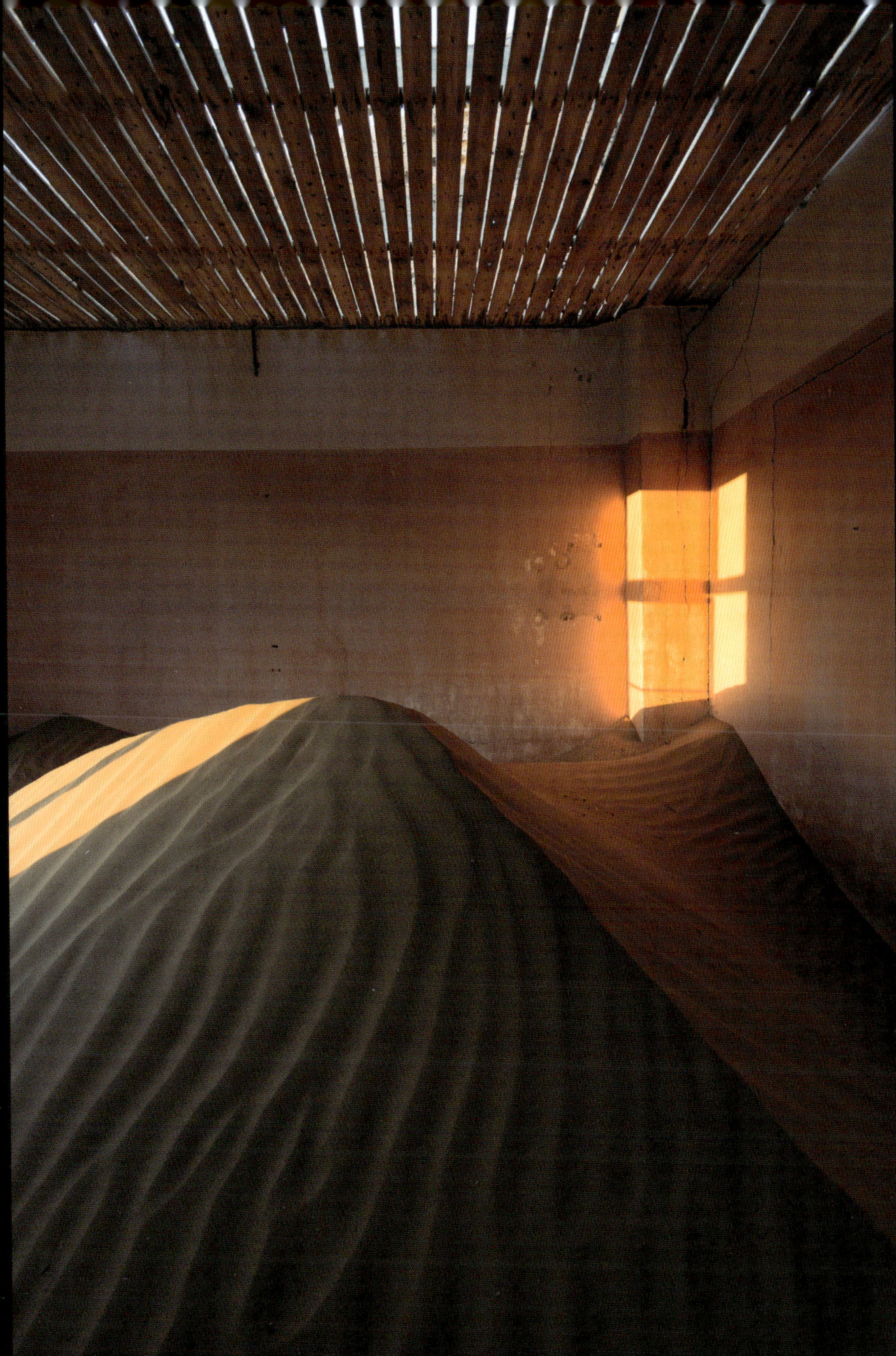

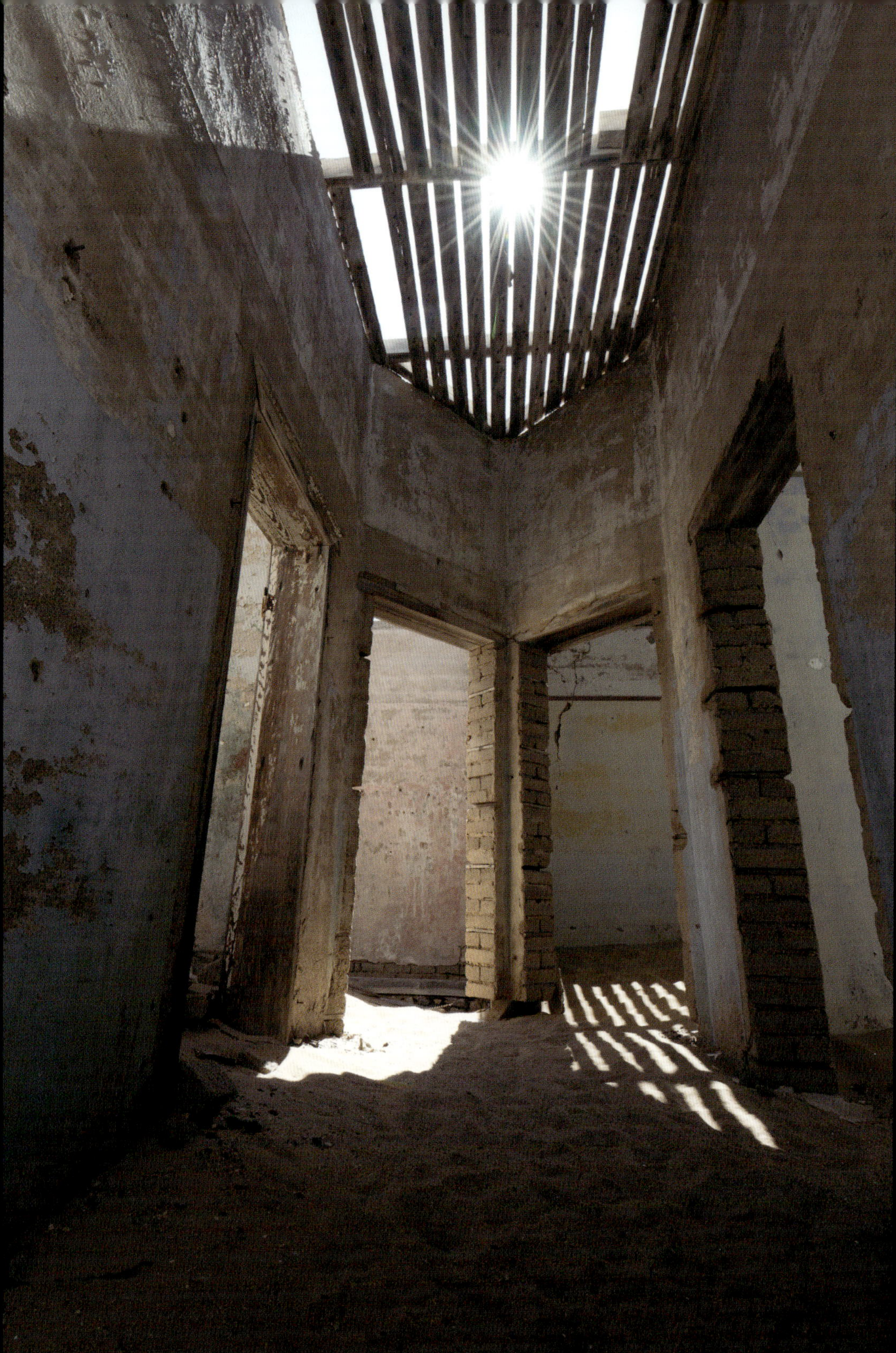

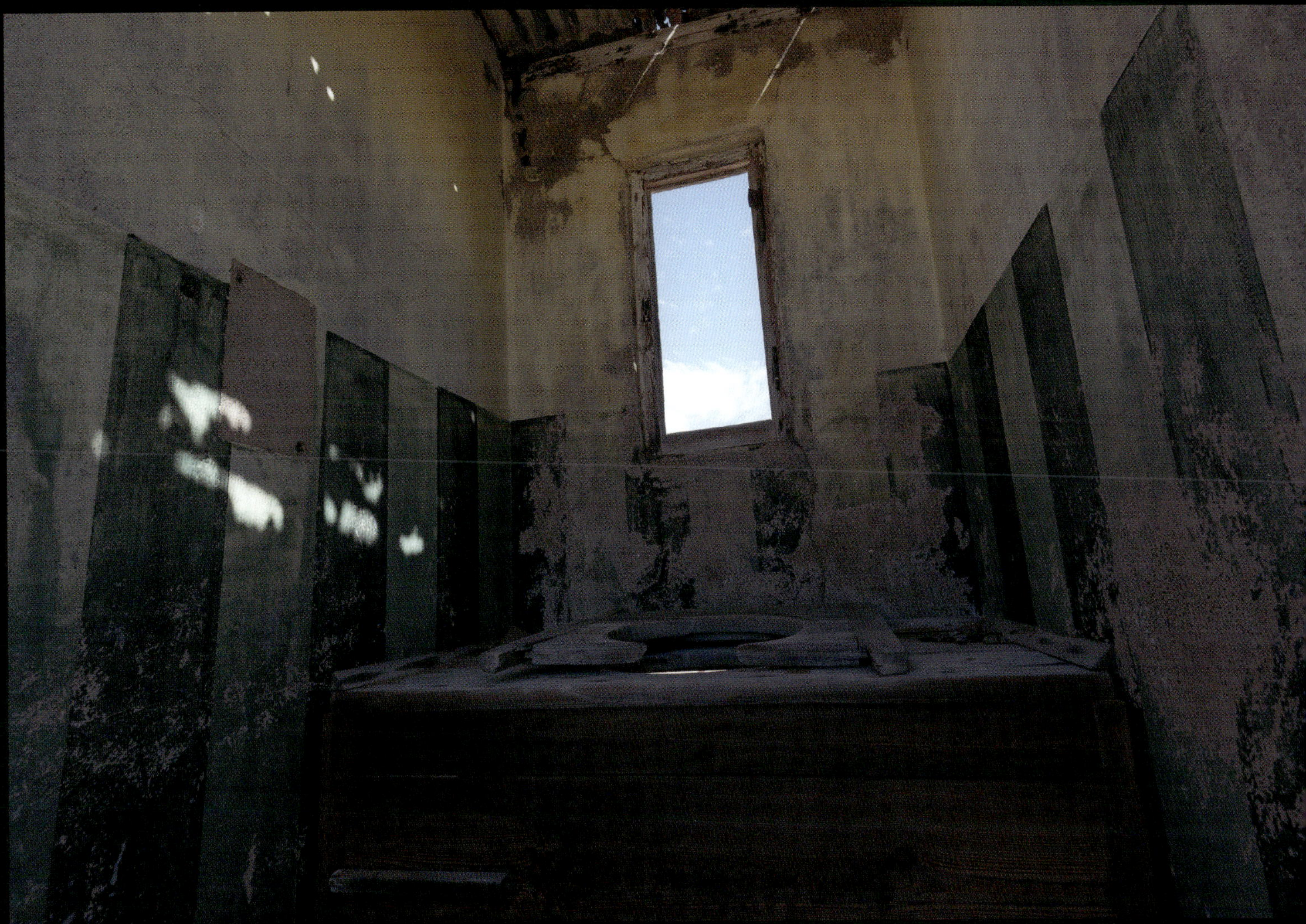

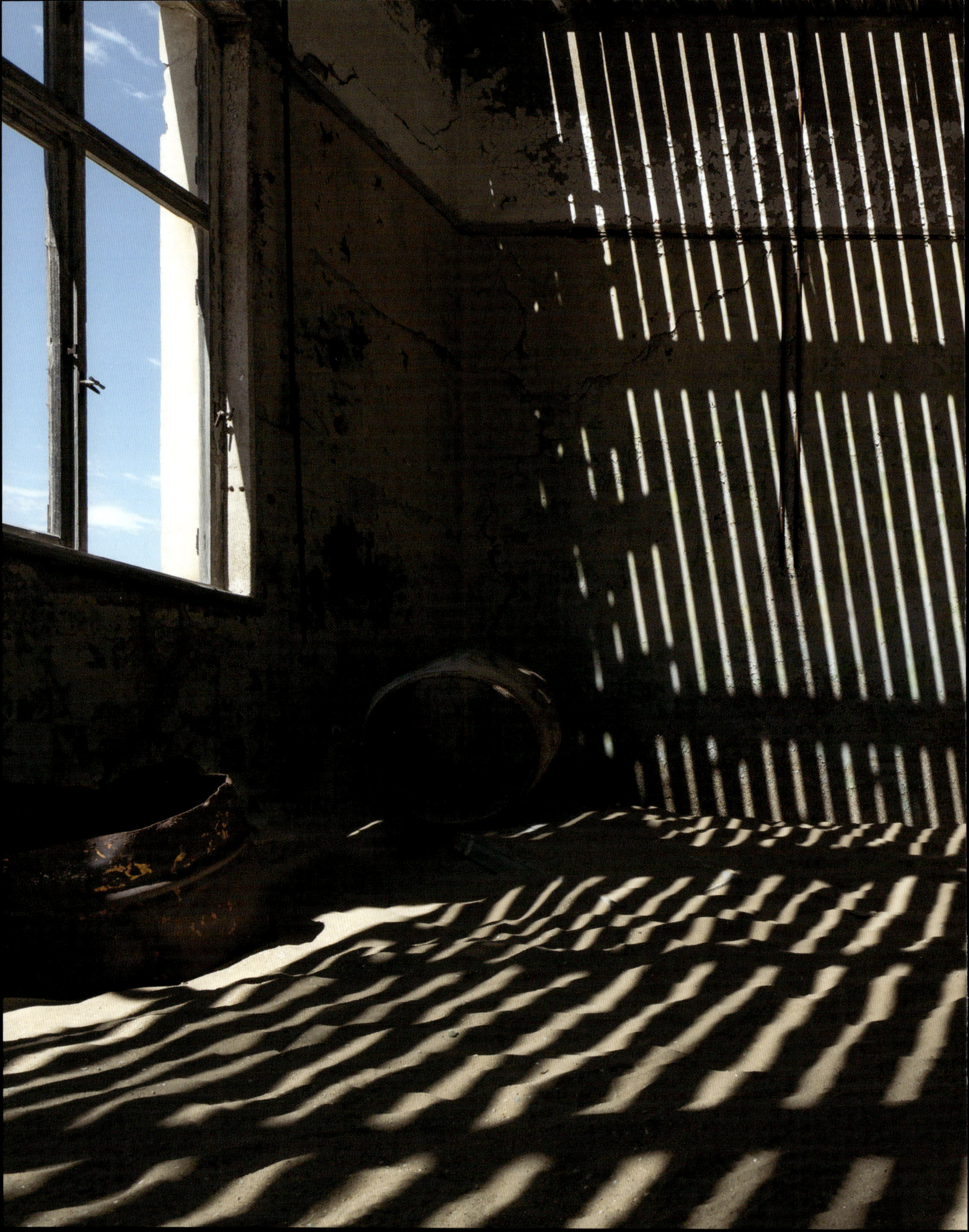

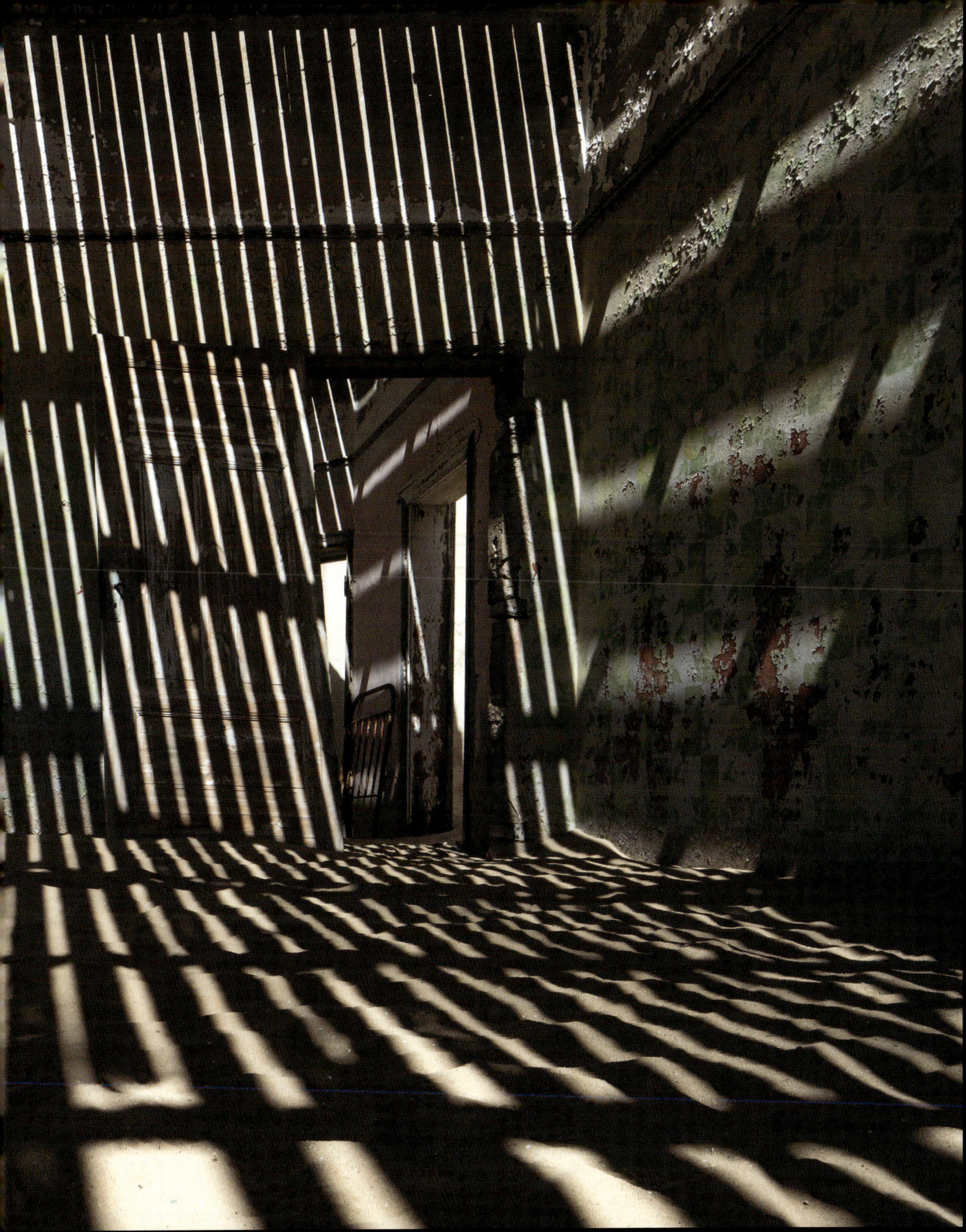

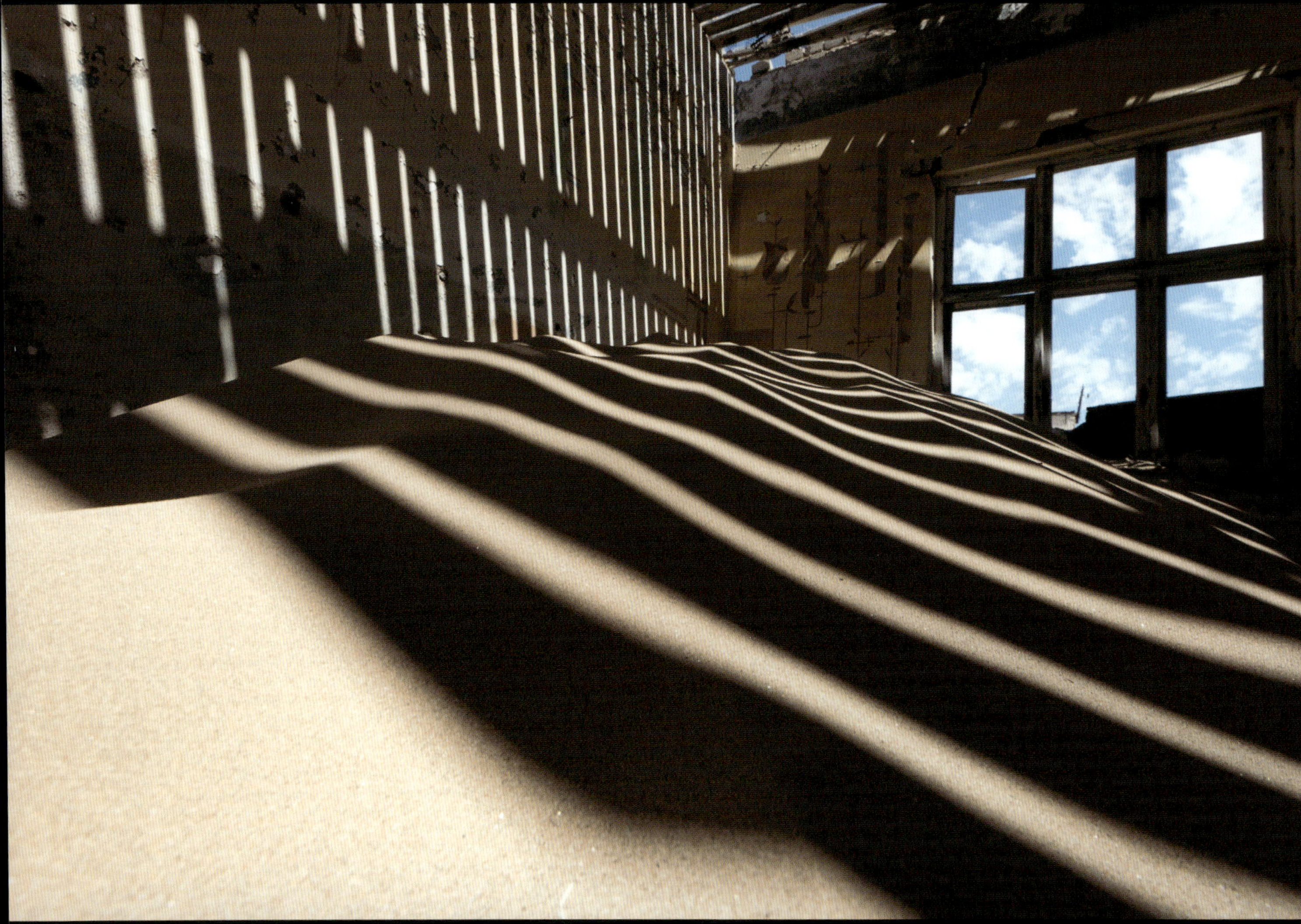

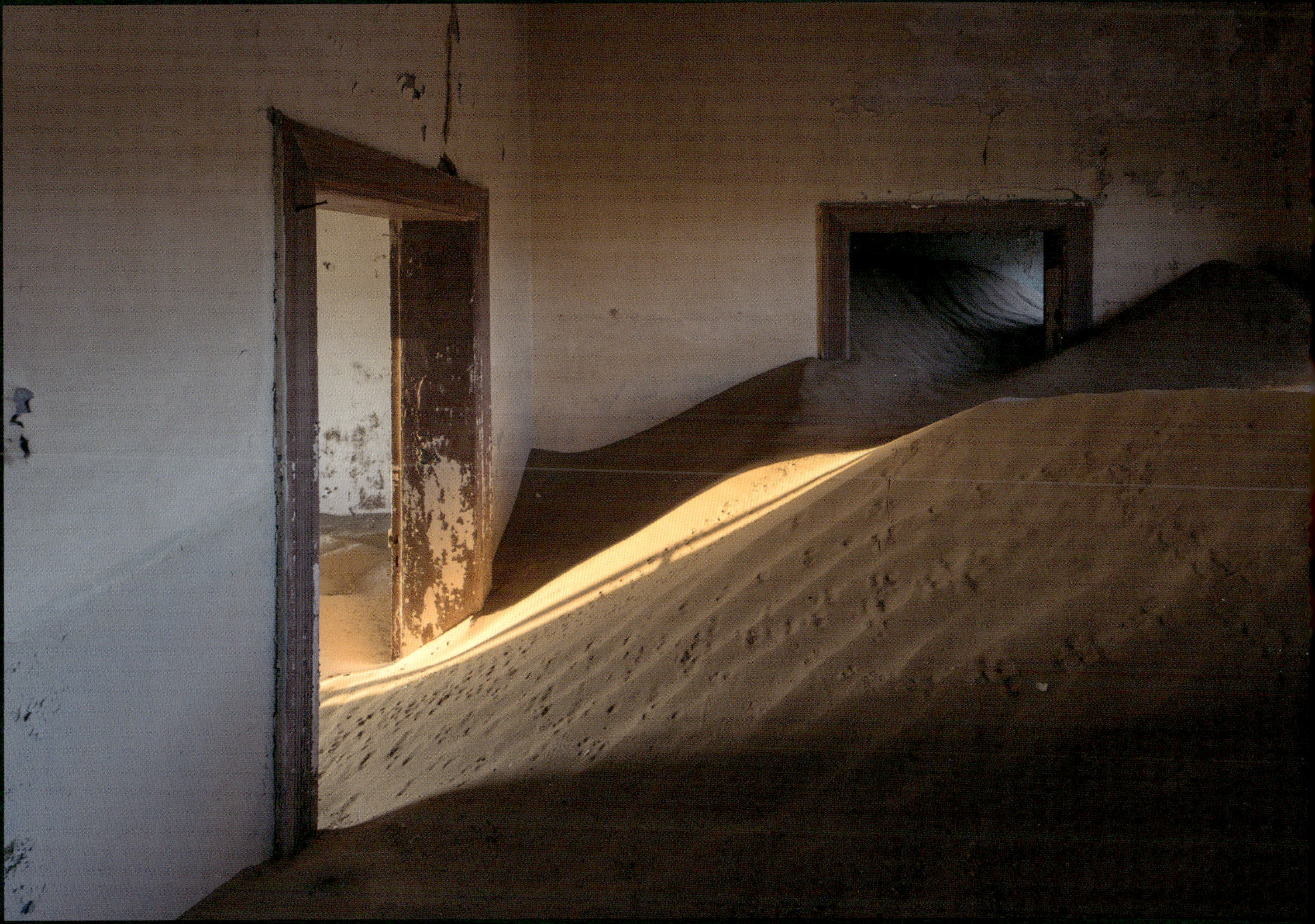

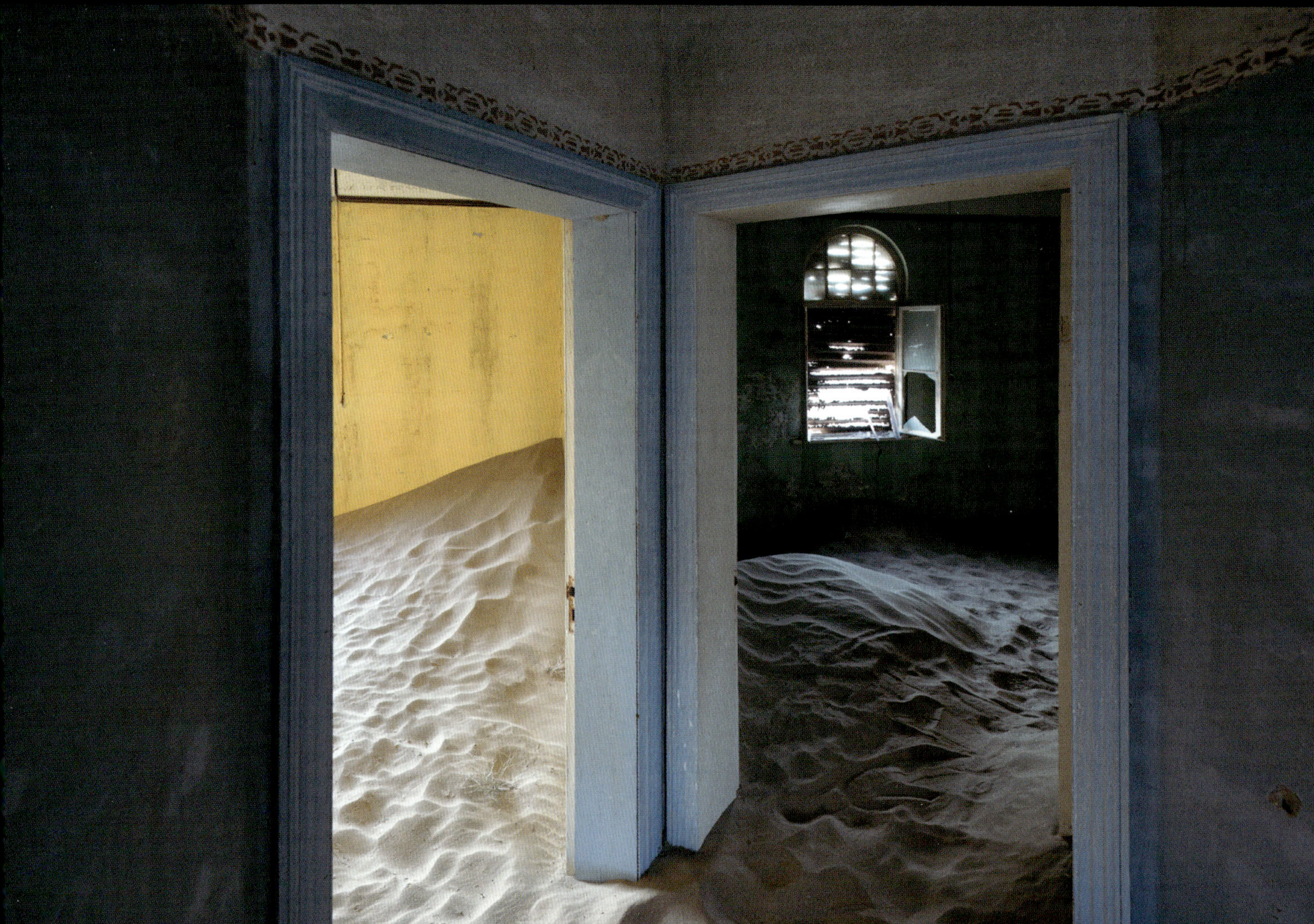

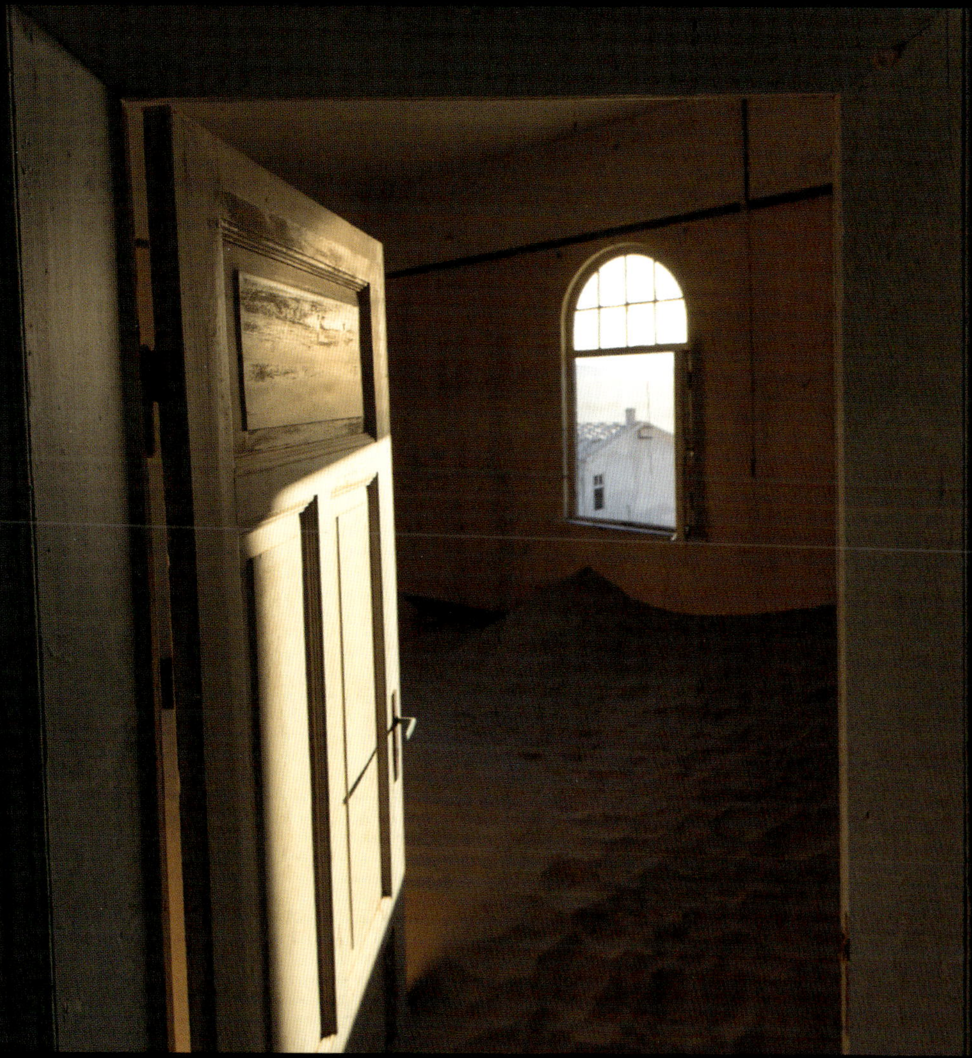

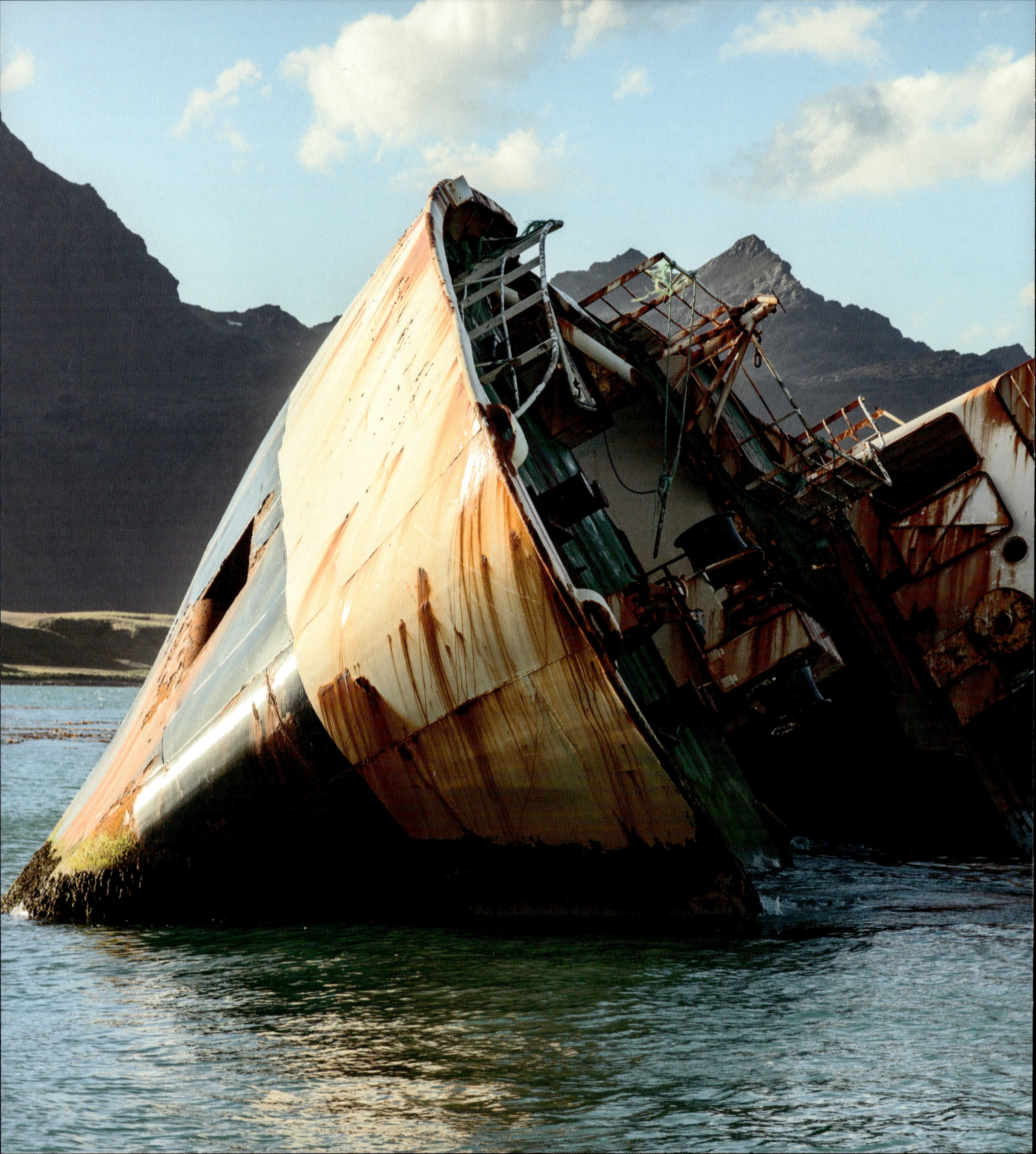

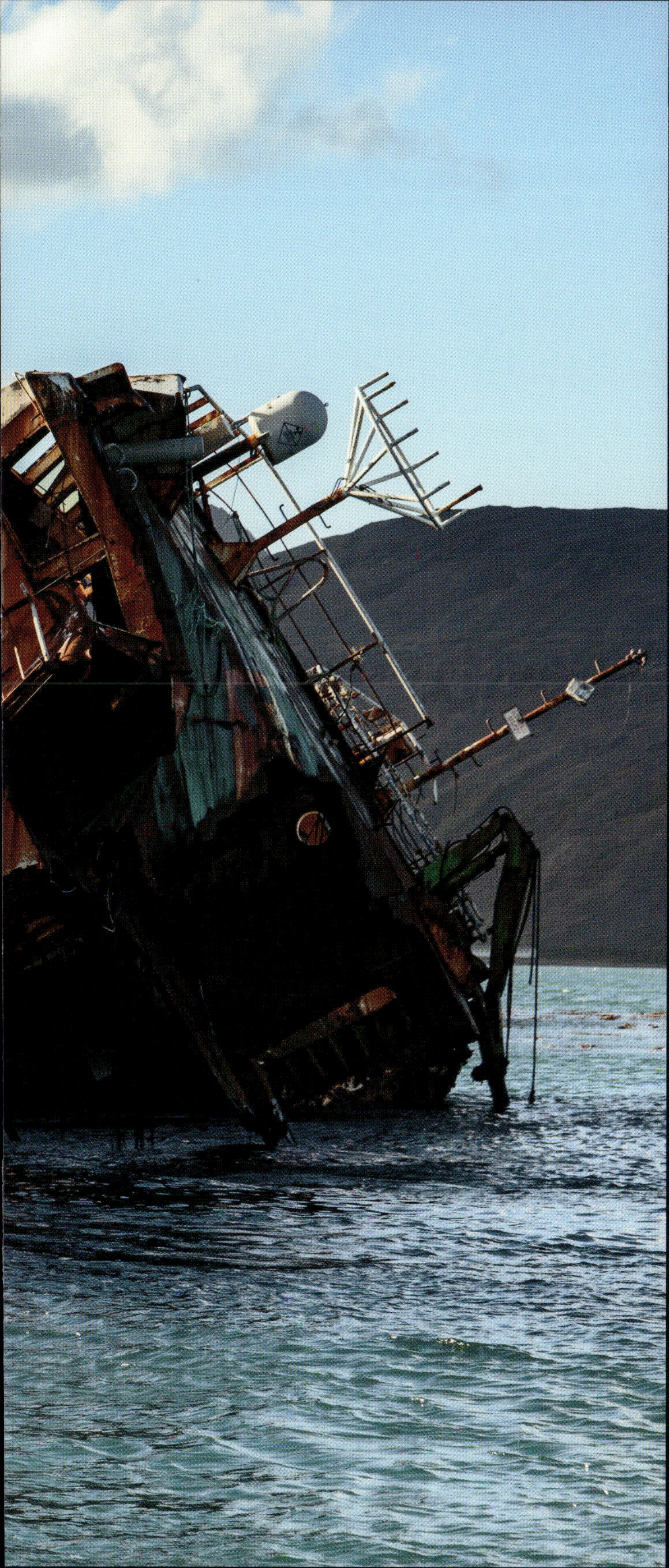

KAP HOORN

CHILE CHILE

FOTOS VON PHOTOS BY JÜRGEN HOHMUTH

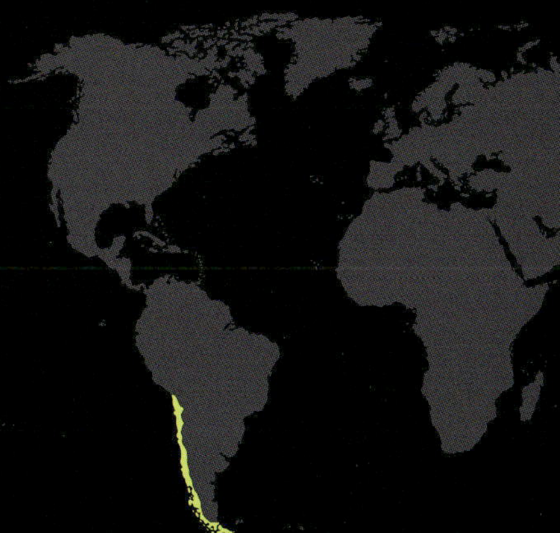

Wenn die Albatrosse über die aufschäumende See vor Kap Hoorn hinjagen und ihre Rufe trotz des entfesselten Windes bis an das Ufer gellen, erzählt eine Legende, höre man nicht die Schreie der sturmerfahrenen Seevögel, sondern die Stimmen der an diesem Ende der Welt untergegangenen Schiffsmannschaften. In Gestalt der Albatrosse, so die Legende, würden die Ertrunkenen nun weiter über die Meere reisen. Das Kap, ein über 400 Meter hoher Felsen an der Südspitze der Isla de Hornos, was übersetzt „Horninsel" bedeutet, liegt im chilenischen Teil des Feuerlandarchipels. Es gilt als berühmtester Schiffsfriedhof der Welt. Und meist scheint es, als herrsche über dem zehn Quadratkilometer umfassenden Bergplateau der „Horninsel" eine beständige Dämmerung.

„Selbst der Teufel erfröre hier", notierte einst Charles Darwin. Orkane, unberechenbare Meeresströmungen, zu geringe Sichtweiten, von den Packeisfeldern der Antarktis auf die Schifffahrtsrouten hinausdriftende Eisberge, Kälte und der schier unaufhörliche Regen verliehen der südlichen Umfahrung Feuerlands bald den Ruf, die gefährlichste Passage der christlichen Seefahrt zu sein. Und Kap Hoorn war ihre gefürchtetste Wegmarke. 800 Schiffe sollen hier gescheitert sein und etwa 10.000 Matrosen mit sich in die Tiefe gerissen haben, erzählt man. Bis zum Anfang des 20. Jahrhunderts blieb die Fahrt um das Kap ein Gleichnis für den Kampf und das Scheitern auf See. Der Bau des Panamakanals und seine Inbetriebnahme 1914 eröffneten dem Seeverkehr eine gefahrlosere und kürzere Route.

Niederländischen Seeleuten war erstmals im Januar 1616 der Weg um Kap Hoorn gelungen. Eine Auseinandersetzung in der mächtigen Niederländischen Ostindien-Kompanie war für die Unternehmung von Willem Cornelisz Schouten und Jakob Le Maire die Ursache. Die Kompanie besaß das Vorrecht für die Niederlande, dass nur zu ihr gehörende Schiffe die Magellanstraße befahren durften. Schouten und Le Maire ging es darum, einen von solchen Einschränkungen freien Seeweg zu erkunden. Wegen der vorherrschenden Westwinddrift war die Durchfahrt vom Atlantik in den Pazifik ein gewagtes Unterfangen. Es verlangte von den Segelschiffen ein ständiges Kreuzen gegen den Wind, trotz hohen Seegangs, schlechter Sicht und der Gefahr auf einen Eisberg zu treffen.

Während der Jahre des kalifornischen Goldrauschs begann man zu vergleichen, wie viel Zeit benötigt wurde, das Kap zu umfahren. Der Rekordhalter, ein für seine Schnelligkeit bekannter Liner namens „Priwall", brauchte fünfeinhalb Tage. Dagegen war der Dreimaster „Susanna" 1905 mehr als drei Monate unterwegs. Immer wieder gaben auch Kapitäne die Passage um Kap Hoorn auf und erreichten über Afrika und Australien den Westen Amerikas. Wem mit einem Frachtsegler ohne Hilfsantrieb die Umfahrung gelang, gebührte ab 1937 die Ehrenmitgliedschaft in der international bekannten Gemeinschaft der Kap Hoorniers. 1949 umfuhr als letzter Handelssegler ohne Hilfsantrieb die deutsche Bark „Pamir" das Kap.

Vom Schrecken, den das Ende der Welt einst einjagen konnte, ist kaum noch etwas zu spüren. Über eine Treppe, deren Stufenkanten sicherheitshalber mit roter Farbe markiert sind, erklimmt der Besucher ein auf 250 Meter Höhe angelegtes Podest und blickt auf die Felsenkuppe des Kap Hoorn. Holzwege führen nun über die Isla de Hornos zum Leuchtturm mit Wohnhaus und Kapelle oder zum stählernen Denkmal für die umgekommenen Seeleute, das einen Albatros zeigt.

When albatrosses go hunting over the foaming ocean off Cape Horn and their cries reach the shore in spite of the unbridled wind, a legend says that you're not hearing the cry of the storm-riding seabirds, rather the voices of the crews of ships that sunk at this end of the world. According to the legend, the drowned sailors now travel again over the seas in the form of albatrosses. The Cape is a 400 meter high cliff at the southern point of Isla de Hornos, translated as "Horn Island", which is located in the Chilean part of the Tierra del Fuego Archipelago. It is known as the most famous ship cemetery in the world. And it usually seems that there is constant twilight over the ten square kilometer mountain plateau of "Horn Island".

"Even the devil would freeze here", noted Charles Darwin at one time. Hurricanes, unpredictable ocean currents, no clear view, icebergs from the pack ice fields of Antarctica drifting into shipping routes, cold and the unceasing rain soon gave the southern route around Tierra del Fuego the reputation that this was the most dangerous passage in Christian seafaring. And Cape Horn was the most feared landmark. 800 ships are thought to have been wrecked there and about 10,000 sailors were dragged down into the depths with them. Up to the beginning of the 20th century, the trip around the Cape remained an image for struggle and shipwreck at sea. The construction of the Panama Canal and its start-up in 1914 opened a less dangerous Due to the powerful west wind drift, the passage from the Atlantic to the Pacific was a daring undertaking. It demanded that the sailing ships continuously cross against the wind, in spite of high seas, poor visibility and the danger of hitting an iceberg.

During the year of the Californian gold rush, people began to compare how much time was necessary to sail around the Cape. A liner by the name of "Priwall", known for its speed, was the record holder and took five and a half days. In comparison, the triple masted "Susanna" was underway for more than three months in 1905. Again and again, captains abandoned the passage around Cape Horn and reached the American west via Australia and Africa. Whoever managed to pass by in a cargo sailing ship without an auxiliary drive was honored after 1937 with honorary membership in the internationally known Association of Cape Horners. The German bark, "Pamir", was the last merchant sailing ship to sail around the cape without an auxiliary drive in 1949.

The fear that the end of the world could instill in you can hardly be felt today. Via a staircase where the edges of the steps are marked in red for safety, a visitor can climb the 250 meters to a podium placed there to view the rocky cliffs of Cape Horn. Today, boardwalks lead across the Isla de Hornos to the lighthouse that has an apartment and chapel, or to the steel memorial to the perished sailors in the form of an albatross.

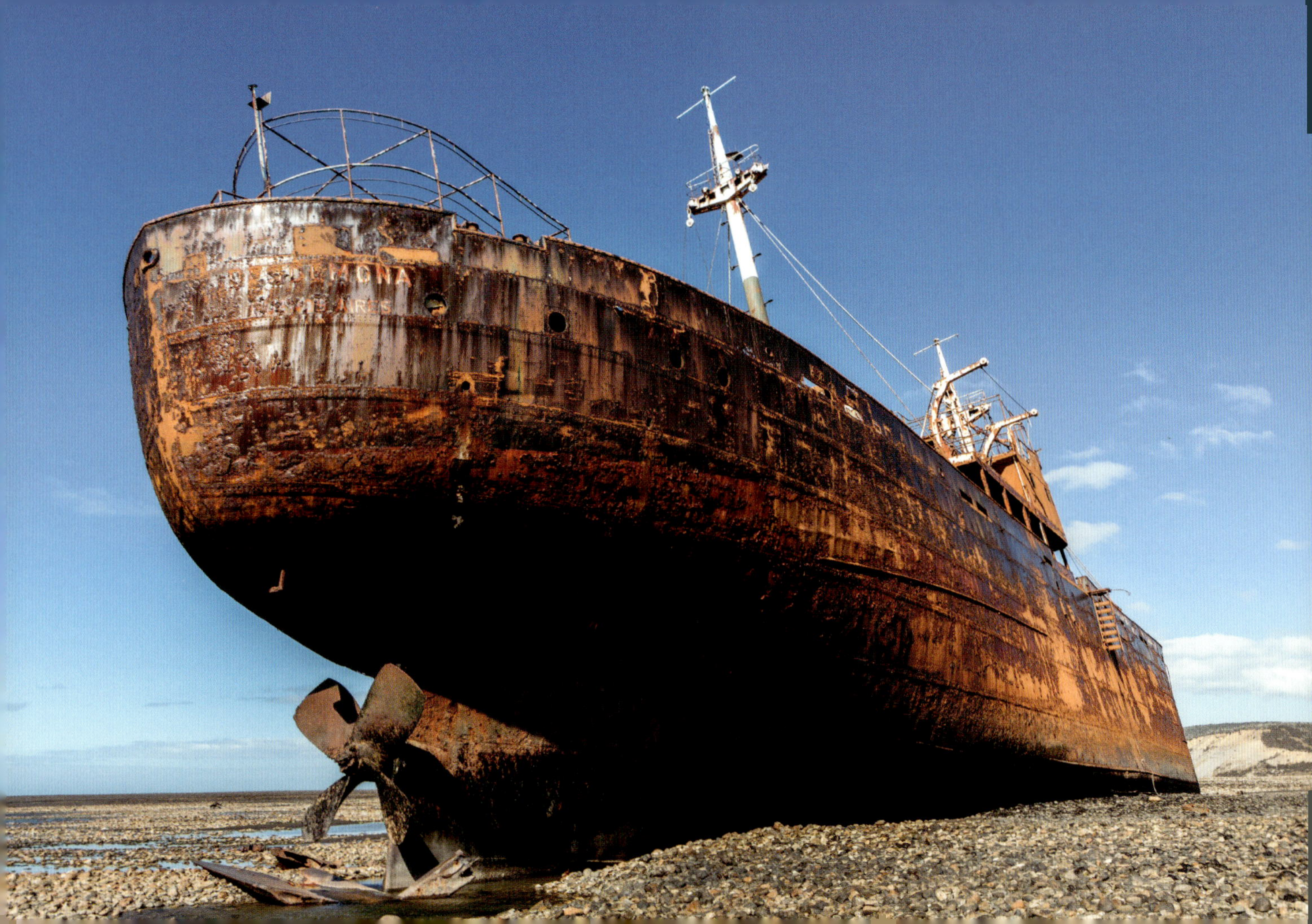

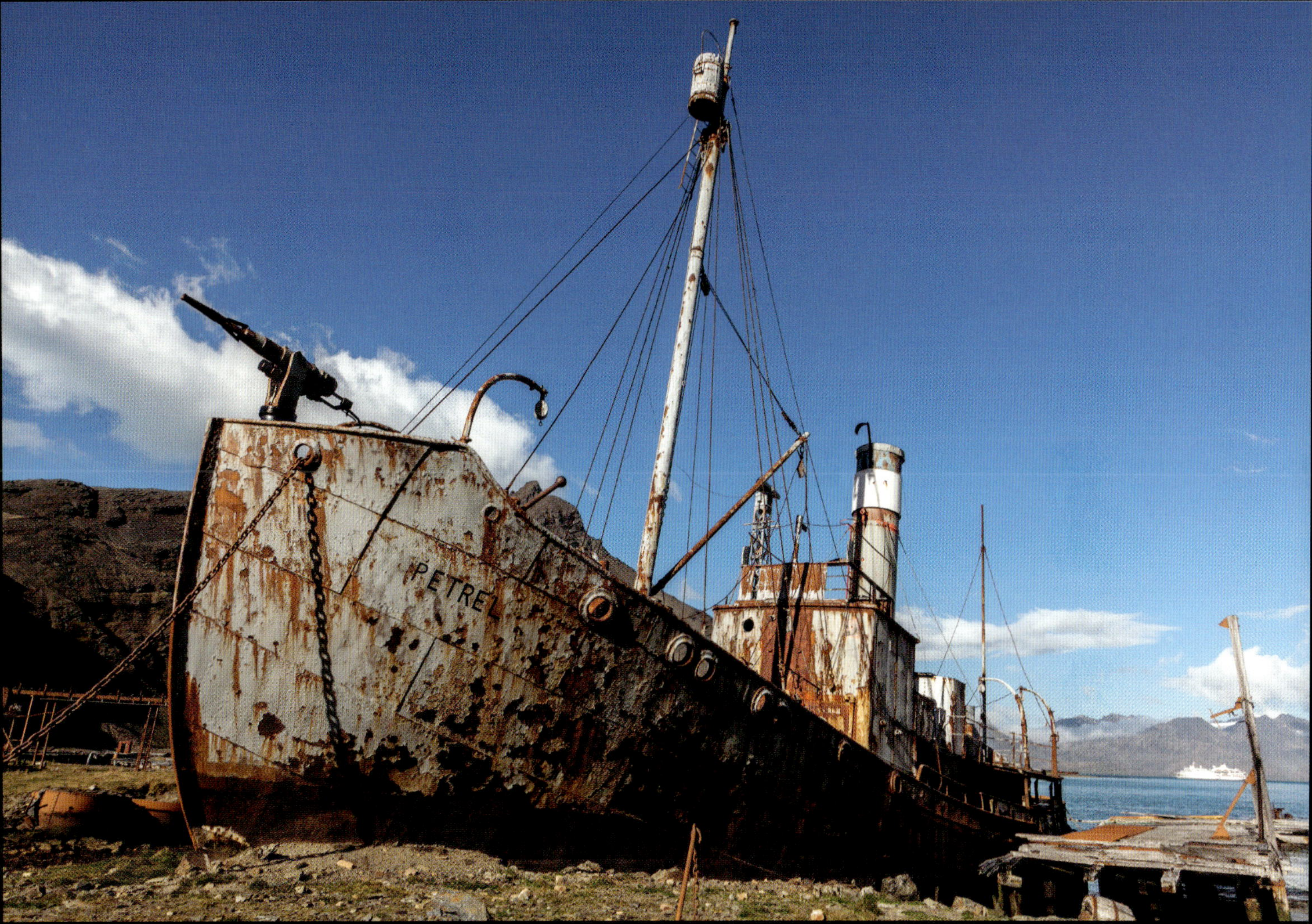
PETREL

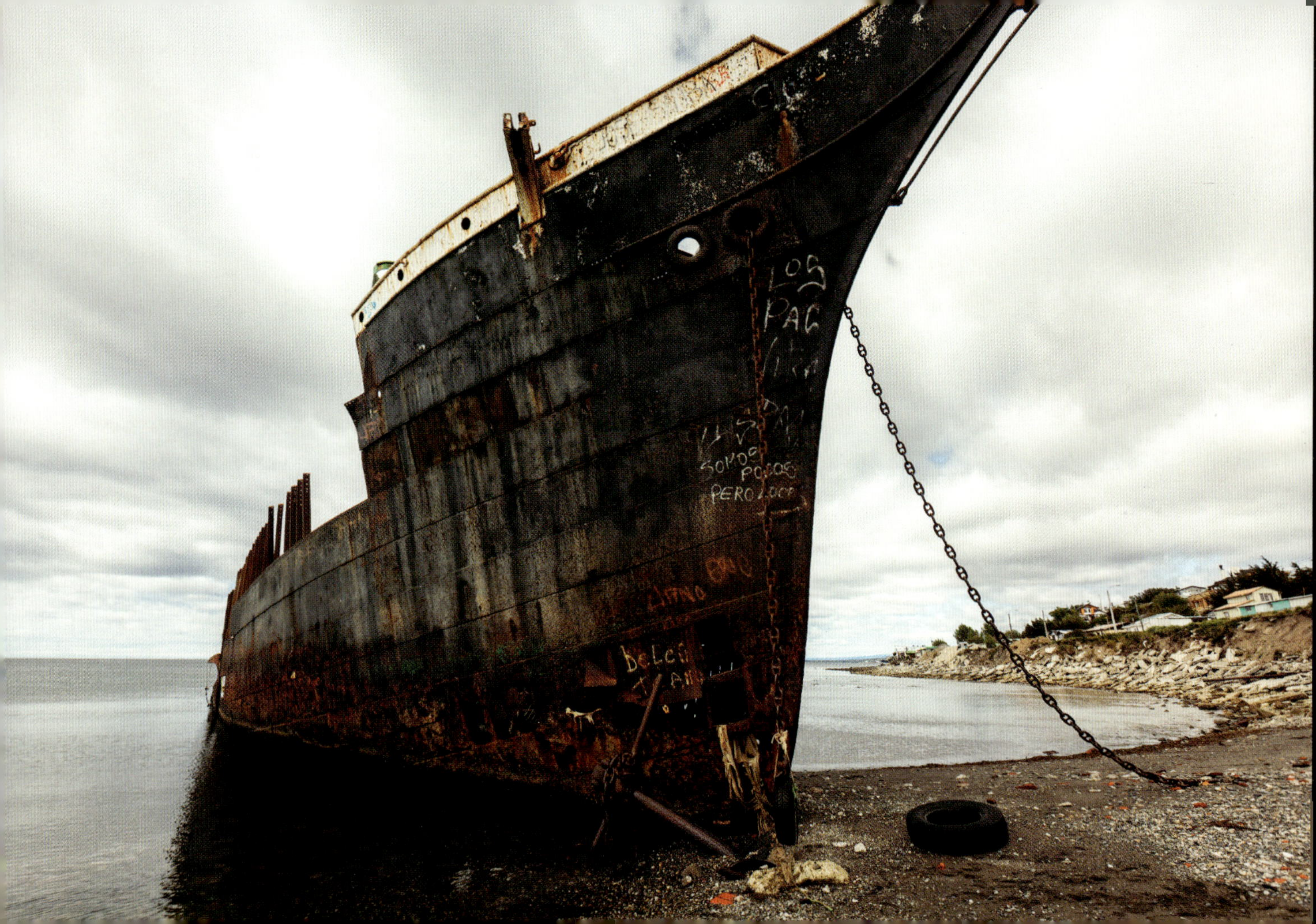
LOS
PAC
SOMOS

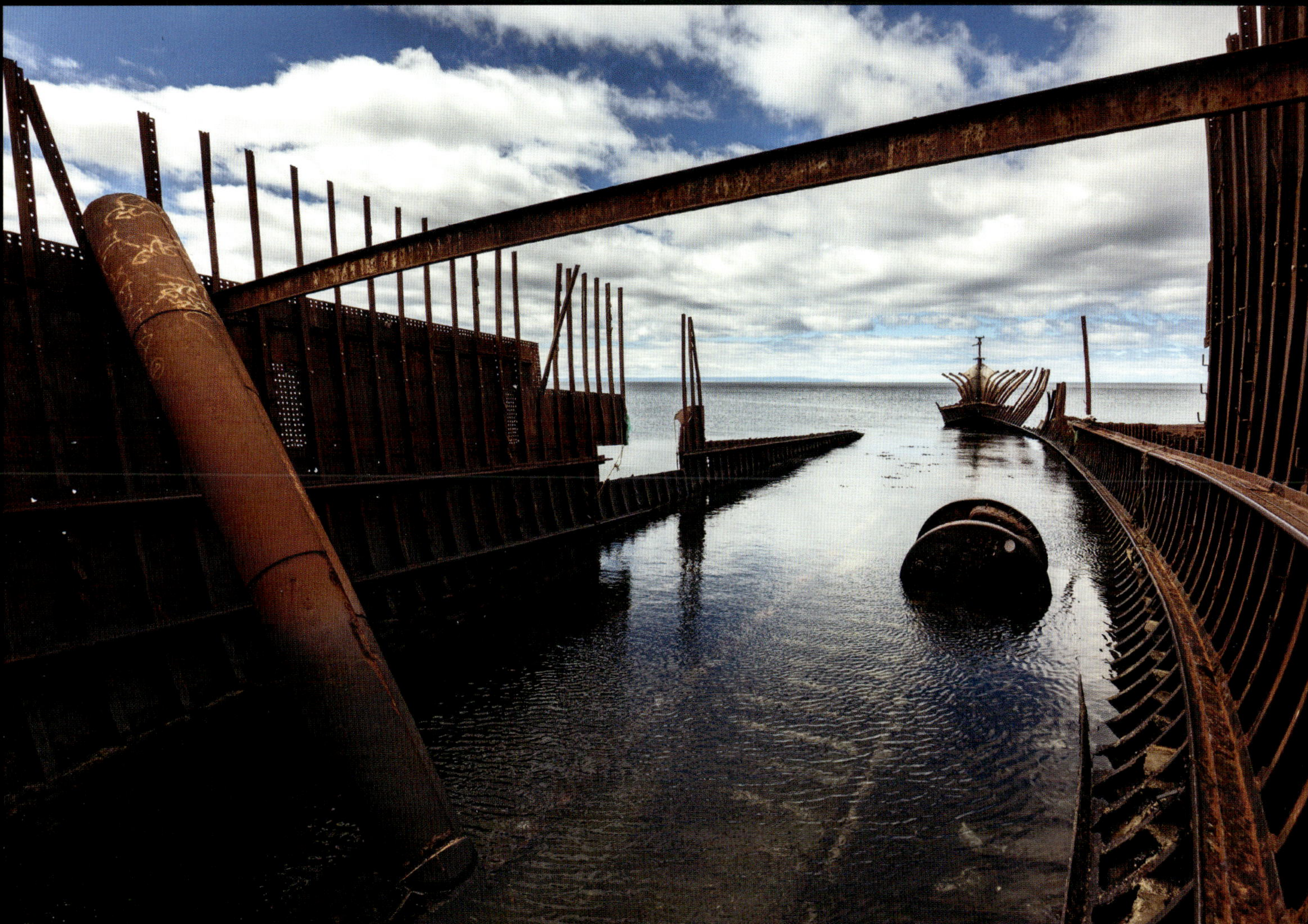

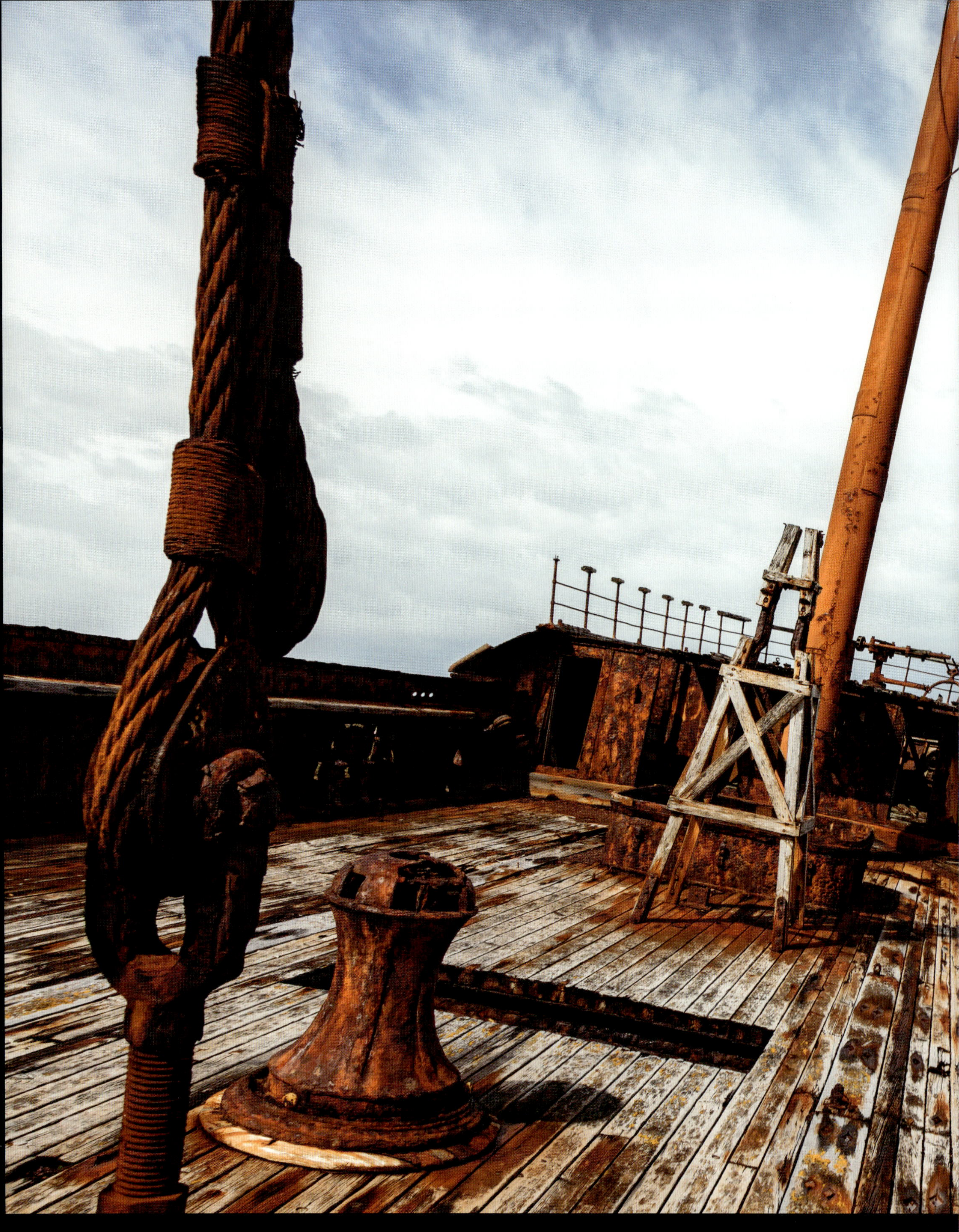

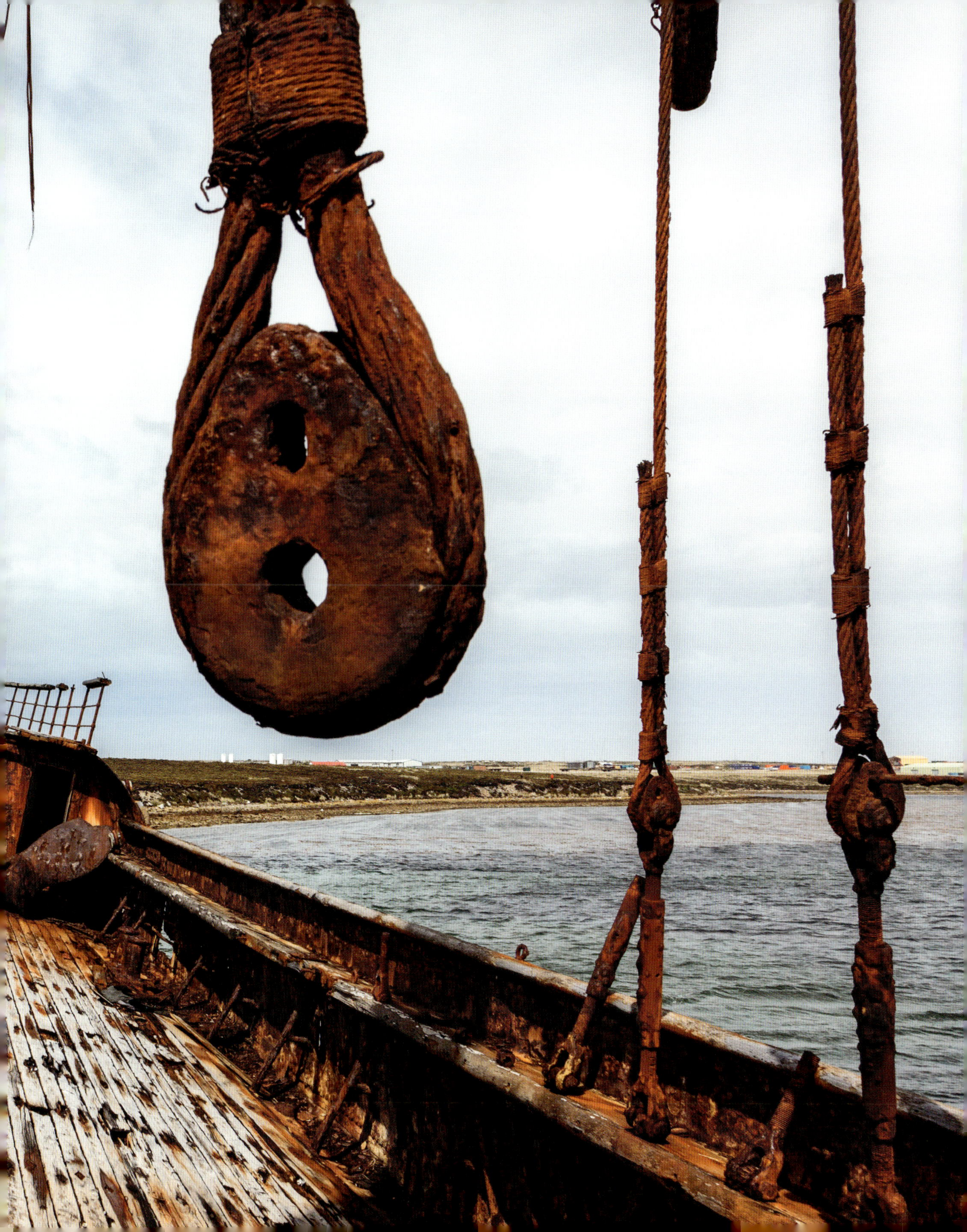

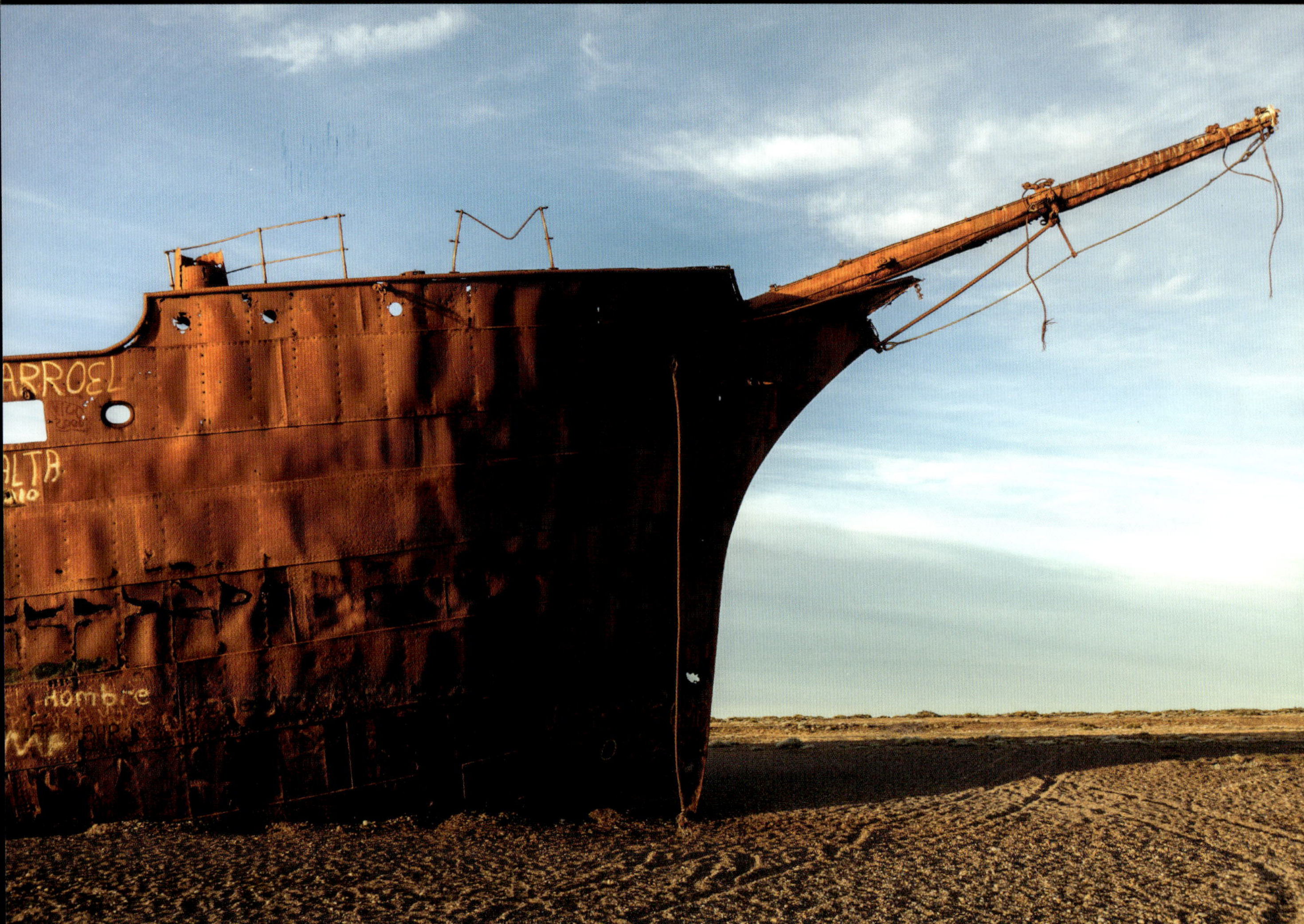
ARROEL
ALTA
hombre

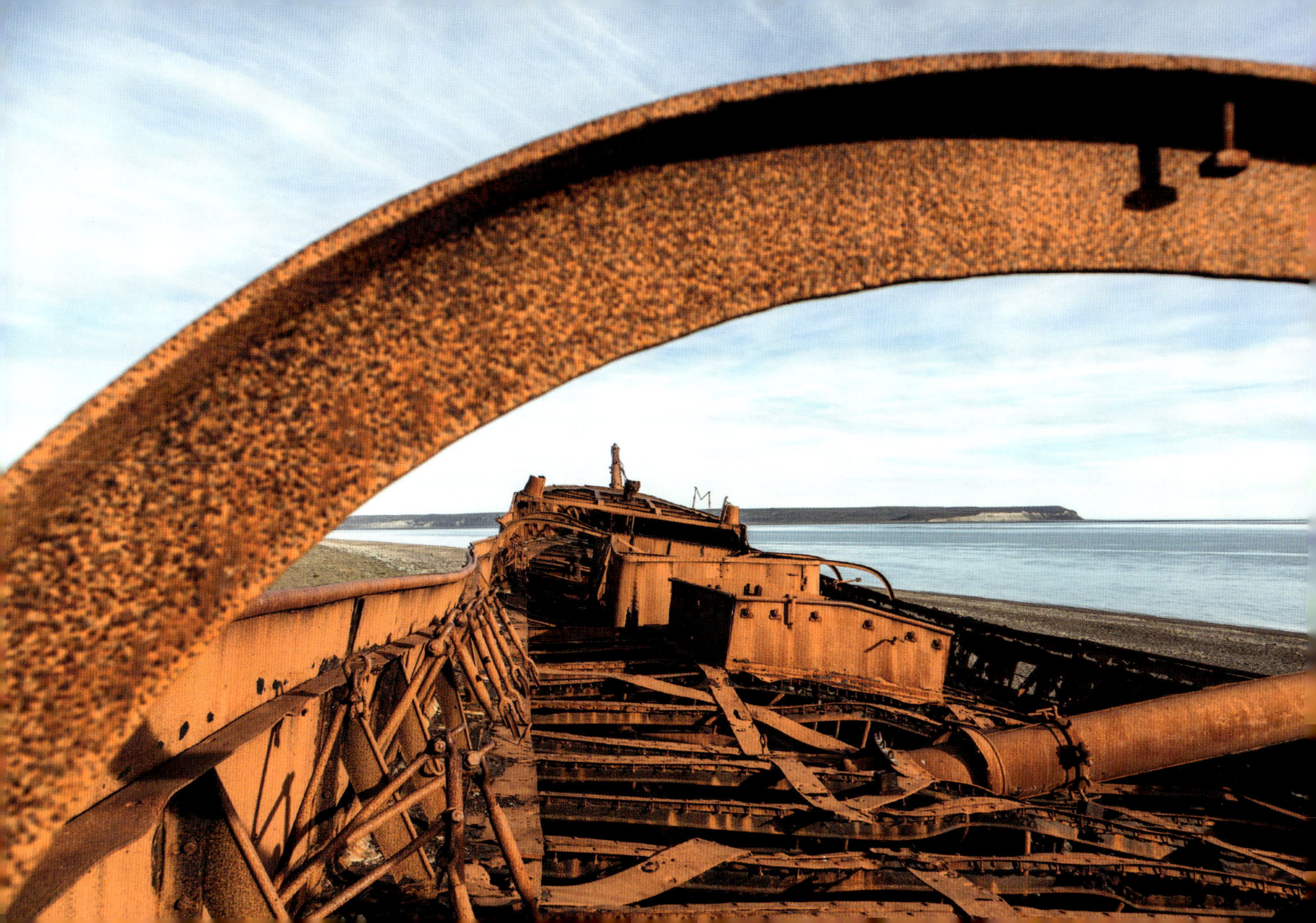

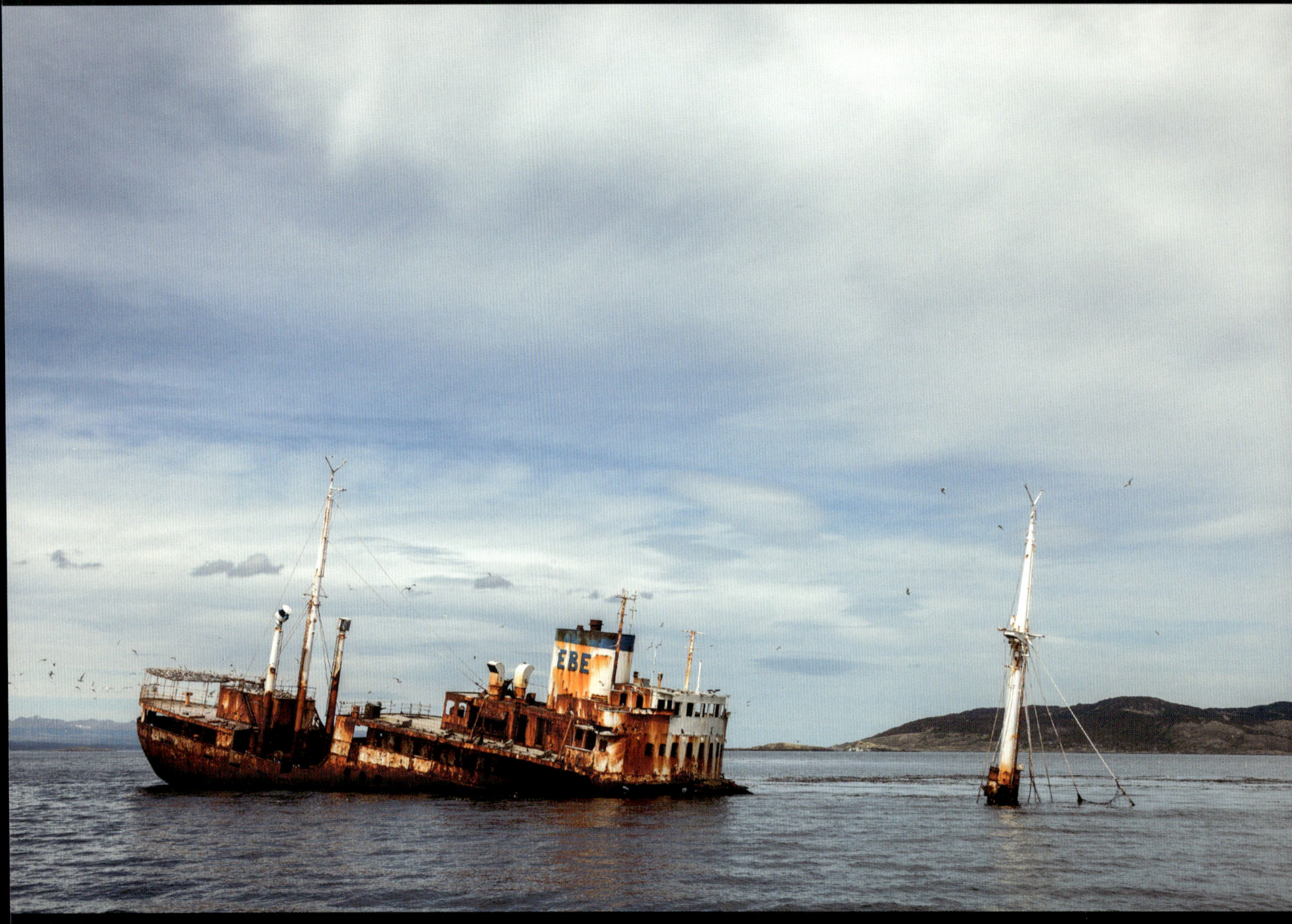
EBE

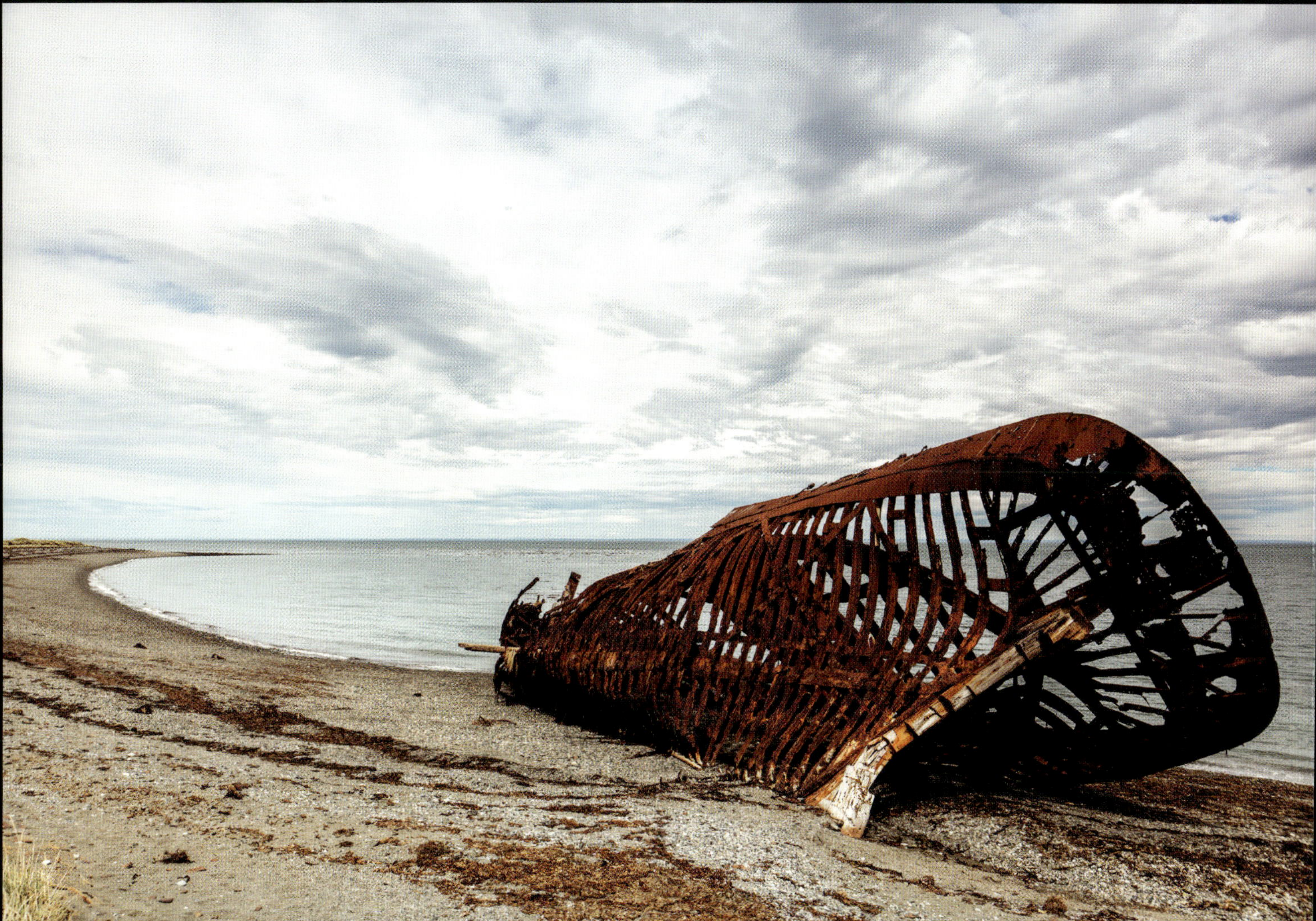

| **Elin Andreassen** lebt als Künstlerin und Fotografin in Trondheim, Norwegen. Ihr neustes Buch: „Pyramiden – a Soviet Mining Town in the High Arctic". www.ruinmemories.org | **Daniel Barter** und **Daniel Marbaix** haben zusammen den Bildband „States of Decay" veröffentlicht, er versammelt verlassene Orte in Amerika. www.facebook.com/odinsravenphotography und www.danielbarter.co.uk | **Matthew Boyer** lebt in Australien. www.flickr.com/photos/krytietv | **Paul Bruins** lebt in Südafrika, fotografiert seit seiner Schulzeit, heute vor allem Architektur- und Landschaftsfotografie. Seine Bilder erschienen in Kalendern, Magazinen und als Buchcover. http://paulbruins.co.za | **Chad Chatterton**, geboren in Australien, lebt in Malmö, Schweden. Er verbrachte einen Tag und eine Nacht auf Gunkanjima in Japan. www.chadchatterton.com | **Alberto Clavería** aus Argentinien ist seit 1997 fotografisch tätig. Er publiziert u. a. in SPIEGEL und National Geographic. www.albertoclaveriafoto.com.ar | **Kris Delcourte** lebt in Belgien und hat als „Mr. Blacksun" in aller Welt nicht nur die Sonnenfinsternis fotografiert. www.flickr.com/photos/krisdelcourte/collections | **Paul Dobraszczyk** lebt in England und arbeitet an einem Buch über tote Städte. Er besuchte Varosha 2013. www.ragpickinghistory.co.uk | **Derek Farr** lebt in Detroit, seine Bilder werden von Eminem, The American Achitectural Foundation, GQ magazine, Conde Nast u. v. a. verwendet. www.flickr.com/detroitderek | **Martin Graf** lebt in Öhningen am Bodensee, Deutschland. Die Historie des Ortes Oradour-sur-Glane, an dem 642 Menschen ihr Leben verloren haben, hat ihn sehr berührt. | **Jürgen Hohmuth** lebt in Berlin, Deutschland. Er fotografiert seit 1981. Buchtipp: „Wracks am Ende der Welt: Der Schiffsfriedhof um Kap Hoorn". www.zeitort.de | **Andy Kay** aus England war drei Tage lang als Fotograf in der „Chernobyl Exclusion Zone". Die Stille in Prypjat ist noch heute seine stärkste Erinnerung. | **Jordy Meow** ist in Frankreich geboren und lebt in Japan. Hier wurde aus dem Hobby Fotografie eine Passion. www.meow.fr | **Marc Mielzarjewicz**, lebt in Halle, Deutschland, Architektur- und Detailfotografie, marode (Industrie-)Architektur. Ausstellungen zum Thema Industrieromantik, mehrere Bildbände. http://marodes.de | **Brian J. Romeyn** lebt in Rotterdam, Niederlande, und ist seit Juli 2010 Urbexer, als er ein kleines verlassenes Dorf fotografierte. www.preciousdecay.com | **Rob Sall** lebt in Chicago und bereist die ganze Welt, stets mit der Kamera. www.robsall.com | **Daniel Ter-Nedden** ist Liebhaber von Geisterstädten und Inhaber einer Agentur für interaktive Medien in Zürich, Schweiz. www.facebook.com/daniel.ternedden | **Peter Traub** lebt in Leipzig, Deutschland, Studium an der Hochschule für Schauspielkunst Berlin/Theater Bautzen sowie am Literaturinstitut Leipzig, arbeitet als freiberuflicher Journalist und Autor. | **Peter Untermaierhofer** lebt in München, Deutschland. Sein Bestseller „Vergessene Orte im Ruhrgebiet" erschien 2013. www.untermaierhofer.de

2. Auflage 2017

www.mitteldeutscherverlag.de

Gesamtherstellung: Mitteldeutscher Verlag, Halle (Saale)
Übersetzung: 24translate GmbH, Hamburg

ISBN 978-3-95462-031-9

Printed in the EU

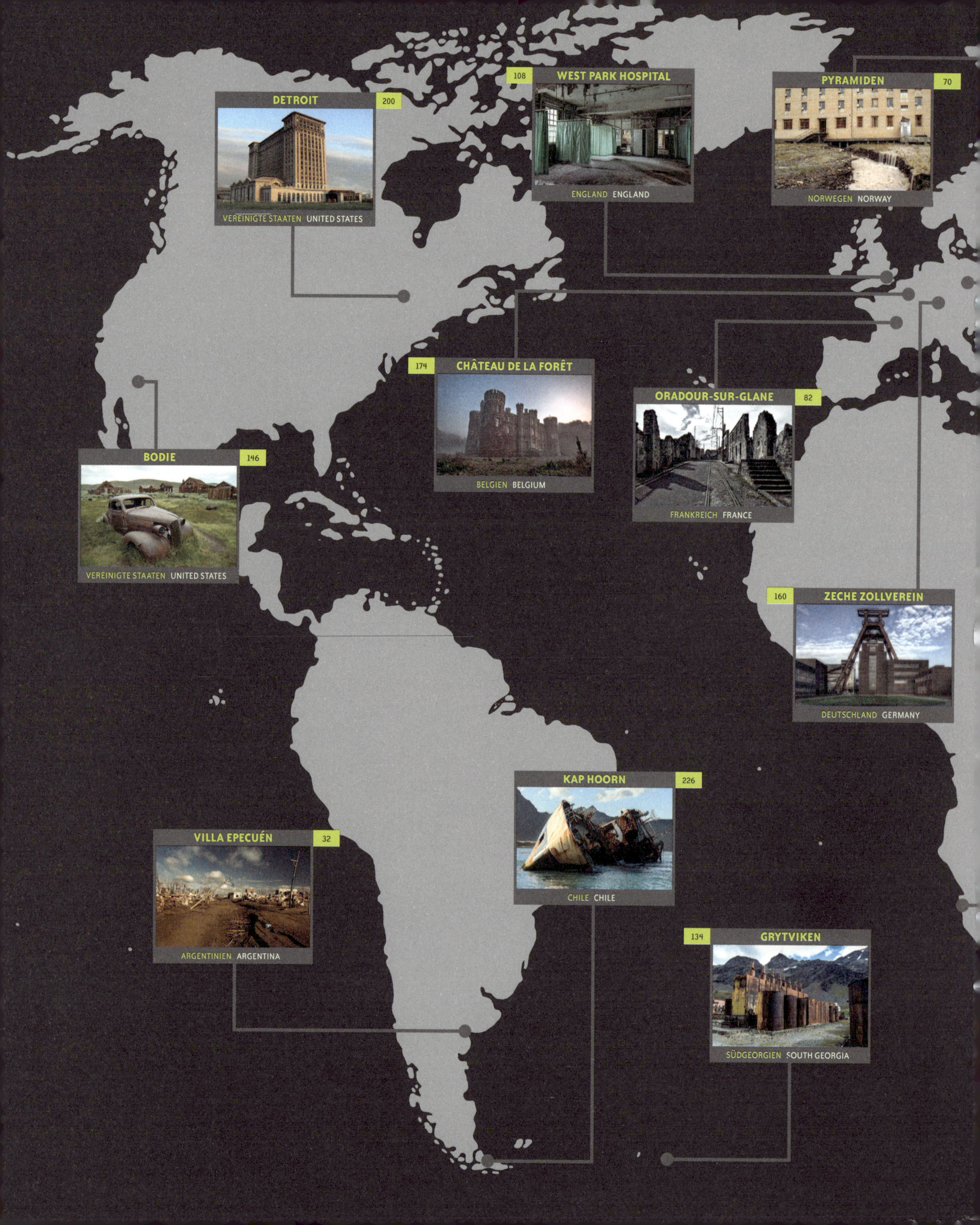

DETROIT
200
VEREINIGTE STAATEN UNITED STATES
108
WEST PARK HOSPITAL
ENGLAND ENGLAND
PYRAMIDEN
70
NORWEGEN NORWAY
174
CHÂTEAU DE LA FORÊT
BELGIEN BELGIUM
ORADOUR-SUR-GLANE
82
FRANKREICH FRANCE
BODIE
146
VEREINIGTE STAATEN UNITED STATES
160
ZECHE ZOLLVEREIN
DEUTSCHLAND GERMANY
KAP HOORN
226
CHILE CHILE
VILLA EPECUÉN
32
ARGENTINIEN ARGENTINA
134
GRYTVIKEN
SÜDGEORGIEN SOUTH GEORGIA